SARAH FRASER

The Last Highlander

SCOTLAND'S MOST NOTORIOUS CLAN CHIEF, REBEL & DOUBLE AGENT

Harper
Press

HarperPress
An imprint of HarperCollinsPublishers
77–85 Fulham Palace Road
Hammersmith, London W6 8JB
www.harpercollins.co.uk

This HarperPress paperback edition published 2013

1

First published in Great Britain by HarperPress in 2012

A catalogue record for this book is
available from the British Library

ISBN 978-0-00-722950-5

Typeset in Minion by G&M Designs Limited,
Raunds, Northamptonshire

MIX
Paper from
responsible sources
FSC™ www.fsc.org   **FSC™ C007454**

SARAH FRASER is married to a Lovat Fraser, the son of heroic World War II Commando Shimi, Lord Lovat. She undertook a doctoral thesis on obscene Gaelic poetry, and has since contributed to TV and radio programmes on Gaelic issues, the clans and British history. Sarah has four children and she and her husband live both in the Highlands and London. *The Last Highlander* is her first book.

From the reviews of *The Last Highlander*:

'Fraser treats Lovat with sympathy and understanding. Whatever his faults, he was a remarkable man and a considerable figure, worthy of some respect and even inviting affection. Her picture of Highland society is excellent and the story she has to tell is gripping. Much of it reads like a good historical novel'   ALLAN MASSIE, *Literary Review*

'Fraser's passion for the historic Highlands, the Jacobites and her husband's family carries the book along … Against this picture, Fraser paints a romantic picture of a charming rogue'

BBC History Magazine

'Compelling biography'   *The Scotsman*

'Sarah Fraser recounts all this with verve and great authority, leavening the history with colourful accounts of the clothes, food, customs and cruelty of the times … Hers is a gripping story, compellingly told'

MAGNUS LINKLATER, *Standpoint*

'A grand, Johnsonian figure … handsomely bewigged … animated in conversation, furiously working gnarled fingers and thumbs. Is the man a hero or is he a villain? … He cut a dash to the last … She unravels a complicated tale with skill and tells it with gusto'

JAMES FERGUSSON, *Country Life*

'As family black sheep go, the 11th Lord Lovat may take some beating'

…rier

Simon, Lord Lovat.
Drawn from the Life and Etch'd in Aquafortis by Will.ᵐ Hogarth.
Price 1 Shilling
Publish'd according to Act of Parliament. August 25ᵗʰ 17..

For Kim
&
For Arabella Vanneck
1959–2011

'[The soul] demands that we should not live alternately with our opposing tendencies in continual see-saw of passion and disgust, but seek some path on which the tendencies shall no longer oppose, but serve each other to common end … The soul demands unity of purpose, not the dismemberment of man'

— ROBERT LOUIS STEVENSON

'A son can bear with equanimity the loss of his father, but the loss of his inheritance may drive him to despair'

— NICCOLÒ MACHIAVELLI

CONTENTS

PART ONE
FORMATIVE YEARS, C.1670–1702

PART TWO
AT THE COURT OF THE SUN KING, 1702–15

PART THREE
THE RETURN OF THE CHIEF, 1715–45

PART FOUR
LORD LOVAT'S LAMENT, 1739–47

ILLUSTRATIONS

Etching of Simon Fraser, Lord Lovat after William Hogarth. (*Scottish National Portrait Gallery*)

James II and family, 1694, by Pierre Mignard. (*The Royal Collection © 2011 Her Majesty Queen Elizabeth II/The Bridgeman Art Library*)
Queen Mary II, *c*. 1685, studio of Willem Wissing. (*Kenwood House, London © English Heritage Photo Library/The Bridgeman Art Library*)
King William III by Godfried Schalcken. (*© The Crown Estate/The Bridgeman Art Library*)

Prince James Francis Edward Stuart, 18th century English School. (*© Scottish National Portrait Gallery/The Bridgeman Art Library*)
Louis XIV in Royal Costume, 1701, by Hyacinthe Rigaud. (*© Louvre, Paris/Giraudon/The Bridgeman Art Library*)
View of Edinburgh by J Slezer (engraved copper plate) produced for D. Browne, London, 1718. (*© The British Library Board*)

Major James Fraser of Castle Leathers, *c*. 1720, attributed to John Vanderbank. (*Private Collection*)

John Campbell, 2nd Duke of Argyll and Greenwich, William Aikman. (*Scottish National Portrait Gallery*)
Archibald Campbell, 3rd Duke of Argyll, attributed to Allan Ramsay. (*Scottish National Portrait Gallery*)

Sir James Grant. Etching by John Kay, 1798. (© *The Mary Evans Picture Library*)

The death of Colonel Gardiner on the field of Prestonpans. Sir William Allan lithograph by E. Walker. (© *The Mary Evans Picture Library*)

George II at the Battle of Dettingen by David Morier. (© *Private Collection/Arthur Ackerman Ltd/The Bridgeman Art Library*)

Field-Marshal George Wade, attributed to Johan van Diest. (*Scottish National Portrait Gallery*)

Prince Charles Edward Stuart, by William Mosman. (*Scottish National Portrait Gallery*)

The Battle of Culloden, 1746. Coloured engraving published by R. Sayer and J. Bennett, London *c.* 1780. (© *The National Army Museum, London*)

William Augustus, Duke of Cumberland, mid 18th century English School. (© *Royal Armouries, Leeds/The Bridgeman Art Library*)

Lord Lovat's ghost. Mezzotint by Samuel Ireland. (© *Grosvenor Prints/The Mary Evans Picture Library*)

Simon Fraser, Lord Lovat. Engraved by Cook after a portrait by Le Clare. (© *The Mary Evans Picture Library*)

MAPS

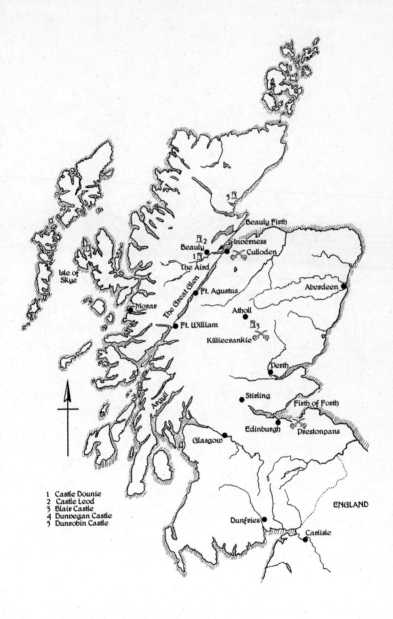

1 Castle Dounie
2 Castle Leod
3 Blair Castle
4 Dunvegan Castle
5 Dunrobin Castle

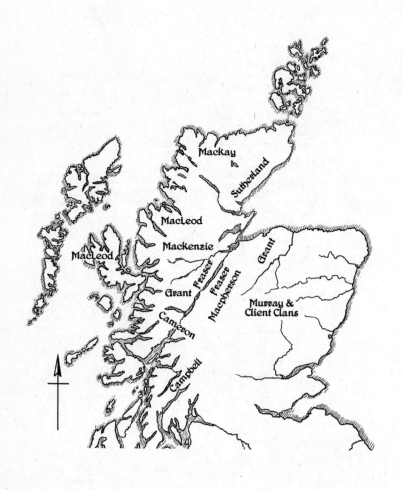

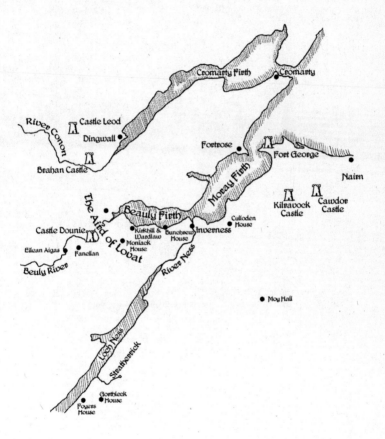

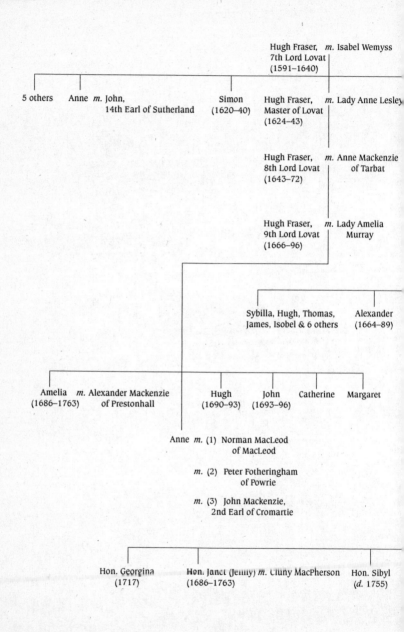

Hugh Fraser, *m.* Isabel Wemyss
7th Lord Lovat
(1591–1640)

5 others   Anne *m.* John,   Simon   Hugh Fraser,   *m.* Lady Anne Lesley
14th Earl of Sutherland   (1620–40)   Master of Lovat
(1624–43)

Hugh Fraser,   *m.* Anne Mackenzie
8th Lord Lovat   of Tarbat
(1643–72)

Hugh Fraser,   *m.* Lady Amelia
9th Lord Lovat   Murray
(1666–96)

Sybilla, Hugh, Thomas,   Alexander
James, Isobel & 6 others   (1664–89)

Amelia   *m.* Alexander Mackenzie   Hugh   John   Catherine   Margaret
(1686–1763)   of Prestonhall   (1690–93)   (1693–96)

Anne   *m.* (1) Norman MacLeod
of MacLeod

m. (2) Peter Fotheringham
of Powrie

m. (3) John Mackenzie,
2nd Earl of Cromartie

Hon. Georgina   Hon. Janet (Jenny) *m.* Cluny MacPherson   Hon. Sibyl
(1717)   (1686–1763)   (*d.* 1755)

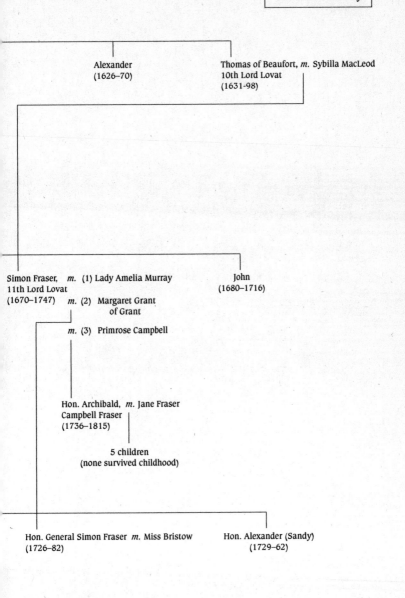

The Lovat Family

Alexander
(1626–70)

Thomas of Beaufort, *m.* Sybilla MacLeod
10th Lord Lovat
(1631-98)

Simon Fraser, *m.* (1) Lady Amelia Murray
11th Lord Lovat
(1670–1747) *m.* (2) Margaret Grant
of Grant

m. (3) Primrose Campbell

John
(1680–1716)

Hon. Archibald, *m.* Jane Fraser
Campbell Fraser
(1736–1815)

5 children
(none survived childhood)

Hon. General Simon Fraser *m.* Miss Bristow
(1726–82)

Hon. Alexander (Sandy)
(1729–62)

PROLOGUE

Death of a Highland chief

His execution was a public holiday. Tens of thousands crowded onto Tower Hill for the entertainment. In the Tower the prisoner raged at his barber. In a few hours he would lose his head. The barber offered up the condemned man's wig, very light on powder 'on account of it being a rainy day'. The prisoner tossed it back to be taken away, properly groomed, generously powdered and then returned. If he 'had a suit of velvet embroidered, he would wear it' today; he would go 'to the block' he said, 'with pleasure'. These sartorial sensitivities belonged to the last aristocrat in Britain to be beheaded.

On this damp, grey, very English, spring day, Thursday 9 April 1747, warders and friends begged his Lordship to petition the King for mercy. 'He was so old and infirm that his life was not worth asking,' he replied.

This was not true. His life, and the ending of it, was worth a lot to many different people.

'For my part,' he claimed, 'I die a martyr for my country.'

The barber returned his wig and his Lordship thanked him. 'I hope to be in heaven by one o'clock,' he said, 'or I should not be so merry now … The soul is a spiritual substance.' It could not be 'dissolved by time'.

The barber wished the prisoner 'a good passage' across. Lovat looked out of the window. He was going to slip through the bars of life and escape to heaven, he was sure of it.

*   *   *

The previous month, Lord Lovat had been impeached for high treason as a Jacobite rebel. The whole House of his fellow Lords, including many former friends and allies, removed to Westminster Hall especially for the trial and one by one pronounced him 'Guilty, upon my Honour'.

Simon Fraser, the 11th Lord Lovat and leader of Clan Fraser – *MacShimidh Mor* in Gaelic – was the son of 'the great Simon' and the last of the great Celtic–Scottish chiefs. The Frasers had fought their way from France onto the beaches of England with William the Conqueror. One of Lovat's forebears was Robert the Bruce's chamberlain. Another had been William Wallace's compatriot in the Scottish Wars of Independence from England; when the English captured him he was hung, drawn and quartered.

Four hundred years after his ancestor's bloody end, Lovat was condemned to suffer the same brutal fate, though in the end he was merely beheaded. Lovat would die for an independent Scotland – or 'North Britain' as many maps now called it – to secure the fortunes of the Fraser clan, and for Bonnie Prince Charlie's lunge at the thrones of his Stuart ancestors. For decades Lovat had maintained a double life, spying for and against the Houses of Stuart and Hanover. He had made fast friends and sworn enemies. His scheming had inadvertently led to the 1707 Act of Union, in which the Parliaments of Scotland and England were incorporated into Great Britain. He cursed it as '*Cette Union infernelle*'.

In Georgian Britain, all convicted felons about to 'be launched into eternity', both common and gentle, were expected to do so showing plenty of 'bottom', a certain gutsy dash. According to the broadsheet reports, in the days before Lovat's beheading, the old man (he was about eighty when he died) faced his fate with 'jocoseness' and 'gaiety'. Smoking his last pipe, he knocked it out into the fire, and gave the pipe away as a relic. The ash from it fell in little clods. He watched the eddying specks as the dust rioted away in the air. 'Now, gentlemen,' he said to his companions, 'the end of all human grandeur is like this snuff of tobacco.'

As he smoked his pipe, ate his last meal, drank beakers of hot chocolate, dressed and prayed, the wooden scaffold grew greasy and slippery in the morning drizzle. London life went on around it. Maids raised fires in the first-floor drawing rooms around the square on Tower Hill, to take the chill from the rumps of the curious rich and rare as they watched in comfort. Tall chimneys smoked.

Before dressing to spectate at Tower Green, a gentleman wrote to his friend over breakfast. 'Lord Lovat is to lose his head in a few hours, and the day being rainy is likely to prove a great disappointment to the crowds that are hastening to see the execution … Perhaps such tragical scenes may do good to somebody: and though this old man be highly guilty and his guilt very inexcusable, yet a considerate spectator cannot but be led to pity and bewail the corruption and infatuation of human nature when he sees a man almost at the utmost period of human life, under no necessitous circumstances … with a plentiful fortune and everything he could reasonably desire without any danger of losing it; and yet not content therewith, he must disturb the peace of the country, and endeavour to overthrow the constitution thereof. Men should consider that when they are endeavouring to break down hedges a serpent may bite them.'

Soldiers marched to the base of the scaffold. Unhurried, they formed up in rows between the block and the mob. Many of the crowd had gathered early, clambering up the stairs to rows of wooden benches, to get a clear view across to the block on the same level as the victim. Towards ten o'clock, one of the packed timber terraces, desperately overcrowded, collapsed. Those beneath panicked and drove themselves back from the splintering beams and planks. Bodies were crushed and impaled. The injured were carted away, some 'screaming themselves to death'. There were nine corpses. The wood was shoved to one side, to be looted for firewood by the poor.

News of the slight delay this incident caused to proceedings reached Lovat. 'Good,' he grunted, 'the more mischief the better the sport.' Sensitive to omens all his life, it was a sign that God was on his side. This execution was a sin.

Lesser players in the drama came and went from the scaffold. One was Mr Baker, the chaplain from the Sardinian Embassy, and the only Roman Catholic priest licensed to practise in England. He knelt now before the image of the crucified Lord and prepared himself to oversee the release of another papist ingrate from the twists and turns of the mortal coil. Government representatives lounged about on the scaffold, chatting with Lovat's closest clansmen and friends. The gentlemen and bureaucrats gazed with distaste on the rabble. The officials were here to get the administration of the sentence right, and to record any last words of inspiration or insurrection. Carpenters hauled an empty coffin up steep steps, and dumped it in a corner. The executioner, John Thrift, laid out and checked the tools of his trade, and fiddled around the block.*

The huge square had the atmosphere of a gala occasion. The Bonnie Prince, Charles Stuart, had slipped the hounds. The Old Fox caged in the Tower was the government's most high-profile prisoner. There was a clamour to see him. The press had kept the name of the unseen 'wicked', 'dangerous', 'notoriously to be suspected' Lord Lovat in the public consciousness. Even though they had him now, he was still talked up as a threat to national security. The masses were beside themselves. The heart of England shouted, kissed, gossiped, ate and drank. Ballads about the drama began to flow from one to another, celebrating victory over 'Old England's Foe'.

> As through the city Lord Lovat did pass,
> The people in hundreds did follow,
> And cryed 'You Old Fox you are catched safe at last',
> While some hissed and others did hollow …

It took about an hour to clear the dead and maimed from the terraces and then the Sheriffs of London sent their message to the prisoner. The axe demanded 'his body'. When Lovat appeared, the tension

---

* A few years later it seemed Thrift had begun to take his work home with him. He was convicted of a horrific murder, and was himself executed in public.

ratcheted up by raucous degrees. Although 'clogged with infirmities and pain', the old man was an imposing presence. 'He is tall, walks very upright considering his great age, and is tolerably well shaped,' reported one news-sheet. 'He has a large mouth and a short nose, with eyes very much contracted and down-looking, a very small forehead, almost all covered with a large periwig; this gives him a grim aspect, but upon addressing anyone he puts on a smiling countenance.'

No longer any harm to anyone, he had to be helped up the scaffold steps by his servants. James Fraser, a close kinsman and executor of his chief's will, struggled to compose himself. 'Cheer up thy heart man,' Lovat patted his shoulder. 'I am not afraid ... My dear James I am going to heaven, but you must crawl a little longer in this evil world,' and gave him his silver-topped cane as a memento.

Lord Lovat looked about him: 'God save us! Why should there be such a bustle about taking off an old grey head that can't get up three steps without two men to support it?' he asked, shaking off his supporters and going to test the axe for weight and keenness.

It was very nearly time. 'Then farewell to wicked Lord Lovat, old Lovat,/Then farewell to wicked old Lovat!' The chorus rose from the ground. The song lumbered along like an old nag beaten up to a canter, thumping out its taunts. '*Don't you love it, Lord Lovat, Lord Lovat?*'

Codicils to Lovat's will prescribed his funeral plans in his homeland, hundreds of miles and a civilisation away. 'All the pipers from John o'Groats to Edinburgh shall play before my corpse and the good old women in my country shall sing a *coronach** before me. And then there will be crying and clapping of hands, for I am one of the greatest chiefs in the Highlands.'

Taking his time, he hirpled over to consider his coffin. The lid, with his name on it, hung open, a door to take his mutilated body down to the underworld. A brass nameplate announced him, '*SIMON DOMINUS FRASER DE LOVAT, DECOLLAT*, April 9, 1747, *AETAT*

---

* *Coronachs* are formal Celtic keening songs. Clapping the palms together, howling, tearing your hair out, rocking, are all signs of lamentation.

SUAE 80'. He leaned against the rails a moment and murmured a line of Horace: '*Dulce et decorum est pro patria mori*' ('It is sweet and seemly to die for one's country').

Lovat took in the restless thousands around him, shouting and singing, all fixed on him. In his mind's eye, he saw his ancestors. From this point on a public scaffold, they moved off from him in a line into the past. They had fought together to make their country independent and free; but Lovat had lived to see that country absorbed into another. He quoted Ovid to himself: '*Nam genus et proavos et quae non fecimus ipsi Vix ea nostra voca*' ('For those things which were done either by our fathers or ancestors, and in which we had no share, I can scarcely call my own').

He knelt down. A kinsman who had helped him ascend to the block knelt near him. They picked up the cloth, a scarlet sheet, to catch his head, and stretched it out between them. The executioner moved his Lordship back a bit. Lovat sat up and the two men spoke. He would bend down, raise his handkerchief and pray, the old aristocrat said. When he dropped the hankie, John Thrift must do it.

Lovat stretched out his short, thick neck as best he could. In under a minute he gave the signal and was launched by the good grace of a single chop. Bonnie Prince Charlie's 'late unnatural Rebellion', the failed second coming of the Jacobite Messiah, thudded a step closer to permanent extinction. The crowd roared.

The style in which Lovat met his nemesis was approved of by supporters and detractors alike. That evening Sir Arthur Forbes wrote to his cousin Duncan, a close friend of Lovat's, in Inverness. 'It's astonishing with what resolution and *sang froid* Lovat dyed today,' he reflected. 'Lovat said he dyed as a Christian, and as a Highland chief should, that is, not in his bed.'

He was born to little of this, however.

PART ONE

Formative Years, c.1670–1702

'He who pays the piper calls the tune'

ONE

Home, birth, youth, c.1670–94

'A mighty man of war had been added to the race'
– THE REVD JAMES FRASER ON SIMON'S BIRTH

The future 11th Lord Lovat was born around 1670, some 550 miles north of Tower Hill, in a small manor house in the Aird of Lovat, the hub of the Scottish Highlands. The lack of a recorded date illustrates the initial inconsequence of Simon Fraser's birth to history.

In Simon's heyday as Lord Lovat his clan territories extended over 500 square miles of northern Scotland. 'My country', as Lovat called it, was bigger than King George II's Hanoverian homeland. Fraser territories fell into two distinct regions: poor Highland and rich Lowland. The estates reaching over to the west coast and heading south-west from Inverness down Loch Ness, were typically Highland: peaty soil covered in rough grass; rushes and heather rising from wind-whipped moors to stony peaks of over 3,000 feet. Between them sheltered valley floors of startling greenness.

Now almost deserted, in Lovat's lifetime hundreds of families inhabited these remote fertile glens: the kindred, or 'family', of up to 10,000 that was Clan Fraser. Many passed their lives without venturing even once to the regional capital, Inverness – though the young men would pour out of the hills to fight if the chief summoned them with the fiery cross. Visitors from the Lowlands or England in the early eighteenth century regarded the Highlands with appalled distaste. 'The huge naked rocks, being just above the heath, resemble

3

nothing so much as a scabbed head,' shuddered an English army officer. The 'dirty purple' heather sickened him. Yet the 11th Lord Lovat's wild hill country produced his most loyal and ferocious fighting clansmen and their lairds, and Lovat returned their devotion with a passion.

The common people's year followed an ancient pastoral pattern. Their stock was their wealth and security; their economy was based on exchange, with hardly any money being involved. Visiting tinsmiths, tailors or cattle dealers received hospitality and, say, cheese, a hide, or wool in return for their services, news of wars and national crises, folk tales and songs. These Frasers struggled to produce enough to survive the snowbound winters. In their calendar, January was *An t-Earrach* in Gaelic – the 'tail' end of the year, not the beginning. By then the grain chest was empty, the livestock emaciated from a winter indoors with too little to eat and from being bled to provide blood to mix with oatmeal. When the spring grass came the poor animals had to be carried out of the byres.

A clan was divided into branches. At the top was the chiefly family, and the families of his close cousins. Each branch was headed by a laird called after his small estate – such as Fraser of Foyers, Fraser of Gorthleck, Fraser of Castleleathers – and held by *tack* (lease) or *wadset* (mortgage). He might be responsible for up to 300 ordinary kinsmen and existed in a state of genteel financial stress. The minor lairds, who managed the Highland parts of the estates, could not make ends meet without the financial support that service to their chief earned them. As a consequence, upcountry men were more old-fashioned than their low-country brethren. Unlike English landowners, clan chiefs such as Lord Lovat kept large bodies of armed men in a state of semi-militarised readiness to protect the clan, and travelled nowhere without a 'tail' of up to a hundred of well-accoutred followers on horse and foot. The hill lairds were the first to make up Lord Lovat's 'tail'. He loved them above all his clansmen.

The other half of the Fraser chief's territories was quite different from the hills and glens and was more familiar to foreigners from the south. The area known as the Aird of Lovat, around the mouth of the

River Beauly on the east coast of the Scottish Highlands, was first-class agricultural land. This part of the Lovat estates provided nearly all the chief's income, and the farms and estates here generated more than enough to meet their lairds' needs. They did not need the extra money earned by traditional service to the chief. The wealthier east-coast lairds might become lawyers, officers in the British Army, politicians in Inverness and Edinburgh, or serve in local government.

Simon's eastern territory stretched from the Aird, ten miles eastwards along the sheltered Beauly Firth to the eye of the Highlands, Inverness. Here, ambitious men, keen to market intelligence about this vast semi-autonomous region of the Scottish state to the authorities in Edinburgh or London, noted everything that happened. Lovat's estates lay at a crossroads between the expanding world of Britain and her colonies, and the self-contained world of the clans.

At the time of Simon's birth, the clan proclaimed widespread loyalty to the ancient royal House of Stuart. The Stuarts ruled in sacred bond with the land, just as a chief was 'married to his clan and country'. However, decades of bloody internal conflict, ending just before Simon's birth with the restoration of Charles II, sowed a horror of uncontrolled violence. However, in the Scottish and English governments' minds, this independent-minded civilisation on its northern frontier, half of whom did not even speak English, posed the single biggest threat to the security of the fast-changing Scottish and British nations. Fraser country was, therefore, of strategic importance to any central authority intent on imposing the will of central government.

As the brother of a chief and great-uncle to another chief, Simon's father, Thomas Fraser of Beaufort, grew up at the heart of this world at Castle Dounie, the historic stronghold of Clan Fraser. At the centre of the Aird of Lovat, the ancient fortress loomed on a manmade mound above the banks of the Beauly River. Towers at each corner of the castle and the thick walls between them offered protection to hundreds of the chief's ordinary kin in times of famine or feud. If necessary, over 400 people could sleep there.

At Dounie, the Fraser chief maintained an entourage of staff, kin and allies who regulated the life of a Highland nobleman and the thousands who depended on him for their safety. One kinsman was *fear an taighe*, the head of the household. He controlled the chaplain, piper, harpist, steward, grooms, pantry boys, cooks, and scores of *scallags* (servants) running around beneath them. The principal Fraser families sent their sons to the chief's household 'to educate, polish and accomplish them'; they were 'exchanged at the yeares end, and others taken ... in their place'. The bonds this fostering forged throughout the clan endured for life and offered mutual protection in the frequent times of trouble that were to be a feature of Simon the future 11th Lord Lovat's life.

Simon was the second son of Thomas of Beaufort. 'Beaufort' was another name for Castle Dounie. An honorary title, 'of Beaufort' was attached to the surname of the second line of the family tree, after the chiefly family, the Lovats. The title expressed the closeness of the connection between the two (Simon's father was often called simply 'Beaufort'). If Beaufort's noble cousin Hugh, the 9th Lord Lovat, failed to raise a living male heir, then the male Beaufort Frasers would rise to be the heirs. Acknowledging their position, they had to prepare themselves for what they hoped would not happen: their cousin's incapacity or death. It followed therefore that the men of the second line of the clan elite filled the most important clan posts.

From this position, in 1650, Simon's father, Thomas Fraser of Beaufort, aged just eighteen, led a thousand Fraser men south to fight Cromwell's New Model Army on behalf of Charles Stuart, recently returned from France. On 3 September 1651 a Cromwellian army numbering 28,000 met 16,000 Royalists at Worcester, in the last battle of the English Civil War. The New Model Army captured over 10,000 prisoners, among them young Thomas Fraser of Beaufort. Cromwell deported Beaufort's fellow Fraser prisoners to Barbados as indentured labourers, or slaves. Simon's father was lucky to survive. He was sent north and 'keeped several years in a dungeon in the citadel that the

English made in Inverness', as Cromwell put Scotland under heavy military occupation.

Scotland eviscerated itself in the religious and dynastic wars of the mid-1600s. The country strained to cope with the thousands of government soldiers garrisoned and quartered on the nation. The troops had free rein to get supplies where they could, with the result that 'be-tuixt the bridge end of Inverness and Gusachan, twenty-six miles, there was not left in my countrie a sheep to bleet, or a cock to crow day, nor a house unruffled'. Women were raped, animals butchered and the harvest carried away. Inverness shrank back 'demure under a slavish calm', economically ruined, said the Fraser chronicler. Lairds and chiefs were bankrupt, or fought ruthlessly to restore their fortunes. Cromwell's victory and his subjection of Scotland gave the Scots a bitter taste of union with England that they were to remember in 1707, when another English ruler pressed them to give up their sovereignty.

After the Civil War, Thomas Beaufort married Sybilla MacLeod, the daughter of another chief, John MacLeod of MacLeod. It was usual for clan elites to intermarry in order to reinforce strategic alliances. Simon's mother, Sybilla, grew up at ancient Dunvegan Castle, towering on a rocky promontory on the Atlantic coast of the Isle of Skye as if carved from the cliff. Sybilla gave Beaufort a child each year of their fourteen-year marriage, dying with the last, when Simon was just eight. Altogether nine of their children died in childhood. The surviving five, in order of age, were: Alexander; Simon; John (who adored his older brother Simon); and the girls, Sybilla and Catherine. Thomas Beaufort lived most of his life within a few miles of Dounie, but whether 'from his numerous family, or want of patrimony, appears to have been in not very wealthy circumstances', said the Reverend James Fraser.

Though there is no date for Simon's birth, the Reverend James, who was also the chiefly family's chaplain, recorded that at Castle Dounie, 'at the propitious moment, many swords hanging in the old hall leapt from their scabbards, indicating how mighty a man of war had been added to the race'. Even in earliest youth, Simon's face

7

expressed force of will. His steady gaze gave the impression of watchfulness, as his eyes scrutinised and his ears listened to his father and the Reverend James Fraser. He and his brothers were tall, vigorous and brave, when many of the older generation were exhausted by wars.

The route that took the Beaufort Fraser children from their home, the manor house 'Tomich', to Castle Dounie, to play with their aristocratic cousins, led them through the village of Beauly. Hugh, the 8th Lord Lovat, assumed his social and political domination of the regional capital, Inverness, in matters of politics and business. However, it was Beauly and the beautiful Aird of Lovat, not Inverness, that defined young Simon's horizons. Here, Simon and his brothers and sisters learned to ride and hunt. The males of the upper reaches of the clan sometimes spent as much as a third of the year hunting. It kept them fit and ready, trained to act in a body. If the fiery cross went up, they could fly together in an instant and chase men not deer.

When clans with territories north of the Highland capital, such as the Mackenzies whose lands bordered Fraser country, wanted to go to Inverness to attend to their affairs, they crossed the River Beauly at the ford in the village. Here they would have to pay Fraser men a toll and declare their business. In this way the Frasers were able to control an important point of access for the northern clans. A strong Fraser chief could use his geographic position to his advantage and help manage the north for the government in Edinburgh. The rewards he sought were the usual expressions of gratitude: perquisites and government positions. Geography blended always into geopolitics.

As well as being a soldier, Thomas Fraser of Beaufort was a thoughtful, scholarly man. When the 8th Lord Lovat was dying, Thomas sat for weeks at Castle Dounie by his deathbed, 'entertaining him with history and divinity'. Simon inherited from his father a passion for clan and national history, theology and philosophical debate, as well as the satisfaction of training and leading a body of armed kinsmen. The Beaufort Fraser children received an informal education in clan history and their place in the world from the Reverend James Fraser.

The son of a laird, Reverend James was at ease with English, Gaelic, French and Latin, and 'had a useful knowledge of Hebrew, Greek, German and Italian'. Simon Fraser would acquire the same languages, becoming fluent in four and competent in five.

In his youth, the Reverend James 'mounted his Highland pony, and accompanied by a Highland servant, spent three years touring Britain, Europe and the Holy Land' in order, he said, 'to rectify the judgement, enrich the mind with knowledge', and give it 'a polish'. Though by turns a Calvinist and Episcopalian, he happily posed as a Roman Catholic to get a room in European monasteries. He visited over thirty European states and on his return wrote *Triennial Travels*, describing every town and city of note, starting with Inverness. He would dedicate his *Chronicles of the Frasers* to Simon when he became chief.

For almost five decades, Reverend James ministered at Kirkhill, a tiny settlement near Beauly, and served as family chaplain to the Frasers. As chronicler the Reverend also occupied the role of *sean-achie*, or tradition-bearer, in the clan. In him the history of Scotland, England, Europe and the clan, actual and mythic, resided; he wove them together like a plaid, surrounding the Beaufort Fraser children with a solid sense of history, their duty to the living and to the dead. Their ancestors had served kings and country. So would they. This intoxicating blend of the literal and legendary fired their imaginations. Some of the oldest Gaelic songs, and even lullabies sung by wet nurses, rioted with bloody narratives of the honour their ancestors defended, and the outrages they avenged. Through such tales the children understood the Fraser loyalty to the doomed Stuart King Charles I.

At *ceilidhs** there would be folk tales, poems, theology, history, politics, agriculture, meteorology, games, riddles, repartee, music and medicine, and gossip – all in the Gaelic they liked to speak at home. Great arguments raged over international and local news. In the

---

* The word *ceilidh* meant simply a 'visit', but implied the whole informal education a child like Simon would receive at home.

martial society of the clans, Simon learned, the chief must loom larger than everyone else, keeping his enemies at bay, whilst earning the respect of close friends and allies.

If *ceilidh* debates grew too heated and threatened to turn bitter or to violence, someone might intervene and call for music, dance or a song – sometimes bawdy. Risqué verse was acceptable at any gathering – though satirising someone's good name could land you in a duel or a feud. One piece of bawdy by the bravura baronet Sir Duncan Campbell of Glenorchy entitled *Bod brighmhor ata ag Donncha* ('Duncan has a Potent Prick') extended to thirty-two lines of self-praise. Typically Gaelic in spirit, the gist of it was this:

> Grizzled Duncan's organ
> I guess is no great beauty,
> Adamantine, wrathful,
> ever ready to do his duty …

> A rheum-eyed hooded giant,
> sinuous, out-thrust face, spurty,
> A cubit out from its bag,
> ravaging, mighty knob-kerry.

Titillation was not the point (though it amused one clergyman enough to copy it into his personal poetry anthology); what this poem conveyed was the nature of a leader, of leadership. Its outrageousness merely educated by entertainment. The hero was a beast of eye-watering proportions and energy; the thought of him made women swoon. The part standing for the whole, the poem described a *proper* clan chief. The Viking culture of the rampaging warrior hero contributed features to the Celtic idea of an ideal chief. 'Victorious in battle and conflict', 'fearsome', 'violent', 'wrathful', with his 'stately-purple … broad back', it was the heroic duty of the 'potent prick chief' to generate and protect his own. He repelled rivals with the baleful glare of his single 'canny' eye, and with his stunning virility ensured the continuance of the natural order.

Laced with humour, verses like this carried a moral to the Beaufort boys, as they sat on the floor fireside in the main room at Tomich, taking it all in. There was no space in this world for a 'sweet' and 'affable' Fraser chief. Rather, the *ceann cinnidh*, the head of the kin, must be King Arthur, the Irish Diarmid, the Viking Beowulf, and Scots Wallace and his companion, Sir Simon Fraser, all rolled into one. The boys practised their swordsmanship imagining they were these great heroes, Simon taking the part of his namesake: Sir Simon the 'Patriot' Fraser – the 'talk and admiration of all Europe' – who was hung, drawn and quartered for his country's freedom on 8 September 1306, a year after his leader, Wallace.

The Beaufort boys were raised to regard their homeland as the heart of the Highland world, connected to all the exotic parts of Europe the Reverend James visited and described to them. But Alexander, Simon, and John would need more than clan stories to perform their duties as future leading men in the modern world. They would need the experience, erudition and confidence that a broad-based education offered. So the boys were put on ponies and sent to school in Inverness to prepare them for university and the battles ahead.

Though barely twelve miles distance, Beauly and Tomich were a world away from the regional capital. Born and bred Invernessians did not much like Highlanders. The Beaufort Fraser boys were a blend of Highland and Lowland. Wild hill men caused trouble to a royal burgh that prided itself on its modern civic and religious values. Townsfolk were terrorised by the 'bare-arsed *banditti*' who 'broke open their doors in the night time, and dig through their houses, plundering and taking away the whole moveables, and oftimes assassinating several poor people in their beds', before heading back to their strongholds in the wilderness.

As civil society settled under Charles II's rule, Inverness was more Lowland in character. Port towns like Inverness, and the sea lanes they sat on, thronged with traffic again. Over a hundred boats and ships could be anchored in Inverness harbour at any time; they strained at their ropes, ready to take scholars, curious travellers and merchants and their goods to and from the Continent. The Baltic ports, the great medical and ecclesiastical centres at Leyden and Paris, and the trading cities of the Hanseatic League, were more accessible and more familiar to educated Highlanders than most English cities and ports. Thousands of skiffs, fishing boats and ships hauling iron, coal and timber, fish and exotic commodities from all over the known world, sailed in and out of the lesser ports round the coast of northern Scotland.

Between Tomich and Inverness, the men and places that shaped young Simon Fraser's outlook were at once insular and remote from Edinburgh and London, but also cosmopolitan and Europhile. Dutch Leyden was closer in every way than English London. Thomas Beaufort wanted to educate his boys to belong in all these worlds – Continental and clan, Highland and Lowland, theocratic and Renaissance humanist. A period at grammar school in Inverness would brush up their Presbyterian theology, and their Latin and Greek. Simon would later study at university in Aberdeen, where he would be taught in these classical languages, as young men were across Europe. He needed to be articulate and literate in both.

The grammar school at Inverness was a room under the roof of the Presbyterian church on Kirk Street. The building stood on the banks of the River Ness. The Kirk Session of Elders that administered the school's business also interfered freely in the lives of the townsfolk. In fact, they saw it as a duty, and ran themselves ragged to keep the people 'godly' in the face of Highlanders' fondness for 'uncleanness, riots, and *extravaiging*' – that is, strolling about the streets when they should be at Divine service. When Simon was a boy, Scotland was a Presbyterian theocracy and men could be hanged for blasphemy, such as denying the reincarnation of Christ or doubting the doctrine of the Holy Trinity.

Along with the Town House, the Market Cross, the Court House, the Gaol and Armoury, the church was one of the matrices of Inverness life. Not only did it house the box pews in which each family shut themselves up to worship; in the body of the kirk, there were also desks for various traders to work from, as well as the school in the attic. Many of Simon's classmates could not buy a seat in the schoolroom, let alone a table. The children would peer through the holes in the floorboards, watching the men below negotiate with locals and strange-looking foreigners. Heather and grass on the floors muffled draughts and softened the boards under their bottoms. A Lowland minister unhappily stationed to the Highlands, described the students crouching there 'like pigs in a sty'. Slates in hand, they gazed up at their dominie, Mr Jaffray, who also yearned to return south as soon as possible from this strange place. 'English ministers did not know much more of Scotland than they did of Tartary,' another Lowlander concluded.

He could have added that they cared less than they knew. They did not see the multi-layered and shifting array of words and images that entered Simon and his brothers' minds. Simon's clan homeland was so remote from the rest of Britain that southerners often made out their wills before venturing there. One traveller to the Highlands returned hugely relieved to get out. 'I passed to English ground, and hope I may never go to such a country again. I thank God I never saw such another.'

It was traditional for the Master of Lovat (the eldest son), any potential heirs, and the principal gentlemen of Clan Fraser to attend Aberdeen University. Simon Fraser went there later than his peers, after a gap of a few years. The young man who arrived in Aberdeen in 1691 to study was about twenty years old, high-minded, intellectually curious, charming, extremely ambitious and proud. Six foot tall in his stockinged feet, he was bright-eyed with a wide, well-shaped mouth half-smiling above a strong, set jaw. A lace jabot foamed at his neck and a toffee-toned extravaganza of a wig tumbled down his back. Every inch of him proclaimed a self-conscious young Highland gentleman, and a Royalist.

In the 1690s half the population of Scotland lived north of the Highland line; Aberdeenshire was the most densely populated county. Aberdeen was divided into two parts: Old and New, the traditional and progressive incarnations of the town. The university had two colleges. Marischal College in New Aberdeen, founded in 1593, which was governed by a modern, Calvinist spirit; and King's College in Old Aberdeen, where Simon came to study, as had his father, Thomas, his brother Alexander, and his mentor, the Reverend James, before him. King's was founded in 1494 to the glory of James IV King of Scots, who died at Flodden Field. Roman Catholic until the mid-seventeenth century, King's was established on a European Renaissance model, mimicking the universities at Paris and Bologna.

On the chapel tower rose one of the glories of King's: an open lantern spire. 'A double arch of crossed stone', its two stone arms cross over. On top of the lantern spire 'there standeth a royal crown ... upon the top of the crown a stone globe; above it a double cross gilded; intimating as it were by such a bearing, that it is the King's College'. Here the Crown of earthly power was supported and raised on top of the House of God. Finally, a double cross perched like a gull on the summit of the globe. No one could fail to read the message: at King's the power of Monarchy, Bishops, Lords and the Lord intertwined. Divine right led to global domination.

As if to sober up the Royalists, God had smitten the crown on the spire in the previous generation, and it 'was overthrown ... by a furious tempest'. The Calvinists at Marischal College cheerfully mocked the Divine pretensions of the King's College Stuart affiliation after the disaster, but Royalists recalled it was 'quickly afterwards restored' and 'in a better forme'.

Simon Fraser lived in its shadow for five years. As a young man of his times he was steeped in this sort of apprehension of the immanence and intervention of the Divine in human life. He had already known four monarchs, despite his young age: Charles II ruled at his birth, followed by the short reign of Charles's brother, James II, before James had fled the thrones three years ago, refusing to renounce his Roman Catholicism and the rights of his Roman Catholic son and heir. By 1691, the solidly Protestant William III and Mary II co-ruled England, Scotland and Ireland. Like Cromwell before them, they maintained an experienced standing army in North Britain, quartered throughout Scotland with no regard for the local capacity to feed, water or house all these extra men.

Haars, the sea mists breathed out of the North Sea when the cold sea air meets the warm air off the land, haunted the mud streets around the King's College buildings, clinging to clothes, wigs and livestock, and drifting against the windows, some glassless, some with tiny opaque panes in the rooms where Simon came to sit, take down his 'dictats and notts', and learn. Tallow candles wavered against the gloom of lecture rooms. The gesture of a fire hissed. Eyes, struggling in the half-light to take down etiolated Latin quotations, were further harassed by the smoke. Simon roomed in cramped chambers in a building abutting the chapel.

The curriculum at Aberdeen offered a mix of academic studies, physical and martial training. It continued the education Simon had received at home from the Reverend James. The Reverend's nephew, Regent (Lecturer) George Fraser, was allocated to Simon as tutor for the duration of his degree. The timetable ran from the beginning of November to the end of June. The 'conveniendums' (times of convening to learn) were from seven to nine in the morning. After a break for breakfast, Simon worked from ten in the morning until midday. If it was 'a play day' he only worked again from five to six in the evening. If not, he sat from four to six o'clock. Before, after and in between all of this were prayers – in the Common School or at the dining table.

Recalling his university years, Simon described the timetable as gruelling. 'I was the youth of this Age that applied himself most to College Learning,' he said with pride. He followed the ordinary degree course in philosophy, yet he disparaged it. 'I read ten hours every day,' he said. 'That four years' study never signified a sixpence to me except to help me to chatter on some such foolish subject as *Ens rationis*.' At other times he conceded that 'the Philosophy class' strengthened 'discourse in arguing, which in my opinion is the most material thing which can be learned at Colleges now'. He could not possibly imagine in 1691 how much he would owe to that ability in later life.

The curriculum gave him more than training in rhetoric and disputation. Many decades ahead Simon would tell a friend: 'I always observed since I came to know anything in the world, that an active man with a small understanding will finish business and succeed better than an indolent, lazy man of the brightest sense and the most solid judgement.' His conclusion reflected his reading list at Aberdeen where they studied the recorded writings of Cicero, who pronounced 'the active life is of the highest merit'. Machiavelli, also on the curriculum, agreed with the Roman: 'An active man can achieve anything if he repudiates half-measures,' he suggested. This was the intellectual discourse of Simon's formative years: Cicero, Virgil, Aristotle, Machiavelli, Erasmus, Petrarch, Pufendorf and Grotius. These men taught Simon the power of human action to direct affairs, and jurisprudence. A strong man could be an agent of change, progress and power thanks to his own efforts – if he was wholehearted, ruthless and prepared. Simon's life was not merely the effect of God's, or godly government's, design. If he needed a rationale for his relentless activity as an adult, Aberdeen and raw necessity supplied it.

After the day's work, the 'Hebdomadars' – a sort of saintly university security force – received the keys of the college gates at nine at night. They would go to check on every room to 'observe the absents', or 'inquire if prayer and reading a part of the Scripture be gone about'. Examination of sacred lessons, and testing students through 'public disputes … in the Common School' on Saturday mornings kept Simon busy, honed his debating skills. Sundays meant mortification and endless opportunities, or obligations, for copious prayers.

All his life – as Episcopalian, or Roman Catholic – Simon enjoyed theological dispute. But he kept 'charity for all mankind' on this matter, he said. Though passionate about politics, society and culture, religious intensity bored most King's College men. Typically, Simon's friends were lovers of the old High Church type of Protestantism. Called 'Episcopalianism' in Scotland, it was roughly equivalent to Anglicanism in England. They preferred to believe in bishops appointed by the King, and both appointed by God. The idea of a clan chief corresponded with the mystique of a divinely sanctioned ruler.

When they could escape observation, Simon and his friends frequented the taverns. Failure to keep up enough praying, getting caught drinking or dallying with the serving lasses (Jean Calvin thought lust a sickness only marriage could cure), playing dice and cards, loud singing, and persisting in holding worldly and semi-seditious conversation in their rooms, all incurred punishments. 'Some crimes are punished corporalie, others by pecunial mulct, and grosser crimes by extrusion.' You were thrashed, fined, or thrown out.

But Simon's claim of time-wasting at university disparages the gifts it gave him: tactics, rationale and strategy for effective resistance. All his life, he never doubted Machiavelli's contention that the ends justified the means. It was not good enough to be merely strong and upright. Machiavelli advised that 'a Prince ... should learn from the fox and the lion; because the lion is defenceless against traps and a fox is defenceless against wolves'.

At the end of his degree course, in the winter of 1694/95, Regent George Fraser offered Simon the chance to continue his studies in a civil law degree, an increasingly attractive route for modern clan leaders seeking to avoid blood feuds. The courts were becoming the more usual battlegrounds for defeating clan enemies, in place of the martial law of the glens. Simon began the course at Aberdeen, but then very suddenly withdrew from it. To understand why, it is necessary to go back nine years to 1685 and the reasons he delayed coming to university in the first place: a wedding – specifically its special marriage contract – and a revolution.

TWO

To be a fox and a lion, 1685–95

'One must be a fox to recognise traps,
and a lion to frighten wolves'
— MACHIAVELLI

In 1685, Simon was at school in Inverness when he learned that his seventeen-year-old cousin, Hugh, the 9th Lord Lovat, had taken a wife. The choice of a chief's bride was of key importance to the political and dynastic interests of the clan, and it would have been conventional for Lord Lovat's closest Fraser kin to advise him, Thomas Beaufort foremost among them. But no Fraser was consulted. Hugh Lovat's maternal uncle, Sir George Mackenzie of Tarbat, made sure of it: he had kept the Fraser cousins apart for many years in order to isolate and control the young boy chief.

Hugh had been orphaned at the age of six, when his father, the 8th Lord Lovat, died at home aged just twenty-nine. After his funeral, the Fraser gentlemen allowed Mackenzie of Tarbat to take young Hugh away. Thereafter he was raised apart from his sisters and his Fraser kindred in Sir George's home, Castle Leod, fifteen miles from Dounie. That the leading Fraser men allowed a Mackenzie to step in and dominate their clan showed how weak the Frasers had become. The Reverend James harangued the clan gentry for tolerating Tarbat's dominance of young Hugh. 'He that hath the blood and spirit of his ancestors running in his veins,' Reverend James thundered, 'cannot be so much turned into a statue or idle spectator … to look what our …

predecessors have been, as well as what ourselves at present are, lest falling short of the imitation of their immortal actions, we so strangely degenerate as not to understand what we ourselves ought to be!' But no amount of eloquent rhetoric by the Reverend could stir Thomas of Beaufort or other principal Frasers to rescue the boy.

A clan could only prosper under a strong chief, but it was clear from an early age that Hugh would not be that person. The Reverend James judged him as 'always but a man of very weak intellectuals'. Bad chiefs came in the shape of weak men, children, women or old men. During Simon's youth, Clan Fraser entered a phase where it got all four – in that order. Two generations of 'virulent Mackenzie women', including Hugh's late mother, had left the Lovat estates rundown and drowning in debt. The Frasers of Beaufort were side-lined and Tarbat inserted his own kindred to manage the clan, handing the Mackenzies leases on Fraser lands. He even gave a profitable little sinecure to the high chief of the Mackenzies, the Earl of Seaforth, as a compliment.

Sir George's standing rose within his own clan as he interfered in that of his nephew's. Tarbat competed for high public office for sixty years, during an era 'of extreme ruthlessness and cunning intrigue', according to one historian of the 1600s, which culminated in 'the final triumph of the various egomaniacs, bigots and embezzlers who' by the final decade of the century would rule the roost in Edinburgh. During the period of his nephew, Hugh Lovat's, minority, Sir George was out of favour and deprived of office.

Tarbat intended to use young Hugh to boost his political ambitions in Edinburgh and build up a local power base from which to launch himself back into the political fray. His search for a suitably connected bride for Hugh took him to Lord John Murray, who had been rising high in the ranks of the Scottish administration in Edinburgh and Whitehall since the accession of King James II, and on to his sister Lady Amelia Murray. In terms of breeding the Fraser elite liked the idea. Not only was Lady Amelia the daughter of the Stuart Royalist champion, the Marquis of Atholl, but she was also related to several Scottish noble families and crowned heads of Europe. The Murrays came from Blair Atholl in Perthshire, fifty miles north of Edinburgh, between the Highlands and the Lowlands. Lord John was married to Katherine, sister of the Duke of Hamilton. These two, the Murrays and Hamiltons, intrigued to dominate Scottish politics and rule the country for absent kings.

Scotland was a sovereign nation, but the Scottish sovereign had resided in London, not Edinburgh since 1603 (when James VI of Scotland also became James I of England on the death of Elizabeth I). In 1685, James II ruled from Whitehall through a rotating oligarchy of ambitious Scottish magnates who dominated the Scottish Parliament in Edinburgh. Lord John Murray was one of these. Murray, son and heir to the Marquis of Atholl, was a favourite of King James's. Atholl and Lord Murray also saw the appeal of the match. Clan Fraser's star may have been waning, but it still had many attractions. The extensiveness and location of Fraser country at the heart of the Highlands could vastly increase Murray influence in Scotland and add handsomely to Lord Murray's growing political profile.

Tarbat only saw the marriage from his own point of view, something he almost immediately regretted. Simon wrote later that the union of Hugh and the nineteen-year-old Amelia, now Lady Lovat, should have 'accomplished the barbarous and long-continued designs' of the Mackenzies 'to win the family of Lovat and extirpate the name of Fraser out of the North of Scotland'. It so nearly did, and undoubtedly would have done, had it not been for Simon Fraser of Beaufort.

Hugh Lovat's marriage naturally affected Simon's standing in the clan, pushing him a step away from the topmost branch of the tree. But the Beauforts expected that. They were 'spares' to the heir, and a chief must marry. What irked Simon Fraser was not the union with Lady Amelia, but an extraordinary pre-nuptial agreement planted in the match that affected the future inheritance of the Lovat titles and estates. It would prove to be of such dubious legality that Tarbat and Murray let it lie dormant for nearly ten years, so as not to draw attention or resistance to their schemes from other magnates. For now young Hugh and Amelia settled to the only job Sir George entrusted his nephew to accomplish without his guiding hand – to make lusty male heirs.

But it was another inheritance problem that delayed Simon from going up to Aberdeen. He was preparing to leave Tomich in the autumn of 1688 and join Alexander at university when news came of the landing of William of Orange and his invasion force at Torbay in Devon. Their Stuart King, James II, had abandoned his thrones and was now rallying support.

Tension had built up over the decade before James came to the thrones of England, Scotland and Ireland in 1685, as it became clear that his brother Charles II was not going to leave an heir. The English Parliament had tried to exclude James from the succession before Charles II died, but failed. By 1688, James II already had heirs. His first wife gave him two daughters, Mary and Anne Stuart, before she died. The girls' mother had been Protestant, and so were they. Mary married William of Orange, and Anne wed Prince George of Denmark.

Then James II married again. The second time he took for his wife Mary of Modena, an Italian Roman Catholic, in a marriage negotiated by France. Parliament's alarm increased when James converted to Catholicism, and reached fever pitch when his papist wife was delivered of a boy. James II refused to bring him up as a Protestant, as he himself had been raised, but promised to respect the Protestantism of his administration and country. His was a rather contradictory position: delicate and full of potential pitfalls.

James refused to let his government interfere in the natural course of the Stuart inheritance of the British Crown: God willed that the King and Queen have a healthy Catholic son. Opposite him, the government refused to contemplate a papist ascending the thrones on any terms. An impasse quickly developed between Westminster and St James's until, just after Christmas 1688, James II suddenly fled to France. His first cousin, Louis XIV, welcomed James, his wife, his son, extended family and entourage, as the victims of a heretical state. James set up a temporary Court in exile, but planned to return within months.

James saw his departure merely as a tactical retreat. He admired the absolutism of the monarchies of France and Spain and assumed his government would not be unable to function without the King to sign laws. Parliament would have to ask him back. Of course he would accept, *if* Parliament backed down over the succession issue that had provoked this traumatic flight.

He was correct that the government required a monarch. But Parliament reacted to the ultimatum of his departure by inviting Mary Stuart, James's Protestant daughter from his first marriage, to become their monarch. She accepted. Her husband, William of Orange, insisted on having equal status with his wife and William and Mary jointly assumed the thrones.

The crisis escalated at speed and within weeks the Highlands exploded into lawlessness and violence. The whole event would trigger the most serious conflict to gnaw at the foundations of Great Britain for the next sixty years. James's departure provoked yet another revolution in a century of revolutions. And it led to the birth of Jacobitism, and its followers, Jacobites, from the Latin for James, *Jacobus*.

All through the winter of 1688/89, Scottish politicians fought for political power in Scotland with growing intensity. In the race to get control of the Scottish Parliament all constitutional principles were dumped. On 17 December, the Privy Council, including Tarbat, now back in government, sent a letter to James II, who had fled and then returned, asking him to call a free parliament. When James fled for a second time, they lost confidence in him. By 24 December they petitioned William, urging *him* to call a free Parliament.

In March the following year, a divided Parliament in Edinburgh passed a vote to support William and Mary against her father, James II. In Inverness, the Presbyterian-dominated Council swore allegiance to the new joint monarchs. But not everyone in Scotland agreed with the ruling. Many of the Gaelic-speaking and Episcopalian Highlanders remained loyal to James, including the Earl of Dundee ('Bonnie' Dundee), and large elements of the clan elites, such as Alexander

Fraser of Beaufort, Simon's older brother. Alexander came home to raise the Fraser host for James II along with clansman Fraser of Foyers. Once more, the four kingdoms stood ready to plunge into battle along religious and dynastic lines. It was a truly awful prospect.

Inverness, harried by Jacobite troops, soon became the scene of 'blood works, riots and fornications', the Council minutes noted with understandable hysteria. Simon claimed that Alexander was the first man in the north to join Dundee's Jacobite army: 'My brother brought him all the rents in Meal and Corn' from the Lovat estates, Simon boasted. Since Tarbat and Lord Murray had abandoned their royal patron to serve a new master, Alexander of Beaufort's initiative incensed them.

Simon tried to follow his brother. He gathered arms, mounted a horse and rode out to join General Thomas Buchan's Jacobite force (consisting mainly of Highlanders and soldiers from the MacDonald, MacLean, Cameron, MacPherson and Invermoriston Grants clans). He did not get very far: he was captured, confined and eventually allowed to return to Tomich. Hugh, Lord Lovat did not accompany Alexander either. As soon as his Mackenzie uncle and Murray brother-in-law had changed sides, he was told to stay at home and prevent his men from joining the rebel Jacobites. This Hugh signally failed to do. When he was told to muster the Frasers for King William he was left gathering the few men who had refused to march for James, to go with him south to his in-laws' Atholl–Murray territory and there to retrieve his clansmen from his cousin Alexander, and put the Frasers under Lord Murray's command.

When Hugh reached Perthshire, his soldiers lined up with some of the Atholl Militia and awaited orders. Hugh went inside to explain why so few Frasers had come with him. As they waited, Hugh's men caught sight of the rest of their clan marching by, Alexander at their head, en route to join Bonnie Dundee. They broke ranks and rushed to the river, scooped water into their bonnets and drank the health of King James VII of Scotland and II of England. Clapping their hats back on their heads, they ran to join their kinsmen, asking Alexander for orders.

Murray and the Marquis of Atholl were enraged; they would not forget this challenge to their authority by one of the young Beauforts. The ineffectual Hugh returned home to Castle Dounie while the Marquis of Atholl packed and headed south to Bath, to take the waters for his health – and safety. The Jacobite head of a traditionally Jacobite clan, he could not be accused of treason by his new King and Queen if he was not in the country. He left Lord Murray, his son and heir, behind to take charge.

The two armies finally closed in on each other on 27 July 1689 at Killiecrankie, a rocky pass ten miles south of the Atholl–Murray seat of Blair Castle. Dundee had 2,500 men, mainly Highlanders – 'the best untrained fighting men in Scotland' – against 3,000 government dragoons, troops and infantry. Supposedly allies by marriage, Murray's Atholl men and Hugh Lovat's kinsmen fought each other at close quarters, and to the death. Though the Jacobites won the battle, inflicting terrible losses of up to 2,000 on the Dutchman's army, over 600 Jacobite Highlanders lost their lives, including their brilliant leader, Bonnie Dundee. His death signalled the end of the uprisings, with government forces scoring a final victory weeks later, despite their losses, in Murray country at Dunkeld.

Amongst the Fraser casualties was Simon's brother, Alexander. Badly wounded, his clansmen 'carried him home in a litter'. Thomas and Simon laid him on his bed to rest, but weeks later Alexander died of his wounds. Simon became his father's heir. Fraser gentlemen gathered at Tomich, wondering if Hugh Lovat at Dounie would mourn the death of his cousin Alexander and the other brave Frasermen who had died with him. Would he lament the defeat of the Stuart King and order the usual magnificent Highland wake for fallen kinsmen? Or would he celebrate with Lady Amelia her Murray clan's share in the victory of William and Mary, and the killing of his kin at Killiecrankie?

Following the battle, the Frasers again suffered. Believing the clan to be Jacobite, government troops were given permission to ransack the Aird of Lovat as they had in the months following the Civil War. After this, Jacobite soldiers came through the Lovat estates: since Lord Lovat had led out men for William of Orange, they assumed the clan had turned Williamite. They plundered freely, robbing the people of anything they could find. By the time peace was declared, the weakness and incoherence in the Fraser leadership had left Fraser country devastated by both sides, more than once. Without a strong chief, everything in Fraser country was open to predation by all comers, apparently.

The Reverend James expressed alarm at Murray–Mackenzie control. These 'strangers', he said, 'prove but spies amongst us, discover our weakness, take all the advantage of us they can, fledge their wings with our wealth, and so fly away and fix it in a strange country, and we get no good of it.' They leased Lovat lands to men from their own clan depriving the chief's own kin of income and breaking up their inherited territories. Then Murray had tried to take the men away and make them fight against their rightful King. These lessons were not lost on Simon. He later claimed that he was nurtured 'to display a violent attachment' to King James from his 'earliest youth'.

The birth of the Jacobite cause had taken Thomas of Beaufort's eldest son and ruined his lands. Thomas could not afford to fund Simon through university until his affairs were in better order and the country at peace. On 1 July 1690, William decisively defeated James II at the Battle of the Boyne in Ireland. James fled for the last time, ending his rule. By the autumn of 1691, Beaufort felt secure enough to send his son and heir, Simon, to Aberdeen.

The Highlands took a long time to settle under the new regime. Simon was in the first year at university when William lost patience with his Scottish subjects' continuing flirtation with Jacobitism and refusal to swear allegiance to him and Mary. He agreed to a gesture to pacify them once and for all, needing to release British soldiers from security duties in Scotland to fight his European wars, as head of the Protestant Alliance against the territorial and religious ambitions of France's Louis XIV.

In January 1692, William signed instructions to separate the Glencoe MacDonalds and make an example of them, by finding a way to 'extirpate that sept of thieves'. The justification was the delay by

MacIain, chief of the Glencoe MacDonalds, in submitting formally to the government's representative and obtaining the indemnity William offered to former rebels. The commander of the Scottish army, Livingstone, wrote to Lieutenant-Colonel Hill, the officer in charge of the garrison nearest to Glencoe. 'Here is a fair occasion for you to show that your garrison serves to some use ... begin with Glencoe and spare nothing that belongs to him, but do not trouble the Government with prisoners.' Hill was horrified. Calling the order 'a nasty, dirty thing', he said the proposed action was uncalled-for: the district where the Glencoe MacDonalds lived was calm; they did not need violent pacification. Too late.

On the night of 13 February, MacIain's people offered shelter to government troops whom they believed were en route to bringing in the rebel Glengarry MacDonalds. At 5 a.m., Glenlyon, in charge of the government soldiers, began the slaughter. MacDonalds were bound, shot and then bayoneted for good measure. After the killings, they burned houses and drove the stock off to Fort William to feed the garrison, leaving 'poor stripped women and children, some with child, and some giving suck, wrestling against a storm in mountains and heaps of snow, and at length overcome' they lay down and died.

The bloodshed at Glencoe blighted King William's rule, and left a deep, long-standing hostility towards him in much of Scotland. To bring Lord Murray back into the government fold and dissolve the stain left on their reputation by Killiecrankie, the Scottish Secretary James Johnston persuaded William to put Murray at the head of the enquiry into Glencoe, and find a scapegoat for the atrocity. That scapegoat was Dalrymple, a rival of Johnston's, who had added the instruction 'extirpate that sept of thieves'. Though William undertook sweeping reforms of his Scottish ministry, the enquiry's report would do little to soothe Highlander and Jacobite anger.

By the winter of 1694/95, after ten years of trying, Hugh Lovat had failed to achieve the one thing required of him. The lack of surviving male Lovat heirs caused Murray and Atholl increasing alarm. Lady Amelia produced both girls and boys, but only the girls (Amelia,

Katherine and Margaret) lived. There was another infant boy, John, but the odds on him surviving were dreadful. Hugh Lovat was the only son of an only son, both of whom had died in their twenties. It was time to return to the marriage contract, and enshrine it in law.

Sir George Mackenzie of Tarbat's family contained a lot of lawyers. He was a lawyer; his brother, Sir Roderick Mackenzie (Lord Prestonhall), was a Law Lord. They reviewed the contents of the marriage contract. The first part of it stated the obvious. The Lovat–Fraser inheritance went through the boys. Then, it asserted that *any* surviving child of Hugh and Amelia would take precedence over the next male heirs, who were the Beauforts. All that an heiress need do was marry someone who already bore the name of Fraser. The normal procedure among the clans suffering the iniquity of an heiress would be to marry her to the nearest male heir. Given Thomas's great age, in this case it would be *his* son and heir, Simon. So far, all this contract did was state the conventions governing marriage at the top of any kindred with a sizeable inheritance at stake. In other words, the contract was completely unnecessary. However it innovated in the next clause.

In 1685, Mackenzie and Murray had stated that if the inheritance did come down to an heiress, all her husband need do was *assume* the name of Fraser to fulfil the requirement that she marry someone 'of the name of Fraser'. Then they would both inherit the Lovat titles and estates. The heiress could be married off to anyone from any clan in effect. This threatened to write out the Beaufort Fraser men, Thomas, Simon and John.

The marriage of an heiress to a man from another clan had the most serious implications for the heiress's clan and its territories. This freshly made 'Fraser' husband would enter his wife's inheritance right at the top and the chieftainship would be conveyed to him. The clan the husband came from, to whom of course he owed all his prior loyalty and affection, could eliminate the Frasers' presence in their own country, and take over their assets. If the heiress married a Mackenzie, the chieftainship would be conveyed to him. If she married a Murray cousin, it would be conveyed to him.

If Hugh died without signing the ratification of their contract, a Fraser with some legal training might easily have this specious document dismissed. Then the Murrays' power base and their exercise of power in the Highlands would be seriously weakened. The old Marquis of Atholl urged his son to get a move on. The Lovat estates are 'the best feather in our wing' he reminded Lord Murray. They must not 'lose' their 'keystone' after a decade of growing influence.

Murray presented the ratification document to Hugh Lovat, who signed it. Murray then took it to the Court of Session to be ratified in law. With the stroke of a pen, Hugh cut Simon from his place on the family tree, and was very likely handing over his inheritance to a girl. He had four; one was going to survive. Letting himself be manipulated by 'natures stronger than his own', as Simon noted tersely, Hugh overturned the tradition and logic of clanship. He opened the door wider to the danger of loss of the clan to another, and put huge power in the hands of whoever controlled the marriage prospects of the heiress. For an ineffectual man, Hugh had created something that had powerful implications for the clan and his family.

In his poky student lodgings in Aberdeen in the spring of 1695, Simon saw that his family were being juggled out of position. But he had to move carefully. Hugh's baby son *might* survive. If so, Simon would only ever be the Laird of Beaufort. Lord Murray could be a valuable connection for someone like him. King William was starting to equip Murray with all the trappings that made power work – royal patronage, commissions and influence at Court. Murray had cash and jobs to distribute. He was networking to get all Scotland and half the British administration in his hands. Simon had to remember that, dislike him though he did, Murray could bring Simon, the scion of a clan now closely allied to Murray's own, forward in the world. For now, Simon needed to be part of his enemy's faction in Scotland.

It was therefore no surprise that after completing his first degree, Simon started on postgraduate work in civil law – specifically property rights. By becoming a lawyer, then a judge, he fought to equip himself should the rightful inheritance of the Lovat titles and estates be questioned. But the sudden ratification of the marriage contract had upset Simon's plans, and now redirected his life. The infant John was Master of Lovat, but Lovat heirs often died young. John's older sister Amelia, and who she married, were of real interest therefore. Simon had a young man's sense of time. Precious years climbing to power in the judiciary might be years squandered. Besides, a growing number of judges, those who were not Mackenzies, owed their appointments to Murray.

Simon felt a measure of contempt for the chief who had exposed his clan to such powerful and ruthless men. Hugh had proved himself incapable of protecting their interests, homes and people. 'Lord Lovat was known for a man of feeble understanding,' he wrote. In Simon's view – fired by principled, naive outrage – the job of preparing the clan's defence against a decisive assault on their name and country had fallen on his shoulders. 'It was my duty to venture my person and Life to recover … [my] ancient family,' he wrote. He bubbled with idealism and bravado. His whole upbringing had prepared him to rise heroically to this kind of crisis and defend them all, he said of himself. 'His duty was inseparable from his Nature.'

Lord Murray saw it all rather differently. As a penniless bystander, Simon posed little threat. Murray did not notice him. Young Beaufort would require a lot more than family pride and passion to halt Atholl ambitions. Simon needed power, money and the backing of his clan. To acquire these he put university ambitions to one side, and headed for Edinburgh.

THREE

'Nice use of the beast and the man', 1695–96

'Your destiny decreed to set you an apprentice
in the school of affliction, and to draw you
through the ordeal fire of trial, the better to
mould, temper and fashion you for
rule and government'

— THE REVEREND JAMES TO SIMON

Simon approached the Scottish capital full of doubts. He knew what to do, but not how to do it. He needed a patron to bring him forward in the world. 'There are two ways of fighting,' Machiavelli instructed a would-be Prince: 'by law or by force. The first way is natural to men, and the second to beasts … So a prince must understand how to make nice use of the beast and the man.' Simon came to learn to fight like a beast and a man.

A young man full of ambition and ability, but without employment or income, Simon lacked prospects. He had connections, but his best contacts in government were also his enemies. His cousin by marriage, Lord Murray, was his obvious port of call. Atholl and Murray were working to tighten their grip on Clan Fraser and would only help Simon if they thought he could assist in their plans to dominate the Highlands. Murray might even readily give Simon a job to control him, even as Murray worked to cut him off. Simon saw little choice but to dissemble with the Murrays, and offer to serve them, as the Murrays dissembled with the Frasers.

Edinburgh was a typical medieval city. Its buildings clung to the high back of a long hill like fleas and burrs on a sheep's back. The old city cooled its carcase in a mire of swamp and loch. When Simon arrived for the first time it was still largely enclosed within its medieval city walls. The scarcity of space meant the old houses towered ten or even twelve floors over the streets below. The High Street ('the Royal Mile') formed the city's spine and central nervous system. It was capillaried with narrow lanes – wynds, allies and closes leading to and from the main street. At the lower end, the east end of the High Street, the Canongate guarded the entrance to the Palace of Holyroodhouse, the image of King William III's presence in Scotland. Heading west, halfway up the High Street, were the Scottish Parliament and offices of the judiciary. At the top end of it, on an extinct volcano, sprawled the massed bulk of Edinburgh Castle. A sleeping giant of military power, it dominated the institutions of the fragile, Williamite Scottish state.

Tall narrow houses flanked Simon as he headed up the High Street towards Parliament to find Lord Murray. He lowered his gaze to skip around the gurgling gutters, overflowing with the effluent of the piled-up city, and skirt the fat pigs rooting excitedly through it. He moved in and out of the piazzas on the ground floors of gaunt old houses. Aristocrats occupied the first floors, clerks nested on the tenth. People lived close up, bound by the economies of architecture, space and a dearth of hard cash. Merchants' wares – woollen stuff, linen, pots – lay in heaps among the pillars, spilling from shops too tiny to do more than keep them secure at night. Ascending the buildings like a row of semaphore flags, colourful illustrations painted on boards indicated where people could find certain wares – a cut loaf, periwig, cheese, a firkin of butter, petticoat stays, from the baker, wig dresser, cheesemonger, dressmaker.

Most men of affairs were on the go by five in the morning. Before the bell of St Giles Kirk struck seven, the pioneering medical man Dr Pitcairne was seeing patients in his underground rooms near the church. Edinburghers called it the 'groping office', because of its darkness and its tenant's occupation. By 6 a.m., Law Lords and lawyers had met agents and clients in the taverns and perused over half a dozen cases.

A fellow politician observed that Lord Murray was 'so great an admirer of his master, King William, that he mimicked him in many of his gestures'. The King loved the way Murray revered him, and he showed it. He gave him a colonel's commission (and the funding) to raise a regiment to defend Edinburgh. William did not feel safe on Scottish soil without a heavy military presence. Only the Stuart-born Queen at his side gave the Dutch Stadtholder any sense of legitimacy in the eyes of most Scots, especially after Glencoe. But the previous winter Mary had died suddenly of smallpox, aged just thirty-two.

In public, Simon echoed the Court Party's expressions of sympathy for William III's loss. In private, he wrote to his father: 'I doubt not you will be in mourning [clothes] for Queen Mary, but I am resolv'd to buy none till Ki. W. dies.' Mourning clothes, he teased, 'perhaps may serve for the next Summer Suit'. He penned similarly jaunty notes to known fellow Jacobites: MacDonald of Glengarry and (rashly) Lady Amelia Lovat's Jacobite brother, Lord Mungo Murray – 'drinking' to the death. Apart from Lord John, the Murrays remained predominantly a Jacobite clan. These letters were a young man's folly and Simon's first wrong move. Glengarry was married to Hugh Lovat's sister, Isobel, and was in Lord Murray's pay. He passed Simon's notes to Murray, who kept them safe. They were Simon of Beaufort's death warrant, if one were ever needed.

Queen Mary's death exposed the tenuousness of William III's right to rule. Many in Scotland felt their suffering was the legacy of removing God's anointed King, James II. A failed harvest in 1695 compounded their discontent. William needed strong support in Scotland: it was imperative that Murray raise the thirteen companies needed to fill his regiment, each under a captain. Every captain received a salary. Out of this he provided the men, paid his company's expenses and kept the balance for himself. Murray offered one to Hugh Lovat. It would bring this Jacobite clan to heel, turn it Williamite, and display to his royal master Murray's growing influence in the Highlands.

Hugh was not interested. It would mean leaving his wife and family, mustering in Edinburgh and becoming politically active in a way he had never desired. Murray had pressured Hugh to take the oath abjuring the Stuarts in favour of William. Now Murray wanted his brother-in-law to take a captaincy, and provide 300 Frasers for Murray's regiment. Murray insisted. Lovat caved in, and then failed to fill the company. He had never led his men.

Simon Fraser unleashed 'the bitterest invectives', criticising his chiefly cousin for accepting the 'infamous commission'. Alexander had died resisting King William; now Lord Lovat was asking them to sign up to join his killers. Behind the scenes, Simon worked to discourage Frasermen from enlisting. Above all, Simon wanted the captaincy for himself. He approached Murray's recruiting agent, Dollery, and offered to fill the Fraser Company of Murray's Regiment of Foot in return for Hugh Lovat's captaincy commission. Dollery wrote to Murray recommending Simon: 'I think him a very hopeful young man ... and may be very serviceable to your Lordship.' Simon had told him that with anything less than a captaincy he could not 'do anything to distinguish him from the rest, which I find he very much aspires after'. Dollery picked up on the ambition, but not the scale of it; and he missed the potential irony of his observation. Murray did not.

Simon duly filled the 300 places his clan chief had failed to achieve. Pleased with himself, Simon asked for his captaincy and his money, a pound per soldier. Murray refused: he recognised that Simon was attempting to use clan operational norms – where clansmen served their leading kinsman's cause, not a distant representative of the Crown – and subvert British regimental ones. Murray allowed Simon into his fold, but at the lowest possible level – as a lieutenant, where he believed he could not cause any trouble. Simon found himself outmanoeuvred. He 'did not fail to be extremely disgusted', he wrote, 'having suffered himself to be over-reached by Lord Murray, whose treason he conceived to be of a very infamous nature'. By the end of December 1695, Lieutenant Simon Fraser was in command of Lovat's Company of accoutred, martial-souled, Jacobite Highlanders. Some days they formed the Palace Guard at Holyroodhouse; others they marched to the other end of the High Street to form part of the force to defend the Williamite regime in Edinburgh. On their uniforms they wore the Murray badge (a mermaid with comb and mirror, and the words, *Tout Pret*, 'Quite Ready'); and they carried the Murray colours. Simon's saddle blanket and holster cap were embroidered with the cipher 'WR'. It was as if the Frasers had been printed all over with the stamp of the enemy's seal. Where was the Fraser badge of stag's head and motto *Je suis prest*, 'I Am Ready'; the Fraser of Lovat coat of arms – crowns and strawberry leaves – the last indicating the French origin of the clan.

William III desperately needed his Scottish soldiers: the British Army was chronically overstretched because of the King's European campaigns, particularly his obsession with countering French aggression on the Dutch borders. High war taxes, the poor harvests and the continued heavy-handed quartering of troops was crippling the Scottish economy. William needed stability in his territories in North Britain. The King's Private Secretary, Johnston, requested Murray come to London, and to come with panache. 'If you have company at hand to come with you, My Lord Lovat, or Glengarry, it will look well, but no time is to be lost,' Johnston counselled. That was Hugh Lovat's purpose in life, Simon thought to himself – to gild another man's lily and make a usurper feel secure. But Lovat would not leave his fireside in the middle of a hellish Highland winter. So Murray travelled south alone.

When Murray arrived he found he was to be well rewarded. On 13 January 1696, the King appointed him Secretary of State for Scotland. 'He told me I owed it only to himself, which indeed is passed doubting,' Murray purred with pleasure to his wife.

In Edinburgh, Murray's officers fell over each other to congratulate their colonel. Simon led the cheers. 'All your Lordship's friends here are overjoyed for your Lordship's new preferment,' he gushed. 'God grant your Lordship health to enjoy it!' And ended his huzzahs with a request: 'I hope your Lordship will not forget my captain's act. It will certainly do me good until your Lordship is pleased to bestow better on me.' He had his eye on the colonelcy.

Another officer simply asked Murray for the whole regiment straight out. The Secretary of State would not be expected to keep it in his own hands. Even without the personal motivation of the clan, it was not surprising Simon pushed so hard. In the lower reaches of the establishment, men like Simon saw too clearly the kind of oblivion that lay just below them. Except for a tiny minority of aristocrats, everyone was on the make. Simon, born to a little portion of privilege, knew there was a path down the social ladder that offered no one, except maybe his chief, a foothold. The weak went down; the strong rose.

Poor and failing harvests dominated the rest of the decade in Scotland. 'The living wearied of burying the dead,' and the population was forced to fight for scraps. These were 'King William's ill years'. The term showed who the Scottish people thought had brought God's anger on them. In London and Edinburgh, Jacobite presses poured forth propaganda: 'I hear the angel guardian of our island whispering in our sovereign's ear ... Rise and take the child and his mother, and return into your country, for they are dead who sought the life of the child.' The 'sovereign' was James II, and his flight had taken him and his wife, Mary and their baby boy into 'Egypt'/France. The biblical analogy showed the strength of feeling in the two kingdoms on the issue of rightful kings and usurping tyrannical governments.

Murray's pleasure in his political success was interrupted in February when the government received intelligence about an invasion plot from France that would terminate 'in an assassination' of the King. Other informants spoke of co-ordinating action by Jacobite officers embedded in regiments guarding Edinburgh Castle. Murray's Regiment of Foot was one of those mentioned. Murray galloped north to hold Scotland steady for the King.

The castle was 'in a very defenceless state', Simon noted, as he trotted his company of clansmen up the Royal Mile from Holyroodhouse. He too had been plotting – with Lord Drummond, active Jacobite and heir to the Duke of Perth – and was in communication with both of them. They agreed that 'as soon as the King [James II] should arrive in Scotland … they should make themselves masters by a *coup de main* of the unarmed garrison, and shut the gates … They should then declare for King James.' In the end the scheme came to nothing. But plotting made disempowered men feel powerful. If James returned, he would sweep Lord Murray away.

Murray gathered his officers. They 'were regarded by the common men in the light of Jacobites', he stormed; all officers must swear the Oath of Abjuration, compelling their loyalty. The oath forswore loyalty to James II and the exiled Stuart Court, and swore allegiance to William and the Revolution settlement. Simon was outraged. 'Officers, highly attached to King James, were forced to sign … in order to preserve to themselves the means of subsistence,' he said, disgusted that Murray insulted good men by forcing them to square up to the competing interests of their souls and their sporrans. He was one of them, and signed.

The following March, 1696, King William summoned Murray south again to reward him further, creating him Earl of Tullibardine, so that he could be a King's Commissioner in the next session of the Scottish Parliament. Murray insisted he must have his brother-in-law at his side this time and summoned Hugh to London. The Earl promised Hugh he would be presented at Court and said he would ask the King to make the whole Regiment of Foot over to him. Simon pushed to accompany his cousin. He and Hugh had grown close since Simon left university and Simon now occupied a traditional place in the clan hierarchy: commanding his chief's soldiers. Murray reluctantly agreed.

After nearly two weeks on the roads, Hugh Lovat, Simon Fraser and their servants reached London, long black boots, full-skirted thick wool coats, linen and wigs all caked with sweat and muck. They found their lodgings and prepared to enjoy the city, keenly anticipating their royal audience. It was the perfect opportunity to make a favourable impression on the King, and who knew what 'gratification' might follow – the regiment, a government post perhaps? At Kensington Palace, they met Tullibardine who conducted them into the King's presence. Lord Lovat was 'one of the most ancient peers of Scotland … head of one of the bravest clans'. Tullibardine announced. Lovat and Tullibardine 'could venture to assure his Majesty of their fidelity'. As the Highland chief stepped up to speak, Tullibardine told Hugh to 'fall upon one knee and take leave of his Majesty'. Ever 'of a contracted understanding' Hugh 'did as he was directed', Simon later wrote of his cousin. Not for the first time, Simon despaired of his chief's passivity. Some men did not merit their opportunities.

Before Simon could urge Hugh to re-present himself at Court, Tullibardine was recalled to the Scottish Parliament to deal with the ongoing fears of invasion and assassination. The Earl briefed Hugh and Simon that, all things considered, this was not the moment to bother the King with personal requests. He would be forced to hold on to the Regiment of Foot, he said, 'till the fears of an invasion should be blown over'. They had heard all this before, Simon told Hugh. Had they come all this way, at great expense, to show the King of England that a great Highland chief would dance a jig before him, to the Earl's tunes? When Tullibardine ordered them to return to Edinburgh, both young Frasers ignored him.

Instead they met with Tarbat's son and Alexander Mackenzie, son of the Earl of Seaforth. As a Guards officer, Alexander was familiar with London's best clubs and watering-holes. It would be chance too for the Mackenzie men to pick up the threads of their relationship with their Fraser cousins. Since the Murrays had taken over, Mackenzie influence at Castle Dounie had ceased.

Hugh and Simon, choked by Lord Murray's condescension, patronage, expectations and favours, now threw 'themselves into the hurly-burly of fun-making, love-making, noise-making' offered by the English capital. 'Come at a crown ourselves we'll treat,/Champagne our liqueur and ragouts our meat', the Highlanders joined in with the songs in the alehouses. 'With evening wheels we'll drive o'er the park,' then 'finish at Locket's and reel home in the dark'. Locket's, near Charing Cross, was a popular gentleman's club. The area roughly bordered by the Strand, Covent Garden and Charing Cross teemed with life. The theatres around Drury Lane brought taverns, coffee houses and bagnios in their wake. Socialising levelled all the classes, aristocrats, intellectuals, merchants and tradesmen, foreigners, Gaels, and the people who fulfilled all whims and desires. When the young men spoke Gaelic, very loud and very fast, they could talk treason with impunity, though many taverns and coffee houses welcomed Jacobites.

Simon worked on his chief, showing Hugh 'very plainly, that Tullibardine made a jest of him, and had brought him to London, in order to make *his* court to King William at Lord Lovat's expense'. He and the Mackenzies counselled Hugh 'to break with' Murray, and free Clan Fraser from its predators. For once, Hugh openly defied his brother-in-law. He sent out a waiter for pen and paper, wrote to Murray, and resigned his commission. 'I hope ... you will be so kind as to bestow it on my cousin Beaufort,' he added. Simon clapped his cousin on the back. This was the spirit they had looked for in him all these years. Simon followed up Hugh's letter with one of his own. 'If your Lordship have use for all my Lord Lovat's men, I have, next to himself, most influence on them.' It was a thinly veiled threat to take them away. Tullibardine made his own brother captain of Lovat's men.

A worried Tullibardine wrote to his wife Katherine, sister of the Duke of Hamilton, who had remained in London, and asked her to find out what the young Frasers were up to. 'I am extremely angry Lovat is not come off,' he wrote. 'I blame Beaufort who I believe occasions his stay till he gets ... [Lovat's] captain's act.' Katherine replied that she had seen Hugh. 'O! He is a sad creature, and keeps the worst of company. It is not fit to tell you here the way he lives,' she told her husband, 'but he says ... he'll stay here, and spend of his own, and take his pleasures a while ... I'm afraid he'll fall into some inconveniency.' Besides the 'inconveniency' of drink, Hugh was whoring himself to a physical breakdown and keeping other very 'inconvenient' companions.

The merry-making soon stopped with news from Dounie that Hugh's only son, three-year-old John, had died. He still had his girls, but now no male heir. Simon could not help but be aware that with the infant's death, the Beaufort Frasers were once again the only male heirs *if* the illegitimate marriage contract could be overturned. Simon discussed it with his cousin. The Fraser inheritance was nothing to do with an alien clan, he said. Murray had been deceiving him for years about what was best for the Frasers and disguising his real intentions. Even this trip: there was no colonelcy of the regiment or meaningful royal recognition for Hugh Lovat. Retrieve some loss of face, Simon urged him, and use the law to put right and undo what the Murrays had put wrong.

Hugh conceded that his in-laws probably 'despised him'. He was an easy-going fellow and he had let them do as they liked with his titles and estates. The worm now turned. On 26 March, 'Lord Lovat obliged' Simon 'to send for an attorney … Convinced of his Error, and the injury done to his own family, he … executed a Deed, in favours of Thomas Fraser of Beaufort, his Grand Uncle, Father to … Simon, upon the Failzie of Issue-male of the Marriage, and restored the Succession to the ancient Channel of the Heirs-male.'

While he had Hugh pointing in the right direction, Simon also persuaded him to draw up a legal bond. Lord Lovat bound himself to pay 50,000 Scottish merks to Simon 'for the special love and affection I bear to my cousin, Master Simon Fraser … and for certain onerous causes and others moving me'. Were Simon to enforce this bond, it would utterly ruin his heavily indebted cousin. Fifty thousand Scottish merks was about £2,750 sterling (or £350,000 in today's values).

Simon's motives were so mixed. On the one hand he believed a weak chief threatened the very existence of the clan. He also believed in the unbroken male inheritance of Clan Fraser, and was determined to throw off the over-mighty Murrays. This bond was the Frasers' security should the Murrays trespass too far and try to marry the heiress, Hugh's eldest daughter Amelia, away from the male heir, Simon Fraser.

Eventually Tullibardine wrote to Simon. He coldly commanded his lieutenant to escort his cousin home, and then report for duty. Tullibardine was Master of the Privy Council, King's High Commissioner and ruled Scotland with 'the authority of a monarch in right of his office, and sometimes a greater power in virtue of his abilities'. The man representing the constitution and the King was supreme. Simon could ill afford to defy him openly. To his face Simon hailed him 'the Viceroy of Scotland'. Behind Tullibardine's back he was learning to plot with more craft.

Simon and Hugh did not return to Edinburgh until 30 June, when Lord Lovat inspected his old company of Frasers. 'To my singular satisfaction,' Simon told Tullibardine, 'there is none of … his company deserted … My Lord Lovat told two or three that he saw of them that he would hang them without any judgement if they offered to go home without their pass.' Simon made sure his colonel knew that the Fraser men only stayed loyal because their chief ordered it, not their new captain, Tullibardine's brother, James Murray.

Hugh Lovat continued his journey north from Edinburgh alone. He had left London with a chest infection. By the time he reached the borders of Murray territory in Perthshire, some forty miles north of Edinburgh, his illness had developed into something like pneumonia. He managed to get to a Murray house at Dunkeld. There he received a letter recalling him to the Scottish Parliament. Obediently, Lovat turned south, but only got as far as a tavern at Perth. Some Murray ladies despatched a physician for their in-law, though they never offered to take him in. They had heard from Katherine Tullibardine that Hugh had annulled his marriage contract with their family, and had debauched himself, spending money he did not have. The old Marquis of Atholl visited Hugh: he had drawn up another marriage contract, reversing the annulment. The Murrays looked down on Lord Lovat in his sickbed, and forced him to sign.

Reports of Hugh's collapse and the Murrays' presence reached Simon, who rode to Perth immediately. He had to defend his new interests and protect his chief. By the time he reached Dunkeld, Hugh was delirious. He 'quite lost the use of his reason for several days, and lay in his bed in a manner incapable of motion', Simon informed Lady Lovat. It was hard for Lady Lovat at Dounie to gauge precisely what was going on in that airless little box-bed in a Perth tavern as the only eyewitness account she had was Simon's. However, she did not come.

On the morning of 6 September, the fever left the clan chief's body and Hugh cooled down. Simon lay next to him and wrapped him in his arms. He might now start to recover, and things could be different. This crisis must cast off the Murray yoke. Hugh slept quietly. Every now and then there erupted from deep in the young man's body a roaring, snorting breath. After one harsh intake of breath, like a wave rushing over shingle, Hugh's heart stopped.

Simon lay there a while. The room echoed his chief's stillness. Poor Hugh. His father had died aged twenty-nine. He had barely made it into his thirties. Simon escorted his cousin's body home where it was interred in the family mausoleum at Wardlaw. He then went to his father, bowed, and addressed him as 'My Lord Lovat'.

FOUR

'No borrowed chief!', 1696–97

'Men must either be pampered or crushed'
— MACHIAVELLI

There was no time to lose. Under feudalism, Atholl–Murray interest in the Frasers died with the late chief. Therefore, 'my father did take upon him the title of Lord Lovat, and possessed himself of the estates', wrote Simon.

Captain Simon Fraser, now the Master of Lovat, returned to his regiment. He had precedent and history and the desire of much of his clan on his side. He possessed youth, determination, righteous indignation, courage and acute financial need to power the claims of his birthright. This might not be enough. But Simon had already asserted the cause of the thousands of the ordinary Fraser clansmen, and of their chief, more vigorously in a couple of years than the Fraser chiefs had in a couple of generations.

As soon as he had the chance, Tullibardine came for Captain Fraser. Manipulating the Privy Council, Tullibardine obtained the gift of his niece, nine-year-old Amelia, 'in a trustee's name', though the child had a mother and close Fraser kin, and did not need an externally appointed guardian. As trustee, he would manage her clan and choose her husband. It was his duty to make the most advantageous match possible for her. This was usually the male heir.

Simon returned to command the guard at Holyroodhouse. Late one night Tullibardine arrived. Simon heard a shout from the guard, saw the flaring of torches, and watched the Earl clatter into the palace courtyard, calling for light and 'a bottle'. He then summoned Simon to join him. 'Having drunk to a good pitch,' Tullibardine 'took a paper out of his pocket and called for pen and ink'. He wanted Simon to sign a retraction of his claims. Simon must know, he said, how he entertained an 'extreme friendship' for him, a mere 'Cadet of the family of Lovat, but of no Manner of Estate'. Tullibardine was aware of the 'meanness' of his situation, he told Simon, who sat there stony-faced. However, 'I am told you have assumed the title of Master of Lovat, and that you have sent the opinions of [legal] counsel to your father, recommending him to take possession of the property of my late brother-in-law.' Tullibardine ended on an accusatory note.

Simon put down his drink and forced himself to be civil. Of course his father Thomas, Lord Lovat, enjoyed his inheritance: the honours and estates of his late great nephew. Why would Simon consult lawyers about a natural course of events, and send results north?

Tullibardine too had gone to the law. His lawyers agreed Thomas had a right to the title. They would all call the old fellow 'Thomas, Lord Lovat'. Why not? However, under the terms of Hugh and Amelia's marriage contract, ratified and signed by the late Lord Lovat, the property and estates belonged to his ward and niece, Amelia.

Simon countered: he either had 'a just right to the succession, or ... had not'. It was quite simple. 'If he had *no* right, it was to little purpose to' renounce his claim to nothing. 'But, if he had a right, he would not renounce it for the revenues of Scotland.' It was his birthright.

Tullibardine convulsed with 'violent passion'. He had always known Simon 'for an obstinate, insolent rascal', he raged. 'I do not know what should hinder me from cutting off your ears and throwing you into a dungeon, and bringing you to the gallows, as your treasons against the government so richly deserve!' Tullibardine referred to Simon's treasonable letters on the death of the Queen, which were now in his hands.

Although he felt awed by 'his formidable person, in the midst of his state and authority', Simon knew he had to stay calm. He stuck his hat on his head. He was off. 'As for the paltry company I command in your regiment ... it is the greatest disgrace to which I was ever subject to be under your command, and now, if you please,' he said, jerking his head towards a lackey in the corner, 'you may give it to your footman.' And out he strode, shaking with emotion. Simon resigned from Tullibardine's regiment.

The next day Tullibardine sent to the King the letters Simon had written on Queen Mary's death. Tullibardine demanded that young Beaufort be arrested, court-martialled and hung for high treason. William consulted the commander-in-chief of his Scottish forces, Sir Thomas Livingstone. Men much more highly placed than young Simon Fraser could be compromised by their ambivalent stance to his rule, he counselled the King. William would be advised not to reagitate feelings that had led to the plotting in Scotland the previous summer.

The King ordered Livingstone to cashier Simon Fraser. Livingstone obeyed but told his Majesty that he suspected 'the Viceroy' was abusing his public position in a private vendetta against Simon Fraser in his and old Atholl's lust to acquire the Lovat estates. It was a view Simon had keenly encouraged. Tullibardine's growing number of enemies believed that 'if the Secretary of State could turn out and in officers at their pleasure, upon their private pique, no officer in the army was sure of his commission'. With this sort of reportage, Simon cleverly and noisily drew attention to the Murrays' pursuit of him and his clan. Men such as Archibald Campbell, the 10th Earl of Argyll, were keen to ally themselves to Simon, to prove that Tullibardine was too eager to use the tools of public office to build his personal power base. By favouring him so completely, it looked as if King William was colluding in the schemes of the Atholl Murrays to extend their territorial and political power in Scotland.

Argyll murmured to William Carstares, a Presbyterian minister and one of the King's most trusted confidants, that Tullibardine's activities around Inverness threatened national security. If 'Tullibardine be allowed to go on ... it may occasion a deal of bloodshed; for if one begin, all the Highlands will in ten days fly together in arms … I am most particularly concerned in Highland affairs,' he said. Simon Fraser had called on the right man to help him. The Frasers were historically 'sword vassals' of the Campbells. It meant that in exchange for protection by the bigger clan, the Frasers brought out their men to fight Campbell battles. To bring down Tullibardine's over-mighty schemes to dominate Scottish politics, men who otherwise supported William's rule would go into opposition.

Tullibardine did not meet with this growing barrage of criticism calmly. He was, said a contemporary, 'endowed with good natural parts, tho' by reason of his proud, imperious, haughty passionate temper, he was no ways capable to be the leading man of a party. He much affected popularity,' but his 'kindest addresses were never taking: he was selfish to a great degree, and his vanity and ambition extended so far, that he could not suffer an equal. He was reputed very brave, but hot and headstrong.' He would destroy Simon Fraser.

At the end of the summer, Simon left Edinburgh. Scottish law had not been able to solve his problems and Simon struggled to see how the traditional path – a clan feud – might be avoided. Everyone feared a feud, 'for Highland feuds never die', as the Reverend James Fraser counselled him. If it came to a feud he could not see how he might expect to win. Over the last two decades the Murrays had amassed a regiment and a militia force of their own. Tullibardine, as King's High Commissioner, enjoyed huge power over the courts and Parliament. If Simon provoked the Murrays, they would surely attack. In the end the solution seemed obvious. The two sides must be brought together. He and the heiress, young Amelia, must be contracted to marry. This was the path of peace.

In April 1697, Simon headed to Castle Dounie to negotiate with Hugh's widow for the hand, at puberty, of the heiress Amelia. Tullibardine reacted immediately. He ordered the girl to be whisked from her mother, the dowager Lady Lovat, and be taken to his Perthshire stronghold, Blair Castle. Simon meanwhile moved into Castle Dounie itself and sent his father to a safehouse on the Lovat Stratherrick estates.

When Simon said of his kin that 'the Highland clans did not consider themselves as bound by the letter of the law, like the inhabitants of the low country' around Inverness, 'but to a man would regard it as their honour and their boast, to cut the throat, or blow out the brains of anyone … who should dare to disturb the repose of their laird', he had his Stratherrick clansmen in mind. High above Loch Ness, Stratherrick concealed itself and its people behind the trees and rocks scaling the steep slopes along the south shore of the loch. Fertile fields around lairds' houses nurtured cattle and rigs of corn in a sea of moorland wilderness. The Frasers who lived there existed in accordance with the values of the clan system. Financially, they depended on a traditional chief of the sort Simon desired to be. The elderly Lord Lovat would be safe among these men.

From Dounie, the dowager Lady Lovat complained to her family: 'Young Beaufort is still here and does not intend to go from this place till his own time. They are more obdurate than ever, and delude the people extremely.' Simon, the chief's son, felt that the chief's son living in the chief's stronghold was not delusional. The widow of a dead chief had to make room for the living one, or move to a dower house.

'The neighbourhood are all knaves, and for him,' the Marquis of Atholl growled when he read his daughter's letters. It maddened him that they had failed to kill young Beaufort in Edinburgh when they had the chance. After seizing Amelia, Atholl wrote to the Fraser lairds advising them to trust him rather than rally to 'Captain Fraser'. The old Marquis 'would find out a true Fraser and a man of handsome fortune that would support their whole name'. This was a dangerous time for the Murrays. Removing young Amelia gave them possession of a serious claimant to the inheritance, but it removed her from the objects of her claim.

Simon was dismayed to find that some Fraser lairds from the rich low-lying country around Inverness were hesitating to enlist for him. Others, such as Robert Fraser and his brother – both lawyers – had thrown over the ties of clanship in order to advance themselves. Even they advised the Murrays it was a step too far not to bring in a Fraser as chief and suggested they could find an alternative within the impoverished Saltoun Frasers from along the coast towards Aberdeen. Simon cursed the two lawyers like an Old Testament prophet. 'Robert, the prime author of these misfortunes, died under the visible judgement of God,' he wrote. Robert's brother 'may yet be overtaken with the just punishment of his crimes', he added hopefully.

The response Atholl received from the Highland lairds was unequivocal. They 'would have no borrowed chief!' Moreover, if Saltoun 'dared to enter their country in hostility to Thomas, Lord Lovat … his head should answer the infringement … We have put on a full resolution to defend our lands, possessions, goods, lives, wives, children, liberties and privileges of free subjects which lie at the stake against all invading and insulting avaricious ambition and oppression *pro aris et focis contra omnes mortalles.*' The judicial phrasing in Latin (suggesting Simon's hand in it) sealed the threat of an old-fashioned Celtic clan feud.

The letter left Lord Saltoun windy about his venture into Lovat territories to arrange a marriage between his son and Amelia Lovat. He wrote to Simon, claiming disingenuously that he only desired to help arbitrate in the Murray–Fraser dispute. Simon thanked him, and suggested they meet. Lord Saltoun agreed.

At the end of September 1697, Saltoun and Lady Lovat's youngest brother, Lord Mungo Murray, rode to Beauly. They looked forward to their time at Castle Dounie working out the details of a pre-nuptial agreement. They would hunt, dance and feast. The intention was then to go back via the Murray stronghold and celebrate the contract by letting the young people meet. Simon, meanwhile, hoped to dissuade Lord Saltoun from acting as go-between for Tullibardine's schemes.

At daybreak, Simon and his lairds set out to rendezvous with Saltoun from the Stratherrick estates, where he had been enlisting gentlemen to his cause. As their party crossed the River Ness and headed west towards Dounie, 'the inhabitants, observing their alert and spirited appearance lifted up their hands to heaven, and prayed God to prosper their enterprise', Simon wrote. Dollery, Tullibardine's recruiting agent, confirmed their support. 'It is certain the generality of the country about Inverness favours' Simon, Thomas and their followers, he told his master. 'In the very town of Inverness I hear they call the young rogue the Master of Lovat.' Even the professional classes were coming over to Simon's side.

The party rode on with confidence. The Beauly Firth sparkled on the right as they entered the woods of Bunchrew, about three miles out of Inverness. Suddenly, one of Simon's lairds noticed a group of 'running footmen' scampering out of the woods. These runners accompanied gentlemen of any standing, holding their stirrups as they mounted and dismounted; opening gates in their path; fording rivers and burns and leading the gentleman's horse to steady its progress. Simon was shocked to see that they were followed by the Lords Saltoun and Mungo Murray and their tail of armed followers. Saltoun was very chatty, apparently 'in great hopes to have his son [become] Lord Lovat when the girl was ripe'. Seeing and hearing all this, Simon erupted. He and Saltoun had arranged to meet that day to prevent this very thing. He, Simon, was the obvious candidate for young Amelia's hand. The Lords were reneging on their agreement on every count.

Simon's reaction was phrased in the clan rhetoric of pride and 'face': such 'an affront was too atrocious ... not to exact satisfaction for it, or perish in the attempt', Simon later wrote. William of Errochit, a Stratherrick laird, shot forward and levelled a carabine at Saltoun and Mungo: 'Stop, traitor, you shall pay with your hide your irruption into this country in hostility to our laird!' The party skidded to a halt. Simon cantered up to Mungo Murray, yelling at him, 'Fire traitor, or I will blow out your brains!' Mungo dropped his reins and threw up his hands. 'My dear Simon,' he retorted. 'Is this the termination of our long and tender friendship?'

Simon looked at him along his pistol. 'You are a base coward, and deserve no quarter,' he replied, 'but I give you your life.'

Simon's men moved among the group and disarmed them all, 'without the smallest resistance from any individual', except Lord Saltoun's *valet de chambre*, who only gave up his weapon after Simon 'struck him a blow on the head with the flat side of his sword'. The two Lords and their company of gentlemen were rounded up and taken to Fanellan, two miles from Castle Dounie, where Simon ordered the party to be locked up. A gallows was erected outside Lord Saltoun's cell window. The unhappy noble sat alone in a tiny room and, in between the sawing and banging, listened to his fate being discussed. The door of Saltoun's cell opened and another of Simon's lairds, Major Fraser of Castleleathers, entered, swathed in plaid from top to toe, his face as red as his tartan. Taunting him, Castleleathers instructed his Lordship 'to prepare himself for another world … He had but two days to live.' The pro-Murray Frasers who had called Saltoun in to their country were then made to cast dice, 'to know whose fate it was to hang with him'. This was ritualised violence, a tool in old-fashioned clan diplomacy; a display of seriousness of intent.

Lord Saltoun did not react well, Castleleathers recorded. As the effect of the news sank in, 'the poor gentleman, finding this a hard pill to digest, contracted a bloody flux, of which he almost dyed'. Saltoun passed out cold, crashing to the floor. 'Upon his recovery he begged his life, the gallows having stood all the time beneath his window – and 500 men waiting on in arms.'

Not wanting the death of a nobleman on his hands, Simon released them all immediately, though not before pressing his sword under Saltoun's and Mungo Murray's chins and making them swear never to come back to Fraser country. Happy to agree to anything, the nobles touched the tip of his weapon, swore the oath and fled.

The kidnapping had started out as what most Highland Scots recognised as a clan raid – a wild spree by the young bloods of one clan against another. However, the Murrays went to court to move the insult into quite another quarter. They declared the Frasers had risen in 'open and manifest Rebellion'. This was a capital charge. The Murrays demanded legal endorsement – a 'Commission of Fire and Sword' – to send in soldiers to arrest the Beaufort Frasers and devastate their lands. The court had to distinguish between the private and public offence in all this. The government had an interest in rather than a monopoly on violence as a tool of justice in North Britain. Representatives of the Crown knew Tullibardine was trying to use Scottish law against a kindred he himself was provoking into a clan feud. The Privy Council in Edinburgh hesitated.

To Simon the kidnapping and high jinx was a Highland, private matter, between the Master of Lovat and the Murrays. He did not see himself as being in rebellion against the Crown. It might all have been diffused, had British justice not been even more vexed by what Simon did next.

FIVE

'The Grand Fornicator of the Aird', 1697–99

'The Lady not yielding willingly,
there was some harsh measures taken ...'
– MAJOR FRASER OF CASTLELEATHERS

Simon did not stop to think. He did not know what would happen or leave enough time to scheme at every twist and turn. On 15 October, days after freeing Lord Saltoun, his Frasers galloped over the hill from Fanellan. Runners fanned out across the slopes around them, like the clan's hunting dogs, and fell on Castle Dounie. Simon ordered a guard to be placed on all the avenues to the castle 'to prevent the Dowager from sending to her father', or brother. Simon made Lady Amelia pen a soothing note to Colonel Hill, the officer in charge of the government barracks at Fort William. 'We are still in hopes to take away this riot friendly,' she reassured him.

Meanwhile, the Sheriff of Inverness-shire did what was required to mollify the victims and rein in the aggressively exuberant Fraser youth. Simon and his associates would appear before him to answer for the kidnapping of Lords Saltoun and Murray. Simon travelled to Inverness, accompanied by his father, where he was rebuked by the Sheriff for letting things get out of hand, told to quieten down and dismissed. The Sheriff Court did not care to consider the issue of Simon's occupation of Castle Dounie. Impatient heirs often bumped against a dowager trying to hang on in the old family home. Besides, Lady Amelia seemed cross, not terrified.

In Fort William, Colonel Hill relaxed. Brigadier Alexander Grant, the Sheriff of Inverness-shire, was a competent man and chief of Clan Grant, friends and neighbours of the Frasers for hundreds of years. Grant was a follower of the Earl of Argyll and 'is judged competent for the Riot', Colonel Hill assured Tullibardine. 'I conclude there will be no more trouble about that affair,' Hill said, turning his mind back to organising supplies. The campaigning season was drawing to an end, and his troops needed to winter in at the garrison.

Tullibardine threw Hill's reply aside and composed a cold note. Hill should not act as if the feuding Frasers and Murrays were just two barbaric clans locked into a territorial dispute. 'Not only on the public account, but also on mine,' he said – as if Scotland and the Murrays were mirrors of each other. The colonel must use government troops to quell this 'uprising against the King'. He *must* send a 'strong party of the King's soldiers amongst them … to apprehend the Beauforts … which,' Tullibardine gritted his teeth, 'I wish you had sent on the first account.'

At Dounie, Simon had thought of another way to settle the feud, as audacious as the first. If he could not have Amelia the daughter, he would have Amelia the mother. Then he would have both of them. He walked through to Lady Lovat's chambers. She loved and esteemed him. They had known each other most of their lives. They must marry. Lady Lovat refused. 'He urged the more, fearing that troops' from the Atholl Murrays 'would march against him'. Still she would not yield.

Simon considered for a moment, then shouted for a couple of men and despatched them to Inverness. They returned after dark. In their wake, they towed an inebriated Episcopal minister on a pony, the Reverend Robert Munro of Abertarff, a 'poor, sordid fellow'.

'The Lady not yielding willingly,' Fraser of Castleleathers noted with foreboding, 'there was some harsh measures taken, a parson sent for, and the bagpipe blown up.' Too late, Lady Amelia realised how vulnerable she was. Two men hauled her, in tears, before Reverend Munro, Simon taking his position grim-faced by her side. The deafening groan of the pipes bounced off the walls of the small room. The minister kept his head down, and pronounced Amelia and Simon man and wife.

An overwrought Amelia was dismissed to her maids. Simon joined his men to drink the health of bride and groom, and the settlement of their troubles. The clan was safe. The Master of Lovat sent a man to Stratherrick to tell his father the news.

Early next morning, at around two o'clock, Simon and a group of armed guards entered his bride's apartments. A drunken Simon instructed the maids to undress Amelia for bed, and then withdraw. When he returned nothing had happened, so he ordered two clans-men to remove the serving women.

Amelia 'cried out most piteously' as two men lifted her to the bed, and struggled to prepare the lady for her wedding night. Bending over her, Simon held aquavitie* to her nose. One man fumbled at her shoes. A maid rushed to her lady and attempted to untie Amelia's clothes. Lady Lovat kicked her away. Determined, Simon searched for a dirk to cut his wife's stays, found none, and told one of his men to do it.

Impatient for this to end, they 'put my Lady on her face and spread her arms' and cut the laces of her corset, and finally left Amelia and Simon alone. Versions of what happened that night circulated almost immediately. In one account the piper played in an adjacent room to drown Amelia's screams, and in the morning a servant found her speechless and out of her senses. Others denied it. By dawn, however, silence hung over the castle. Simon had put the bachelor state behind him.

The Murrays erupted in fury. The sister of Scotland's most powerful man was the 'most violented lady' in the kingdom, they said. Amelia's father, the Marquis of Atholl, commanded Lords James and Mungo to get her away. Atholl pressed Tullibardine to obtain an order for

---

* Aquavitie – a strong spirit, flavoured with dill or caraway – was traditionally used to settle upset stomachs and aid digestion.

government troops to 'catch that base creature, Simon Fraser, and his accomplices'. From Inverness to Edinburgh and London, gossip and letters argued the question: had he raped a Marquis's daughter? If he *had* forced her, and was not mad or stupid, what had driven him to do it?

Major Fraser of Castleleathers recorded that very quickly Lady Amelia made up her own mind. 'Whatever new light the lady had got,' she desired her husband to 'send for Mr William Fraser, minister of Kilmorack, to make a second marriage (not thinking the first valid)'. The hell of that night left her not knowing where she stood.

Simon said he hoped the marriage would allay 'the Marquis of Atholl's fury against him', but the news that Atholl had acquired Simon Fraser as a son-in-law, unsurprisingly, sent the old man into a frenzy. There 'was nothing in his mind but the business of the base Frasers', wrote his wife. Old Atholl was adamant Tullibardine must make their quarrels a government concern at the highest levels. For the next two years, the records of the Privy Council chattered with Inverness and the Frasers.

The forced marriage and consummation were brutal errors of judgement that Simon would regret all his life. Again he had used a lamented but tolerated old tradition and pushed it to new levels in order to force a match with a Marquis's daughter *against* her family's will. The practice was normally used to make a girl fall in line *with* her family's wishes, against her will.

Thomas Lovat wrote to the Earl of Argyll, explaining first that the Saltoun incident had been settled by the Sheriff, and second, that his son and Amelia were now legally married. It was better to let it all die down, he said. Besides, he observed cannily, the Murrays' 'design of appropriating the estate and following of Lovat to themselves, is made liable to more difficulties by that match'. Argyll agreed entirely. Tullibardine's political enemies stood by Simon as a way to attack the High Commissioner and curtail his vast ambitions to rule all Scotland with his brother-in-law, the Duke of Hamilton.

In order to convince the legal establishment in Edinburgh to act against Simon, the Murrays required their star witness: the victim of the alleged crime, Lady Amelia Lovat. Rumours buzzed around Inverness that the dishonoured Lady was now dead. When Lords Mungo and James Murray rode to Castle Dounie they found it empty. Simon and Amelia had withdrawn, with a company of armed men, to the isolation of Eilean Aigas, a wooded rocky islet in the middle of the River Beauly. Simon hoped the black, fast-flowing tangle of currents surrounding the island would make their retreat impregnable.

They stayed here for several weeks. Simon wrote to a friend in Inverness explaining he was struggling to keep up his wife's spirits. 'I know not how to manage her,' he wrote unhappily, 'so I hope you will send me all the advice you can.' He was not used to coping with a woman, a mother, who was just a few years older than him. For a lady of rank to live an itinerant life, adjunct to a fugitive and far from her children, was very hard. Simon soothed her as best he could.

Amelia Lovat's position was a confused one. A 'shamed' lady, even the daughter of a Marquis, was a social outcast; she knew this. Besides, she had sworn a deposition that her marriage was genuine when the Reverend James had visited them at Dounie. When Amelia's father found this out he was furious, shouting that the Fraser clerics were all 'false prophets and wizards'. She yearned to see her brothers, perhaps to find out when she might come back, or to get some degree of acceptance from her family. Though Simon did not trust them, he allowed Amelia to travel down the glen to meet with her brothers. He would never see her again.

At Castle Dounie, James Murray greeted his sister tenderly, and asked if she was 'lawfully married to Captain Fraser of Beaufort?' She answered that she was. Lord James pulled away, raised his foot and 'gave her along the belly', yelling at her that she was a bitch. Lady Amelia doubled over. An Inverness laird, Fraser of Culduthel, rushed forward to aid her, but Murray men overpowered him. They pushed Amelia onto a horse and galloped off towards Inverness.

With Lady Amelia on her way to Blair Castle, Tullibardine persuaded the Privy Council and Court of Session to issue 'Letters of Intercommuning' forbidding anyone to 'commune' with the Frasers.

In effect, 'whatever slaughter, mutilation, bloodshed, fire-raising or other violence, shall happen to be acted', by anyone who assisted the law in 'seizing, reducing, and bringing them in dead or alive … the same shall be held as laudable good and warrantable service to his Majesty', but even more to the Atholl Murrays.

Colonel Hill warned Tullibardine that local people on both sides 'talk very slightingly of the matter and say now there is no need of sending forces'. The issue was settled; no one wanted to stir it up to a savage feud where the more powerfully ambitious side used the law to inflict crushing blows and the other eventually responded in kind, having nothing to lose. Tullibardine ignored him. A first wave of troops was sent in, commanded by Amelia's brothers. The ordinary clansmen, weakened by the famines of King William's ill years, found increased troop numbers quartered on them and could not cope. The people began to starve.

Over the next few weeks, the Murray ladies at Blair Castle pressured Lady Amelia to condemn Simon Fraser. 'My Lord and I has told her … over and over,' her sister wrote to Katherine Tullibardine, 'that if she has any regard to her own honour and reputation, she will for once lay aside her reserved humour … and tell, to all she speaks with, the abhorrence she has of that base man.' If Amelia maintained she was married to Simon, there was no case.

Her refusal to come to court and declare she had been raped drove her family mad with frustration, and her despair is clear from her letters. 'I have the comfort in my extreme misery to be owned by such relations … which is God's goodness to me … one so unworthy and so unfortunate.' If she assented to her family's description of her as ruined, what sort of future would she face? By condemning Simon, she condemned herself. Her shame would feed scandal sheets from Inverness to Paris. Her family pushed on oblivious. She was their political pawn. Lord James Murray believed that Tullibardine and his eldest brother were prepared 'to ruin my sister's and niece's interest' – the Lovat estates – to exact vengeance, kill Simon and regain control.

* * *

Simon escaped Eilean Aigas and haunted the hill country, moving and hiding from glen to glen. At the end of the year, Simon sent his father to safety from the Stratherrick estates, to Thomas's brother-in-law, the MacLeod chief, at Dunvegan Castle on the west coast of the Isle of Skye. The Murrays now had about 600 soldiers – government and Murray men – in the Inverness area. Lord James Murray wrote to his father, Tullibardine: 'Except to satisfy you, I confess I expect neither honour nor credit by turning a plunderer.' Atholl and Tullibardine worried that Lord James did not have the stomach for the fight to waste Fraser country and reduce the clan to submission.

Tullibardine had failed to secure from the Privy Council a Commission of Fire and Sword, the licence he needed that allowed him to eliminate the Frasers. Some Councillors 'were opposing the case', Dollery informed his master, 'as judging it not proper to give a direct commission to one clan over against another, and others said that it was not agreeable to law either'. The government read this principally as a clan feud. The central authorities manipulated feuds as a control valve to maintain a power balance in the region, but were wary of elevating one to a matter of national security. It might all backfire. They all lived with the national outrage after Glencoe.

In Inverness, even the weather conspired to conceal Simon. 'Severe frost and snow' filled paths and tracks. The Murray soldiers shirked from going out on forays. No matter how much the Marquis of Atholl offered in lures and bribes, officers could obtain no reliable intelligence from turncoats. All his army could do was destroy the clan's property, which, given 'the most tempestuous weather of snow and great frosts', brought more starvation to ordinary Frasers. Unless the country people, the poor, 'be made to suffer for his being among them', wrote one of Tullibardine's officers, and those among the professional and landowning classes 'that go along with him [be] punished in their goods', they were sure it would be impossible to get hold of Simon Fraser. Tullibardine ordered the devastation to continue. It was futile. One officer spelled out the situation – 'the whole country are entirely addicted to him' and they should call a halt.

Atholl and Tullibardine would not relent. As the winter of 1697/98 ground on, it proved impossible 'to march against them from a town that favours them … through a country that is friendly to them, and intangled with them, without being discovered'. The Murray spy network was proving a disaster. Simon's functioned beautifully.

The Murrays subpoenaed scores of Frasers from all ranks to go south and testify against their chief. The road south led them by Blair Castle, thirty miles north of Perth. The old Marquis forced the military escorts to bring the witnesses to him and put them in his dungeons. The Lord Chancellor, the Earl of Annandale, sent tetchy letters requesting the forwarding of his witnesses. The Marquis of Atholl let the witnesses go, while he whinged that the court in Inverness, run by Brigadier Grant, was biased 'to the prejudice of our family … It is all our enemies that has it in their hands' – a breathtaking complaint from a man who intimidated witnesses daily and whose son manipulated the Edinburgh judiciary. Atholl asked Tullibardine to make sure the Frasers were sent back to him on their road home, 'so that I may make them perfect what they have begun'. They know, the Marquis said, 'they would be ruined if they did not' appear for the Murrays, 'which is the best argument to Highlanders'. If they 'should fail', he added chillingly, 'they will still be in my power to take amends … All this has been my business night and day.'

Revenge consumed the old man. 'I hope I have got the chief [men] of the name of Fraser who live in Stratherrick broke and divided,' he told Tullibardine. He was determined to break Simon's core support. Yet the Murray chief was no longer young. He carried stress in his belly, making him prone to belching and 'gout in the stomach'. He put himself under terrible pressure to settle Simon on a gallows, before allowing himself to die a happy man.

By the spring of 1698, Atholl declared with satisfaction that 'the estate of Lovat is altogether ruined'. Although the outlaws remained at large, the Murrays had amassed enough evidence to start their trial. Simon was cited to answer two charges: first, forced marriage and rape. Second, raising men in arms and resisting the King's forces.

The court 'compered' Thomas and Simon and their followers to appear three times over the summer, with increasingly dire threats every time they declined. On 6 September 1698, the court found them guilty of the capital crime of rebellion, and they were declared forfeit in King William's name. Tullibardine got his Commission of Fire and Sword. (The Crown prosecution refused to have anything to do with the private charge of possible marital rape.) Simon, his father and their main adherents were now 'outlawes and fugitives frae the lawes'. They were to be 'executed to the death ... Their name, fame, memory and honours to be extinct and their armes to be riven furth and delate out of the bookes of armes.' For the rest of time, none of their heirs could enjoy titles, positions and dignities. In effect, anything that anyone did to the Lovats and their men, since they were outside the law, would be ignored by anyone within the law. The Murrays had free rein to pursue Simon any way they chose. His family were to be wiped from the pages of history. The Lovat estates lay tantalisingly within the Murrays' grasp.

Simon wrote to Argyll, asking that he secure a pardon from King William to let the Lovats live at peace, enjoy their estates and serve his Majesty. Someone had to control the Murrays. Argyll went to the King.

While at his brother-in-law's castle on Skye, Simon received news that his father, Thomas, Lord Lovat, had died and been buried in the graveyard of his wife's family. Simon could not risk bringing the body of the Fraser chief home, or honour him with the traditional huge Highland funeral and burial at Wardlaw. In hiding, Simon had no time to grieve. He believed the Atholls had hounded the old man to death. Simon now assumed the titles of MacShimidh Mor, the 11th Lord Lovat, chief of Clan Fraser – though these were worthless to a young man who was now an outlaw.

Armed with a death warrant, the Murray hunt heated up. At the head of hundreds of Athollmen and Lowland soldiers, Lord James Murray, accompanied by his brother Mungo, planned a night attack into Stratherrick where they believed Simon was hiding. 'Having the authors of his father's death, and of all his personal misfortunes before his eyes, he would now revenge himself in their blood, or perish in the attempt,' Simon swore. He galloped to Stratherrick to stop more ill-treatment of his people. The hunters would become the hunted.

The Murrays struck camp for the night against a rocky crag. When they mustered the next morning, Simon calculated he had something under 300 men to their 600. Given the numerical disadvantage, a full-frontal attack would fail. Simon ordered one of his men, Alexander MacDonald, to take sixty Frasers and string them out in a thin line in front of the enemy, so they would believe his whole force faced them. Meanwhile, Simon led the rest around to their flank.

Realising late they were to be ambushed, Lord James ordered his troops to fall back towards a 'terrible defile', six miles in the direction of Inverness, called *Allt nan Gobhar* – the Blacksmith's Burn. Alexander MacDonald guessed their goal and raced ahead of them to block the way through. The fighting men under Simon broke rank in pursuit.

Simon Fraser fought as MacShimidh, a Highland chief; not as the bewigged and breeches-clad British peer petitioning in the law courts of Edinburgh, but wrapped and belted in a plaid over the top of his linen shirt, like his ordinary kinsmen. He put a bonnet on his head, and stuck the Fraser emblem, a sprig of yew, in it. With the battle cry *A'Chaisteal Dhunaidh* – 'for Castle Dounie', and the scream of the pipes, they charged to battle. 'Lord Lovat ran for three miles alongside them, on foot, and almost naked.' The howling chief of Clan Fraser stampeded the government troops towards the men hidden in Blacksmith's Burn. Drawing close, the Murrays saw what awaited them and suddenly 'impressed with the most lively apprehensions' of impending slaughter, most Murray men tried to surrender. Simon observed Lord James yelling at them to engage but they 'laid down their arms and covering their heads with their plaids, cried out for quarter'. A Murray fighter came running towards them, 'with a white handkerchief … neckcloth tied to a bludgeon, crying out for mercy'.

'Lord James,' Simon wrote with grim pleasure, 'was beside himself at this declaration.' Simon's first response was not to take the surrender. He surveyed the noisy, trembling and quarrelling bunch of regular and irregular forces whose commanding officers had 'deprived him of lands and title by violence, injustice, and fraud … [He was] outlawed and condemned to death, hunted on the mountains,' he reflected. The last couple of years had not encouraged the philosophical, university-trained side of his character. They drove him in on most animal resources, to survive and fight, protect his territory. His father had died without elegy and obsequy; without his life being properly honoured. He would 'avenge the death of his father, and the tyranny of Lord Athol and all his family'. Since birth, these men had tried to manipulate his destiny. Now Simon was clan chief.

Though his first instinct had been to massacre the lot of them, older heads among his advisers made him understand that if he did, 'not a man in the Kingdom would either assist or pity' the Frasers' cause, so he contented himself with humiliation. He lifted his sword tip and made James and Mungo kiss it and swear upon it that 'they renounced their claims in Jesus Christ, and their hopes of heaven, and devoted themselves to the torments of hell, if they ever returned' or occasioned 'Lord Lovat the smallest mischief'. He then lined up his men in two files and made the enemy troop run the gauntlet jostled like criminals, and sent them out of his country.

At bottom, Simon was in desperate need of a pardon to end this feud before his whole inheritance was torched beyond resurrection and his people all starved to death. More in hope than expectation, Simon Fraser thereafter took as his motto *Sin Sanguine Victor*, 'Victor without Blood'.

SIX

Victory and loss, 1699–1702

'I despair of saving myself or my Kindred'
— LOVAT TO THE EARL OF ARGYLL

The Reverend James had educated Simon in his responsibilities to his clan, always to keep going, and to determine his own fate. He conjured,

> In spite of malice you will still be great,
> And raise your name above the power of fate.
> Our sinking house which now stoops low with age,
> You show with newborn lustre on the stage.

Typical of Celtic eulogies, the hero is praised and cajoled to ever-greater sacrifices. Other chiefs had passed by this destiny. But it inspired Simon and, as the century drew to a close, left him facing a death sentence. He believed passionately that fate or God had laid on him as a sacred duty the salvation of Clan Fraser. It was, he always said, inseparable from 'his Nature'. Primogeniture and his personal qualities confirmed fate's decree. Sir George Mackenzie of Tarbat and then Tullibardine had tried to break and remake Clan Fraser in their own image, using all the skills and resources they could muster. Now Simon sought to restore the clan using his gifts and training.

Without heavyweight political backing, Simon could not win. He faced a long guerrilla action, a ruinous feud, fought on and over his country. While Tullibardine influenced the Edinburgh judiciary, the courts offered no path back inside lawful society. For eight long months the Atholl Murrays had harried and hunted the Frasers, trying to capture or crush their leader, but without success. In a desperate attempt to flush out the Fraser chief, Lord James, smarting from his defeat at Lovat's hands, had his men drive off stock, smash boats, nets and fishing gear, spinning wheels and looms, and fell trees – anything that might allow the Frasers to live or do a little business. But Simon was still at large, and his messages were getting through to the south. His successes and the substantial levels of support he clearly enjoyed impressed many who sought to bring down Tullibardine and stop him (in the Highlands) and his brother-in-law Hamilton (in the Lowlands) exercising almost unassailable power in Scotland. The Duke of Argyll advised Simon to 'lay down his arms and come privately to London' to seek a pardon, informing William III that Tullibardine created chaos and hostility to the King in Scotland in the service of his greed. Lovat and the trouble in Fraser country were Argyll's proof.

Late in 1699, two weeks after setting out, Simon Fraser entered London for the second time in his life. It proved a wasted trip. The King had left the country and was at Loos in Flanders. By the turn of the century, William was in a stronger position in Europe. In 1697, Louis XIV of France had abandoned his previous war aims and sued for peace. As part of this he now acknowledged the Prince of Orange as William III, King of England and Scotland, thereby denying the claim of James II. Even the Pope proclaimed William III 'the master; he's arbiter of all Europe'.

King William was now in Flanders taking part in another struggle provoked by Louis XIV's ambition. The future of the thrones of Spain and the Holy Roman Empire was at stake. At present the ailing King of Spain, Carlos II, sat on both thrones. The rest of Europe was divided between whether to keep the thrones united, or split them up when Carlos died, and on who would sit on either or both thrones. Competing European interests battled over a settlement, until Louis XIV insisted on having both titles for his second grandson, the Duke of Anjou. Relations between William III and Louis XIV, only recently nosing above freezing point after three years of peace, plunged to a glacial impasse and stayed that way while Carlos II lived.

William needed a relatively peaceful and united Britain to be able to concentrate on defeating Louis. And while no government needed the entirety of its peoples on its side, it did need enough capable supporters to maintain law and order locally, raise taxes and supply soldiers for these international affairs. To be one of the regional managers, Lovat explained, he needed to live as a magnate, not an outlaw. He and his people could then 'serve your Majesty as they are full ready to do', as he outlined to King William in a letter Carstares read aloud to his monarch.

Argyll supported Simon by adding his voice. 'The persecution [Tullibardine] exercised against Lord Lovat and the clan of the Frasers, is capable of exciting all the clans, and even the whole nation, to revolt against the government,' Argyll asserted. 'The King cannot do a more acceptable thing for the generality than send [Lovat] his pardon for the convocation of men in arms.' More people only hesitated to speak out against Atholl and Tullibardine because 'they threaten so hard and bite so sore', finished Argyll.

The Murrays vehemently opposed this. 'It will be a great reflection on the government if there be not a speedy course taken to apprehend' Simon Fraser, Tullibardine lectured his King, justifying the turbulence and suffering he brought about in Fraser country. Other Scottish politicians petitioned Carstares, emphasising the wider British political element in Lovat's case. 'Although I cannot justify Captain Fraser in his proceedings, but yet, the rendering of so many men desperate is not at all to the government's interest,' wrote Sir James Stewart, the Lord Advocate.

Simon reiterated that the Frasers wanted peace, 'to live the more comfortable under the rays of your Majesty's protection, and thereby be more encouraged to serve your Majesty's interest'. William listened to the increasing volume of this sort of talk, of Tullibardine's abuse of his position for private gain. Tullibardine had maintained his following with the promise of positions and pensions to clever, ambitious men. The King decided to stop promoting men put forward by

Tullibardine to fill posts in the Scottish executive. Tullibardine reacted by resigning from the government in a fit of humiliated fury. Having the deepest confidence in the counsel of Carstares and Argyll, the King agreed to pardon Simon for his crimes against the Crown and accepted the Fraser chief's offer of devoted service. However, William refused to enter into the murky business of the forced marriage. The Crown had never charged him with it and logically William could not pardon him for it. He was happy to curb Murray ambitions, but he told Argyll he did not want to 'disgust' them too much.

It had taken nearly two years, from Argyll's first letter to his last, for the Earl to be able to write excitedly to Simon Fraser's friends that he was brandishing 'Beaufort's (now I may say Lord Lovat's) pardon' in his hands. Simon was free, and now officially the 11th Lord Lovat. As the chief, MacShimidh Mor, Lovat could return home and relieve his people's sufferings.

In Europe, three deaths threatened further political instability and affected Lovat's plans. First, the British Protestant succession failed again when, in July 1700, the surviving Protestant Stuart child of Princess Anne and the Prince of Denmark, the eleven-year-old Duke of Gloucester, died.

The ramifications of Gloucester's death spread north to Scotland, and far south to the Courts of Versailles and St Germains when, the following summer, Mary and Anne Stuart's father, James II, died in exile. With his eye on Spain and the Holy Roman Empire, Louis XIV no longer had reason to appease William. Happy to aggravate political tensions within Britain, he proclaimed that James II's son would be 'King James III of England and VIII of Scotland' on the death of Princess Anne. Anne had not even succeeded yet. The third death was the passing of Carlos II, King of Spain and Holy Roman Emperor.

Meanwhile, King William's grasp on Scotland was slipping. The whole country was breaking down after five years of failing harvests and a famine that had killed up to fifteen per cent of the Scottish population. Politicians racked their brains for schemes to stimulate life in the economic mud in which Scotland drowned. Their suffering was proof of God's displeasure at the overturning of the natural order and at the anointed Stuart ruler having been driven away. The massacre at Glencoe, the quartering of government troops on starving people, and a series of economic disasters all blighted his rule.

The most recent crisis went back to 1696, when William Paterson, Scotsman and founder of the Bank of England, had suggested to his fellow Scots merchants and landowners that they should start a foreign trading company to stimulate their weak economy. Scottish businessmen set up 'The Company of Scotland' to trade with Africa and the Indies. Scots flocked to invest and sank a quarter of the nation's tiny liquid capital into the venture. Inverness merchants contributed £3,000. They almost beggared the town on the gamble of massive returns. When the profits rolled in, it was said, investors' wives and children would rush to demand luxuries from local merchants. The economy would boom. This was Paterson's vision for Scotland.

The Scots plumped on Darien, on the Isthmus of Panama, as the cradle of their hopes, christening it 'New Caledonia'. The Spanish complained angrily and claimed the territory – close to Spain's silver mines – for themselves. William III agreed to withdraw English support for New Caledonia on one condition: that Spain refuse Louis XIV's demand to make his grandson King of Spain and Holy Roman Emperor.

Spain agreed. The English Parliament pressured English merchants to withdraw all their capital from the Darien Venture. The English Navy, rather than protecting its sister nation's merchant shipping, harried and captured it. To the Scots, William was putting his English subjects' interests over those of Scotland. The collapse of the Darien Venture induced national economic breakdown. The Scots went into shock.

The whole nation seized on Darien and the colony at New Caledonia as the image of Scotland's impoverished world standing. The Lord Advocate – the most senior lawyer in Scotland – Sir James Stewart, tried to impress on Carstares the level of grief and despair felt in the kingdom William had never once bothered to visit. 'Disasters increase, and the weakness of the government is more and more discovered … Was ever a people more unhappy?' The Scots asked themselves what they gained from the Union of Crowns. Independence looked like a solution to the succession and economic crises.

Sir James Stewart identified three groups fighting to dominate the Scottish Parliament: the Jacobites, the 'Malcontents', and the 'Williamites'. The Jacobites wanted to 'break the army ∴ [so] that, when the King dies, and neither the Princess Anne nor he having any children, they may the easier embroil the nation, and do their own business'. That is, to restore the Stuarts from France. 'The Malcontents that are not Jacobites,' he explained, were aggressive place-seekers. They just wanted to disrupt proceedings in Parliament and disrupt government in Scotland, to force the King to promote them to power. However, 'the Williamites … I think, must be more numerous than the other two. Their aim solely is the peace and security of the government and the good of the country, by an industrious pursuit of honourable and profitable trade …' This last comment was wishful nonsense to make the King feel better. William's credibility in North Britain was disintegrating.

Simon, Lord Lovat, moved into Castle Dounie and began collecting such rents as he decently could from starving clansmen and semi-bankrupt lairds. He took debts on himself and let the ordinary tenantry off their rents for that year where he saw they had nothing.

He was not left for long to try and sort out his estates. Goaded by Lovat's reappearance, the Murrays hurtled back to the law courts. This time they forced 'Sister Lovat' there with them. They petitioned the Court of Session to summon 'Captain Fraser' (they would not call him Lord Lovat) – to answer the private charge of '*rapt* and *hamesucken*'. Relative to rape, *rapt* was a watered-down assault. Lovat explained it to one of the King's advisers. 'They do not [charge] me for ravishment, but for carrying her by violence from place to place.' They hound me 'as if I had murdered the King!' Lovat complained. *Hamesucken*, loosely speaking, was socking (*sucken*) it to someone in their own home (*hame*). A crime against property rights, it was a capital crime, unlike *rapt*. *Hamesucken* also covered 'the ravishing of

67

persons of rank in houses of consequence'. They had to charge Lovat with both to get a death penalty.

Argyll told the King that the court summoning Lovat was 'not composed as it ought to be'. While the Lord Advocate warned Argyll if Lovat 'is found tomorrow in Edinburgh, I would not give a sixpence for his head'. Years of Tullibardine infiltration of the law courts favoured the Murrays securing the clan chief's conviction. There were 'such wicked and abandoned judges', Lovat wrote, 'the innocence of an angel of light would be to no avail!' And Lovat was no angel. Lovat did not appear and on 17 February 1701 was found guilty *in absentia*. He was outlawed yet again.

Argyll advised Lovat to forget Edinburgh and the Scottish legal system and come south, persuade the King to extend his pardon to cover the 'private charge' and fulfil William's intention to pardon Lovat. He must demonstrate that the Atholl Murrays subverted the King's wishes.

In the summer of 1701, William raised Argyll to a dukedom, a great sign of royal favour. Lovat, an Argyll man, waited for his patronage. He wanted Argyll to place him somewhere in the Scottish government. There he could do the King's business and his own.

Roderick Mackenzie, Lord Prestonhall, on the bench of the Court of Session, was a Scottish Law Lord, the brother of Sir George, now Viscount Tarbat – and therefore the uncle of the young Amelia Fraser presently living at Blair Castle. Tarbat and Sir Roderick had voted for Tullibardine to declare Lovat's forced marriage with the dowager Lady Lovat null and void, and also to condemn Lovat to death because of the '*rapt* and *hamesucken*'. Now Sir Roderick presented the Mackenzies' bill. He offered his son, Alexander Mackenzie, as husband to young Amelia, now rising thirteen and of marriageable age. On his ward's behalf, Tullibardine thought about it, and accepted. It might help reduce the Frasers to obedience. It meant that Simon Fraser could never marry her and it brought the Mackenzies back on side. Tullibardine was rebuilding his power base. Those wily old Mackenzies could be useful allies.

There was a problem: even in the terms of the corrupt marriage contract of 1685, the husband had to be a Fraser. So the bridegroom's father made him into one. Alexander was henceforth 'Alexander Mackenzie of Fraserdale'. It was a mockery, but it mattered little. The bridegroom got ready to wrest the chieftainship of Clan Fraser from its natural chief.

On 7 March 1702, Lovat borrowed some money from Inverness lairds and merchants and prepared to go to London to raise an action in the House of Lords against this malicious twist of fate. Everything he had tried thus far the Murrays had countered using the might of the state. They had each resorted to force, corruption or violence to crush their opponent. He needed to stop the marriage and clear his name.

The next day at Richmond Park, William III's horse put his hoof into a molehill, stumbled and threw its rider. The King broke his collar bone and contracted a chest infection. Two weeks later he was dead. Lovat had not even left Inverness.

In March 1702, Princess Anne of Denmark ascended the thrones. The great and good rushed to London to confirm or acquire places in her administration. Lovat headed south to join them, arriving in late April. As he skulked in London to get an entrée to the new Queen's presence, news came of the marriage of young Amelia Fraser and Alexander Mackenzie. In his absence they had moved into Castle Dounie. The news 'was decisive in shattering and reshaping his plans'. As if to confirm the blow to his hopes, Queen Anne then raised the Earl of Tullibardine to the Duke of Atholl.

Lovat wrote to Argyll asking for his help. His old patron replied he had to tread carefully; Argyll was not favoured by Anne. He could or would not do anything. 'I despair of saving myself or my Kindred in this government. So I am resolved to push my fortunes some elsewhere,' Lovat wrote. 'The restless enemies of the family of Lovat', and the 'indifference' of his allies and protectors filled him with pain and disillusionment. 'Though I have now lost my Country and Estate, I do not value my personal loss, for I can have bread anywhere.' He predicted, though it tortured him to say it, 'that after I am gone, in ten years there will not be ten Frasers together in Scotland'.

Scarcely eight weeks after Queen Anne ascended the thrones, her ministry opened hostilities against France in what would become known as the War of the Spanish Succession. On Carlos II's death, Louis claimed the thrones of Spain and the Holy Roman Empire for his grandson. Should he succeed, Spain, her colonial empire, and the loose confederation of European states that made up the Holy Roman Empire, would all fall within Louis XIV's sphere of influence. Louis would interfere in Spanish colonies and overseas trade through French ambassadors in Madrid. On France's northern frontier lay the Spanish Netherlands, buffer between France and the United Provinces. Louis would quarter his troops there if he could, and menace the Protestant Low Countries. To the south, if France influenced Spanish-held territories in Italy – such as Naples and Sicily – then Anglo-Dutch Mediterranean trade would be disrupted. In England's nightmares, Louis XIV achieved his wildest dream, to be the first 'universal monarch' – effectively, ruler of the known world. That world would be largely Roman Catholic. The consequences for Protestant Britain and her allies would be dire.

Alone, Lovat concluded he could hope for nothing from Edinburgh or Whitehall and must leave the country for a short while. He lodged for a few weeks in Harwich and thought things over. While there he took a lover, a young woman called Lucy Jones. Little is known of Lucy other than her notes to Lovat. He asked her to write to him as 'Captain John Campbell', showing he felt the need to adopt pseudonyms, fearing perhaps that the new Duke of Atholl would hunt him down. She told him she worried about the effects of his 'melancholy'. She counselled the sort of stoicism that showed she did not know her man very well ('life has such mixtures, that sure all wise people must despise it. It is the mart for fools and carnaval of knaves'). When he left, Lucy disappeared from the record of his life.

Lovat collected himself. He straightened his cuffs. He must think more flexibly. The weakness of the British succession might be the key to reverse his phase of bad luck. The Stuarts' quest for Restoration to their inheritance seemed to chime so neatly with his own. If Anne died, her nearest relative was her half-brother, James. Instead of missions to hold the line of the Highland chiefs for William or Anne, perhaps he should sway the clans to support James's claims? The Scottish Parliament was calling officially for the end of the Union of Crowns. The Jacobites in Edinburgh saw independence as the preliminary to bringing in James. Scotland and England seethed with intrigue, action and possibilities. There must be something in all this for Lovat; his family had always supported the Stuarts.

The blending of the personal and political reinvigorated him. 'My nature,' Lovat explained, 'obliged me to expose my person ... in such a ventorious or rather desperate manner that none of my enemies or even my own friends and Relations thought that ever I would be able to accomplish my design,' to save the Fraser clan from disappearing, 'but that I must die in the attempting of it.' Lovat told some clan members and supporters in Inverness-shire that he was going to the Continent for a few months, to gather arms and money, and maybe commissions, to buy support in the Scottish Parliament to vote for independence.

He left his young brother John Fraser as his deputy, with instructions to defend their interests and resist the Mackenzies should they try to encroach. They did. John haunted Stratherrick, still the centre of support for Lovat's claims. From there John led a band of men into the Aird of Lovat and garrisoned Beauly. He and about thirty minor Fraser lairds and their sons roamed the Aird for months, threatening those who looked likely to accept the new incumbents at Dounie. When the government at last forced the Atholls to recall their soldiers, much of Fraser country was laid waste. It seemed to Lovat, as he prepared to leave, that all he had predicted was fast coming to pass. But he dared stay no longer.

His destination was the exiled Stuart Court outside Paris. Except for a few stolen weeks on the run, it would be fifteen years before he was back among his Fraser clan again.

PART TWO

At the Court of the Sun King, 1702–15

'A Perfect Romance'

– GUALTERIO TO LORD LOVAT

SEVEN

The Stuart Court of St Germains, 1702

'The dismallest place in all Europe'
– THE EARL OF MIDDLETON

Lovat trotted out through the forests west of Paris. His goal was the palace at St-Germains-en-Laye, twelve miles out of the city, and ten miles north of the new and still-expanding Palace of Versailles.

It soon loomed above him. Birthplace and childhood home of Louis XIV, the French King had only moved from St Germains on the completion of Versailles seven years earlier. Until then it was the premier royal palace in France, fit for a king-in-waiting. Louis XIV and James II's grandparents, Henry IV of France and Marie Medici, laid out six formal terraces descending from the palace in huge, graceful steps to the Seine. Mary, Queen of Scots, lived at St Germains as Queen of France when she was married to Francis II. By offering James II sanctuary and a pension at St Germains after he fled England in December 1688, Louis showed how highly he regarded his Stuart cousins, and how acutely he felt their injury. James had died the previous September and spent his final years depressed and obsessed with religious devotions. His body was buried in the chapel at St Germains, and his brain in a sarcophagus at the Scots Chapel in Paris.

The Stuart Court had been looking for a way home, scanning the vistas from the palace's uppermost terraces, across northern France, for almost fifteen years. The hills of Montmartre lay in the distance to the east. Below the chateau, deep avenues cut long ago, lined with chestnuts and oaks, disappeared into the forest. The woods nurtured wild boar, deer and birds. Louis XIV's children came regularly from Versailles for the sport. It was imperative Lovat improve his prospects. He had borrowed money from Principal Carstares to go home and from the Fraser lairds and merchants to return to London. He was 'in a starving condition' and needed funds and protection. He tormented himself with thoughts of what his life should be: Dounie and all that went with it, the chief at ease in his own hall. Instead, Amelia and Alexander Mackenzie of 'Fraserdale' sat in his chairs and made heirs in his bed.

Lovat's first contact was a cousin, Sir John MacLean. The two had communicated as soon as Lovat landed in France. Sir John addressed his letters to Lovat's new alias, 'Donald Campbell', or 'Dole Don, Ambassador Extraordinaire of the Devilish Cantons' as he was in MacLean's crazy demotic. (*Dole* is the phonetic rendition of the Gaelic for Donald, *Domhnall*. *Donn* is dull brown – in hair or mood. The 'devilish cantons' were their beloved Highlands.) Lovat was *vic mo chri*, 'son of my heart', and 'I am yours and yours I will be to all eternity or may God confound me. Your own, *In saecula, seculorum. Amen*.' Sir John mixed Gaelic, English, French and Latin promiscuously.

Before Louis XIV moved to Versailles, he had spent years upgrading the irregular pentagon of his grandparents' medieval palace to the sprawling monster Lovat now gazed on. Louis's architect, Hardouin-Mansart, added five projecting wings, regularising each façade. To allow for the crush and scramble of courtiers milling around the French King as he moved from room to room, the architect collapsed walls dividing the cramped medieval rooms. Wind-tunnel passages now stretched from end to end of the vast building, creating walkways for processing, parading and plotting in. Dogs, servants, politicians and courtiers tripped over each other as they jostled to keep close to the Sun King, his family, his favourites and his succession of mistresses. Then one day they all left for the new palace at Versailles.

Neglected, St Germains fell fast into disrepair. The 'Accounts of the Royal Buildings' record the condition of the empty palace when James

II arrived in winter 1688/89: broken glass; dried-out, un-waxed, shrunken parquet flooring heaved out of line; locks stuck with rust that bled down doors and windows in damp weather; blown plaster and warping woodwork needed repairing. St Germains reeked of neglect. Nevertheless, in 1702 the new war and Louis's opportunistic proclamation of 'James III and VIII' gave Lovat optimism: plans and counter-plans changed as news of the progress of the war arrived.

The layout of the palace made day-to-day management hard. Louis's half-completed building works failed to open up a way to allow internal communication between the royal apartments of the Queen Regent, and sixteen-year-old James, and their ministers. The royal accommodation spread over most of the *bel étage* (the second floor was the 'beautiful floor'). Everyone here was forced to live modestly. Lovat wandered with counsellors and royalty alike, scurrying rat-like from one suite to another between floors via exterior gangways. He would soon understand that the palace's rambling and incoherent structure mirrored deep problems amongst the leading Jacobites at St Germains.

Lovat was introduced by Sir John to one of the most senior politicians and nobles, the Duke of Perth. An energetic man, 'always violent for the party he espoused, and … passionately proud', Perth was impatient for the Jacobite call to action. He was very sociable and open hearted, lively but quixotic. He 'tells a story very prettily, is capricious, a thorough bigot, and hath been so in each religion while he professed it', observed one of the British Secretary's spies. Perth converted – more than once – and dashed through a spiritual palette that took in Presbyterianism, Episcopalianism, and Roman Catholicism.

Lovat's reports about the discontent in Scotland and England were sweet music to Perth's ears. Perth was happy to make the Scottish throne available to James as a first step, whether by Act of Parliament or at the point of a sword. Lovat claimed to have met 'the chiefs of the clans and a great number of the Lords of the Lowlands' before he left Scotland. Never deserted by the rhetoric of self-promotion, Lord Lovat claimed he had pleaded their Majesties' case 'in so spirited a manner ... urged with so much force' that the leading men of the Highlands begged him to go and represent them in Paris, and tell their King to come now, and rule over them. The country suffered grievously under the yoke of the Union of Crowns, Lovat said. Hence, he 'arrived in Paris with this important commission'.

If this accorded exactly with Perth's hope, it was anathema to the other dominant character at St Germains. The Earl of Middleton was a moderate Jacobite and an English Protestant. He had come over in 1693 to be James II's chief minister. The Duc de Saint-Simon, recorder of everyday life in Louis XIV's Court, described Middleton and his wife as 'fiendishly spiteful and scheming, but Middleton, because he was admirably good company, mixed on equal terms with best people at Versailles'. Though the Earl hated St Germains, calling the palace 'the dismallest place in all Europe', he remained ferociously loyal to young James and his mother, Mary of Modena. Guided by Middleton, devout Catholics though they were, the Stuarts were committed to preserving the Protestant settlement in Britain, and offering religious tolerance to all. Middleton's secretary recalled the late James II counselling his son that 'if ever he came to Rule over that People, to be a strict Observer of ... the Laws of England ... that he might not split upon that Rock which had been so fatal to him'.

In Middleton's judgement, strict observation of 'the Laws of England' and diplomatic exchanges between magnates – *not* threats of violence by Gaelic-speaking Highlanders like Perth's kin – was the correct strategy for restoration. When speaking to Middleton, Lovat emphasised the need to strengthen resistance in the Scottish Parliament, to vote for independence and then the restoration of the male Stuarts. Someone should be sent back with money to buy votes, he argued. He, Lovat, could do it.

By living at daggers drawn ('like cats and dogs' was how Louis XIV's daughter-in-law put it) Perth and Middleton terminally weakened the Jacobite ruling council. Lovat tried to avoid taking sides, or being treated with contempt by one side or the other. However, the minute Middleton heard of Lovat's strategy for restoration and the key role of the Highland clans, he opposed it. The Earl then worked to ruin Lovat's credibility, gleefully repeating at Versailles gossip about 'the Grand Fornicator of the Aird'. Lovat hit back that the Earl's strategy had slowly suffocated the cause: his many missives lay smothered under a mountain of paperwork in the English administration. While some English ministers nodded and gave verbal support to Middleton, they prevaricated with questions, delaying commitment to bring back James, even as they worked to proclaim George of Hanover King of England and Scotland when Anne died. Their measured, meaningless exchanges with the Court at St Germains damped down the Jacobite threat while satisfying their own residual Jacobite sympathies.

Middleton soon hated Lovat for his views. He truly believed the Fraser chief was wrong. Yet it was plain to Lovat that Middleton's group were out of touch with national sentiment. They had been away from the British political and social scene for at least a decade and more. What Parliament might have accepted then was not so obviously attractive now. Bringing in Anne instead of James, and negotiating with other claimants to the thrones, should have alerted old hands at St Germains to the new political realities. Only force would carry them home.

Perth countered, citing Lovat, that only a rising in Scotland, backed by France, would give them what they wanted. He bemoaned 'the counsel that prevails here is that which advises inaction and waiting for a miracle'. The ultra-pious Mary of Modena liked to believe waiting for a miracle was a viable policy and would retreat frequently to the convent at Chaillot to pray for one.

Middleton had some reason to pursue the policy he did. Even pro-Hanoverians admitted the level of support for James in both English Houses of Parliament. 'There is a party in this Kingdom for the Prince of Wales,' they wrote to the Elector of Hanover. Even his enemies called Young James the Prince of Wales. Their 'boldness is founded, not only on their confidence in the King of France, but on an assurance with which they flatter themselves, of being countenanced and supported by the present government'. Many of the most powerful men in Queen Anne's administration – Godolphin, Marlborough, Bolingbroke, Ormonde – engaged in friendly communications with

St Germains. It did not mean they would actually vote to bring 'King James III' back. Lovat declared in frustration that 'while her Majesty implicitly followed the advice of the people who were at the head of the English Parliament, Jesus Christ would come in the clouds before her son would be restored'. Middleton recalled the Queen Regent to the reports he had from Scotland, that Lovat 'joined insinuating talents to low manners and a profligate character'.

Lovat lost patience. He had intended to be in France just a few weeks, obtaining money and stirring up opposition to Anne in the Scottish Parliament and the Highlands. He urged the Jacobites to catch hold of the opportunity the war presented and persuade Louis XIV to back them. It offered the sort of chance that might not come again for *another* fifteen years. An invasion of Scotland would merely be part of Louis's larger strategy, and divert some British troops menacing his northern border through the Low Countries.

Though Mary disliked Lovat's arrogant tone, the logic of his argument tempted her. She agreed that Middleton's policy was not working, and if the war suddenly turned against France, Louis might recognise Anne, and then George as her successor. She would ask Louis to back an invasion.

Before she could act, the Queen Regent was distracted by a bizarre religious conversion. Middleton claimed to have been woken in the night, 'hearing the Blessed Sacrament carried along with the sound of a little bell before it, to the apartment of his son, Lord Clermont, who was at the point of death'. Middleton's son suddenly felt better. He was convinced it had been Mary's husband, the late James II, ringing to exhort him to convert to Catholicism. Middleton declared that the keys to the offices of state were incompatible with the keys to heaven, and theatrically handed them back to the Queen Regent. He needed to go on retreat to clean his soul.

Mary's attention swung ecstatically away from Perth, Sir John MacLean and Lovat, and back to her dear Middleton. She told everyone that Middleton's conversion gave her the only joy she had experienced since the death of 'our Saint King', as Mary now called her late husband. It was almost beyond belief. Up to now, Middleton 'had so mean an opinion of converts, that he used to say, "A new light never comes into the house but by a crack in the tiling". It *was* a miracle, said the Queen, the first her dead husband had performed. Middleton slid back into Mary of Modena's favour, and slipped the keys of office back into his pocket. Mary waited for another 'sign'.

Living with the infighting at St Germains for even a few months made it clear to Lovat that he must go straight to the real decision-maker, or he would be trapped inside this melodrama for years. Only Louis XIV could provide effective support for an uprising. However, the French King would not meet with a heretic. All things considered, it was a good time to consult one's religious conscience. Besides, it was clear that conversions were *de rigueur* for ambitious politicians at St Germains.

Lovat went to Brother McLoghlan, a priest at St Germains, and declared his intention to convert. Brother McLoghlan advised the Scot to retire to a convent to think it over. Lovat did not need to go that far: this was not a huge leap of faith for an Episcopalian, and not a very devout one. Without Catholicism he did not have the support of the Queen Regent or a recommendation to Louis XIV. By early the following year, Lovat was writing to Italy to offer the Pope his service to the Holy Mother Church 'to the spilling of my blood … With this object I go to hazard my life and my family.' The Pope replied, thanking Lovat and welcoming him into the Church of Rome.

Lovat's persistence had paid off. In the autumn of 1702, he had heard that Louis XIV would grant him a private audience. Immediately Lovat started penning a grandiloquent harangue for the edification of 'The Greatest Prince in the Universe' from the self-appointed spokesman of his Scottish allies – *les chefs des tribus montagnards* – the chiefs of the Highland clans.

EIGHT

Planning an invasion, 1702–04

'The Greatest Prince in the Universe'
− LOVAT TO LOUIS XIV

Lord Lovat, MacShimidh Mor, had abandoned his clan for exactly this sort of opportunity. As for his Most Christian Majesty, the Stuarts were loved relations. Schemes to benefit them had bubbled out of this chiefly milord for months before Louis granted him an audience.

He clattered into the courtyard at Versailles, his nerves steeled by need. Lovat felt the Sun King's presence all round him, monumental-ised in the buildings Louis had raised and the gardens he had laid down, beautifying the face of the earth and glorifying God as Louis had been glorified by the Almighty. When Louis walked in the gardens, fountains sprang to life. To bring off the effect, other fountains had to die down behind him. The plumbing was not up to his vision. Nothing quite worked as hoped.

Lovat chivvied himself down miles of corridors towards his private audience. He was shown into a small chamber off the Hall of Mirrors. Standing in his stockinged feet 'Louis le Grand' was just five feet five inches of global power. Lovat, broad and long, loomed over him by seven inches. He had to bow very low. The Court flunkies retired leav-ing just the Marquis de Torcy (son of the great Colbert), who placed himself behind the King, now seated in the royal chair, and giving the Highlander space to speak. Torcy was keen for the invasion of Scotland to happen. It would pull thousands of British troops out of the

Continental field of operations and weaken the Duke of Marlborough's army.

Addressing the King in good French with a Scots accent, Lord Lovat enlarged 'upon the ancient alliances between Scotland and France'. He expatiated on genealogies: Louis XIV's, ancient and connecting him intimately to the royal House of Stuart; and Lovat's, 500 years old, connecting him to French aristocracy. The Frasers were originally a French family, Lovat reminded the King: they went to England with the last successful French invaders, the Normans. This Fraser could go with the next, the greatest Bourbon. Lovat knew Louis adored genealogy.

'At a thousand hazards to [my] ... life,' Lovat accepted the commission of the Highland elite to come here, he said. If the Highlanders rose in rebellion and were 'honoured with the protection of the greatest King that ever filled the throne of France', he said they could not fail. Lovat drew to a close. 'With a look of much benignity,' he noted happily, Louis assured him the 'whole French nation had their hearts unfeignedly Scottish'. The two men speculated about invasion plans. It pained Lovat to be looking back towards his homeland through the spyglass of an invading soldier, pointing out opportunities to attack it.

Back at St Germains, Lord Lovat's mind flitted between France and home. With Louis behind him, his hopes of his own restoration had been revived. He broadcast the news of his success to the Duke of Perth, Sir John MacLean, and MacLean's cousin, Alexander. 'The King promised at all times to assist the Scots with troops, money and everything that might be necessary to support them against the English,' he told them. The men were overjoyed and raised their glasses. Lovat looked at the old men around him. They had all come here to this place as optimistic young men; he was determined not to get stuck, like them, for a decade and a half.

The Middletonian faction took little notice of Lovat and his claims until gifts from Louis XIV began to arrive for Lovat, including a valuable sword and a pair of beautiful pistols. His new friends admired their lovely workmanship, with the head of 'His Most Christian

Majesty' cast in silver on the handles, and Lovat's full coat of arms, coronet and all. The steel barrels were richly inlaid with figures in gold with the Fraser motto, *Je suis prest* [*prêt*] and the crest of the Fraser chief at the muzzle. The presents suggest Lovat made quite an impression on the French King; and a slightly different one on Louis's *maitresse en titre*, Madame de Maintenon. She saluted the tall, dashing Highlander as '*un homme ravissant*', a loaded compliment in the light of his conviction for 'ravishing a lady of rank in a house of consequence', but also perhaps an amused allusion to his gift of a beautiful weapon engraved with 'I am Ready' on it.

Lovat retired to his room to prepare for his meetings with Louis' ministers. The cogitations emerged in another of his memorial letters to the Sun King. 'What is necessary to carry on a vigorous war?' Lovat asked rhetorically. His answer was quite specific: 6–7,000 men, including 600 cavalry and 1,200 dragoons, 'who must have their accoutrements carried along with them'; 18,000 arms, 'firelocks with bayonets, and not muskets'; also, ammunition for an army of 30,000 men, plus artillery, plus ammunition for three garrisons and artillery for them too, 'to be a safe retreat in case the army be obliged to winter in that country'. Finally, Lovat required about £40–50,000 cash 'to gratify those that bring in forces … and to buy provisions' – there would be no more quartering of troops on poor Highlanders. 'The sooner this is done,' Lovat continued, 'it is certainly the better because of the season of the year and the present commodious weather.' Spring was campaign time. No one fought through the winter if they could possibly help it. Everything got bogged down in the mud. Men and materiel rotted like turnips.

Lovat's invasion plot was born of impatience and ambition: he had been away nearly a year and was increasingly restless to return to the Highlands. Ships with men, war chests and arms must land on the west coast of Scotland, he said, and others on the east. They could sweep through the country gathering men and seizing Edinburgh before the English were properly alerted to the threat. Sir John MacLean looked over the plans. He cavilled. Cousin Lovat had been a bit creative with the figures, he thought. He had rated some of the chiefs at about double the number of troops they could actually bring out. Lovat dismissed his criticisms; the French needed encouragement, he said.

Lovat could not hope to succeed if he did not involve Mary of Modena, young James and the Earl of Middleton. He petitioned James for gratifications. Lord Lovat 'expects a letter of thanks from the King for the service of his family wherein he should promise to make him Sheriff of Inverness'. Wherever he was, home was the backcloth against which Lovat stood and spoke. The Sheriffs of the shires dominated both elections and the county law courts. 'My enemies grow great in the Prince of Denmark's [Queen Anne's] government,' he complained to James, 'and they accomplish the ruin of my estate and family.'

Letters from the Highlands told of a worsening situation. At St Germains, Lovat requested a patent for the title of 'Earl of Inverness' from the Stuarts, though a duke's coronet might sit better on him. Above all, he wanted to be restored to his inheritance. In his imagination, he could be the premier duke in Scotland, and unassailable. In reality he was a broke and dispossessed fugitive.

The young king-in-waiting was all in favour of Lovat's dashing schemes, but Mary of Modena could not decide what to do. In theory, she would undertake whatever was needed to get the two of them back to the Palace of Whitehall, though she also believed that God would provide, and she must prevent her son exposing himself to danger. The Duc de Saint-Simon observed of James's mother, 'for all that she was so pious, loved power, and had been too strict and narrow in his [her son's] education, either from misguided affection or because she wished to keep him obedient and fearful of her'.

The Earl of Middleton drifted through the corridors like a cloud, growing blacker and heavier. Rumours reached him that Lovat had been urging the Queen Regent to 'use all her interest with the King of France to embrace the offers of the Highlanders'. Lovat told her the Highlanders 'are certainly the strongest party in the three kingdoms to bring home the King or make a diversion for the armies of the Allies by a war in Britain'. Middleton's view of them as cateran bands was wrong, Lovat explained. 'The Highlanders' power and loyalty is so frightful to the usurping government' of Queen Anne, 'that those in authority always come to them and make great offers to come into their party'. This was partly true. 'Management' by 'offers' was a recognised government tactic: ministers bought the loyalty they could not command by affection, or compel by fear. Some impoverished chiefs simply offered themselves and their men to the highest bidder. There was an element of this sort of opportunism in Lovat's presence at St Germains.

Lovat counselled Mary of Modena against the policies of 'a *politique* party in England who promise to call home the King on conditions'. 'They are not to be believed, though they write and swear never so much. For knave will be knave still to my certain knowledge.' This was daring – the 'knaves' flirting with restoring James included the Earls of Godolphin, Marlborough and Bolingbroke.

Middleton argued against Lovat's plan as soon as he saw details of it. Lovat is 'full of ambition and enterprise' and has been 'gained' by the French to stir up 'a civil war in Scotland', he said to Mary. It was 'extremely advantageous to France', since it would draw British troops home, but 'it would ruin instead of advancing the affairs of the King her son,' he judged. Lovat challenged Middleton to prove his claim that the English administration had made a 'promise to call home the King' on the death of Queen Anne. Middleton could not produce proof. Lovat suggested the Queen Regent set a deadline. If the English ministers refused to fix a term for persuading Anne to nominate her half-brother James as heir, then 'it was incontestable proof' they never would. Lovat told Mary 'that their promises were intended only to amuse and lull asleep the Court of St Germains, as they had successfully done for fifteen years past'.

Middleton hit back, persuading Mary and Louis not to invade until Lovat could provide firm evidence to substantiate his claims about the Scots' readiness to rise. Gualterio, the Papal Nuncio in France, through whom Lovat had been communicating with the Papacy and Louis XIV, advised him to make peace with the Earl. Middleton seemed ready to conciliate him and suggested that Lovat might find one of his English confidantes an amusing and informative diversion for an evening or two. Her name was Mrs Fox.

'Mrs Fox' was a practised spy, who moved between Middleton and the various English noblemen at Whitehall, and 'who promised to cause the Queen [Anne] and the Parliament of England to declare for King James the third' when Anne named a successor. Middleton asked her to 'open up' Lovat's mind and make him see what solid backing the Earl had.

Lovat had heard rumours of Middleton's association with Mrs Fox. The Earl enjoyed the use of a '*petite maison* hard by the convent of the Benedictines at Paris, where he would often retire in pious seclusion from the world, and hold his conferences' with his spies. On one side of the wall, nuns knelt on stone floors, their lips moving intimately over their beads. On the other, was Mrs Fox. When Lovat called on the her, 'she was alone, and negligently reposed upon a kind of bed'. He made her sound like some sort of courtesan.

'As she had a kind of wit,' Lovat recalled, Mrs Fox 'entertained [me] ... very agreeably for two hours. At the end of that time Lord Middleton arrived, and Mrs Fox quitted the apartment.' The two men began to talk about what sort of information the Scotsman might try to gather from the Scottish Jacobites.

Lovat and Mrs Fox corresponded after their meeting: flirting, flattering and probing. She cajoled him about his health. 'Pensiveness' threatened to lower his spirits, she said. She advised him to do nothing to compromise his honour, and laughed to scorn his 'fantastical' invasion schemes. (In fact, Lovat's plans would form the basis of *two* invasion plans adopted during his lifetime, in the uprisings of 1715 and 1745.)

The Jacobite ruling council at St Germains concluded that 'the most effectual means of securing the succession of the Crown of England to the King, after the death of his sister, would be to put him in possession of the Crown of Scotland'. That meant adopting Louis XIV and Lord Lovat's invasion plans, and dropping Middleton's futile diplomacy.

* * *

While finances were being gathered, Lovat attempted to firm up other alliances at Court, and devoted some time to wooing the Duke of Perth's daughter, Lady Mary Drummond. He composed the following piece of doggerel for her:

> By the merited reputation
> You have in this nation,
> I have a mighty inclination
> To become your relation
> By a legal copulation.

She did not seem very interested. He persisted,

> Thou Sylvia kills me, I'll never complain
> Or demonstrat my love, since I know it's in vain.

He gave it up. He liked women, but had no time to take them seriously.

In Scotland, Sir Roderick Mackenzie had turned up an old debt that young Amelia Mackenzie (Lovat's) grandfather raised in the late 1660s. The old Lord Lovat secured the debt against some Fraser property, but never repaid it, and it sank into the background for thirty-five years. Sir Roderick found the debt and bought it off the creditor's heirs, who were astonished suddenly to have the matter settled. Sir Roderick sniffed about for more. Miscellaneous Fraser debts, mostly paltry sums, lurked in corners of solicitors' offices. Sir Roderick bought up the lot. He went to the Court of Session (on which he and his brother sat) for the right to enforce repayment to himself immediately as creditor of all these debts. The Lovat estates did not pay – Sir Roderick must have instructed his son to default – and Sir Roderick raised an action before his legal brethren (including his brother) to claim the assets of the Lovat estates in lieu of the money he was owed. He won. Sir Roderick Mackenzie was judged to be 'in rights of the Lovat estates'. Ostensibly, Sir Roderick had dispossessed his own son, daughter-in-law and grandsons.

Mackenzie had trumped them all, both the male heir, Simon, Lord Lovat, and Amelia's ambitious Uncle John, the Duke of Atholl. He drew up an entail of his new properties – the whole 500 square miles of Fraser country – in favour of his son and grandson. In France, Lovat was stunned. How could an outlaw Highlander, practising treason at an exiled court, challenge a senator of the College of Justice in Edinburgh? Sir Roderick's timing and execution were faultless.

Lovat was desperate for any mission that gave him money and reason to leave France. By the spring of 1703, Middleton gave it to him, recommending that Louis XIV send the clan chief back home to obtain proof of the situation on the ground. Louis agreed and requested that Lovat obtain written pledges from the Highland chiefs that they would rise if France invaded. Lovat was apprehensive about the mission. He relied on the Duke of Perth to maintain the French King's enthusiasm for action. Lovat was to tell the Scots that if enough troops took to the field, Louis would back them with experienced officers, money, arms, and munitions. Mary and Middleton told Lovat to keep quiet and only find out the level of support in Scotland. Louis and Torcy issued passports for Lovat and another Jacobite, Johnny Murray, the son of a Perthshire laird. They were unaware that Middleton had already despatched his own spy ahead of them, a man named James Murray.

Middleton instructed James Murray to reach the Scottish Jacobites first and prepare the ground *against* Lovat's mission. Lovat would tell them France was on the brink of invasion, but James Murray was to warn the Scots that the French would never 'venture on matters that are not decisive'. The Scots would have to do it all alone, before French support came.

The Middletonians also wanted Murray to sound out Atholl's brother-in-law, the Duke of Hamilton, in whose leadership of the Scottish Jacobites they put unlimited faith. 'Assure Lord Aran [the Duke of Hamilton] of the great sense we have of his sufferings, services, interest, and prudence, in advising, managing and performing what is practicable in the present conjuncture: that you have orders for our friends to use all their credit in opposing abjuration, Hanover and Union.' They must vote against naming George as successor to Anne in the Scottish Parliament, and vote young James Stuart onto the throne of Scotland as his half-sister's heir – as if the English would ever accept their decision.

The virus of the incapacitating factionalism at St Germains was being spread to Scotland. The two groups of spies took it with them when they left.

NINE

'A disposition in Scotland to take up arms', 1703

'The first thing to be done was to make an Invasion
upon Scotland; to facilitate which, it was necessary
to foment an Insurrection in the Highlands'
— JAMES FRASER, *A GENUINE NARRATIVE*

Lovat and Johnny Murray left St Germains in May 1703, accompanied by Major George Fraser, Colonel Graham and servants. Lovat knew he faced major obstacles. His standing in France was not replicated in Scotland, where he was an outlaw 'under sentence of death ... [and] with whom,' sniffed a Scottish minister, 'no honest man in Scotland would converse'. From this position, Middleton sent Lovat to persuade chiefs to rise in arms against the Queen, and fully expected him to fail.

For a month Lovat and his fellow plotters lurked at the sea ports in northern France, prevented from crossing by the war being waged in the Channel. Eventually they sneaked away in a prison boat, disguised as English prisoners of war being exchanged for French ones, and sailed out of Calais under cover of darkness. The sea slopped and sighed; the men hunched their shoulders against the cooling air. Lovat recalled his last conversation with Mary of Modena. He was *not* to make plans 'till you have particular orders from myself'. It was to be an information-gathering exercise only. If it became anything more interesting, he would have to make it so.

Lovat listened to the water slapping at the boat's sides. Daylight and the open road always seemed denied to him. Ever since the marriage of his late cousin, Hugh Lovat, almost twenty years earlier, his eye had had to adapt to the darker corners of intrigue. In the shadows, men could not easily make him out. Even to his allies, he was a puzzle. Few saw how events at home positioned him in the world, and at best only partly understood his motives. His friends advised him to ignore slights and minor quarrels and to get on with the main task of regaining his titles and lands and restoring his 'true King'.

The little 'prison ship' approached the English coast with caution and the party was landed during the night 'at some place in the neighbourhood of Dover'. From there they sped straight to London.

By 12 June, Lovat had already gathered intelligence from the capital, telling St Germains that 'the big merchant' – the Duke of Marlborough – is cooling. Lovat never missed the chance to pour cold water on Middleton's policies. And even if hit upon unconsciously, to codename the 'the big merchant' suggested both Marlborough and St Germains saw the great General's loyalty as a potentially tradable commodity. Lovat inferred that Marlborough needed an explosion of action – an invasion – to spur his interest. Meanwhile, Marlborough led Queen Anne's armies out against Louis and the Jacobites. From London the conspirators decided to head north, to pursue their commission.

The group reached Northallerton in Yorkshire without attracting unwelcome attention and stopped at an inn, where the gentlemen retired to a private room to discuss progress. Edinburgh was a few more days' ride away. The inn keeper served the servants beer and food and asked about their journey. Travellers' news was an attraction of the inns. Local people would gather there to get news of the outside world. The country being at war, there was an especially large interest. Lovat's servants remained vague in their talk of business north of the border, except for their French valet de chambre. Intoxicated on beer and attention, the man boasted that 'Mi'lord' is a man of substance, a passionate 'partisan of James III'. They were on a mission from the French Court, he said. Lovat, John Murray and the other officers sat in an upstairs sitting room, drinking and smoking and talking while the servant blabbed beneath their feet.

Sitting quietly in the valet's audience was the local Justice of the Peace. He slipped out, roused all the constables he could find, armed them and marched with them to the inn. One of Lovat's guards heard whispers and clattering. He looked from the window and ran to warn his master. The gentlemen leapt up. Lovat said they would have to fight and break free, or die in the attempt. John Murray shook his head. He was a naturalised French subject and they would not dare harm him. The reprisals would be terrible for English prisoners in France.

Lovat dismissed his friend. If this was not his fight, then Murray should retire to his own room, and wait and see. Lovat had no choice, 'since,' he shrugged, he 'expected no better, if ... taken, than to be hanged and quartered'. The noise of the constables and their officer grew louder. Lovat pointed to the table. On it lay two pistols and a 'blunderbuss that carried eight bullets'. Take those and go onto the stairs, Lovat instructed his men, while arming himself to the teeth.

Soon they heard the Justice at the foot of the stairs, the crowd of constables shuffling in behind him. It was the middle of the evening. Most of these part-time government servants had been dragged from their firesides by their superior's excited summons. Lovat listened behind the door. The Justice moved towards his prey, confident of the element of surprise.

Lovat whispered to his men that the minute they heard fire, they could assume their chief had shot the Justice. One soldier should then immediately 'discharge his blunderbuss upon the constables on the stairs'. They had seen that most of the local men bore nothing but long staves. Then, said Lovat, they must run for it, forcing their way through the injured men blocking the stairwell. 'The night was very dark,' and moonless, Lovat noted. 'Once gain the street, [then] nothing would be easier than escape,' he reassured them. His men took heart and waited. The one hovering in the recess at the stair head cocked his weapons.

Moving in silence to the fireside, Lovat checked his pistol, and took a moment to review their position. There was a crash at the door. The latch clicked up. The Justice piled in and opened his mouth to shout to the occupants to disarm and surrender. Lovat glared. The two stood ready to blow out each other's brains.

In a blink, Lovat's face dissolved from outrage into a hundred creases of smiling recognition. 'My dear Sir, how happy I am to see you,' Lovat began, coming towards him, his arms akimbo. It had been two years since he had 'had that pleasure – with the Duke of Argyll – at the races near this town', he said, trying to conjure up happy days. The Justice looked stumped, then relieved. He cast about his mind for some memory of this big, mobile face. Nothing came. Although he could not place him, the man was obviously noble. It was a simple matter for Lovat to slip a frame or two of false memory past his well-greased vanity.

The Justice 'begged him to be seated' so his Lordship could be served with a bottle of wine in this town, where, the JP said with a bow, he was 'a man of some consequence'. The Justice darted ahead of him. The Justice insisted on finding the wine himself and left the room. He dismissed his constables and sent for their hostess to fetch up the 'best Spanish wine she had in the house'. The two men enjoyed a bottle together, and exchanged gossip about their smart mutual friends.

A few hours of deceit and chat accomplished what bloodshed might have failed to. The men sat on either side of the fire and talked and talked. Lovat drank hard – but drink never seemed to affect him. He thought he had never been drunk. Not so the Justice, who by midnight was 'obliged to be carried off without sense or motion to his own house'.

Alone again, Lovat advised Johnny Murray and his gentlemen they must all take to their horses and 'quit the town', though it was one o'clock in the morning. They galloped away, furious with the valet who had exposed them to such danger. It gave Lovat 'more trouble to hinder … Murray from stabbing the French valet' than 'to outwit the penetration, and escape from the hands, of the Justice of Peace', he grumbled.

* * *

After a tense and weary ride, full of half-imagined voices and fearing the rattle of pursuers' bridles, they came to Durham. Lord Lovat was within a hundred miles of Edinburgh, and less than half that distance from the Scottish border at Berwick-upon-Tweed. It would be madness to cross the Tweed with the Murrays' price on his head. Lovat sent Colonel Graham and Major George Fraser on to Edinburgh to scout ahead.

At Northumberland, Lovat visited the major Jacobite families. He showed them a portrait of their exiled monarch. They had never seen a picture of him. It was a typical Stuart face – long and thin, full-lipped, with a prominent nose and dark benign eyes. They gazed at it, knelt down, kissed it and prayed before the image. Lovat watched and listened. They bent at the knee, but their minds were far from 'supple', he thought. Not liking what he saw he accused them of being frightened to tell their rightful King they would fight for him. They retorted they were ready to venture everything on the day James came home with an army, and raised his banners. Lovat could not get any of them to commit their treason to pen and ink.

The men returning from Edinburgh carried more bad news. James Murray, whom they all knew from St Germains, had been there for two months, alerting the Duke of Hamilton to their arrival. Hamilton was about fifty, wealthy, swarthy, energetic, and full 'of good sense ... haughty and ambitious' and 'covetous'. He led the anti-Union Cavalier Party in the Scottish Parliament. Lovat's men told him the Duke of Atholl was often with Hamilton, although Atholl, who now held the post of joint Scottish Secretary of State with the Earl of Cromartie (formerly Viscount Tarbat), was a member of the Court Party under the Queen's High Commissioner, the Duke of Queensberry. The Cavaliers, many of them old Stuart-style Royalists, inclined to Jacobitism. They favoured an independent Scotland and perhaps thinking back to the fiasco of William III, a different monarch. Another Atholl ally, the Duke of Montrose, was Lord President of the Privy Council – one of the great officers of the Scottish state. How could Lovat possibly find a space here?

Queensberry and the Court Party represented the wishes of Queen Anne's ministry. Their instructions were to force the Scottish Parliament to vote for a full Union with England, and to accept George of Hanover as the heir to Queen Anne in Scotland. Lovat's men said Atholl was increasingly disillusioned with Scotland's prospects in a fully united kingdom under the Hanoverians, and was irritating his boss, Queensberry, by associating so much with his brother-in-law Hamilton's Cavaliers. Another big political grouping in the Scottish Parliament was the Country Party. They were firmly Scottish nationalist and might come in with the Cavaliers, except for the religious issue. Most Country men were Presbyterian, and vehemently anti-Catholic. The Cavaliers' Jacobitism carried with it the whiff of Rome.

Mary of Modena had asked James Murray to 'break [the news of] Fraser's business by degrees, the Queen apprehending [that Hamilton] would be averse to it'. The minute Atholl heard about Lovat's involvement he called an extraordinary meeting of the Privy Council to reissue Lord Lovat's death sentence. How this man was not dead and buried twice over amazed and infuriated the Duke.

Meanwhile, failure to get agreement on the government's measures was causing Queensberry frustration. Endless letters came to him from Westminster; the government was getting anxious. As the Queen's High Commissioner he needed to know what was going on behind the scenes. Queensberry made friends by making promises. He would reward good intelligence handsomely. One Queensberry man said he had found 'there was nothing he had promised to do for me but what he made good'. His enemies thought him in 'outward appearance and in his ordinary conversation … of a gentle and good disposition, but inwardly a very devil, standing at nothing to advance his own interests and designs'. Queensberry was, they said, both grasping and lavish with the money he received; both sincere and deceitful in the handling of his power.

As he waited near Newcastle, Lovat knew he had a problem. He could not work within the system because of Hamilton, Atholl and the Mackenzies. He could not work underneath it to foment rebellion because of Middleton, Mary of Modena and even Louis's fluctuating enthusiasm for an invasion. Yet there was no doubt Scotland was approaching a crossroads – on into full Union, or off towards independence. The Scottish Parliament was roaring against its handling by Queensberry. The majority were determined to resist her Majesty's Commissioner until he guaranteed certain concessions, and demonstrated he worked for Scottish interests as well as London's. The destabilising mix of passions and empty purses made for a Scottish legislature that rocked with turbulence and resistance to management. One good push and they would all rise and break free, thought Lovat.

In Paris, Louis had asked his trusted intelligence adviser, Eusebius Renaudot, to interpret developments for him. Renaudot told his Majesty there was no enterprise 'more certain, easier or more speedy' for restoring James to the throne in Edinburgh than 'to profit by the general disposition of the whole of Scotland to take up arms'. This view of the situation was 'so public', Renaudot concluded, 'that none doubt of it, except the Ministers at St Germains'. Back in Edinburgh, the Duke of Queensberry could not steer debates his way. He looked across at Hamilton and Atholl and wondered what was behind their vehement opposition. Outside Newcastle, Lovat listened to his officers' reports and mulled things over.

The pressure on Queensberry steamed to a head in the late summer of 1703. Debates in the Scottish Parliament about the succession drowned beneath shouts of 'Liberty!' 'Honour!' 'Religion!', and above them all 'Trade!' Even the Almighty appeared to take an interest in Parliament's business. 'While the rolls were calling upon this question, there fell the greatest rain that was ever seen come from the heavens, which made such a noise upon the roof of the Parliament house … that no voice could be heard, and the clerks were obliged to stop. "It was apparent that the heavens declared against their procedure," one member said.' God directed them to refuse Hanover and Union.

The MPs' formal answer to Queensberry came in two bills 'intended to secure their liberties and freedom from the oppression they

97

sustained thro' the influence of English ministers over Scots counsels and affairs'. The Scots debated an Act of Security, and an 'Act *anent* [concerning] Peace and War'.

This second Act stated that no monarch of England and Scotland could declare war on behalf of the Scottish subjects without the specific consent of their Scottish Parliament, which, they said, 'was absolutely necessary, considering how much the nation had lost by being brought into all England's wars'. The two countries were approaching a peak of bitterness towards each other. The Scots deeply resented the way they had been hustled into the War of the Spanish Succession. It was partly a trade war. They accepted the English must fight to protect their trading empire; but why should Scotland have to pay and fight for it when, as the Darien Venture showed, they were to be excluded from this trade? Ordinary Scots would be paying for decades to get over that economic catastrophe.

The other Act, the Act of Security, legislated that the Scottish monarch was expressly *not* to be the person occupying the throne of England – unless England consented to conditions that would 'secure the honour and sovereignty of this Crown and Kingdom, the freedom, frequency and power of parliaments, the religion, liberty and trade of the nation from English or any foreign influence'. Scottish grievances had piled up in the years following the Darien fiasco, economic ruin, famine, the harsh tax burden that the wars laid on Scots and English alike; and the late King's insensitive response to this chain of social and economic depressions that strangled Scottish life in the last decade of the seventeenth century. The Scots were fed up with Whitehall mandarins and City traders.

By September, the Scottish Act of Security had been debated but not passed when Queensberry granted a first reading to an Act of Supply. The Supply was the Scots' contribution to the maintenance of their Queen, her administration and her foreign policy. MPs packed the House for the reading. In the debate that followed, all sides raged at each other into the night. Candles were lit and for two hours nothing could be heard but a cacophony of contrasting voices with two phrases dominant: 'Liberty!' and 'No Supply!' Did Parliament meet 'for nothing else than to drain the nation of money, to support those who were betraying and enslaving it' someone yelled? Queensberry would not call the vote. He feared, rightly, he was losing control of the Scottish Parliament, and losing this vote would wound him fatally. The Earl of Roxburghe suggested to his fellow parliamentarians that if they could not obtain 'so natural and undeniable a privilege as a vote' by the normal way, 'they would demand it with their swords in their hands'. Cheers greeted him.

Queensberry sent out an order to footguards to stand ready in the Netherbow Port, one of the gateways to the medieval city. A Lieutenant-General Ramsay sneered 'in his cups that "ways would be found to make the Parliament calm enough"'. The Scots were stunned. Would Queensberry really use Scotland's soldiers to take away Scotsmen's control of their own legislature?

The English Parliament punished its riotous neighbour in Edinburgh. It invoked punitive 'Navigation and Aliens' Acts. The countrymen with whom the English wanted to share King and Country were now 'aliens' on English soil, and their meagre trading efforts were to be given no encouragement. Such measures further infuriated the Scots. The High Commissioner was at his wits' end. Atholl, Cromartie and other important figures crossed the floor from the Court Party to the Cavaliers. Queensberry watched in anger and dismay, and did not forget it. His enemies accused him of 'having undertaken and promoted every proposal and scheme for enslaving Scotland, and invading her honour, liberty, and trade, and rendering her obsequious to the measures and interest of England'.

Queensberry had to strengthen his hand. The Court Party was the largest single party, but when the Country and Cavalier parties united behind the big aristocratic leaders, the opposition groups dominated the House. Queensberry needed to form an alliance to get enough votes to carry his measures through. The other obvious political group was the Scottish Church, and its leader, the chief of Clan Campbell, Archibald, 1st Duke of Argyll – Lovat's old patron. Queensberry formed the alliance with Argyll and his party. Despite this coalition, the opposition, allied under Hamilton, forced the

Scottish Act of Succession through the house. Queen Anne refused to ratify it. The Scots refused to vote her any Supply. Anne wrote to Queensberry and advised he prorogue the Scottish Parliament for a year. This would prevent the working of government north of the border. The English wanted to punish the Scots. Years later, Queensberry recalled 1703 as the stormiest session of his parliamentary career.

At the height of the trouble, Queensberry's new political ally, the Duke of Argyll, sent him a message. 'There was a person come from France,' he said, 'who was willing to make great discoveries, providing that he got a pardon, and some establishment for a maintenance, and that his name should be kept secret till these were obtained' – all fairly conventional in the churning waters of early-eighteenth-century politics. Argyll said the intelligence would give Queensberry evidence against their common enemies, Hamilton and Atholl.

On 11 August, Queensberry wrote to Queen Anne. The informant was a man of rank, who had personal dealings with the exiled royal family, and with Louis XIV. 'If that person shall apply to me and be willing to own what he has said, how shall I use him?' he asked her Majesty. He waited for a reply, and went to tackle the Scottish Parliament again.

TEN

The 'political sensation', autumn 1703

'O, what a tangled web we weave,
When first we practise to deceive'
— SHAKESPEARE

The 'man from France' was Lovat, of course, as Queensberry must have been aware from the very first rendezvous. He had met Lovat before, and not many others fitted his Lordship's notorious profile. Queensberry probably concealed it from Anne in the likely event of his correspondence being opened by one of his enemies' spies, forcing his informer to flee.

After making initial contact in August, Lovat and Queensberry arranged to meet the following month. Lovat did not sit twiddling his thumbs. He rode west and sneaked into Argyll, where he met Rob Roy MacGregor, the Stewarts of Appin, and other Jacobites. He despatched a rider to invite his brother John and the leading Frasers to come and meet with them. Their chief was on his way home and wanted to see them.

Lovat assured the chiefs and nobles he met that Louis XIV would send them 'every kind of succour' if they rose in arms. 'They were perfectly ravished' by this news, he said, and clamoured to make 'a thousand protestations of fidelity' to James. The air resounded with their 'resolution to hazard their lives in the cause', but they would not commit themselves to it on paper. The big chiefs did not even appear, but sent proxies. Meeting up with his brother John, Lovat learned of the harassment of those Fraser clansmen who had rebelled, but also of the clan's growing acceptance of Mackenzie rule. It was even rumoured that Sir Roderick's son would resume his own family name. Lovat was aghast and asked himself hard questions as he rode through Scotland, about whether the path of invasion and restoration would lead him back to Castle Dounie. Queen Anne had issued an indemnity to her Jacobite subjects in exile. The penitent and the two-faced conspirator mingled together. Could Lovat benefit?

On 21 September, Anne assented to her High Commissioner meeting the anonymous informer from France. Argyll summoned Lovat to his house outside Newcastle, and gave him Queensberry's pass to cross the border into Scotland. The old Duke did not live to enjoy his errant protégé's turn as a thorn in the side of the establishment. On 25 September, after being pleasured in his private brothel at Chirton, near Whitley Bay, Argyll got into a scuffle. Reeling between fornicating and a fight, the old man died of his injuries. Lovat described being 'touched to the bottom of his soul' by the death of his old patron.

Under cover of darkness, Lovat slipped up the stairs to the Commissioner's apartments in the Palace of Holyrood. Insisting on concealing his face in the shadows, Lovat talked. His information confirmed everything Queensberry feared and hoped. The 'stranger' spoke about Louis XIV. France was planning an invasion. (As the architect of it, Lovat could provide details.) It would not happen until the French navy was repaired and mastered the sea. Queensberry could tell the English ministry to relax their vigilance.

The informer said he knew that Hamilton was corresponding with the French Court. Lovat and James Murray had travelled with letters. He said James Murray's correspondence to the Duke of Hamilton and the Duke of Gordon had been already delivered. Hamilton would draw on his influence in the Scottish Parliament and the almost universal discontent in Scotland with the English and their attitude to them, to make them vote James Stuart onto the throne of Scotland, easing his path to England on Anne's death.

Queensberry hung on every word. The Jacobite ruling council had boundless faith in Hamilton and pushed the Scottish Jacobites to 'enter into a league with France'.

The third letter he still had. He produced it. It was, he claimed, from Mary of Modena to the Duke of Atholl. Queensberry checked the signature. The 'M' was Mary's. Yet the letter was not addressed to anyone by name. This was natural, they both agreed, to protect the receiver in case it was seized. Lovat drew Queensberry's attention to the front of the paper. It said 'To L. J. M'. The Duke of Atholl was known at St Germains as Lord John Murray. One thing niggled though. The cover was written in a different hand to the letter inside. Queensberry was so thrilled to be offered proof of Atholl's treason, he did not query further.

The British Ambassador in The Hague had reported to London gossip about large sums, in gold, forwarded to men in Scotland via a Dutch commercial house. Queensberry asked where all the cash that Hamilton controlled originated? In Rome, explained Lovat, from the Papacy itself. The money then moved through France to Rotterdam and then across the sea into the hands of opposition magnates in the Scottish Parliament. Lovat had Queensberry's full attention. The involvement of the Church of Rome in Scottish affairs would repel the Country Party – full of Protestant clergy and Whigs – and of course the Church Party, and split the Cavalier–Country coalition.

Lovat could confirm 'by ocular demonstration', he declared, that Hamilton had accepted a general's commission from 'James III'. Queensberry asked what else the two men had corresponded about. Lovat replied he had seen a letter from the Earl of Cromartie to Middleton. It prophesied the downfall of Queensberry and the passing of his seals of office into Cromartie's hands. Queensberry felt a wave of relief at the informer's intelligence. He knew he was right when he smelled conspiracies and Jacobite plots around these magnates, the heart of the resistance to him. Lovat observed Queensberry, and how 'the duke ... breathed the most inveterate hatred' against Lovat's enemies.

All Queensberry needed was hard evidence of bribery and corruption, especially concerning Hamilton and Atholl. As they fell, the tall trees would crush the smaller ones growing around them. The informer agreed to spy; his price was to be given back the territories taken by the men who, he could prove, were traitors to Queen Anne and the Revolution settlement. He said he would need a pension for life also. Queensberry replied that some reward would come.

The two men parted. Despite Queensberry's excitement, something made him hesitant. He reported to Queen Anne. 'I confess it hard to know how one should know or be ready to reveal so much. Yet the delivering of that principal letter' to Atholl, or 'L. J. M.', 'and the showing his own commission under the hand and seal of the Prince of Wales as King James III and VIII, these do give credit to what else could not have been so well trusted'. Queensberry wanted so much for it all to be true. He wanted to see replies in their handwriting. Lovat had nothing like this and said he would return to London and France to spy for him and obtain the incriminating material.

By 25 September, Queensberry had ordered the prorogation of the Scottish Parliament. It had refused to vote the Queen her Supply, or agree to settle the inheritance issue in accordance with England's wishes. The MPs had merely re-presented the cursed Act of Security for royal assent. On a more positive note, Queensberry told the Queen he had found the key to breaking the deadlock with her Scottish Parliament – the anonymous double agent. Queensberry asked for her Majesty's permission to reward the man and let him go back to France to get the proofs of treason.

Lovat now turned his attentions to the commission from Mary and Middleton. He was playing a very complicated hand. Queensberry assumed he sat and waited for his pass to go to England and France. In fact, Lovat crossed the Firth of Forth and rode thirty miles north to Perth, to Drummond Castle, home of Lord Drummond, the Duke of Perth's son. Summoning the leading Jacobites, Lovat talked of rising in rebellion. If they concerted their rising, 'in a little time they would make an army that would master the kingdom; and that then he was sure the King of France would send home the King, and all the necessaries that were requisite to put him on the throne'. Lovat listened to their answers, and took in the sight of empty seats and gloomy faces on the few who had come. No one wanted the leadership because they did not want to rise. No one wanted anyone else to have it for the same reason. They did not even want to be asked to make a decision. Lovat plugged away at their recalcitrance for three days. Half of them had come only to ask him to leave.

One notable absentee, whose presence would have given a significantly different feel to the gathering, was the seventy-year-old Earl of Breadalbane. Lovat sent a co-conspirator, a man he was quickly calling the dearest of all his cousins, Colin Campbell of Glendaruel, with a letter to ask him to come. Breadalbane turned his kinsman away testily. Chief of a branch of the mighty Clan Campbell, Lovat had described him to Louis XIV as *un homme solide et trés sage*. Such qualities led Breadalbane to reject these emissaries from France. An English spy described the old man as 'cunning as a fox, wise as a serpent, and slippery as an eel'. Breadalbane sent a message to tell Lovat he 'was too old to turn papist'. Besides, 'no man who was a real Protestant, could meddle with a popish interest and be secure of either his Life, Liberty, or Estate'. Breadalbane intended to stay securely in possession of all three things, even at the cost of his Jacobite principles.

Privately, Lovat was beginning to agree with Breadalbane. He rode back to Edinburgh thinking over what he had heard. Maybe St Germains and the Stuarts could not deliver either his titles and estates, or even his rightful King. Johnny Murray reported from his mission that 'none of the Low Country would stir without commissions'.

With a mixture of relief and weariness, Queensberry returned to Whitehall, and arranged to meet Lovat in the south. A few weeks later, in the October half-light, Lovat and his co-conspirators clopped through the mire of a city steaming in the early winter sun. The gleaming dome of the new and almost-finished St Paul's Cathedral drew them. Lovat sought the house of a Jacobite apothecary called

Thomas Clarke, who kept a shop in Watling Street in the shadow of St Paul's. The party split up to avoid attracting the attention of the authorities, but met or corresponded every day. Lovat's intimate was the fellow Jacobite, Colin Campbell of Glendaruel. In letters, several each day at times, Lovat unguardedly expressed his dreams. He conjured Glendaruel to aim for greatness. 'Let you and me take example, and let us do brave, gallant things while we live ... Adieu. My dearest of all the world. Farewell.' Clarke the apothecary was impressed by Lovat, whom he described as a 'tall, pretty Gentleman' with a 'sanguine Complexion, fair Hair or a Periwig'.

Lovat's brother John arrived in London to inform him that Sir Roderick Mackenzie's latest move had been to secure Amelia Mackenzie of Fraserdale, nee Fraser, the legal right to use the title Lady Lovat. Argyll's death had removed his most powerful patron. Lovat had no money, as usual, and even fewer options. He told John to disrupt the Mackenzies' management of the Lovat estates as best he could. But the continual progress of Sir Roderick showed Lovat he could ill afford these long drawn-out exchanges of intelligence that might lead to something, or nothing. Unease of the mind emerged in aches and pains. Lovat begged physic from Thomas Clarke to ease his physical discomfort.

To add to his burdens, rumours of Lovat's double-agenting began to circulate. They reached Clarke the apothecary's ears, though he refused to believe them. 'If Fraser were not true to the King's interest' (meaning 'James III's') then Clarke 'would never trust any man', he said. Dismiss it as he did, the gossip endangered Lovat. It was recalled that before he came to St Germains he had been an officer in William III's army. Lovat hoped he had not backed himself into a corner.

In talks with fellow conspirators, Lovat was quite open about his meetings with Queensberry. He explained that he met the High Commissioner to allay Queensberry's fears of invasion and make the English less vigilant. Lovat challenged his critics, 'had he not the heads of all ... [King James's] friends in his pocket?' If he had been out to betray the Jacobites, he could have brought some mighty oaks crashing to the ground. Yes, he told the Commissioner of a plan to invade

– but Louis continually considered an invasion that never happened. The English knew it. He had revealed certain Scottish magnates had Jacobites sympathies. Again, it was nothing Queen Anne's administration did not know. All he did really was repeat Queensberry's suspicions back to him.

What Lovat could not explain was his motivation, that is, his odyssey back to Fraser country. Without adding that piece of the puzzle, his dealings with the High Commissioner looked very odd, to say the least.

Lovat met in secret with Queensberry again, to request passports to travel to France and obtain intelligence. It was now imperative to get out of England. Queensberry agreed the passports must be made out 'in an unknown name', since Lovat 'was declared a rebel', and his identity must be protected if he were to continue spying. Secretary of State Nottingham issued them in false names and sent them to Glendaruel to deliver.

London was home to more of the Scottish nobility than usual that winter. With no Parliament sitting in Edinburgh, many nobles came south. They 'waited and attended the English ministers … without knowing what was to be done'. The wound of the unresolved Scottish succession festered. After six or eight weeks' increasing frustration, gossip about the problem of Scotland began to home in on one thing. One minute it was a secret; the next, it was everywhere. A terrible 'plot had been discovered'. No one was quite sure of the details, but it involved a French-backed insurrection in Scotland to restore the Stuarts and bring down the government there, and perhaps threaten the Protestant succession, and even to break up the Union of Crowns. Scotch gossip buzzed about London coffee houses and alehouses. Some of the most highly favoured nobles were implicated in treasonable dealings with the exiled royal family. The intelligence had come from an outlawed Highland chief, rumour had it it was Lord Lovat, otherwise known as Captain Simon Fraser of Beaufort. Some claimed he was working as a double agent, controlled by the most powerful man in Scotland, the Duke of Queensberry.

The gossip made Colin Campbell of Glenadruel very jittery. He feared to deliver the passports himself and sent the apothecary Clarke in his place. Alone in his lodgings, Lovat's spirits sank at the thought of leaving for the Continent again, without having accomplished any of his ambitions. He brooded over his situation. 'My dear, for God's sake take care of yourself,' Glendaruel counselled him by letter. 'The standing of your family is in your person ... You must consider the insupportable loss it would be to your friends if you should distress yourself with melancholy.' He was worried his cousin might lose his mind and become suicidal.

Lovat packed and confided the most precious of his intimate possessions to his beloved Glendaruel: a little self-portrait 'James III' had given him, his commission and the papers of the Lovat estate. He planned to be back in a few weeks and did not want to take much with him. He left everything else at Clarke's shop.

Another plotter, called Ferguson, learned the Fraser party had passes to fly out of reach. It was time to use what he had picked up. Ferguson went to the Duke of Atholl and sold him what he knew about the movements of Lovat. He had worked out that the plot was more 'mischief' than danger. Ferguson repeated Lovat's accounts of his exchanges with the Duke of Queensberry. The information showed Atholl that his fellow minister, Queensberry, schemed to ruin him. In a towering fury, Atholl demanded redress against the malice of the Duke of Queensberry, her Majesty's representative in Scotland, and his villainous lackey, Captain Simon Fraser of Beaufort.

By the end of the first week of November 1703, Lovat was still reluctant to abandon England. It only added to his troubles when he was told that Sir John MacLean, his wife and family, a few servants and the spy, Mrs Fox, had fled France, landing on the Kentish coast near Folkestone, and been immediately arrested. Weary of the poverty, bickering and inaction at the Stuart Court in exile, Sir John had obtained permission from Mary of Modena to take advantage of the indemnity from prosecution that Queen Anne had offered to Scottish Jacobites if they returned and swore loyalty to her. Lady MacLean could barely stand, having given birth to a baby eleven days earlier. Goodness knows what Mrs Fox wanted back in England. MacLean's children and servants fretted and sniffed. Sir John straightened himself on the crumbly Kent shingle. Could he make terms and live in peace at home, he asked?

The short answer was, no. The indemnity had expired. The soldiers arrested the lot of them. A lachrymose Lady MacLean wailed to her husband to get them out of this dreadful situation. Sir John was taken to London, locked up in solitary confinement and allowed neither ink nor paper till he told the authorities what he knew of the activities of Simon, Lord Lovat, and of a conspiracy to overthrow the Queen in Scotland.

Sir John was frightened out of his wits and in a torment of anxiety over his family's well-being. 'I am confounded to know that your brother [-in-law] is prisoner,' Lovat wrote to Glendaruel. 'His only business is to give them fair words ... I'd rather see him shot and damned than that he should do an ill thing,' he growled. A few days later Lovat's nerve broke and on the 11th he bolted from Billingsgate to Gravesend with his brother John and a couple of followers. Lovat's actions caused pandemonium, but he thought he had control of the game.

ELEVEN

The 'Scotch plot' exposed, winter 1703–04

'All the Discovery is laid to your Charge'
– DUKE OF PERTH TO LORD LOVAT

The government snapped into action. In the Tower, in solitary confinement, security experts from the Office of the Secretary of State for the Southern Department accused Sir John MacLean of bringing his family to England as a blind for his covert mission to overthrow the monarchy. Threatened with trial and a traitor's death, the suffering of his abandoned wife and family, Sir John collapsed in horror. He offered to become an informer, 'upon assurance of his pardon and being treated like a gentleman'. Lovat had told him he should be ripped in two by wild horses if he ever spilled the beans.

Directed by the informer Ferguson, soldiers raided Clarke the apothecary's shop and seized all papers, correspondence and possessions relating to his secret guests. That led to Glendaruel and Ferguson himself being taken into custody and thrown into Newgate gaol. The soldiers found a silver box with Lovat's crest on it. Inside was a commission signed 'J. R.', addressed to the Duke of Hamilton. The authorities were not disposed to think it genuine: they wanted to muck out the political stables without throwing too many big beasts on the dung heap. The administration weren't quite sure what had been going on, but Atholl, Hamilton, Ferguson and others insisted 'Simon Fraser' was at the heart of the problem. The search for him intensified.

In Edinburgh, Captain Neil MacLeod, in whose house Lovat stayed when he first met Queensberry, was arrested, but said nothing much. In fact the investigators struggled to get an uncompromised source to condemn Lovat. Queen Anne's new Secretary of State, Robert Harley, wrote to Carstares, William III's old chaplain and confidant. Harley's anger descended on the whole of Scotland. 'It is grievous to … find the chief [men] of the Scots nation so averse to any discovery of the French correspondence,' he raged. Carstares replied that the most important thing was to find Lord Lovat, and bring both Queensberry and Lovat together before Harley. He agreed the mutual dislike and suspicion between the Scots and English at present left some men unwilling to add to the negative commentary about the Scots circulating in Westminster.

All this animosity was laid on Lovat's shoulders. High-profile public figures sought to defend themselves by further blackening Lovat's name. The impression of many at Westminster – that most Scots were practising duplicity, evasions, obstructions, and treasonable longings for independence – found expression in the image of Lord Lovat and his activities. Certainly, he had opened himself up to attack. He was guilty and a scapegoat. 'Nothing is wanting now but Lovat, Fraser (I mean), to be found,' Harley complained with irritation. 'Cannot the person who knows where he is, be persuaded to let him be found?' Neither money, nor threats of torture and execution, 'persuaded' anyone to produce the Fraser chief. Besides, he had already left the country.

Lovat and his small party of Fraser men had left on the *King William*, bound for Rotterdam. Queensberry knew roughly where he was. 'We are come safe here,' Lovat reassured the Commissioner when they landed. 'I will have a most dangerous journey … for all the roads are full of parties and partisans, and the French insult now because of their last victory at Speirs.' The French had just won a naval battle. Queensberry folded the letter and hoped his trust was not misplaced.

To the French, Lovat rejoiced in the naval victory at Speirs, their gains compounded by a storm. 'A mighty English warship broke to

111

pieces on the port at Halvent and most of its equipment drowned. Another has been destroyed on the coast with two Dutch warships lost.' Wreckage and corpses bobbed and bumped to shore. 'I have such a dangerous journey to make, and I fear perishing,' Lovat added poignantly.

The grey sky was tucked in from horizon to horizon, as far as his eye could see. This flat land chilled his soul. Without the Highlands and home, he was one in the teeming colony of place-seekers, spies, and information-brokers to the merchants of power and pensions in Whitehall and Edinburgh, St Germains and Versailles. He could not shake off the melancholy that had descended in London. Letters came now to 'John Smeaton, c/o Mr Vincent Nerinx, merchant of Rotterdam'. The man who wanted to be known as one thing, My Lord Lovat, chief of Clan Fraser, had acquired myriad aliases. Unaware that Clarke the apothecary was in the Tower, he wrote and asked him for more physic. 'I endeavour to banish my melancholy; but I have this minute, and all day, a fever by drinking bad wine. I wish I was out of this unwholesome country.' It seemed he could not even drown his sorrows successfully.

Early winter winds swept handfuls of rain across the land, scratching and stinging, belching foul air and water. The apothecary had nothing to relieve Lovat's ailment, he said: exile, chronic wear and tear of the emotions, repeated failure, continual regrouping of forces, strategic adaptation. 'That air that you are going to' – French air – might help, suggested Clarke. Was the vagueness in the phrasing someone being careful not to betray him, or an enemy agent trying to draw Lovat into naming names and places? Clarke said he doubted a full recovery was possible until Lord Lovat returned to breathe 'your own native air' in the Highlands.

When Lovat recovered his spirits he wrote to Glendaruel, unaware he too was under arrest. 'I bless God I am well in my health … I strive to recover from my melancholy every day. And I entreat and conjure you, as you love your soul, body, honour and friends, strive against melancholy,' he advised, 'for if anything ruin me, it will be grief; so forsake it my dear.' When his spirit failed, it nauseated a body that was otherwise, at the age of thirty-one, in peak condition. The grip of low spirits haunted him like some febrile diseased part of him; it whispered that he had squandered his chances and there would be no success.

On 13 December, a carriage took Queen Anne to the House of Lords. She addressed both Houses of Parliament. 'I have had unquestionable informations of very ill practices and designs carried out in Scotland,' she announced to a packed House. They were being carried out 'by Emissaries from France, which might have proved extremely dangerous to the peace of the Kingdoms'. She instructed the House of Lords to set up a commission to look into the furore stirred up by Captain Simon Fraser of Beaufort, erstwhile 11th Lord Lovat. The Lords and Commons agreed they must all 'look on the Protestant Succession as your Majesty's best security', as well as their own.

Lovat was cited to appear. Queensberry had to admit he let Lovat go to obtain evidence to support his claims; Atholl accused him of helping Lovat get away, to remove the evidence of the High Commissioner plotting against his personal enemies. Queensberry thought Atholl wanted Lovat under lock and key in order to carry him to Scotland and execute his old death sentence on him – before Lovat could prove Atholl and his allies were traitors.

By the run-up to Christmas 1703, Lovat's letters had become painfully delusional. 'If we both live a year,' he wrote to a Fraser kinsman, 'you will, by God's help, see me the greatest Lord Lovat that ever was. I am so already out of my country, and I hope to be so [with]in my country very shortly.'

The Fraser party arrived in Paris on Christmas Eve, and settled at lodgings in a suburb of the city. Lovat despatched a long memoir of his mission's findings to Mary of Modena. From his meeting in the west of Scotland he had brought petitions from men such as the MacAlpine Stuart chief, who confirmed Lovat as their envoy. Middleton discredited them. Lovat had even better news from 'a general council of war' at Drummond Castle. He had 'proposed to them to take up arms immediately, with an entire confidence of being speedily succoured from the Kingdom of France'. When Mary and Middleton heard such talk they were shocked. Lovat had been ordered not to make plans, but assess sentiment on the ground, and report back.

Mary was, however, delighted to hear of the Scottish Parliament's resistance to settling the Scottish succession on Hanover. She sent Lovat a warm letter of encouragement. Louis XIV too expressed his pleasure. Middleton had to follow suit. What satisfaction to hear he was back, the Earl wrote; especially, he added spitefully, 'after the apprehensions I had from the malice of our enemies'. Lovat was mad to come back trumpeting like an elephant if there was any truth to the rumours from England.

In London, the 'political sensation' of the winter 1703/04 worked itself to an unsatisfactory climax, as a Parliamentary Committee was set up by the Queen to look into the 'Scotch plot'. All Lovat's intimates were rueing their friendship with him, including Lovat's beloved cousin, Glendaruel, who groaned from captivity, 'I wish to God I had never seen him.' When he heard, Lovat was devastated. Glendaruel's betrayal hit him hardest. 'Unnatural monster, this perfidious traitor, this execrable villain,' he howled. David Lindsay, the Earl of Middleton's secretary, who did qualify for protection under Queen Anne's indemnity from prosecution to former Jacobites, said Lovat allied low cunning and an insinuating nature. The Lords demanded evidence against Lord Lovat. Lindsay admitted he had never met the man, but he heard an awful lot about him. The Lords dismissed Lindsay as a Middletonian stooge.

Despite all this, there were few hard facts about any danger 'to the Peace of the Kingdoms'. The Committee seemed wilfully recalcitrant about pursuing suspects. When one witness offered to bring things to the light of day that remained hidden, their graces threw him into Newgate gaol. The Committee preferred to believe that the conspiracy was a chimera and typical of many government enquiries, no one was prosecuted as a result. One bishop concluded that some of the intended prosecutions were deliberately 'managed ruinously' to leave

Lovat to bear most of the blame. Lovat had drawn on the Jacobite sympathies that ran deep in vast swathes of the British people. Those with vested interests in establishing the claims of the German Protestant regime knew what they were up against – an old guard, hoping to let the Stuarts back in, and yearning for old certainties. However, as long as men behaved in public, examiners did not need to expose the muddled contents of their hearts. There was an active desire *not* to expose the extent of the correspondence of British grandees with the Court of St Germains. It seemed Lovat's worst crime was to have stirred the mud at the bottom of the political pond so vigorously and so successfully.

In early spring the enquiry closed. The Parliamentary Committee's report concluded that two things had caused the crisis. First, it was 'that after your Majesty ... the immediate succession to the Crown of Scotland is not declared to be in the Princess Sophia' of Hanover and her son George. When that was settled, 'the House will do all in their power to promote an entire Union between the two kingdoms for their mutual security and advantage'.

Entire Union. When the Scots read this, they were mortified. Nothing led them to believe the English cared a hoot for 'their mutual security and advantage'. The Scottish Parliament resented these loose and bullish comments by one legislature on the behaviour of an independent neighbouring legislature. They whipped up a response, accusing their English counterparts of 'an undue meddling with our concerns, and an encroachment upon the honour, sovereignty, and independency of this Nation'.

Lovat had read the mood of the nation better than most, but his stock at St Germains and Versailles collapsed when the Parliamentary Committee's report arrived from London with his name mentioned everywhere. It got worse when Middleton's spy, James Murray, arrived in the capital on 14 February. Lord Lovat was 'wicked, dangerous and notoriously to be suspected', Murray reported. *Johnny* Murray knew all this, said the Middleton spy, so Lovat had had him killed. That explained why he had not returned with the Frasers. Middleton translated James Murray's report into French as fast as he could and submitted it for Louis XIV's perusal. Lovat was a traitor to France and possibly a murderer. There was only one punishment for capital crimes.

TWELVE

'You walk upon glass', 1704–14

'They flee from me,
that sometime did me seek'
– THOMAS WYATT

Middleton demanded Lovat's arrest and execution. The Papal Nuncio warned Lovat that he 'walked upon glass'. If not a traitor to the cause, there was no doubt he had abused grossly their trust in him by meeting with Queensberry.

Just in time, Johnny Murray reappeared at St Germains – bearing letters that supported all Lovat's reports about the clans and an uprising. His return had been delayed by the war, he said. He had been forced to make a detour through Northern Europe. Lovat's hopes revived and he wrote to Louis XIV's minister, Torcy, 'I come tomorrow to do obeisance to your Excellency, and receive orders.' Now was the time to go home and raise the clans.

The war over the Spanish Succession was dragging on and the French, predictably, were keen to revisit the scheme for an invasion of Scotland, to coincide with an uprising there. Louis asked the Queen Regent to issue commissions to the Jacobites, to let them serve under the French officers involved in the invasion. To Louis's disgusted amazement, sticking by Middleton's ineffectual diplomacy, Mary refused.

Lovat was as aghast as the French. The time was so ripe 'there was nothing but the immediate interposition of heaven, the strange imbecility of his mother, and the ignominious perfidy of the Earl of

Middleton, that could have prevented the restoration of King James to the throne of the three kingdoms', he argued. Lovat would not draw sword in the service of the royal family again until her son came of age. Mary demanded Louis lock up Lord Lovat.

As the weeks passed, Lovat found it hard to retrieve his reputation at St Germains, despite Johnny Murray's return. The scandal of the Queensberry, or 'Scotch plot', stuck to him. Louis ran out of patience with the entire Jacobite cause and banished Lovat to political exile. A horrified Lord Lovat had no choice but to obey. He and his brother John, with Lovat's pageboy, sloped out of Paris at midnight on 27 May 1704. Lovat was banished to Bourges, in the centre of France, the former capital of the province of Roman Aquitaine.

From Bourges, Lovat wrote to the Papal Nuncio expressing feelings of disorientation, in a 'place completely unknown … and which already looks very sad in my eyes'. He had little money, and had left unsettled bills in Paris. He worried about when he would be recalled. He appealed to Mary of Modena, apologising for his 'cruel frustrated outbursts' and begging her forgiveness and restoration. Mary did not reply. Lovat pleaded with Versailles for a pension to reflect his status and pay off his debts. Torcy eventually answered that Louis would give him a gratuity of 300 *Louis d'or* on top of his pension so he could pay off his bills and live at some ease. For the time being, however, he had to stay put.

Lovat weighed the purse in his hand, wondering if he could make more of this. He felt 'obliged to distinguish myself' in Bourges, he told a new friend, a local aristocrat and courtier at Versailles called the Marquis de la Frézelière. Lovat greeted the Marquis as 'cousin', acknowledging the French root of Fraser, from *fraise* (strawberry). The Frasers came originally to England with William the Conqueror and worked their way north. Lord Lovat's coat of arms showed strawberry leaves in the first and fourth quarters, and ancient crowns in the other two. The French King had ordered a *Te Deum* to be sung in every major town to give thanks to God for France's victories in battle against the Duke of Marlborough. A dazzling gesture to flatter Louis might earn him forgiveness and liberty, Lovat thought. As soon as he had his freedom then he and John could return home and rid Clan Fraser of Mackenzie control for good. He had to admit his time in France had not advanced his cause one step.

To distinguish the *Te Deum* of Bourges, Lovat organised a huge fête. He printed and distributed lavish invitations to the city's entire population, all 15,000 of them. Lord Lovat, it announced, 'will make a liberality of several barrels of wine ... where the people are assembled to see the fireworks that will be let off at the end of the *Te Deum*' – the fireworks to coincide with music in a spectacular *son et lumière*. To dispense the wine, 'this grand seigneur has made a contraption out of the fountains that will tumble abundantly with wine at the ceremony and during the best part of the following night'. Drink was running in the streets. Lovat intoxicated the whole city. Revellers 'carried away wine in full buckets, finding themselves at last sick of drinking, several remaining vessels, still full, will be carried the following morning to the hospital'.

Lovat explained to the people of Bourges that in Scotland, 'Milord Lovat' was chief to 600 gentlemen and 5,000 others of varying professions. He threw himself with relish into playing the chief and mounted a military tattoo, dressing some of the townsmen in Highland dress, fully accoutred with typical weaponry of the Fraser Highlanders – a rifle, two pistols, a dagger, sword and targe. Lovat was acting out his dreams. Everyone had a wonderful time. The townsfolk were 'exhausted with drink'. Lovat was exhausting.

Afterwards, he wrote an account of the extravaganza to the Marquis de la Frézelière. De la Frézelière talked about Lovat's magnificent feasting and show of loyalty to Versailles. The first sign Lovat had miscalculated came when the Papal Nuncio read Lovat's publicity material and dictated a reproach. At St Germains, where life was so frugal they sometimes hardly had enough to eat, the report electrified them with rage. Here was Lovat, in disgrace and penury, throwing a fête for an entire city and flaunting himself as if he were a prince. Riled, Middleton and the ruling council at St Germains obsessed with getting written proof of the Scotsman's treason from England; then

Louis would have to have him killed. '*On néglige le reste,*' one French minister said, bored by the Stuart Court: 'everything else is neglected'.

Louis did not respond well to Lovat's signs in the sky over Bourges. Once again, the Fraser chief, left to his own devices, had exceeded his brief and pursued his own agenda. The money had been there to pay his debts, nothing more. The King ordered Lovat to be removed from Bourges and put in gaol, the bastille at Angoulême fifty miles south of Paris. Lovat sent John home to hide in the hills and keep their kinsmen loyal.

Since Lovat left the Stuart Court in exile, some odd realignments had taken place at St Germains. It was even more important to keep Lovat out of the way. Middleton and Mary of Modena argued it was now in France's interest to take active steps to restore 'James III'. The appeasers had turned warmongers. The French victories Lovat celebrated so extravagantly, the intelligence about the levels of support for James in Scotland, the resistance in the Scottish Parliament to Queen Anne's order that the Scots declare for George on her death, and negotiate to enter a full Union with England: all this let Middleton see Lovat had been right all along. The English ministers who penned gracious letters about restoring James had led him up a blind alley.

At Angoulême, Lovat was 'thrust into a horrible dungeon', which had, he claimed, 'since time immemorial been the unviolated habitation of coiners and murderers'. His little pageboy 'conceived so extreme a horror at this dungeon' that he became ill and had to be put under a physician for six months. The boy's physical illness mirrored his master's mental anguish.

The cell door banged shut. 'Lord Lovat remained in this apartment, shut up for [the first] thirty-five days in perfect darkness, where he every moment expected death and prepared to meet it with becoming fortitude.' He was convinced someone had moved him here to silence him for good and all, where no one would see or protest. At the same time, he 'listened with eagerness and anxiety to every noise'. When the door creaked upon its hinges, '[I] believed that it was the executioner come to put an end to [my] ... unfortunate days.' As time passed and nothing happened, he 'thought proper to address himself to a grim gaeloress, who came every day to throw him something to eat, in the same silent and cautious manner in which you would feed a mad dog'. Lovat begged for paper, ink and light. If they were not going to assassinate him he must stay in touch with friends, if he still had any.

He sweated through July into August 1704. 'I am sad and melancholic,' he complained, 'shut … in an evil tower'. He repeated that he had not betrayed France and the Stuarts' cause to Queensberry. Months turned into years. No one came.

By 1706, Lovat was desperate. From the Highlands John wrote to him that Sir Roderick Mackenzie had taken another step towards the absorption of the Fraser clan. Sir Roderick had written a letter to the Fraser gentlemen. In it, he described the Fraser coat of arms. The eminence of the Fraser strawberry leaves and current diminution of Mackenzie stag's head on it, offended their new chief, his son. It must be reversed. Amelia Lovat, as she could be called, and his son Alexander Mackenzie of Fraserdale had been blessed with a son, named Hugh after her father, the late Hugh Lovat. Sir Roderick suggested that if his grandson Hugh 'shall think fit, in the place of the surname of Fraser, to carry the surname of Mackenzie, and to alter the … coat of arms' then these moves are 'expressly ratified and approved'. The consequence would be 'that the said surname and arms', of Fraser of Lovat, 'once being altered, and recorded so in the books of Heraldry … then it shall not be in the power of the said heir … ever thereafter to return to the name of Fraser'.

Lovat had always maintained that the Murrays and Mackenzies sought to swallow up his clan and its territories. This letter set out the process of final elimination.

Frantic to go home, Lovat tried to keep abreast of European politics by begging for newspapers and pamphlets; he needed to be properly prepared if a recall to Court came. He learned that they were now using his invasion plan again. It was tantalising. If only the French had let him 'go home and organise an uprising', three years ago, 'Marlborough would not today be in Bavaria,' he told Torcy when he heard of how the war swung in favour of the Protestant Alliance. 'In spite of my youth and my faults I know best the situation [in Scotland]', he said. The grindingly slow pace of Middleton's preparations had killed the momentum time and again. Lovat wondered if that was still Middleton's goal in fact, and wrote from Angoulême with haughty disdain that such 'watery-souled' revolutionaries would always fail.

Lovat greeted the New Year, 1707, from inside the bastille with good wishes to the Papal Nuncio: 'I wish your Excellence a good and happy new year … I have passed the worst year of my life. I hope that this will be more favourable.'

The Nuncio replied that it was not likely to improve soon.

'I see clearly … The violence of my persecution is not passed,' Lovat responded wearily.

Marlborough had marked 1706 with victories at Turin and Ramillies, driving the French back towards their own borders, and out of Italy and the Spanish Netherlands. The English fleet dominated the Channel. England and France gradually emptied their coffers on the war effort: both countries were on a very long march towards military and financial exhaustion.

At the beginning of 1707, the bill for a treaty of full Union between the Kingdom of England (including Wales) and the Kingdom of Scotland was forced through the Scottish Parliament. Bribery with huge sums of money, intimidation of dissenters, clauses to enable Scotland to retain an independent Church and judiciary, and the prospect of entry to 'the bowels of the hive' of British trade to revive Scotland's economy and society, all helped shove it onto the statute books. A few decision-makers approved it, in the teeth of the fury of hundreds of thousands of ordinary Scots. The sovereign Scottish nation would disappear on 1 May 1707. Tens of thousands of Scots took to the streets, shouting that their liberties, their identity and independence were being traded away in shame and perpetuity.

Lovat had to pace out his patience at Angoulême, agitated and stuck fast. No plan ever equalled his for practicality and coherence, but he could not take advantage of his talents. He had lost everyone's trust. In prison, Lovat raged against 'cette Union infernelle'.

On 14 August, after three years in gaol, Lovat finally received an order to move – to Saumur on the River Loire. He was to be made more comfortable, on an increased pension, but was forbidden from returning to Paris or Scotland. Lovat ordered his servants to pack his belongings, and bid farewell to a black period of his life.

At Saumur, the horses shouldered their way between tight, packed streets of medieval houses. First-floor windows overhung the shops, entrances to inns and the ordure below. The carters sought the next residence to which Lord Lovat found himself banished at the pleasure of the King of France. As his prison walls expanded to include the town and surrounding countryside, his pain progressed from acute to dull and chronic. He recognised his own alienation, isolation and impotence. He no longer had the spirit to attempt the sort of gesture he had made at Bourges. The years at Angoulême had trained him into submission, as they were intended to. Lovat's brother and heir, John, whom he hailed as the 'Chevalier Frezel of Lovat', visited again, and accompanied him to Saumur.

At Versailles, Louis XIV welcomed back an Irish spy in his pay called Colonel Hooke. He had just returned from a mission to sound out British Jacobites about an uprising. Hooke carried a memorial letter from the Jacobite leaders in Edinburgh. Bitterly aggrieved with the aftermath of the Union, they promised Louis that 30,000 men would rise to support the invaders, if James Stuart came to lead them. Post-Union Scotland was deteriorating further, swamped by the bigger English economy. The new Scots MPs at Westminster felt poor and irrelevant when they protested that England rode roughshod over Articles of Union and were totally ignored. With renewed hope, Lovat bombarded Torcy with letters and tactical advice as revived plans to invade Scotland finally entered the final phase.

In early 1708, John rode to Paris to await orders to join the invasion. Lord Lovat was ordered to stay where he was. Within a month they would be back, 'after the entire failure of the unfortunate enterprise'.

* * *

It felt doomed from the start, the operation being first delayed when James Stuart was struck down by measles. Then, the minute Marlborough's intelligence chief Lord Cadogan heard that the French were preparing to embark ships and the nineteen-year-old James out of France, he informed his senior naval commander Admiral Byng. The British Admiral found the French expeditionary fleet lying at Dunkirk and blockaded the port. Forbin, head of the French force, realised the Royal Navy was anchored nearby and wanted to call it all off. James badgered Louis XIV not to lose faith, and when a thick fog descended, cloaking the coast, the invading force slipped away. When it lifted, Byng saw the birds had flown and gave chase.

The would-be 'James III of England and VIII of Scotland' stood in the lifting mist on the deck of the *Mary*, 'bound for my ancient kingdom' of Scotland. The former enemies, Perth and Middleton, stood with him. The young prince was going to the country for which he was born, of which he knew nothing but reports and assessments from people, most of whom had not seen it for over twenty years. James pondered how his subjects would receive him. He consulted the Duke of Perth and the Earl of Middleton, but particularly Perth, the passionate Scot. The *Mary* creaked up the coast of England, passing Newcastle and then the ancient monastic foundation of Lindisfarne on Holy Island.

The aspiring invaders crossed paths with British troops returning from Europe. As Lovat had been predicting for five years, when they heard of an invasion, the British marched ten regiments of foot soldiers from the front line to Ostend. Marlborough ordered them north to Leith to defend the Protestant succession and the Union. The Jacobite expedition was fulfilling the strategic goal: divide British forces and distract the concentration of the commander-in-chief. The invasion force neared the Firth of Forth, with Edinburgh halfway along its southern coast, and the coastline of the Kingdom of Fife on its northern shore. Forbin misread his sightings, badly, and overshot Edinburgh's port at Leith. Instead of landing James, they kept sailing north, a hundred miles from Inverness. By the time the French admiral realised the extent to which he had miscalculated his location, the pursuing British fleet had pushed him further north leaving him unable to land James safely. Forbin, over-cautious with his instructions, lost his nerve. The French navy turned and made a run for France chased by the English who were only a day behind him.

James had sailed so close he could smell his land, and see it, but not stand on it. Now he was carried back to the only real home he had ever known – the grim grace-and-favour palace of St-Germains-en-Laye. Lovat commented ruefully: 'It seemed as if this prince had always been followed by an unfortunate star.' How would these men wrench a kingdom back out of its possessors' hands with that spirit? Were such indecisive men worth his loyalty, he asked himself?

He wrote to Torcy again, begging him to put an end to his banishment. No reply came. Lovat was no longer worthy of even a line. 'What was nearest to my heart was now to return to my beloved clan and to live and die in the midst of them,' he said. Right now he felt he 'would not merely have enlisted himself in the party of the house of Hanover', but 'any foreign prince in the universe, who would have assisted ... in the attainment of his just and laudable design', to regain his clan.

Lovat wrote to the English ministry. He offered to make peace with Queen Anne's administration and fished for an amnesty to let him come home without the risk of the extant death sentence being carried out. He would 'demean himself like a good and faithful subject to her Majesty', and abandon the Jacobites and Louis XIV's France. He offered to help keep the Highlands quiet, accepting that it meant telling his clan George of Hanover would be their next King. Secretary of State, Robert Harley, rejected him. They did not need someone like him.

By 1711 the invasion threat had receded. On 27 September, France and England agreed to preliminary articles of peace. Both countries were sick and tired of war. Louis XIV recognised Anne and the English succession in the House of Hanover. He agreed to make James Stuart leave France, since England could not negotiate with a country that harboured a usurper. James left for Lorraine, a duchy in the Holy

Roman Empire. His mother stayed at St Germains. Jacobitism was a dead issue.

The following year, a peace agreement was signed. In 1713, Lovat again sent his brother John home to keep his family's presence there alive. Lovat loaded John with letters, among them one to Lord Leven, a trusted former ally and colleague of the late Duke of Argyll. He told Leven to lead the clan in case of trouble. John must place his Frasers at the disposal of the Duke of Argyll, John Campbell (son of Lovat's former patron and one of Marlborough's generals), whichever side he espoused. Unknown to Lovat, Leven had turned Jacobite. He sent the letter straight back to James Stuart, by now the guest of the Duke of Lorraine. Middleton repeated his call for Lord Lovat to be executed.

During 1713, Queen Anne had become ill and by the end of the year her 'ailment appeared dangerous'. The news provoked fresh fears including rumours that the clans were getting ready to rise for James and throw off the wretched Union. In 1713 a vote to break the Union had failed by just one vote in the House of Commons. John Fraser wrote pleading with his brother to come and give the Frasers a lead 'upon the eve of a period when the whole kingdom would be full of war and confusion'. His clan did not know whom they should support. But Lovat dared not break out of exile and offer his enemies the reason they needed to kill him.

He was in a low state in the house at Saumur, in July 1714, when he heard someone ask for him in a Highland accent, using his Celtic patronymic – MacShimidh Mor. His heart skipped a beat as his French valet announced a visitor, and a man in thick tartan breeches walked in and greeted him in Gaelic. It was Castleleathers.

THIRTEEN

The end of exile, 1714

'Come to fish in Drumly Waters'
— CASTLELEATHERS TO LOVAT

Major James Fraser of Castleleathers sweated heavily under his tartan bonnet, a woollen plaid flung over his shoulders. He fell on one knee to greet his chief, his button eyes sparkling as they took in this sorry situation. On 1 May 1714, at four o'clock in the morning, he explained, he had taken 'journey from his dwelling house with his habersack and left his wife and children spralling on the ground in tears'. He had no tongues to navigate through France but English and Gaelic. Desperation brought him here. He had come to bring his chief home.

Lovat looked at him. How could this be true? Was it a plot to make him go on the run so he could be killed as an outlaw? He hardly dared let himself hope after more than a decade in exile.

Castleleathers explained that after the marriage of Amelia Fraser to Mackenzie of Fraserdale, 'the poor name of Fraser was then looked down upon by all the neighbouring clans. Encroachment made on them daily by the Mackenzies' wore them down, until Lovat's brother John appeared last year, to tell them their chief was alive and in trouble. Up to that point, most of the clan 'knew nothing of the natural chief's being in life'. They were amazed to discover he lived. The Reverend James – Castleleathers's father-in-law – died five years ago, he said, and had dedicated his chronicles to Lovat, their absent chief, hoping he might come back and raise his people.

No one had talked to Lovat like this for nearly fifteen years. The clan elite felt that 'if Lovat could be stolen out of France, he might come to fish in Drumly Waters', said the Major – 'Drumly' meant all churned up, like a river in spate, the water murky but full of nutrients and attracting the biggest fish and best fishermen.

Suddenly, Lovat leapt up and started hugging the Major, finding he 'could not express himself for joy'. Castleleathers was delighted with his success thus far. To complete his mission all he had to do was repeat the thousand-mile journey in reverse and get his Lordship back to Inverness-shire. It worried him to see Lovat so 'very low in his person'. Encouraging him as much as he could, he 'asked him if he had any thoughts of ever returning home?'

It was the purpose of his life, Lovat snapped back, shocked that Castleleathers needed to ask such a question. But he could not go without permission from St Germains, he said. It was too dangerous. The Major settled in and over the next few days he and Lovat walked by the Loire and thrashed out a plan. His Lordship was not the reck-lessly confident youth the Major remembered. He now hesitated, wary even of Castleleathers. It puzzled the Major to hear him talk about the Highlands and then decline every plan to get there. A return to Castle Dounie and the Fraser lands seemed a remote dream. Castleleathers humoured his chief, saying the obvious solution was for him to go to Versailles to plead for his chief's release. The man who had never been imprisoned, condemned to death twice, cut off, alienated from all that gave meaning to his life, could not understand his illustrious prison-er's guardedness. But Castleleathers had not come here to be his chief's companion in exile. He had journeyed through two foreign countries on foot, in wartime, to release his Fraser chief. He made Lovat write long letters of memorial to James Stuart, protesting his loyalty and pleading for permission to go home, rescue his clan from usurpers and stir up the Jacobites at this propitious time of Queen Anne's illness. As far as Castleleathers was concerned, James 'III' was the Pretender not the King. But Lovat was still a Jacobite, a fact Castleleathers would ignore until he got him to England; then Lovat must reconcile with the British authorities.

Packing the letters away, 'the poor Major walked off on foot in his shirt, with his cloaths on the hilt of his sword'. Days were slipping into weeks; Castleleathers had to press on. Worse, they wasted time at exactly the moment when an opportunity arose for Lovat to make his peace with the British authorities. The news was spreading through France that Queen Anne had died.

The English Parliament proclaimed George I King of Great Britain. On the streets all over England, Tory Jacobites yelled and protested against the accession of a German Elector who spoke no English. Over eighty riots erupted to cries of 'No Hanover!' 'No cuckold!' Were Lovat to come now, as someone imprisoned and despised by the Jacobites, and offer George his loyalty and service, he might be accepted.

From Lorraine, 'James III and VIII' wrote an open letter to the 'people of Britain'. In it he plumbed ancient fears and allegiances, charging his erstwhile subjects that the 'People ... voted themselves a parliament, and assumed a right of deposing and electing Kings, contrary to the fundamental laws of the land, and the most express and solemn oaths that Christians are capable of taking.' Barely anybody in the kingdom would fail to feel some anxiety on reading this. The symbol of the King was sacred. 'Whensoever it should please God to restore us, we would make the Laws of the Land the Rule of our Government, and to grant to our Subjects a general Indemnity for whatsoever has been done contrary to those Laws; And all the Security and Satisfaction they could desire, for the Preservation of their Religion, Right, Liberties and Properties.' Dispossession had schooled James to be a profoundly tolerant man. Whitehall did not extend the same toleration to him. They had tried the male Stuarts twice. The trust was gone.

Castleleathers was granted an audience with James Stuart at the Duke of Lorraine's palace on the French eastern frontier at Lunéville. Playing the Jacobite, the Major offered Lovat's long memorial. James took it, pocketed it unopened, and asked Castleleathers how he had got this far without a word of German or French. The Major replied that he had three sentences. James asked to hear them. When we are alone, the Major said, embarrassed. James insisted. In the first phrase the Major asked the road, the second for a bottle of wine, the third: to beg a bed. Hearing his accent they all 'burst out a laughing'. Castleleathers replied that 'he was glad to come twelve- or thirteen-hundred miles to make his Majesty laugh so hearty'.

James then informed Castleleathers that Lord Lovat would never regain his favour or confidence. He was 'well and authentically informed that the Frasers would pay as much respect to the recommendations of Lord Atholl, and that they would assemble under the orders of Mr Mackenzie of Prestonhall'. Castleleathers was stunned. He had come all this way to free his clan from under the heels of Mackenzie of Fraserdale and the Duke of Atholl. If the Frasers did not want to live with these two, they were not going to die for them. Castleleathers told James that if 'Prestonhall were mad enough to put himself at their head, he would be so saluted with musket bullets, that light would be seen through every part of his body'. Did James know the clans that poorly he could not remember they were 'so attached to their natural chiefs' they would oppose neighbours – that was why Castleleathers was here after all? Kings came and went. Government, remote in Edinburgh, had retreated even further to London. Clan bonds were the most meaningful thing to which a man could give his heart and arm.

James retorted that *he* would be chief to the Frasers himself before he allowed Lovat to leave France. Castleleathers repeated that if James would give them their natural head and chief, 'they would venture their lives and fortunes in his cause; and if not, that they had declared that if they should die to a man, they would never draw sword for him or any of his'. Whereupon James 'took the Major by the button of his clothes, and with a smile told him he was sure he would fight'. Castleleathers replied that 'he behoved to do as the rest of his clan did'.

James pushed him away. He would give leadership of the Frasers to 'any other commander they pleased', but *never* to Lord Lovat! Castleleathers shook his head. He now knew he and Lovat would have to make a run for England, in spite of James Stuart.

The next day, Castleleathers set out in the balmy early morning air, mounted on a horse given to him by the Duke of Lorraine and sucking a fine pipe from the Duchess. This was the vision that greeted Lovat when the Major eventually arrived back at Saumur on a late summer's night. Lovat was relieved to see him, but his good mood did not survive the bad news. The two men retired, knowing they had difficult decisions ahead.

Next morning, Major Fraser rose and went to salute his chief. Lovat glared at him. He 'looked like a Tyger on a Chain, and asked the Major if it was to betray him that he came to that country'. The way Lovat saw it, Castleleathers had returned after some delay from his time with James, smoking luxurious tobacco and riding a beautiful fine horse, saying 'the King' would never free him. Years of imprisonment and the attempts by Atholl and then Middleton to have him executed had left him paranoid. He was sure Major Fraser had been paid to assassinate him the moment they left.

Castleleathers ignored his chief's outburst, suggesting they send Lovat's valet to England to 'see what encouragement his friends would give him to go home'. Lovat wrote to a friend from his youth, his clan neighbour Brigadier Grant, who had forgiven Lovat his youthful crimes – the kidnappings, the forced marriage. Grant was a follower of the 2nd Duke of Argyll's faction at King's George I's Court. Now a British MP and army officer, the laird of Grant would be a useful ally. Lovat hinted at rumours in France of an uprising in Scotland. 'We will see very soon a time in which true friendship will be useful and necessary. For tho' all the possible appearance be for King George, there is a great storm that hangs over Scotland, and will break out sooner than people expects.' I am, Lovat promised, committed to 'live and die with the Duke of Argyll and his family' and need 'his Grace to ask and obtain my full remission'.

The valet returned with good news from Brigadier Grant and John Forbes of Culloden and people in the north, but no word from Argyll and his brother the Earl of Ilay. Castleleathers was stumped. He had anticipated difficulties with the journey to and from the Highlands, but not with getting his chief to move one mile. The Major pointed out to his chief that Louis XIV's heir, the Duke of Orleans, who would rule as regent on Louis's death, hated Lovat. The King was ill and probably dying. 'The next day after the King of France's death, he might expect the bastille for a closet.'

With some trepidation, Lovat gave in. He sold his possessions and accompanied Castleleathers to the French coast at Boulogne. England was a mere twenty-five miles away. They thought 'to hire an open boat' for fifteen pistoles. The crew of the boat 'did not favour' the Major's horse, but Castleleathers refused to leave without it. Lovat could not go without the Major, so eventually the crew gave way. They all lifted the animal into the boat, and weighed anchor at seven o'clock on the night of 14 November 1714. The wind blew up. The sails were soon taut and they whipped along. By nightfall, conditions hit gale force, 'the storm being so great they all despaired of their lives'. The horse 'turned so unruly at the sea coming over him, that he had to be bound with ropes; in which situation he lay until they were landed'. By two the next afternoon, the party arrived at Dover, and fell exhausted onto the dock.

FOURTEEN

A necessary change, 1714–15

'Grant me your protection and friendship'
– LOVAT TO THE EARL OF SUTHERLAND

After reaching London along the Thames, Lovat's party hid out in a Jacobite haberdashers in the City. Next morning, Lovat sent Castleleathers to the Earl of Ilay to ask what encouragement he might expect from him and his brother, Argyll, the two sons of his old patron. But Ilay would talk to Castleleathers of nothing but 'the Young Pretender'. Britain remained unsettled. Ilay quizzed the Major on what he had made of James. Having gone round and round in circles hundreds of miles wide in France to free Lovat, now the Major went round and round in slightly smaller circles to try to make progress from London.

On 19 November, Lovat wrote to Brigadier Grant from his hideout in the haberdashers: 'I must own I am the most unhappy of mankind, to have been barbarously treated as a Hanoverian by the Court of St Germains this twelve years by past without intermission.' Now the Argyll Campbells held back because they thought he was a Jacobite. 'They tell me … my life is not safe!' he cried, and 'that they know not what to say to procure my remission'. They could not see how he could be pardoned for his crimes. 'It's a very desperate case; but there is nothing but a stout heart to stay brave. I did foresee all the scaffolds that could be before me.' The fear haunted him and left him constantly under stress.

Brigadier Grant, Sheriff of Inverness-shire, chief of the Frasers' neighbours and an old friend from his youth, came to wait on Lovat. Ilay had confessed to Grant he hardly knew what to make of Lovat's reappearance. With the country so turbulent, the arrival of a notorious spy and intriguer like Lovat to offer intelligence and service tantalised the Campbell brothers. Lovat pressed Grant to 'convince the Duke of Argyll and the Earl of Ilay, that the Rosses, Roses, Monros, and all the Moray lairds', who supported the new King, would address George I, and say they would 'be overjoyed to have me join them when the Pretender comes to that country, which they may depend upon, in spite of their security and precautions'. What the Highland chiefs should do, said Lovat, was ask the King for a 'remission' of the sentence against him. Then he could at least travel without fear of a knife being plunged into his neck. Without a pardon, he could not relax his guard. Atholl, whose spies had already alerted their master to his enemy's presence, wanted another chance to arrest Lovat and execute the old death sentence: it seemed Atholl always underestimated Beaufort's tenacity. No matter how they stamped on him, he sprang up again.

When Mackenzie of Fraserdale heard the news of Lovat's return and that he was petitioning for a pardon, he sped to Edinburgh to see the Justice Clerk and obtain a copy of the 'Extract of the Process and Sentence against' Simon Fraser. The second most senior civil judge in Scotland, the Justice Clerk Adam Cockburn had been a close friend of Fraserdale's father, Sir Roderick Mackenzie, and he was still on good terms with Amelia Lovat's uncle, the Duke of Atholl.

Atholl paid informers to scour London for Beaufort. A Tory 'tainted with Jacobitism', Atholl was falling from favour with the government and the Court, but he could still bring down Simon Fraser as he fell. Lovat had been spotted 'in a remote coffee house at the far end of the City', Fraserdale told Atholl. 'I am informed there are several of our Scots Commoners at a great deal of pains to procure a remission for these two brethren [Lovat and his brother John].'

The 'Scots Commoners' were the MPs Grant and John Forbes of Culloden. 'I must beg your Grace will once more write to your friends in London in this matter, and I am satisfied if they are unsuccessful this time,' getting his pardon, then 'we shall be free of any further trouble this way'. He signed his letters, Alexander Mackenzie now, without a hint of the lumbering designation 'Fraserdale'.

Ilay and Argyll were not indifferent to Lovat. They were well aware that support for the Stuarts was most passionate in the north, strengthened by anti-Union sentiment. Much better let the natives control their own region than import foreigners from the south. There was no successful tradition of government-appointed outsiders to manage the Highlands, and the Frasers and Campbells were traditionally allied. Now, when Brigadier Grant called on Ilay again, the Earl told him he had spoken to the King about Lovat. The King's ministers required an address to King George I, signed by the friends of whom Lovat boasted in Scotland, as security for the Fraser chief's good behaviour and loyalty.

Lovat got to work, writing to Duncan Forbes and his brother John in Inverness. Duncan was a rising lawyer in Edinburgh, and John was laird of Culloden. The Forbeses had known the Lovats for generations; they used to serve the Lovat chiefs. Bit by bit they rose to be landowners in the Inverness area and numbered themselves among the strengthening Argyll interest in Scottish politics. They were just the sort of men who might help Lovat.

Astutely, Ilay ordered Castleleathers into Scotland when Lovat's address to the King was ready, so he could collect the signatures from Highland chiefs. Castleleathers and his brother-in-law, Fraser of Phopachy, trudged through the five counties of the Northern Highlands – Caithness, Sutherland, Ross-shire, Cromartie and Inverness-shire – 'in the winter storm, and got the subscriptions of every leading man' in a land divided into Whig and Tory clans. Both sides signed. 'When they met with the Jacobites they made them believe that this address was from the Pretender. To King George's friends [they] unravelled the story,' the Major reported, and wound it round the other way, 'telling them the whole plot, and that the paper was drawn up by my Lord Ilay to work out Lord Lovat's remission with King George.'

While Castleleathers and Phopachy travelled through the Highlands in January 1715, George I dissolved Parliament and called a general election. Since his accession the previous autumn, the King had been settling scores, rigorously dismissing Tories and reappointing Whig supporters of his foreign policies. The Argyll Campbells rose. George believed all Tories were covert Jacobites. Whigs like the Argyll group colluded in this prejudice. The Forbes brothers, ambitious to exercise political domination of the Highlands, realised that an enfranchised Whiggish Lord Lovat might serve their ends very well in a constituency teeming with Jacobites. Culloden (John Forbes) was seeking to hold on to the Inverness-shire seat at Westminster. 'I cannot well be returned,' he calculated, 'unless Lovat has his remission and is in this Country at the time of the Elections.' He calculated that a restored and grateful Lovat would bring in all the votes the Fraser chief controlled, and hand them to the Forbeses.

Despite the widespread dislike of George I, the election on 24 February 1715 was a landslide for the Whigs and swept the Tories from power. In Inverness, Fraserdale 'makes a great bustle here against his clan', Culloden told his brother Duncan, 'because they disown him for their chief'. Rumours of the return of their real chief buzzed in everyone's ears. No one knew when he was coming, but they knew his wishes and most voted for Culloden. John Forbes held his seat, but the Jacobites retained their domination of Inverness Burgh Council. 'Were Lovat in this Country,' Culloden ruminated gloomily, 'we would not be browbeaten by the Jacobites on every hand, as we now are, nor half the trouble that now is in our Elections … We look for the Pretender with every fair wind, and let me tell you this, If he does come, there will be bloody bricks … and they,' the Jacobites, 'will have raised a devil that they cannot so easily lay.'

The 'devil' was civil war. The region divided itself violently between support for George I and James Stuart. It was odd, Lovat said, how the administration delayed his pardon 'at a time when the Kingdoms are like to swim in blood, for now, you may fully depend on it, that the Pretender will be over in the month of March next'.

But the Pretender did not come in March and the country was no calmer. When the new Parliament met to vote money for the Civil List on 14 May 1715, Culloden wrote to Duncan in Inverness that he had just come out of an eight-hour session in the Commons. The money was at last voted 'after a very hot debate that was stuffed with a deal of scurrilous reflections from both parties', he wrote. 'You may perceive that though Jacobitism be decaying with you, as you think,' in Scotland, 'yet it is prevailing here ... much more than ever I thought it would have done ... I cannot express the endeavours that are used to alienate the hearts of the people from his Majesty' by the Tories. Culloden hoped to God nothing would come of it.

Spring drifted into summer in the English capital. Castleleathers returned to his chief in London, his mission not yet accomplished. Still the Frasers scuttled among the dust and shadows of the day. It could not last. In the middle of a June night, troops under the Duke of Montrose's direction ran them to ground in a house off Soho Square. Montrose was joint Secretary of State with Atholl, and they were close political allies. At 3 a.m., 'two baillies and so many constables came into their rooms, and desired them to surrender themselves prisoners in the King's name'. Castleleathers grabbed his weapons and demanded they declare 'if they were for King George'.

The baillies retorted that of course 'they were for, and in the name of, King George'. Major Castleleathers replied that all of the men of that room were so too. Probably, said one baillie, but 'his orders was to bring them as prisoners'.

Castleleathers knew his chief 'lay close within the curtains' of a box bed, 'and heard all this debate'. The Major was nervous about 'some *pater nosters* and *ave marias* ... [his chief] had got about him in his pockets, and if a search was made would bring him timely to Tyburne'. They would signify Catholicism, loyalty to the Stuarts (and France), and treason.

Castleleathers darted behind the curtains and told Lovat to get up. Spotting Lovat's breeches, he searched them and removed all his papist paraphernalia. Where could he conceal them? He spied 'a *house of office* near my Lord's bed'. A chamber-pot that had done its work recently – the perfect thing. He opened the lid and poked the incriminating bits and pieces beneath the surface. The troops escorted the Highlanders out and marched them to a 'sponging house' – a secure holding house for debtors in custody – until they came before the courts.

The capital was on fire with news that James, the Young Pretender, was on the move. Lovat's 'great friends' were going to drop them, in the Major's view. They needed another plan of escape. Lovat was nervous and asked Castleleathers to sleep by him. It was hard to stay calm when everything was so different from 1703. He did not know who had ordered him to be locked up – Atholl or Ilay?

None of them slept 'over the next few nights, but talked, contriving how to make their escape'. Other than that one subject, they were very quiet and heavy, with 'no friend coming near them'. The best they came up with was to make a run for it. They could bribe the Frasers on the door to make up a party of Highlanders and 'carry them off with flying colours' to the north. Lovat felt depressed. After fifteen years it looked as if he was going home the way he had left: on the run from the law.

On 6 September 1715, the Earl of Mar raised his standard at Braemar and declared for 'King James III and VIII'. The rebellion so long dreaded and rumoured, had started. This was a home-grown uprising. For this reason it caught the British authorities unawares. Lovat had warned them it was coming more than once, but they detected no military preparations on the Continent, and there had been no flare-up of diplomatic hostilities with a foreign power. The Earl of Mar did not know what to do next, however. His King seemed worse than useless. James had issued an order countermanding his previous order to rise, but issued it too late for it to be obeyed. The chopping and changing left Mar, a reluctant rebel commander, dizzy with indecision.

As he raised the banner proclaiming James, the flag, newly made for the occasion, unfurled and was tugged this way and that by a brisk breeze. Suddenly, a gilded wooden globe on top of the standard popped off. The men standing round watched it thud into the mud. They looked on it as 'a bad omen and did call to mind the story of King Charles the 1st whose staff head fell off when he stood before the judges'. Bad harvests, good ones, infant death, disease and fine weather, all life thrived or withered under the pitiless gleam of the Divine gaze. Someone picked up the golden ball and screwed it back on. Mar's banner billowed above his lodgings. On one side, the pennant showed the Scottish arms embroidered in gold; on the other was the thistle, and the motto *Nemo me impune lacessit*, 'No one attacks me with impunity' (later the motto of the Black Watch) and under it the words 'No Union'.

Mar's rebellion ignited a series of local uprisings up and down the kingdoms. It showed the new King how widely he was rejected. The hardships the country 'groaned under since the fatal Union' brought them, said Marshal Keith, one of the Jacobite commanders; the men had 'taken arms by orders of their lawful Sovereign, to free them from a burthen they were no longer able to bear'. Dynasty and religion were harnessed to the economy and pulled the people into rebellion. 'The common people flocked in from all quarters, but there being no arms yet arrived, no use could be made of their zeal, and therefore they were dismissed,' Keith wrote of his potential fighting men. Thousands milled about carrying hoes and scythes looking for leadership, a strategy, weapons, uniforms. Mar planned to seize Perth as a good supply base, and stop to wait for his King and the French.

At this critical juncture for the Jacobites, God called Louis XIV to him, and 'James III and VIII' delayed embarking from France. In Scotland, Marshal Keith observed his commander-in-chief dithering in the face of setbacks. Mar's problem, he thought, was that the Earl was not raised to war but 'to the pen, and was early brought into business … [He] had good natural parts but few acquired'; he was not a soldier and could not learn. Mar had not wanted to lead a rebellion. The Duke of Atholl had turned James down. James's half-Stuart, half-Churchill brother, the Duke of Berwick, urged James forward, but also refused command. '[Go] with what you can get or scrape …

Providence will do the rest,' he said. Berwick, a naturalised French citizen, could not accompany him. James pleaded: 'You know what you owe to me ... of what vast consequence your accompanying me is.' James never forgave Berwick, a brilliant general, for failing to come to his aid.

In overall command of the British forces was John Campbell, the 2nd Duke of Argyll, who had served under Marlborough. Argyll apologised to the Earl of Sutherland, Lord Lieutenant of the Northern Counties, for the lack of arms. He could not let the Earl have more than 300 firelocks and ammunition for twenty-four charges. Just 'make the best of your way' north, he ordered Sutherland, 'gathering what number of men you can ... Follow the enemy in the rear, and annoy them as much as possible you can.' In this lacklustre way, Sutherland was to take command of the army and crush Mar.

Lovat wrote to Sutherland: if the Earl would 'countenance him' and procure him liberty and become bail for his good behaviour and loyalty, he engaged to 'be very useful to him at the head of his clan in the North for King George's interest'. Sutherland decided to take a risk and use the Fraser chief. The principal Whig Unionists in the Highlands joined in a bail bond of £5,000. Lovat was 'fully resolved to expose my life for the Royal Family of Hanover', he said, and hoped Sutherland would ask the King to pardon him. 'Grant me your protection and friendship,' he beseeched Sutherland.

King George instructed his Lord Advocate, Sir David Dalrymple, to Scotland, to prepare a judicial statement about the case of Lord Lovat. The Argyll Campbells and Sutherland wanted to use him. Others wanted to hang him. The King needed to be told his story. Dalrymple's report was a model of circumspection: Lovat had been charged with 'a riot and a rape' in the late 1690s. He did not appear to answer the charge, Dalrymple noted, and 'what followed I do not remember, nor the substance of the evidence then given'. Yet another lawyer said Lovat's standing in the north was 'of no small consequence' to the King. On the other hand, there were the Atholl Murrays to consider. 'What may engage the one to his Majesty will disoblige the other.' The Earl of Ilay asked the King to consider if 'the good the

Duke of Atholl may do, may be equal to the loss the King's service suffers for the want of Ld Lovat's pardon'. He doubted it. Ilay also pointed out that, with regard to these old Scottish lawsuits, 'there is a point in Lord Lovat's case which I believe his enemies in Scotland have not considered, *viz.*, that he, being a peer' of the British Crown, 'could not be tried in Scotland' for those cases.

Lovat was grateful to Ilay, but it was a sobering moment to consider that so many of his travails could have been prevented if this sort of information had come to the fore earlier, in 1698/99. Lovat was bailed from the sponging house by his old Fraser allies, and the men who hoped to benefit by his presence in the north. But the bail came with conditions. First, he must wait in London until October.

Castleleathers observed to his chief that 'the greatest friends you expected to have, look upon you as a Jacobite and Roman Catholic, and will do so till you show yourself in another shape'. The Major needed to leave for the Highlands at once, to defend his home and family. On 13 September, just a week after Mar raised his baubled standard, Inverness fell into Jacobite hands. This time Castleleathers would go with or without his chief.

FIFTEEN

Return to Scotland, 1715

'A hundred to one at least in their interest'
— ARGYLL TO TOWNSHEND
ON JACOBITISM IN SCOTLAND

Lovat and his friends learned that Inverness had not so much fallen, as offered itself, to the Jacobites, having first supplied them with food, arms and horses. At 4 a.m. on the 13th, a signal sounded and the town's guard stood down. By 4.30 a.m., there was no one on duty when the din of men and horses echoed in the streets. Lachlan Mackintosh – son-in-law of the town's Provost (mayor) – his kinsman Mackintosh of Borlum, and 250 armed Jacobites marched into the town centre and proclaimed King James at the market cross. No alarm bells rang. No drumbeat roused the slumbering citizens.

Next morning, at Brahan Castle, the Earl of Seaforth, high chief of all the branches of the Mackenzies, set out the fiery cross to raise his clan for the Jacobites. The Mackenzies prepared to march to Inverness through their kinsmen Mackenzie of Fraserdale's Lovat lands, absorbing Mackenzies and Frasers en route.

In Inverness, Jacobites moved about uplifting the goods of pro-Hanoverian businessmen and gentry. The magistrates handed over most of the public funds available in the town and the people of Inverness woke to an occupied Highland capital and a Town House full of toasting and speechifying Jacobites being entertained by their Provost. The celebrations went on into the afternoon. Lachlan

Mackintosh installed another Mackenzie, Sir John Mackenzie of Coul, in Inverness Castle as Governor of the town for King James. When the magistrates met again, they paid an Episcopalian minister to lead prayers for success of the rebellion. They opened the Tolbooth by the bridge across the Ness to the Mackenzies and Mackintoshes, giving the rebels access to the town's arms and ammunition and control of the lowest crossing point of the river. Jacobite soldiers led out horses under cover of darkness, loaded with supplies for rebel groupings outside the town. In the wake of the general election, Culloden had warned the government that the Highlands were still too Jacobite and they must have men like Lovat who could sway whole clans.

Culloden was still at the Houses of Parliament when the rebellion broke out. He too immediately left for Inverness to protect his home and family. At Culloden House, two miles to the east of Inverness, his wife and servants had to hold off a force of armed men. She pleaded neighbourliness and the good manners due to a lady. They spared her – she had known most of the officers all their lives – but the ordinary men were licensed to pillage her fields and granaries.

For Lord Lovat and the Frasers, leaving their Soho sponging house without permission meant breaking bail. But if they did not go, the Fraser lairds holding out against Fraserdale and waiting for their chief in the hills of Stratherrick above Loch Ness might give up hope or be attacked by the Jacobites. Lovat had to go. In the Aird of Lovat several hundred fighting men had already answered Fraserdale's summons to muster at Castle Dounie and march away under the Earl of Seaforth with the rest of the Mackenzies. Fraserdale was effectively the Fraser chief: he had been married to the late Lord Lovat's daughter for ten years, managed the lands every day and lived at Dounie. He referred to himself as their chief. This was probably Lovat's last chance to haul his clan back from the brink of destruction to be rebranded as a branch of the Mackenzies.

The allegiance of Inverness – 'the gateway to the north' – was seen as a vital part of national security. Inverness would be the 'glittering prize in all that was to follow' in the northern theatre of war. Lovat agreed they would go there. Castleleathers obtained passes for the rest of them to travel from the Secretary of State for the Northern Department, Townshend, and an alias which he gave to his chief, who remained an outlaw. They packed up and rode out of London up the Great North Road, with Lovat disguised as a servant to avoid detection.

By the time Lovat and his little band reached Newcastle, the rebellion was already a month old. Newcastle was in an uproar. Several Jacobite families in the north of England, including Lord Derwentwater and the Northumberlands, had taken up arms. The Earl of Kenmure had risen in the north-west.

The Frasers dismounted, stiff and cold in the fading autumn day, having ridden almost 300 miles. The mayor of the town arrived to get their news. He advised the Frasers not to take the east coast 'post road', the main road north. Jacobite forces under Derwentwater and Thomas Forster MP controlled it, he said. Though Newcastle held out for King George – the natives coming to be taunted with the name 'Geordies' – it was surrounded by Stuart sympathisers. Hundreds of expatriate Scots lived and worked in the region. Jacobites concealed themselves behind the façade of work and family everywhere, including here in the town. The Whig Geordies expected a bold rebel strike to seize Newcastle imminently.

Next day, the Frasers crossed the country and headed into Scotland via the west coast route. Unknown to the Geordies, Derwentwater and Forster had decided not to siege Newcastle. They thought it too well defended, and went off to pursue softer targets at Hexham and Kelso. The rebels needed to take a major northern English city though. Much of Scotland as far south as Perth was Jacobite. Gaining a major English stronghold would trap the rest of Scotland between two Jacobite armies. They could probably take the whole country before moving south into England. Yet the Earl of Mar allowed the English rebel leaders to spend 'two weeks meandering from town to town, and otherwise dawdling' wherever they found a congenial billet. The Jacobites 'really had no idea what to do after they failed to take

Newcastle'. Combined with Mar's dithering, the lack of an effective leader meant the Jacobites began to lose the great advantage their popularity and the shock of their rising initially gifted them.

The Frasers reached Dumfries, turned north and eventually came to Stirling and the main Hanoverian camp. At Stirling, the Duke of Argyll was in overall command of British forces. *Eoghan Dearg nan Cath* or 'Red John of the Battles' to his Campbell kinsmen, Argyll was also Lord High Commissioner for Scotland. The reports of insurrection from every corner of Scotland and the north of England filled him with gloom. He reported to Secretary Townshend: the Jacobites 'have a hundred to one at least in their interest'. He complained about the inadequate number of men and arms sent to him. Argyll's war council was contemplating the possibility they would have to lose Scotland in order to establish the new German regime in England. There was simply too much turmoil in too many places north of the border. He could not fight everywhere at once. Argyll hated the Stuarts. 'That family … owes me and my family two heads,' he wrote. Perhaps this war would add his own to the debt, and pass it on to his son, though not without a fight. Argyll was in his late thirties and still in his prime.

Lord Lovat was also still in his prime. At about forty-three, he was a little older than Argyll. If only he had stayed in the army when he was a young man, and climbed the ladder of service and promotion, he reflected, he too might have been here as a highly decorated senior officer. Instead, his youthful misdemeanours meant he was in Scotland as a bail-jumper, prison-dodger, ex-Jacobite agent and freshly painted Hanoverian, and still an outlaw in Scotland. Lovat observed the levels of support for 'King James'. By all accounts, the new regime should lose, and that would be the end of the Hanoverians and the Union in Scotland.

Castleleathers was sent ahead to announce the arrival of Lord Lovat and request an audience with the Duke of Argyll. Lovat had left London, Castleleathers told Argyll, because he knew he must go home and prevent his clan joining the rebels. They wanted permission to go to Inverness. 'There are 300 of his name to join [Lord Lovat] … when he goes home,' Castleleathers told Argyll. Moreover, 'such of his name that joined Fraserdale, if we were at home this night, shall all desert Fraserdale from Perth'. This would be a substantial blow to the Jacobites. Argyll had to give him a chance. Lovat had waited for many years for someone to respond to his offers. In his heart a Jacobite, he must now dedicate himself to the Hanoverian cause, for his own and his clan's survival.

Also in Stirling, waiting to go north, was John Forbes of Culloden. Their fellow Hanoverians around Inverness were not putting any pressure on the rebels, who were reinforcing Inverness, and expanding into the north and Western Highlands. Sutherland's attempt to engage Seaforth and stop the Jacobite advances had failed pitifully. Seaforth, the Mackenzie high chief, had engaged and routed Sutherland on Munro clan lands (which lay north of Inverness, between Mackenzie's and Sutherland's territories). Sutherland fled thirty miles north by sea to his stronghold Dunrobin, and was still there, but very little blood was spilled. Only one person died in this encounter.

Highland warfare – clan warfare in other words – appeared very strange to southerners. Large bodies of militarily competent, armed men marched up to each other, as Sutherland's and Seaforth's men had, stated their demands, threatened each other with the nightmare they would inflict on each other to the tenth generation of their seed if they were not satisfied, reached an agreement that prevented this scenario, and marched home again. This was an over-simplification, but a considerable element of Highland warfare was a war of lurid words and violent displays by men in arms. The reason was obvious to all: the horrors of a full-blown blood feud and chaos. Partly as a result of this ethos, only two men would die in the northern theatre of war – the arena of clanship – during the entire rebellion.

News-sheets reported that some of the wild MacDonald kindred, Jacobite to their marrow, smelling weak and undefended enemy lands, were swarming out of the Western Highlands to raid Hanoverian estates around the Highland capital. All their houses and families lay in their path. Argyll ordered the Highlanders to Edinburgh to find a boat home. Reaching Inverness, the Duke said they must raise their clans and revitalise the campaign to reverse the Jacobite progress. On 18 October, Brigadier Alexander Grant wrote to his brother, Captain George Grant, who lived near Inverness: 'My Lord Lovat is now gone north. There's no doubt but his clan, who had loyalty enough to withstand the threats of a bullying rebel,' their Mackenzie usurper chief Fraserdale 'will most unanimously join him in the support of his Majesty King George's person and Government.'

Grant urged his brother to bravery. 'If any handsome thing is done, there's no doubt but you'll be rewarded for it. I wish with all my soul I could be with my friends and kinsmen on this occasion,' he mused. 'Let them take example of the name of Fraser, who future ages must praise for their loyalty to their prince as well as love and friendship to their chief.'

Lovat's enemies still painted him as 'that outlaw' Captain Fraser of Beaufort. But the most powerful soldiers in Britain now cited him in his full rank; and his kin as a model others might copy. Lovat climbed another step up in his own and the establishment's hopes. He watched and listened and contributed advice about the defeat of the Jacobites as diligently as he had plotted their victory. Lovat would not fall from favour again. He was determined on that.

Approaching Edinburgh, the city seemed oddly quiet. Lovat recalled it in the 1690s, when the whole carnival of an independent nation shouted and jostled, gossiped, plotted, formed alliances and slandered their enemies all around him. Edinburgh now appeared tense and subdued. Many of the towering medieval houses on the Royal Mile lay half empty, some having run to semi-ruin for want of gentle tenants. Post-Union, the economy had not sparked to life. Society tightened its belt and did not spend. Allan Ramsay, poet, Jacobite, antiquarian bookseller, and the father of Ramsay the portrait painter, complained that the Canongate, previously heaving with market traders, stock and customers, had become a 'Poor eldritch hole!/what loss, what crosses' it bore.

Lovat gazed up at the castle and down towards the Palace of Holyrood. The contrast between Edinburgh as the capital of a sovereign nation, and Edinburgh as a poor cousin to London, struck him, a passionate Scottish nationalist, as a scandal. He seemed to have travelled thousands of miles and suffered years of imprisonment and exile merely to end up where he started – a minor officer in an alien King's service. But to think like that might drive him mad.

At Leith, Lovat, his brother John, Castleleathers, Culloden, their servants and a party of cattle drovers carrying gold in their saddle bags to fund the resistance to rebellion boarded a boat and set sail at night on a full tide. The boat nosed its way into the Firth of Forth, and made east for the open sea. Their course would take them north to Peterhead, and then west, to land eventually at some point close to Inverness.

SIXTEEN

Fighting for the prize, 1715

'Lovat's arrival on the scene
transformed the situation'
– DANIEL SZECHI,
1715: THE GREAT JACOBITE REBELLION

The night gave them some cover. They crossed the Forth and began to tack out of the firth up the Fife side of it. Lovat and Culloden retired to sleep, leaving the boat's skipper, a sailor and Castleleathers at the helm. The men on deck chatted quietly about the unsettled state of affairs, the interruption to commerce and agriculture and so on. Suddenly Castleleathers felt his skin prickle. He hissed for silence. The skipper chatted on. In the dark, behind their conversation the Major was certain he caught sounds drifting in and out of earshot. He told the others to hold their tongues. A boat, said the helmsman, coming close.

Out of the darkness, a shot rattled through the sails. Castleleathers drew his pistol. Mar's men, the skipper told them, asking if they were friends. 'If you are friends, as I hope you are, we will slack the sail till they come up,' the skipper looked at him with curiosity. Not liking the man's drift, Castleleathers put his pistol to the skipper's breast. Raise all sails 'or you are a gone man', he whispered.

Hearing the shot, Lovat appeared. Castleleathers told him to stay below. The captain of the Jacobite boat might have tipped someone off about the drovers' gold being taken north for their Hanoverian chiefs. In full sail, under cover of the dark, they soon pulled away from the Jacobite raider. The skipper tried to pull in next at Aberdeen. He had some business there, he said. Castleleathers growled that he should sail on. 'It was not time to stop their passage with such a fair wind,' in the heart of rebel-held territory.

Halfway along the coast between Aberdeen and Inverness, the weather 'turned a pick teeth' and they could not make progress against it. They landed and rode the last sixty miles through Jacobite-held territory until at last the huge bulk of Kilravock Castle – twelve miles west of Inverness – loomed before them. Hugh Rose, chief of the clan, shouted to his clansmen to throw open its doors. Rose of Kilravock, staunch Hanoverian, brother-in-law of Lovat's friend and patron Brigadier Alexander Grant, strode out to welcome them. Lovat and Culloden were family and childhood friends of the Roses.

Kilravock could hardly believe it, the sight of Lovat standing there: heavier, older; not the slim, open-gazed youth he recalled. The eyes still shone, large and prominent, but bags cushioned them below. At the bridge of his nose, experience had pinched his brows down into a two-pronged frown, but deep laughter lines reached from each side of his nose to the sides of his mouth. Lovat had always had a watchful expression, as if he looked at the world from somewhere deep behind the surface of his face, keeping his counsel in the shadow of himself. But the gaze had sharpened, become more focused. This was a big handsome returning prodigal. They embraced with warmth. Kilravock then praised Castleleathers, who had set out nearly eighteen months ago to retrieve his chief. A fool's errand, many had then commented.

That night they were all 'very boisterous'. Lovat rested the following day, exhausted but exhilarated. He thought he had not relaxed for twenty years, and even now could not be certain that his kin were coming to him, as he had promised the Whig grandees. Argyll's decision to support Lovat's mission rested in part on assurances that the chief of the Frasers' sudden reappearance in the Highlands would have a galvanic effect, like a man back from the dead. Argyll desperately needed something to revitalise the war effort in the north.

Kilravock informed Lovat that over 300 of his kindred were holed up in Stratherrick, waiting for their 'natural chief's' call. Lovat began to feel an upsurge of the old purpose, grit and energy. These Stratherrick lairds had remained and kept faith with him. Their spirit moved Lovat to his core. He could never leave them again, no matter what it cost him personally. He would set aside his nationalist longings while he climbed to power, a mature and enfranchised peer of the realm and strong Highland chief. Lovat asked Castleleathers to go and bring his men to him. They would meet at Culloden House.

Once reunited with his men, Lovat could not be held back. All the energy the other Whig officers lacked over the last two months focused in him. He had everything to gain – his pardon, his whole inheritance – and nothing to lose since he was still officially 'obnoxious to the law'. The Jacobites were making ready to sit out the winter in Inverness until spring renewed the campaign season. They quartered the Highland Jacobite troops on known rebel families, and any foreign soldiers on known Hanoverian sympathisers.

At Culloden House, Lovat and his fellow officers planned their next moves. Lovat had to make capital out of this crisis. The same tactical skill he applied to his invasion plan for Louis XIV and the Stuarts he now applied to the problem of retaking Inverness for the Hanoverians. He headed up a force based around his clansmen and camped on the edge of the town, throwing down a challenge to Sir John Mackenzie to come and give them battle. Sir John was astonished. He could not think what had changed in the government camp that gave rise to this burst of bullish activity. His intelligence told him their commanding officer, Sutherland, still crouched at Dunrobin Castle, nearly fifty miles away. 'Not shapen to be a warrior,' according to Castleleathers, 'though a very honest man in all other respects,' Sir John declined the offer. In Inverness Castle and the Town House, the Jacobite commanders looked across the river and felt a little nervous for the first time since the rebellion began.

Inverness Burgh Council sent a messenger to Coll MacDonald of Keppoch asking for help. The chief of the Keppoch branch of the

Jacobite MacDonalds was marauding through the Hanoverian Grant lands, halfway down Loch Ness. Answering the call from Inverness, Keppoch turned to veer north along the north bank of Loch Ness and attack Lord Lovat in the rear.

Lovat walked among his men at their camp at the old horse market, the Merkinch, on the opposite bank of the Ness from Inverness Castle and town centre. He stopped to talk to all ranks with love and curiosity, enquiring after their fathers and kin. Sir John Mackenzie did not like their proximity. From the castle battlements, he watched as his lovely herd of cattle, which grazed on the Merkinch, was taken for food by the Frasers. He sent a message to the Mackintosh chief at Moy Hall, ten miles south of Inverness, requesting 500 Mackintosh fighting men to reinforce the 300 Mackenzies in the Highland capital.

Lovat dealt with the threats he identified one by one. He despatched the Reverend Thomas Fraser of Stratherrick, 'as good a soldier as a minister', with the Stratherrick men to parlay with the MacDonalds and persuade Keppoch that the town was now under siege and he should turn away. Keppoch MacDonald did not want to fight his way into Inverness to incarcerate his men on the wrong side of a siege, surrounded by government troops. Keppoch avoided Inverness and headed south through the hills.

Lovat then switched his attention to the Mackintoshes mustering at Moy Hall. He must prevent them marching north to help defend Inverness. Lovat ordered his troops to break camp. They crossed the Ness and advanced to the south side of Inverness, threatening to descend into Mackintosh country, and waste it. The Mackintoshes backed down at once, and hurried to 'make apology, swear they met to defend their land against Keppoch and that they will not assist the rebellion, upon which they promised to disperse'. No one wanted to shed his neighbour's blood. Lovat seemed unstoppable. According to one historian, his 'arrival on the scene transformed the situation' in the northern theatre of the rebellion.

The Fraser chief returned to his camp on the north bank of the Ness to blockade Inverness from that side. This was the road that led to the Aird of Lovat, Castle Dounie, Fraser country, and beyond that into Mackenzie country. It was important to his future that Lovat was clearly visible in the vanguard of any action, even standing out as 'the first man that appeared in the field', as he changed his image from fugitive to ruler.

There was one other thing to do before he moved. Lovat despatched a man to ride south to Perth. The messenger announced to the Frasers serving under Mackenzie of Fraserdale that their chief was back, and ordered them home. Almost to a man the Fraser fighting men deserted and left Mackenzie of Fraserdale sitting in his tent, a rebel and colonel with hardly any men to command. At long last the Whigs were engaging the Jacobites in earnest, eager for a victory over the Jacobites in the Highlands. When he heard, Argyll was delighted.

Lovat then met in council with the gentlemen of his clan. 'What would you think if I would go immediately, and attack Inverness?' he asked. His fellow Whig lairds preferred a siege to starve them slowly into submission. Forbes of Culloden and Rose of Kilravock had blockaded the town from the south and east. Maybe a siege was not dramatic or eye-catching enough to suit Argyll's or Lovat's style. 'I know it would put me in great favour at Court that I be the first man who appears in this country,' said Lovat. The Earl of Sutherland was still trying to make his men come back out from their homes. 'It will be thought a very bold action for us to attack Inverness with only 300 men,' Lovat concluded. The government sorely needed such bold thinking from its officers. 'So my good friends, let me have your solutions,' he asked.

'March!' they responded with pleasure. They too could see that a successful attack and reoccupation would earn rewards for them all, and many Frasers were ready for a fight with the Mackenzies. But before Lovat could attack, Kilravock's younger son, Arthur Rose, set off to speed up the siege. In the depths of the night, on 10 November, Arthur, his brother Robert, and a handful of men drifted in a little boat towards Inverness harbour, intending to seize all the boats and cut a major supply route into the town. In the darkness, they suddenly made out the shape of a guard. Arthur Rose put a pistol to the sentry's breast and told him to edge, quiet as a cat, in front of him and take them to the town's main guardhouse. Most of the town was asleep. No one noted their passing. If they did, they kept quiet. It was wartime, and better not to interfere. They crept up from the river towards the Tolbooth, and reached it unchallenged.

Their captive called 'Open!' to the men within. Rose held the sentry before him as a shield, and nudged him forward. The two men moved slowly. When the sentry got in clear sight of his fellows, he shouted 'An enemy! An enemy!' and threw himself forward. Rose stormed the room, sword and pistol in hand. As the sentry leapt away Rose was exposed to the Jacobites. They shot him twice at close quarters, and crushed him between an old wooden door and stone wall. Arthur Rose took several hours to die of his injuries, the second – and last – fatality in the northern war. Castleleathers lamented the loss of 'a bold resolute man'.

In the morning, Sir John Mackenzie of Coul wrote a letter of condolence to Arthur's father, Kilravock. Mackenzie enclosed passports saying he wanted them all to feel free to come into the town to bury their kinsman. Kilravock was so choked with grief and fury, he refused. He fired off a message to the magistrates of Inverness and his son-in-law, Sir John Mackenzie of Coul. All the Whigs were in a fury to burn 'the town at all ends'. The Inverness Jacobites at last woke to the reality of war. In the end, Kilravock's remaining son, with John Forbes of Culloden, Lovat, other government officers, Sir John Mackenzie of Coul and the rebel officers attended the burial. One of the government officers took Sir John to one side and advised him to render the town to the government, or Kilravock was determined to abandon the siege and reduce the whole town to little more than smoke.

The two men met the following day at a small burn to the east of the town. Sir John Mackenzie agreed to surrender Inverness, if his father-in-law would let him and his men go to join the Earl of Mar. The Earl had moved south-west of Perth, in the direction of Stirling and Glasgow, and had struck camp on the plain of Sheriffmuir. Kilravock brushed his son-in-law away. Mackenzie could go home in peace, but without his weapons and goods. The Hanoverians occupied Inverness on 12 November.

The next day, Sunday 13th, Hanoverian forces under the Duke of Argyll fought the Jacobite army under Mar at Sheriffmuir, outside Stirling, forty miles west of Edinburgh. After months of skirmishing, in the end their meeting was a messy and indecisive encounter: the two sides almost walked into each other by mistake, approaching from either side of a hill. But it was *the* battle the Jacobites needed in order to consolidate their great gains. After five hours of fighting, nightfall left the two armies at an impasse. They retired, both sides claiming victory. Argyll had fought an army two and a half times the size of his own to a standstill. The price was huge, costing him forty per cent of his effective forces.

Argyll held a council of war. His troops could not take another day like that. If Mar came on tomorrow, as surely he must, sheer force of numbers was going to deliver him victory, and with it all of Scotland. There would be no one to stop them marching into England, with Scotland at their backs to supply them. Faced with this vision, Argyll saw no option for him but to retreat to Stirling and risk the Jacobites slipping through his fingers as they marched south.

The Jacobites had lost about seventeen per cent of their men but still with around 4,000 in their number could have regrouped to finish the business 'without too much trouble'. Mar assembled his senior officers and the heads of the clans to debate whether they should attack again. Some of the leaders, like Marshal Keith, insisted they must regroup and seal the victory. Others reported, wrongly, that Argyll's numbers were now equal to the Jacobites', adding that the Highlanders, Mar's bravest and most committed troops, were exhausted 'and had eat nothing in two days'. They were 'averse' to re-engaging Argyll's forces. The defeatists carried the day. 'It was resolved ... to let the enemy retire unmolested ... The loss of colours was about equal on both sides; but the enemy got five piece of our cannon.'

Thus, the battle was decided by Mar in his tent. 'Neither side gained much honour,' Marshal Keith recalled, but the decision was 'the entire ruin' of the Jacobite campaign.

A massive surge in desertions now compounded Jacobite losses. Fighting clansmen poured north and west. To them this was not desertion, but their terms of engagement. When the chief called them out, they answered, did their duty, picked up spoils of war and, full of honour, took it home to their wives and mothers. They would certainly come out again when summoned. Mar's regular army officers were horrified.

Not only had the ordinary men of the clan left. News of the fall of Inverness reached the Jacobite high command at Sheriffmuir very fast. The Earl of Seaforth packed up and went home, taking his men with him, fearing for his lands and properties close to Inverness. His kinsman Mackenzie of Fraserdale was appalled to learn that Simon Fraser, calling himself Lord Lovat, had reappeared and was playing an essential part in resurrecting the campaign around the 'the key to the North'. Fraserdale now followed his high chief to attempt to secure his estates against the outlaw Beaufort.

In the face of desertions and excuses to withdraw, Mar could offer no intelligence where or when the inspiration for this whole, substantial but wavering insurrection was going to arrive and take charge, and bring back those now riding away. Where was 'King James'?

In Fraserdale's favour, at least Lord Lovat was still outlawed, though how long he would remain so was doubtful. Argyll told Secretary Townshend: 'I find Lord Lovat's being in the north has been of infinite service to his Majesty … I am informed our people there have possessed themselves of Inverness, which is certainly owing to him, and I am persuaded he will do all that is possible to spirit up our people there to make a diversion.'

Before Lovat arrived, King George's men had not even attempted to retake Inverness. Within ten days of his return they had achieved the first significant Hanoverian victory of the rebellion. Now reports came in daily about their movements all across the northern

Highlands, securing targets with speed and efficiency. Argyll, a very experienced general, knew this was no mere coincidence. Lovat's energy and tactical acuity had given the Hanoverians' northern army the confidence to snap into action. Now Lord Lovat demanded his prize: a pardon and freedom; the Fraser titles and estates back in the line of the heir male. The Mackenzies and Murrays prepared to do anything to hang on to them.

PART THREE

The Return of the Chief, 1715–45

'Yet still the blood is strong,
the heart is Highland'
– FROM EMIGRANT SONG

SEVENTEEN

Home, 1715–16

'There was nothing done for the government till I took
arms … I obliged the rebels to desert this town'
— LOVAT TO SECRETARY OF STATE TOWNSHEND

Lovat rode to Castle Dounie with hundreds of Fraser fighting men. As
he walked through rooms he had not seen for years, he found himself
in a singular position of having no pardon, or title to the castle and
all the lands leading in every direction from its doors and windows.
He despatched Lady Amelia and her children to a nearby farmhouse,
and noticed the family silver was missing. He determined to discover
what had happened to it.

From one point of view, he occupied rebel property on behalf of
the government. He anticipated it would be assigned to him perma-
nently in due course, as reward for his role in crushing this rebellion,
and as a key aspect of the pardon that he was sure must soon be
granted. Titles to parts of his patrimony were bound up in four-foot-
long, legal documents tied with red ribbons in Edinburgh lawyers'
offices. Tactical indebtedness by Sir Roderick, continued by his son,
left wadsets (mortgages) hibernating in the charter chests of Mackenzie
lairds. Lovat had no idea whether money had actually always changed
hands, or if they were a device and Mackenzie's cousins merely agreed
to say they were creditors, should they ever need to stake a claim on
the assets of the Lovat estates. Certainly, when he looked into it, it
seemed to Lovat that some creditors had not pressed for any repay-

ment for twenty years. Others, when he examined them, were obviously the ordinary debts any gentleman owed money lenders.

He sat at his old desk, trying to work out what had been happening. Frequent interruptions called him away: he spoke to soldiers arriving from Inverness with instructions and requests from the other Hanoverian leaders; his fellow officers came to Dounie to hold war councils with him, to ask his advice in planning the next phase of the campaign to crush the claims of the royal family Lovat had hoped to restore for two nearly decades, and to reinforce the strength of a Union he believed cursed Scotland.

The seeming rehabilitation of Lovat had sent Fraserdale into a frenzy of anxiety. They were both outlaws now. Who would the authorities favour? The longer Lovat kept possession of Castle Dounie the harder it was to throw him out legally. He and Lovat raced to ingratiate themselves and accuse each other. Fraserdale surrendered to government forces and begged not to be prosecuted, desperate to stop his estates being forfeit to the Crown and assigned to someone loyal to King George.

Lovat stressed to Townshend: 'There was nothing done for the government till I took arms ... I obliged the rebels to desert this town ... All my people, whom Mackenzie of Fraserdale forced by open violence to go with him to Mar's camp, deserted all and came and joined me when they heard I was in my country,' and Fraserdale 'pretends now to submit himself' to British justice. It was vital Lovat introduce the element of pretence into Fraserdale's submission, and talk up the power of his own authority in the area.

Fraserdale responded with urgent pleas to his Edinburgh supporters for help with his release. Foremost among his allies was his wife's uncle, the Duke of Atholl. Atholl called on the Scottish Secretary, the Duke of Montrose, and requested his niece's husband be brought to Edinburgh, where the courts were full of friends and inclined to be lenient with rebel gentlemen who offered guarantees of good behaviour and signs of repentance. Cockburn, Justice Clerk of the Court of Session, was prepared to do all he could to keep Lovat out and make sure the estates were not forfeited to the crown.

Good luck and cool planning had given this branch of the Mackenzies the sort of prestige birth had not assigned them – not to mention properties and income that only a fool would relinquish without a fight to the death. The couple's son, Hugh, thrived, and was set to inherit the titles and estates after Fraserdale's death. If the boy changed his name as Fraserdale's late father had advised in his 1706 letter to the Fraser gentlemen, then this boy would be Hugh Mackenzie, 12th Lord Lovat. If they could not kill Simon Fraser of Beaufort by law, perhaps they might slowly smother him into failure and insignificance by law. He would waste his life in semi-scandalous obscurity, walled in by legal documents, some sound, some unsound. It would take him decades and cost him a fortune he did not have to unravel it all.

A week after the taking of Inverness, a soldier arrived at Dunrobin to tell the Earl of Sutherland his subordinate officers had achieved what Sutherland failed even to attempt. The Earl realised it was time for him to resume active command of his forces in Inverness. He did not want his name to be conspicuous only by its absence from reports of the victories in Scotland.

Others were already too active that way for Sutherland's liking. He wrote to King George that he was preparing to come and lead his forces when the Inverness junior officers took the initiative and attacked without his authority. 'The Earl of Sutherland was greatly disappointed that he was thus deprived of the honour of taking Inverness,' Sutherland reported. 'This treatment was very provoking, yet I stifled all resentment, the better to go on with your Majesty's service.' He had no generous word yet of how well his fellow officers had done. He went on, recasting his defeat by Seaforth into a wonderful and self-sacrificing diversionary manoeuvre. His unequal force of 1,800 tackling 4,000 enemy soldiers interrupted the Mackenzies' march to join the rebels; the 'diversion I gave them for some time was probably the ruin of their cause', Sutherland judged confidently. 'I may say, without vanity, that God was pleased to make use of me, as an instrument to prevent' Argyll being crushed by weight of enemy numbers at Sheriffmuir. Sutherland had performed this heroic act, he reminded the King, 'long before Lord Lovat and some other assuming gentlemen came to the north and joined me'.

At the same time Sutherland wrote to Lovat and asked him 'to send some of his force to meet them, as they were afraid that the Earl of Seaforth, returning from Sheriffmuir with a great following of the clans, would attack them at the head of the Mackenzies and MacDonalds', and defeat Sutherland again on his way south. Lovat obliged and sent men under Castleleathers to escort his wary commanding officer to Inverness.

In this way, the story of the capture of Inverness became a battle in itself. When he had some peace, Lovat meant to put his version to the King. In the hinterland of the rebellion, they were all boasting and seeking royal favour in the shape of promotions and pensions. How else could a man get ahead? Lovat needed to go further than most. Sutherland was merely making the best of his advantage as commanding officer.

From the government camp at Stirling, one of the Grant elite wrote to Lovat. 'I hope when the King is *rightly* informed of the part you acted in recovering the castle and town of Inverness he will reward you suitably to that great and important service.' In London, he warned, the Highland victories were talked of 'as if nobody had acted any part but the Earl of Sutherland and those he brought with him'. In addition, Grant promised to try 'to stop anything that may be intended to be done for Fraserdale', by Atholl or Montrose. The Brigadier told Lovat he wanted 'an impartial account of facts, with the people who were there ... People at London are surprised ... when I tell them that had it not been for the appearance made in Inverness-shire by Lord Lovat and others, that the Earl of Sutherland nor any of the others would have ventured to cross' out of their own clan lands. They all needed payment for their services. When the time came, Grant did not want the King to look back over the reports and read only the name of Sutherland everywhere, when he was not within fifty miles of the town.

At home, Lovat plunged his nib into his ink with delight, and set his mind to establishing peace in his region and publicising his opinions and activities. The mid-winter weather was appalling. Yet Lovat was exuberant, declaring 'we are resolved to make our graves in the streets rather than yield this place, till it is in flames about our ears, and we will sell our lives as dear as we can, for we know that this place is the centre of the rebellion and the key of the north'. Their intelligence told them Mar was planning his retreat north. If he did, the centre of rebel activity would move with him. All his life friends had asked him to keep quiet, not to speak up. Grant invited him to lift his trumpet to his lips and announce his presence and the renown of his services. He did not need to be asked twice.

It had been quite a year after decades of reverses. In twelve months, Lovat had gone from exile in France, to a London gaolhouse, to commanding hundreds of Fraser men now encamped below his battlements at Dounie. He was back in the clan chief's house, amused each evening by the respectful and lively table talk of peers and gentlemen. Reading his reports, the government would breathe a sigh of relief that he was there, one of their own, comprehending what was needed, and holding the line. King George's ministers would hesitate to suggest an effective and committed nobleman should be moved out again because a proven rebel, Fraserdale, craved rehabilitation. But the sentence hanging over Lovat shaded his joy.

In the middle of these negotiations James Stuart appeared – long expected, but in the end unannounced. A poor seaman, he landed at last at Peterhead near Aberdeen, in the north-east corner of Scotland. On 8 January 1716, he addressed the Earl of Huntly. 'My presence will inspire,' James hazarded; 'I do not doubt, new life and vigour into the troops you command.' Actually, most Highland troops had gone home for the winter after the debacle at Sheriffmuir. 'It is of the last consequence … that in conjunction with the Earl of Seaforth you lose no time in reducing Inverness … I heartily wish you … satisfaction.' Thus James discharged the full fire of his rhetoric – slightly ponderous, slow moving, considered.

The Jacobite earls listened to their King with dismay. 'Now there's no help for it, we must all ruin with him,' groaned the Earl of Huntly. 'Would to God he had come sooner.' For four months they linked the coming of the King with inspiration and success. Now Huntly connected his late arrival with catastrophe for all his supporters, some of whom were already negotiating the terms of their surrender to British justice. Seaforth promised James he would raise his Mackenzie clan again to retake Inverness, and also asked the Dowager Countess of Seaforth to persuade Lovat to help him to submit to King George. The Hanoverians' council of war in Inverness had resolved to lay waste Mackenzie country, to bring the clan to heel.

In Perth, James worried over the lack of action. He knew his northern magnates were trimming – talking to representatives of George I, as well as planning to come out for him again – and that Lord Lovat was at the heart of it, tactically. While he talked to Lovat, the Earl of Huntly renewed preparations to go to Perth and join James. He repeated his request for men and arms. The Earl of Mar repeated his refusal. 'We are unable to supply your wants at this time,' he said, but added that 'Lovat has it now in his power to reconcile himself to the King, which I am not without hopes he will do, and if he did, it would make the work easy.' Mar told James miserably that Lovat was the 'life and soul' of the Whigs in Inverness, such that 'the whole country and his name dote on him'. James agreed this gave his own prospects 'a very melancholy aspect'. Having denied Lovat for so long, suddenly the Jacobite leadership realised they had totally underestimated him. Now he held the key to the north. Lovat had always maintained that the Gaelic-speaking Highlands, semi-independent since time immemorial, a huge swathe of them passionately loyal to the Stuarts, was an obvious place to look for loyalty and forces. If James could link Perth and Inverness with a broad belt of support that spanned the Highlands from Inverness in the east to Fort William in the west, and with his rule secure north of that line, the Highlands would serve as a base from which he could spread his influence south in the spring. James's senior officers should try to turn Lovat back to them.

* * *

Lovat wrote to his old friend and university colleague, John Glenbuchat, one of the Gordon gentry. Moustaches reaching to his shoulders billowed to either side as he moved. Old Glenbuchat's fierce gaze seemed compelled by something very irritating on the horizon. 'When all this is over, men of honour will be known, and whatever comes, though we should fight against one another, that will never make me forget our old comradeship,' Lovat wrote, signalling his affection, but that he was on the other side. Their old comradeship was based on shared hopes for the Stuart kings and perhaps an independent Scotland.

A week later, Glenbuchat replied bluntly, 'I heartily regret that your opinion is so much changed ... "Bad companies corrupt good manners", and I am sorry you are so trysted.' Glenbuchat had seen James a week ago. 'I had the honour of kissing the King's hand at Scone,' he told Lovat. James 'asked concerning your behaviour particularly. If I could wait on you in safety I would give account of his sentiments. None can persuade him that you will draw your sword against him ... I am very much concerned to be contrary to you,' Glenbuchat observed with some sadness, 'though I hope it will not be for long, for I am convinced you believe I have the just side.' His appeal was severe and seductive. He had known Lovat for thirty years.

Lovat was mindful of the time he was a very different man. For years no one had wanted him. James Stuart had told Castleleathers he would never free him or bring him to Court. Now everyone wanted him. Correspondence with James would damn him in George I's eyes. Yet, he could not resist finding out how far the Stuarts would go to woo him back. He cast a fly over the Jacobites. He might come over if asked personally by James and if rewarded with enough titles and honours to requite the humiliation, pain and loss of the last two decades. James replied, eagerly writing out the required petition and gilding his offer with patents for useless Jacobite titles. He offered Lovat a dukedom.

When Huntly discovered there was a chance Lovat might return to the cause, he added his own effort to bring his former comrade back round to his old self. 'When we were young I knew your sentiments of loyalty and love to your country so strong that I could not believe anything could have altered them, till I heard of your being in Inverness … It's not only for the King's sake I write so pressingly, but old acquaintance and friendship contracted by young people cannot easily be forgot, which ours was.' The letter breathed affection, regret, longing. It appealed to a youthful idealism about their future, the old confidences, memories, and hopes held in common.

Isolated from all he had ever known of this 'old comradeship' for so long, rejected by monarchs and governments, his clan degraded, their natural chief outlawed on both sides of the Channel, in February 1716 Lovat could not bring himself to burn these letters, though it was madness to keep them. He put them away in his private chest, and went out to fight for his property rights and to impose British rule in the Highlands.

The arrival of Castleleathers at Saumur eighteen months earlier had forced a decision on Lovat. He had answered the Major's plea that he come back to save his people any way he could – abandon France and the Stuarts and throw in his lot with the new regime. What could he say in twenty lines now, to explain the last two decades of exile to these friends? It was laughable. Castleleathers had said the times offered clever fishermen 'good sport in Drumly waters' and the chance to pull out the big fish. Lovat had not imagined that both the Hanoverians and Stuarts would want him.

From London, King George I wrote to congratulate the Earl of Sutherland for 'the good services which you are rendering me and of the skilful dispositions you have made to defend the important post of Inverness'. Cadogan and Argyll had since attacked the Jacobites in Perth. The Secretary of State, James Stanhope, added: 'I have it like-wise in command from his Majesty to tell you that in consideration of Lord Lovat's zeal and services on this occasion, his Majesty will grant him his pardon.' On 4 February, his friends Captain George Grant, Colonel William Grant, Culloden and Duncan Forbes, Deputy Lieutenants of Inverness-shire, added their voices, declaring that since the 'open rebellion of Mackenzie of Fraserdale, the Estate of Lovat lately in his possession becomes forfeited to his Majesty King George', and his representatives are 'requiring and commanding all' Lovat estate tenants and tacksmen pay their rent in the usual forms to 'the Honourable Simon, Lord Lovat ... authorising him or his factors to grant receipts and discharges'. Things were moving steadily Lovat's way.

Fraserdale panicked. It was the eleventh hour. Once the pardon was confirmed, Lovat could claim back his inheritance. The Edinburgh judiciary's amenability to corruption had worked well for him in the past. He now appealed to it, to save his home, his wife, his heir and all that he had acquired.

EIGHTEEN

The legal battles begin, 1716

A Fox may steal your hens, sir,
A whore your health and pence, sir,
Your daughter may rob your chest, sir,
Your wife may steal your rest, sir,
A thief your goods and plate.
But this is all but picking,
With rest, pence, chest, and chicken;
It ever was decreed, sir,
If Lawyer's hand is fee'd, sir,
He steals your whole estate.

— JOHN GAY, *THE BEGGAR'S OPERA*

All through the spring of 1716, legitimate merchant creditors, all kinds of money lenders and Mackenzie wadset holders began to agitate at the sight of the Lovat estates being taken over by Simon, Lord Lovat. Mackenzie of Fraserdale was their debtor; the Lovat estates were offered as his and his creditors' security, a guarantee of Fraserdale's ability to meet his repayments. Fraserdale asked his wife to canvass their influential friends in the Scottish judiciary to come to their defence and delay answering queries about his part in the rebellion. He had to hurry.

Fraserdale's father, Sir Roderick, had made plans for Lovat's possible return. Fraserdale contacted the men Lovat asserted were illegitimate creditors, and asked them to prepare to stake a claim on the

Lovat estates, in case they were taken away from their cousin on a more permanent basis. In general the Scottish judiciary was reluctant to dismiss creditors' claims on forfeited estates. If would-be money lenders believed a government might suddenly withdraw the security for their loans for political reasons, they risked interrupting the supply of credit on which the healthy running of the economy depended.

Without the complication of Lovat's return, Duncan Forbes, deputy of the Court of Session, might have argued for a pardon for Mackenzie of Fraserdale. The government simply was not going to deal with the underlying causes of Scottish discontent. Better to have the political nation without resentment if they were also without satisfactory address to their post-Union grievances, thought Forbes and Dalrymple, the Lord President of the Court of Session. Given his and his brother's ambitions to control the Highlands, however, Duncan Forbes supported Lovat. The expectation was that in return, Lovat would support Duncan and Culloden in their political activities.

The Reverend James used to say he prayed 'of our Lovat' it would 'prove what the prophet saith, "I will overturn, overturn, overturn it, and it shall be no more until he come whose right it is, and I will give it him"'. The chronicler implied 'our Lovat' was the Chosen One, and God would 'overturn' the usurpers when Lovat came back into his kingdom. Clan MacShimidh Mor – 'the children of the son of the Mighty Simon' – would emerge into the sun from under the dark 'Hesperus cloud' of Murray–Mackenzie usurpation. No wonder Lovat saw his role as fulfilling a duty ordained by God and history. His ancestors had taught him by example. The Reverend praised 'the true splendour, nobleness, worth, wisdom, virtue, graces and antiquity of your renowned ancestors ... centred in your excellent self, their surviving stem'. Lovat concluded he could not achieve glory by staying at Dounie. He must go to the source of patronage – London and the Court of King George I – to ensure it.

Lovat's allies urged Westminster ministers to speed up his pardon. Whosoever secured the favour of the Crown would get the Lovat estates. Lovat associated himself with Argyll's clique, the Argathelians, a faction vying to represent George I in Scottish affairs. Their followers included all Lovat's Inverness friends, Grant, Kilravock, the Forbes brothers. Competing with Argyll was the Squadrone faction, which included the Earls of Sutherland and Montrose, the Duke of Atholl, and the Lord Justice Clerk, Adam Cockburn. They enjoyed backing in London from the Duke of Marlborough. Fraserdale naturally appealed to the Squadrone to support him and undermine Lovat.

Lovat's ambitions simplified early in February 1716 when James Stuart and his leading advisers slipped out of Montrose Bay on the *Maria Theresa* and returned to Lorraine. James's followers were in disbelief when they woke next morning to the rumour that God's anointed one had gone from them like a thief in the night. 'In the greatest confusion imaginable, running from house to house seeking their King,' the Jacobites were in disarray. Even Argyll pitied them when he and the Earl of Cadogan caught up with them. Cadogan was a Marlborough man through and through, and competed with Argyll to be the man credited with ending the rebellion. In Lovat's favour was Cadogan's special loathing of all Mackenzies; they represented everything he hated in clanship. Against Lovat was the political antipathy between Argyll and Cadogan. They were all Whigs, all loyal to the Hanoverian settlement. However, beneath the surface some very large ambitions and egos were at play.

Lovat now went to press with his account of the action at Inverness. It dominated the front page of *The Flying Post*. When the uprising began, Lovat wrote, the Whig forces 'marched towards Inverness in order to its relief. But finding themselves at that time greatly outnumbered by the Rebels … they thought for his Majesty's service to' flee and 'wait for a more favourable opportunity for advancing that way' again. Lovat mocked Sutherland's retreat home. 'About the 3rd of November, the Lord Lovat and Culloden arrived in that country. As soon as the Gentlemen of his name heard of his arrival, they immediately waited upon him. It can't be imagined what a sudden alteration to the Advantage his coming not only occasioned in the Countenances of them, but in a great measure, in that of every honest man.' It was only after the 'taking of Inverness by Simon Fraser, Lord Lovat', that Sutherland, his son, Lord Strathnaver, and the Munros found the courage to venture from their castles again.

Beneath the article appeared an advert for a new map of Scotland. Hardly a tenth of Englishmen knew what lay north of the English border. Travellers' tales told of high lands, pathless and unmapped, groaning with wild beasts. They concealed Highland bandits who spoke not a whisper of English, but lurked among the horrible crags, competing to maim the unwary traveller, or drown them in a mountain torrent.

Reading on down the front page, readers found light relief from the rebellion in Scotland in gossip about the poet and aphorist William Wycherly. The old man had fallen into bitter dispute with his nephew and heir over his estate, which the youth was due to inherit on the poet's death. Out of the blue, Wycherly, aged eighty-one, had married a very young woman called Elizabeth Jackson, and settled three-quarters of his estate on her. Ten days later he died, to the grief and horror of his heir, the joy of the new heiress, and the glee of the reading public.

At the bottom of the page a health and beauty advert offered the 'true royal chemical washball for the beautifying the hands and face ... without mercury, or anything prejudicial ... By taking off all deformities, as Tetters, ringworms, *morhey*, sunburn, scurf, pimples, pits, or redness of the small pox,' it cured a range of skin complaints. War, political propaganda, celebrity gossip, and health and beauty tips riveted readers from London to the Highlands.

Stern rebuffs to Lovat's self-serving account of the northern campaign appeared within weeks. His brother-in-law, Thomas Robertson of Inches, wrote a public letter decrying Lovat's claims. He would not usually deal in politics, he said, but 'that which excites me more to it [is] that the prints from London seem to attribute any appearance [of King George's troops at Inverness] ... to one who I assure you hath no manner of share in it'. This was not true, but Robertson was of Fraserdale's camp.

* * *

In July, Cadogan ordered General Joseph Wightman to Inverness to stamp out the embers of Jacobite resistance, and impose law and order on the scrapping Highlanders. This would be Wightman's second tour of duty in Scotland. Many of Wightman's soldiers were Dutch and Swiss troops, ill-suited to fighting in Highland terrain. Cadogan asked Lovat to give the General what help he could, in local knowledge and armed men. Lovat had to obey but was impatient to go to London to counter Atholl and Montrose's support for Fraserdale. Besides, until his pardon was signed, he was an outlaw, and could not possibly approach George I and his Court. 'I am very well with General Wightman; but always very much mortified to see myself the servant of all, without a post or character,' he wrote to Duncan Forbes. He imagined all except him were receiving thanks from the King. He worried all the prizes would be handed out to others before he got there.

Argyll and Ilay had the King's ear though, and on 10 March, George I signed the document that left Lord Lovat a free, lawful, British subject for the first time in nearly twenty years. Written in Latin, it pardoned him and enumerated all the crimes for which it would be rescinded.

Cadogan asked Lovat to 'send me your thoughts concerning the properest measures to be taken for reducing' the clans who still evaded submission, 'in case they pretend to make any resistance'. He meant especially the Mackenzies and their client kindreds, whose vast clan territories stretched from the east coast to the north-west coast of Ross-shire, and estate on the Hebridean island of Lewis, from where the Earl of Seaforth was negotiating his surrender.

Lovat's prescription for peace was a violent purgative. The government would never be secure in the unsettled areas, he advised Cadogan, until 'the rebels of those countrys be transplanted'. If not sent to the Colonies, then 'not only their chiefs, but likewise the leading men of every clan, be made prisoners and kept as hostages to guarantee the peaceable behaviour of their people'. Lovat would start with Fraserdale. The minority Whigs were obsessed with security problems. Lovat fed that obsession, stimulating their fears in one breath, and offering solutions in the next. The process of bringing round the peripheries of Britain to the idea of Union and Britishness was moving gradually. The government had been caught badly unawares by Mar's uprising. Still, in the wake of it, they advanced as before: using 'well-affected' locals like Lord Lovat to police their own, while at the same time making an example of selected rebels, ruining them, and forfeiting their estates to the Crown. Lovat understood this perfectly. In his version of the policy, Fraserdale would be sacrificed, and perhaps a MacDonald or two, and Seaforth pardoned.

Lovat recommended the government raise a body of 1,500 Highlanders to supplement Wightman's Dutch and Swiss regulars. The fitness of the Highlanders was vastly superior in mountain conditions, and 'they wade the river commonly better than any horse', Lovat boasted. They would 'be absolutely useful for disarming the rebels' on their native terrain. Three hundred active young Gaels should come from each of the five great clans which had been out for King George, he recommended, under the command of men like Lovat. They could fan out in a line from Fraser country and into Mackenzie country, sweeping west, emptying the last pockets of resistance. This would give Lovat the perfect opportunity for some private mopping up, to eliminate dissident elements from his clan lands: those who served Fraserdale and opposed Lovat's return.

Even as Lovat penned his report, he could see that a company of trained Fraser Highland soldiers would strengthen his power base at home markedly. If Atholl ever thought to attack him again with troops, as he had done when Lovat was young, Lovat would have a properly regimented defensive force to hand.

His plans made sense to his commanding officers. They were the sort of draconian measures Cadogan and Wightman understood. Ministers in London thanked Lovat but told him his more drastic suggestions to transport chiefs and gentlemen of the rebel clans to the plantations were not practical, or desirable.

However, the stream of advice and action from Lovat was paying dividends. His reputation improved and his treasons were pushed into the shadows. Even the Earl of Ilay wrote to congratulate him on his efforts to speed up his rehabilitation, and advised him the time was right to come south: he had spoken to Townshend that day, who said 'your Lordship might come when you pleased; all the Court, I find, are very well disposed to take care of you, and to find out such a reward as I foresaw you would, and now they are all convinced you do, deserve'. That could only mean the gift of Fraser country. Lovat's heart surged with joy.

When Lovat first re-entered Castle Dounie in early 1715, he had immediately noticed that the family silver was missing. The trail to rediscovering it led him, strangely, to General Wightman, who had seized it as a prize of war. Fraserdale had hidden it with Mackenzie of Coul when he went to join Mar, and Wightman had taken possession of it.

Lovat was incensed and fired off an outraged letter to Cadogan, who agreed the silver ought to be Lovat's at least until the King's pleasure was known regarding the Lovat estates. The issue reflected the insecurity of his position. Lovat also asked Cadogan permission to go urgently to London to speak with the King about his reinstatement. Cadogan agreed. Lovat set off just as John Forbes of Culloden reported to his brother that 'Marlborough's dependents at Court are provided for and the others are not … Some here do suppose our Duke [Argyll] is not so much in favour.' This was vital news to the Forbeses and to Lovat. Argyll was their patron.

Culloden reminded Sutherland, with whom he was on good terms, that the Earl had promised to support Lovat's bid for royal favours. Sutherland was as good as his word. On 8 June news came to Lovat that the King was 'pleased to appoint him Governor of the Castle and Fort of Inverness', and captain of an Independent Company of Foot. They were to be a local militia for policing the Highlands, as envisaged in Lovat's memorial to George I, except that the companies would be independent of each other under their captains. The clans contained too many men of divided or unproven loyalty, including Lord Lovat, to trust such a big fighting force to a single commanding officer, especially one so well known for his cunning.

Even this limited recognition was too much for the Duke of Atholl. 'I can hardly believe what is contained in the Edinburgh *Courant*! That Simon Fraser, who is there called Lord Lovat, to which he has no manner of right ... has got an Independent Company!' Atholl was aghast. 'I have also frequently heard that the Duke of Argyll has countenanced that person, which I hope is not true.' What did it take to get rid of the Old Fox!

Lovat rushed the notice of his appointments around the offices of *The Flying Post*. Lovat's notice said the King had rewarded him 'in consideration of my Lord Lovat's service in reducing of Inverness'. Sutherland protested to Lovat that he was 'justly offended at his assuming the sole merit to himself in that affair'. This was the second such article. He insisted Lovat publish a retraction and acknowledge the Earl's dominant role, not only in quelling the rebellion in the north, but also in intervening on Lovat's behalf with the King and his advisers. Lovat wriggled. He denied any involvement in writing the piece and gave vague assurances that he would make sure Sutherland's place was known.

The next edition of the *Flying Post* came and went. Nothing appeared. Sutherland was not going to go quietly again. He summoned one of his dependants, Gordon of Ardoch, and despatched him to tell Lord Lovat to retract this nonsense or face the consequences. Ardoch found Lord Lovat dining with one of Secretary of State Townshend's employees, and had thrust the letter in his face. It came from the Earl's desk, Ardoch said. Lovat took it from him. He read a retraction of his own account of the rebellion in the Highlands. The letter described how the Governor of Inverness abandoned the town when he saw the Earl of Sutherland approach with his men and twelve cannon. Lovat, 'most civilly saying that the letter was stuffed with lies and falsehoods', tossed it back. He was not going to take this fabrication to the *Flying Post* or any other newspaper.

Gordon of Ardoch blustered, 'he durst not have said so of it had the Earl been present'. Lovat retorted that the Earl had not even written this letter. It came from the pen of a Sutherland lackey, Sir William Gordon. Sir William was a Squadrone supporter who fed intelligence to Montrose, his political leader in the Squadrone. Sir William was happy to denigrate Lovat and establish his own claim for rewards. Ardoch could tell Sir William, said Lovat, that if he met him he would cut his throat for his mischief-making.

Next morning, Lovat made his way to the Smyrna Coffee House near Piccadilly. The company was always diverse in the coffee house, not unlike the mix of people at the Court of a Highland chief. 'A couple of lords, a baronet, a shoemaker, a tailor, a wine-merchant and some others of the same sort, all sitting round the same table and discussing familiarly the news of the Court and the town,' greeted his eyes. 'The government's affairs are as much the concerns of the people as of the great. Every man has the right to discuss them freely … The coffee houses and the other public places are the seats of English liberty,' a visiting Frenchman lamented. Lovat joined some friends. Fortified, he regaled them with the previous day's tale, news of his Independent Company and his generalship.

Mid-story, Sir William Gordon strode in, shouting and roaring that Lovat must publish the correction that had been written for him. Lovat refused. His account was more or less correct already. He knew Sir William had asked for £14,000 expenses he claimed he incurred defending King George. Sir William stormed out, but shouted he would be back next morning 'beat up my Lord's quarters and adjust the matter betwixt them'. They would duel. Lovat hurried round to the lodgings of his Highland neighbour, and fellow Argyll factionary, Rose of Kilravock. With great reluctance, Kilravock agreed to act as his second. Gordon of Ardoch was more than happy to second Sir William.

Dawn the next day, Lovat and Kilravock rode from Piccadilly to Marylebone Fields, threading their way through the streets as the capital shook itself awake. Across from the fields drifted a sound of lowing from the Lactarian, a herd of cows that grazed in St James's Park and supplied the city's morning needs. Pewterers, coppersmiths, coopers and blacksmiths began their banging to ring in the start of their working day. The first traders from the countryside plodded or rattled into the heart of the City towards Smithfield, Billingsgate, Covent Garden, their noses assailed by the stink from miles out. Streetside shops opened their doors. The first flies felt their way towards carcases and cheeses, vegetables and fruit, and rubbed their legs together with pleasure. Dust from Lovat and Kilravock's horses coated the whole jolly array in a fine film of grey.

At Marylebone Fields, Lovat, Sir William and Gordon of Ardoch, dismounted and turned to begin. At that moment, a hooded man on a horse appeared out of the early morning haze, levelling his pistol at the cluster of men on the field. He would shoot the first man who drew, he said. The two seconds approached as near as they dared, shouting at the clansman to be gone. The eye of the pistol's muzzle swept across them. The hooded rider refused to move. More men rode up. James and Alexander Fraser, Lovat's cousin and business associate, and four others cantered across the grass.

Choler seized Sir William. Lovat had goaded him to the point of a fight. Sir William was a fighting soldier and he believed he would win. Now the duelling field was full of Frasers urging their mounts between Sir William and his target. Through the thicket of sweating horse flesh, boots, spurs and clanking swords, Sir William roared at Lovat that by ordering his clansmen to come and save him, he was nothing but 'a lying knave and an arrant coward'. Lovat tried to push his way between the riders and draw his sword, but scraped it no more than half out of its sheath. The hooded clansman turned and aimed the pistol at Lovat's chest and the whole crisis teetered over into farce. There was a substantial ritual element to this statement of readiness to defend one's good name and reputation with one's life. The fields now emptied as quickly as they had filled.

Bloodshed had been avoided. Lovat's friends rejoiced. Politics and Fraser matters provoked so much passion in Lovat's bosom, that they feared for him. In his conflicts with Sutherland and Sir William, Lovat loosed the bundle of fears and resentments that burdened him from his youth. It did him no good. His friends advised him to shoulder them more lightly.

* * *

Whilst in London, Lovat received news of the death of his brother, John. Before coming south, he had written to Sutherland, passing on John's 'last respects for he is so dangerously ill with a fever, flux and stitches that there is little or no hopes of his recovery. He was a good-natured and brave young fellow.' Lovat spoke as if John were already dead. 'His fatigue and drinking this winter and the sudden quitting of it has killed him. I wish with my soul that my Lord Strathnaver,' Sutherland's son and heir, 'may give over his drinking in some measure, otherwise he cannot live ... I have been ill too,' Lovat confided. 'Constant fatigue' was wearing him down. John Lovat had lain in bed at Castleleathers' house for his final six weeks. All through the spring, the decline of his loyal brother and heir had lowered Lovat's spirits. 'A simple man', John had lived his life in his brother's shadow, representing him, fighting Lovat's corner while he was in exile.

John's loss thrust into Lovat's mind with painful force fears for the future. Without heirs, what was it all for? Lovat had been caught up in London, fighting himself to exhaustion, only for all his achievements to slip away from his family again upon his own death. His cause was going well, but he now had no family, no wife or children; no heir. He knew he must marry soon, though the forced marriage with Amelia Murray might cause complications.

NINETEEN

Living like a fox, 1716

'Put all the irons in the fire'
— LOVAT TO DUNCAN FORBES

Lovat cast his mind about for a suitable bride. He was forty-four and had very good prospects. Many gentlemen married for the second time at his age, childbirth having carried off the first wife. Lovat already enjoyed the position of Governor of Inverness and command of a company of soldiers. He was a peer of the realm and chief of an ancient clan. He believed King George favoured making the gift of the vast Fraser lands to him. With those behind him, Lovat thought he might seek election to the House of Lords, as one of the sixteen Scottish Lords voted to a seat. He would have a wife and children as well.

Children symbolised stability and continuity. A settled man was attractive to the authorities. After John's death, Lovat's only male heir was a cousin, Fraser of Inverallochy, who lived many miles away from the Lovat estates. To attract the family of a suitably well-connected woman, however, he should have legal title to substantial properties. It was a circular problem. Lovat pressed Walpole and the other Lords of the Treasury for warrants of escheat for the Fraserdale-Lovat estates.

Since Lovat's most powerful allies were the Duke of Argyll and the Earl of Ilay, marrying into a clan connected to the Argylls could serve all his needs. Allied to Walpole, they had increasing amounts of patronage at their disposal. But, as Culloden explained, the Campbell brothers had recently invited the King's displeasure. George I planned to visit Hanover. When Argyll heard of this he told the King bluntly that Britain, and especially Scotland, were far from secure. The King would be leaving an empty throne and a country still shaking from rebellion. George must empower his son and heir the Prince of Wales with decision-making powers as Regent while he was in their German homeland. George, however, loathed his son and ordered him to sit dumb, as a figurehead, until his father's return. He was not to fill any office, not even a lieutenancy in the Guards. Argyll advised the Prince of Wales to refuse his father's limits on his ruling powers. Better than any man in the land, Argyll knew how close the Jacobites had come to winning at Sheriffmuir. They ought to have won.

The King turned on Argyll and Ilay, his staunchest supporters in Scotland, thereby splitting the Whig Party into the King's faction and the Prince's faction. The Scottish Squadrone – Roxburghe, Montrose, the Duke of Atholl, Sir William Gordon, Justice Clerk Cockburn among them – were for the King. The Argyll faction insisted on an effective mandate to let the Prince of Wales rule in his father's absence.

Lovat put his head in his hands. He needed Argyll to persuade the King to sign the warrants granting him his lands to attract a wife. And now the King was cold-shouldering the Argyll Campbells. Being Lovat, he asked to speak with George I in person.

On Saturday 23 June, Lovat wrote to Duncan Forbes explaining, 'I had a private audience of King George this day … No man ever spoke freer language to his Majesty and the Prince than I of our two great friends,' Argyll and Ilay. Lovat assured George that Argyll and Ilay gave the Hanoverians 'more service and were capable to do them more service than all those of their ranks in Scotland', by which he meant the Squadrone.

Lovat was in a hurry to marry. His eye had fixed on Margaret Grant, sister of his comrade and fellow Argathelian, Brigadier Grant of Grant. It was not clear how well Lovat knew Margaret. Dynastic and geopolitical conjunction of the Frasers and the Grants, and the prospect of direct male heirs, stimulated Lovat's passion. The unity of Grants and Lovats would create the biggest power bloc in the Highlands. The clans had known each other for centuries, and by extension Lovat and Margaret ('Peggie') would know each other well enough already. Lovat flattered Argyll that one of his greatest motives to marry Margaret 'was to secure them the joint interest of the north'. It sounded almost as if he was courting Argyll not young Margaret.

Argyll's brother, Ilay, agreed but queried whether Lovat wasn't already married to Fraserdale's mother-in-law, Amelia, the dowager Lady Lovat. 'When I told him that the Lady denied, before the justice court, that I had anything to do with her, and that the pretended marriage was declared null' the Earl was half-satisfied. When Lovat added that 'the Minister and witnesses were all dead who were at the pretended marriage, he was satisfied', and said he would speak to the King.

However, on 28 June 1716, this Highland hegemony they were all constructing – Argyll, Ilay, the Forbeses, the Grants and Lovat – was rocked to the foundations when the King sacked Argyll and Ilay. 'It seems that the best of men must have their ups and downs,' Culloden told his brother. The dispute over the Prince of Wales's regency had done for them. The Forbes brothers reflected on the setback with calmness and reason: they approved of Argyll acting out of principle, even to his and their detriment; they were confident they would not be 'out' for long.

Not so Lovat, who threw off a letter to Duncan the next day in a whirl, and in French. 'The blow fell, the two dear brothers are disgraced … Never have gentlemen left the court with more noise or more regretted; no one knows the reason.' This was wild talk. Everyone knew the reason. Lovat was always at his most unreliable when emotionally overwrought. 'It's said that all their creatures will be treated the same. Goodbye. I don't know what I've written to you,' he gasped in a panic. 'I'm not myself and I don't know what will become of me.' Now his 'freer language' with the King marked him out as one adhering to disgraced ministers. Ilay had feared that scandal from

Lovat's past might affect their standing. If muck from this Campbell scandal stuck to Lovat, he would fall with them.

The news of the dismissal of Argyll and Ilay reached Inverness. Wightman heard it from William Strathnaver, the Squadrone Earl of Sutherland's alcoholic son and heir. The Argylls' disgrace 'was reported by a certain young Lord here ... [whose] head is always steeped in *aqua vitae*', Wightman said to Duncan Forbes. 'On my return home yesterday I meet this sweet gentleman, returning to Dunrobin, and indeed very ill, his face being of as many colours as the rainbow. But, for all that, he hopes to live to have the Regiment of Fusiliers.' That was to be Strathnaver's 'gratification' for his father's services. 'Good God, if it should be so, what a regiment of Flamecutters there will be in a short time.' Wightman shuddered to think of it. Strathnaver boasted he would give no man a commission who did not swallow a pint pot of brandy in one go for breakfast, and whose breath would torch a tree at fifty paces.

Lovat was panicking unnecessarily. The King, in the week before he left for Hanover, remembered his meeting with Lord Lovat and read the memorial from his Hanoverian officers and lairds in Inverness outlining Lovat's case. It urged the King to recall that the rebels, like Fraserdale, 'are declared to incur the penalty of £500 and a single and life rent escheat'. That is, he explained to the German King who might not know what an escheat was, 'the forfeiting all the goods and chattels, and the rents and profits of their estates during their lives'. Its purpose was to prevent the forfeited person from being in a fortunate enough position to raise men and money to engage in treasonable acts, yet without making a martyr of him. He was merely to be impoverished.

Lovat had not seemed to notice the implications of the escheat: it was limited to 'the lives' of the persons forfeit. Lovat walked into the anomalous position of wishing an extremely long life to Mackenzie of Fraserdale. 'The value of the [Lovat] lands is generally said to be about £500 yearly, but are very much encumbered with debts ... It is conceived that the immediate making ... a grant to a person of credit in the country ... would greatly tend to strengthen the hands of the government.' Lovat was 'humbly proposed' as the right recipient of the gift. The King listened and was 'graciously pleased to comply with what is desired in it', Stanhope said. The secretary was preparing the warrants for his signature.

All Lovat had to do was to wait in London for written confirmation of the gift. For the moment Lovat was overjoyed.

One or two of the Squadrone objected instantly: the Duke of Atholl ordered his son, Lord James, a Scottish peer in the Lords, to 'do what you can to have it stopped'. In the north, the creditors of the Lovat estates rushed to their lawyers to lodge objections, fearing for the repayment of the mountain of pretended and real debts. Squadrone allies of Fraserdale queried the competence of English law to resolve these Scottish cases. The Union preserved the independence of the Scottish judiciary. The 'Squad' doubted that Lovat's warrant for the escheat was valid under Scottish law. Lovat started to panic again. He launched a letter to Duncan Forbes in Edinburgh. 'The Justice Clerk [Cockburn], Montrose and all the rest' of the Squadrone 'were resolved to search all means to ruin me'. They had sent to Scotland to try and have his judgement overturned in the Court of Session. 'I beg you may put all the irons in the fire to get my business through ... in spite of the opposition you will meet with. I do not see how they can go against the King's positive orders and the advice of the King's lawyers.'

His missive clattered to a halt as he threw his plea at Duncan's feet, 'My dear General you must be active in it,' he cried. In Lovat's timeta-bling of his life, everything had to be done right now, 'this morning'. The closer he came to achieving his dream, the more anxious he was that someone would keep him out again.

While he waited to hear, he pressed on with his marriage plans, asking Argyll to speak up for him. Argyll agreed. The Duke was too impor-tant a magnate to keep out forever. In the wilderness for a season, he had time to do some favours for his dependants. Argyll was like a sheepdog keeping his sheep together. He wrote to the Grant elite one by one. 'Lord Lovat is one for whom I have, with good reason, the greatest esteem and respect, and as I confide entirely both in him and the Brigadier, I am most earnest that this match should take effect.' He urged the Brigadier's brother, Grant of Ballindallach, to use his influence to bring off the match 'which will, I think, unite all friends in the north, a union which will be very serviceable to his Majesty and his Royal Family, and no less so to all of us who have ventured our lives and fortunes in defence of it'.

Argyll's involvement flattered Grant. 'The Duke of Argyle and Earl of Ilay were both employed by Lord Lovat to speak to me *anent* my sister Peggie,' the Brigadier told Ballindallach when he asked his brother what was happening. The Brigadier consented to the marriage, he said, 'providing they please each other'. Lovat had income and posts. The Forfeited Estates Commissioners listed the yearly value of the Lovat estates at £783. 2s 11d sterling. In today's values, that means they yielded more than £100,000 per annum. It was a start. 'The gift of Fraserdale's escheat is passing in his fa[vour which], with good management and the debts he's already master of, will undoubtedly enable him to make the family estate of Lovat his own.' He knew Lovat had bought some estate debts back off the creditors already. 'These were the reasons, joined to that of so considerable alliance that moved me to consent.' The Frasers were an important clan and Lord Lovat was shaping up to be a powerful chief and British aristocrat.

Having exhausted all avenues of resistance between Inverness, Edinburgh and Westminster, Lovat's enemies could not prevent the law finally coming down in Lovat's favour. Walpole signed the Royal Warrant and Lovat prepared to marry, now able to offer his bride a share in 'all goods, gear, debts, and sums of money, jewels, gold, silver, coined and uncoined, utensils, domiciles, horse, nolt, sheep, corns, bonds, obligations, contracts, decrees, sentences, compromitts and all other goods, gear, escheatable whatever, as well not named as named, which pertained of before to Alexander Mackenzie of Fraserdale' and were now Lord Lovat's. The Lovats were even free to 'labour and manure' the lands. In addition, his Lordship was invested with the 'said Alexander's' life rent of all 'lands, heritages, tenements, annual rents, tacks, steadings, roomes, possessions, and others whatsoever, pertaining and belonging to him, with the whole mails, ferms, kaines, customs, casualties, profits and duties on the same'.

Lovat wrote to the Brigadier that he was ready to marry but understood the decision to accept his offer must be Peggie's. 'I would rather marry her chambermaid than marry her contrary to her inclination,' he told Grant. 'For if there is not a mutual inclination in that life rent bond, it must be a curse rather than a blessing,' as he knew only too well.

'With Lord Lovat I am sure she will be happy in a good man and a better estate,' Grant concluded. No one remarked that Lovat did not own the estate in perpetuity. If Fraserdale died tomorrow, it went to his son. 'Let her want for nothing that may be proper for Lord Lovat's Lady … to put her in the handsomest manner of my hand.'

Lovat obtained official permission to leave London and go home to marry. The Secretary of State approved. While negotiating the dowry, Lovat might check 'if any ill designs are carrying on there', the Secretary instructed him. Lovat noticed how anxiously the government enquired after the situation in the Highlands, and gave them what they wanted – information about subversive elements – and also what he wanted them to have – a slight unease that the Highlands was not properly settled yet, and a feeling they must put some money and positions behind men of proven loyalty and influence there. These men would make sure the area was peaceful and well managed, ensuring London did not need to bother about it.

In the depths of December 1716, the bridegroom, his servants, important household officers, and a tail of gentlemen of the clan set out from Castle Dounie for Castle Grant. Orders for quantities of provisions went out weeks before to the merchants of Elgin: 'Sixteen pound 12 ounces of white sugar at 12s the pound,' hops, raisins, cinnamon, '8 pound rice, at 6d. per pound' and other spices, all amounting to £69. 9s 6d (Scots) were ordered in. Then, half a hogshead of wine, at £7. 10s sterling arrived, with 7½ bolls of malt, and eleven bolls of barley for 'brewing aquavite'; plus '12 stones 3 pound butter, at £3. 6s. 8d. the stone', for baking. The list went on.

For the bride, there was 'cash sent to Aberdeen to buy necessary for Miss Margaret at the time of her marriage, as per Miss Wilson's account – £385. 12s'. A great Highland wedding lasted for many days; every neighbour and kinsman, haughty and humble, would be welcomed into Castle Grant. Lovat insisted Grant publish a letter about it in *The Courant*. If not, they would miss a chance to show the administration how significant they were in the north.

After days of feasting and dancing, the new Lady Lovat, mounted on a fine horse, was escorted by her husband out of Speyside, through the hills to Inverness and on to Castle Dounie. Along the way, cheering clansmen were rewarded with small coin from Lovat's purse. He stopped instantly when he recognised a face, to enquire after his 'cousin's' health. The muddiest hut dweller might merit an embrace, a polite exchange and a coin. They were kinsmen, all Frasers, and in that shared heritage, equals. Lovat loved the pageantry of his chieftainship. If only his father, brothers and the Reverend James were alive to share his triumph.

They celebrated the rehabilitation of a male Fraser with feasting, music, chess, singing, bardic verse, dancing, and good conversation. The kinsmen Fraserdale had not favoured, who had stayed loyal to Lovat, came riding out of the hills to welcome home MacShimidh, their chief. Lovat cemented his friendships with the Hanoverian elites around the Highland capital. He invited them all to share his display of old-style chiefly generosity. The fires blazed, servants rushed to and fro with platters of food, the piper blew up his bag in the hall at Castle Dounie. Lovat's guidons, swallow-tailed banners with crest and motto on them, flapped energetically from each tower.

A few miles away from Dounie, in a small grace-and-favour manor house, sat the ousted Lady Lovat, whom Lovat called Amelia Mackenzie of Fraserdale. She had no husband, and just a few servants and furnishings left. All her property had been gifted to Simon Fraser, whom she hated. She determined to get it all back with the aid of powerful Mackenzie and Murray supporters, creditors and friendly local faces, all now offering to help her lay traps for the Beaufort.

Two hundred and fifty miles south-west of Inverness, Amelia's husband, Mackenzie of Fraserdale, was wintering in gaol in Carlisle awaiting trial for treason. Fraserdale, one of the first to surrender after the rebellion was quelled, protested his innocence to anyone who would listen. He and his fellow rebels asked for an 'exculpation (as they call it) to preserve a livelihood to themselves and families, protesting that, if the government seized all they had, they'd as soon be hanged as be starved'. 'Exculpation' meant taking the culpability, or guilt, away from them. 'What reply can one make to these miserable creatures?' asked Bishop Nicol, who was there to witness the trials.

This was exactly the point Lord President Dalrymple and Duncan Forbes were making as the courts in Edinburgh deliberated over the rebels' cases. If the authorities utterly impoverished the rebels, they would have nothing left to lose, and might conspire again. As the rebel leaders in Carlisle said, they might as well hang for treason trying to restore their fortunes, as starve because they had lost everything that kept them within the pale of law and order. Crushing only worked if you crushed to death. Leaving a vital spark left the rebels room to resurrect themselves. Either be properly judicious, firm but benign – or crush to kill.

Bishop Nicol continued: 'Mr Mackenzie of Fraserdale (against whom an indictment was found by the grand jury on Saturday last) seems to be the likeliest person to bring on the debate,' about the legality of the English courts to try Scottish cases. 'This gentleman's case has been so variously represented that (without a formal trial) nobody can tell what to make of it.' Fraserdale was the test case. 'Some stoutly affirm, as himself does,' not surprisingly, 'that he never bore arms in the Pretender's camp.'

On the other hand, said the bishop, 'Lord Lovat has seized the life rent of his estate, and will probably be desirous to continue in possession.' Lovat did have the estates, but this remark misrepresented the situation. He had not 'seized' them. They were a royal gift, but Fraserdale and the Murrays got their wish. Fraserdale and his case moved to Edinburgh, where Squadrone judges and Law Lords got to work to overturn the guilty verdict, and suppress the gift of the estates to Lovat.

Amelia waited at home with their children to hear the judgement from Edinburgh. She loathed Lovat, and everyone around her said he was a brute and bandit. He led her poor father to drink himself to death; he had forcibly married and raped her mother, which led her to be subjected to a humiliating lawsuit. Her family afterwards had neglected her. The elder Amelia's undoer seemed now to have undone the daughter. This Amelia had many reasons to fight Lord Lovat.

James II and family, though Mary and Anne, James's daughters by his first wife, are not shown here. This is the Roman Catholic Royal Family in exile, the putative James 'III and VIII' on the left.

Mary II, wife of William of Orange, and eldest daughter of James II by his first – protestant – wife, Anne Hyde.

William of Orange, William III, widely loathed in Scotland, a country he neither visited nor understood.

James Stuart, 'The Old Pretender', devout but tolerant, brave but passive, not a man to seize a throne – and enemy of Lovat.

Louis XIV, in red high-heeled shoes, liked Lovat's schemes and patronised but then imprisoned the Fraser chief.

A view of Edinburgh in 1718, economically, politically and socially depressed a decade after the Union with England.

Major James Fraser of Castleleathers, sent by the Fraser lairds to retrieve their 'rightful chief' from exile in France, had a devil of a job rousing Lovat to act.

2nd Duke of Argyll, *Eoghan Dearg nan Cath,* 'Red John of the Battles', instrumental in obtaining Lovat's pardon from George I, after Lovat's service to the new king during the 1715 rebellion.

The Earl of Ilay, later 3rd Duke of Argyll, powerful Westminster politician, and Walpole's Scottish manager. Ilay favoured patronising the Forbeses over the Frasers and Grants, and soured Lovat against George II's regime.

Sir James Grant of Grant, MP, loyal Hanoverian, too amiable and inert by half for his aggressively active brother-in-law, Lovat.

The Battle of Prestonpans, the last battle to be won with broadswords, and the Jacobite victory that determined Lovat to throw in his lot with Bonnie Prince Charlie.

George II, last British monarch to lead his troops to victory in battle.

General George Wade, builder of the first roads to open up the Highlands. Intelligence expert, he liked and distrusted Lovat.

Bonnie Prince Charlie, easy to resist at a distance, but he dazzled and enchanted many who encountered him in the flesh.

Culloden. Last pitched battle on British soil, a total victory for Cumberland that annihilated the Jacobites. Reinforced by pacification of the region, its brutality was fuelled by the fear and anger Jacobite successes had stoked in most Britons.

William, Duke of Cumberland, 'Butcher' Cumberland to the Jacobites, 'The Conquering Hero' to Handel and the British government. He was loved by his men, and determined to do what he needed to ensure the Highlands could never rise again and threaten the security of Great Britain.

Lovat as a barefoot Catholic monk. Scores of cartoons and stories fed the public's appetite for scandal about him after he was captured. This plays on a rumour that Lovat was a Jesuit cleric in France and debauched women coming to him to make their confession.

Lovat as a young man, in armour and ready to defend his king. Which king, was a question asked about him for sixty years.

TWENTY

'What a lion cannot manage, the fox can', 1717–18

'This Gift ... the most precarious thing on earth'
– LOVAT TO DUNCAN FORBES

That winter of 1717, in her small house on the Lovat estates, friends and family continued to comfort and counsel Amelia Lovat on how to get rid of Simon Fraser. She must not accept her loss. There were three ways she could retrieve her properties. The first was already in hand – engineering the exemption of the Lovat estates from being forfeited by her husband's rebellion. This contention rested on the claim that they belonged not to Fraserdale but to Amelia, and she was no rebel.

This first round of judgements in Edinburgh had already gone her way. By a 'Decree of Exception' the court in Edinburgh declared the estate was not forfeited to the Crown. Amelia's Murray and Mackenzie connections persuaded her to lodge a claim for the estates and the resumption of her entitlement to the rents from them, under a 'resuming clause'. The logic was, if 'excepted' from forfeit, she could then 'resume' her ownership of them. If so, the new Lord and Lady Lovat were cuckoos to be dispossessed and evicted. Atholl had then moved in Fraserdale's favour to obtain his pardon, but in this he failed.

Second, she had a fistful of Mackenzie relations who were ready to swear they were her creditors and she and Fraserdale had defaulted on their debts. As her creditors, they were legally entitled to first call on all the rents of the Lovat estates. Coincidentally, they asserted a level of indebtedness that exceeded the total income of the estates and would bankrupt the estates if they enforced their bonds. This was the argument being adopted up and down the country by Scottish Jacobites in order to prevent the government getting their hands on their estates and income.

The third option was to play the long game. Wait for her husband to die, and then everything would revert to Hugh, her son.

On his side, Lovat had three ways to stop her. First, he could claim that most of the asserted debts were 'trumperies'. Second, he could try to get the honours and titles of Lovat back in the male line. Third, he needed to change the terms of King George I's gift to him from Fraserdale's lifetime to perpetuity; he was upset this had not been the original term anyway. Without perpetual title to all he gained, he might just as well give up now; Fraserdale could die any day.

He was too determined to be down hearted for long though. He had seen such a marvellous reverse in his fortunes in the last year, he was sure it must continue. The Frasers' preference for their natural chief had brought him back, out of exile; but one glance at the contents of his desk told him it was the machinery of the British state that would most likely let him and his family stay. It would mean more lawsuits, more time, money and energy. He already had debts. The funds just did not exist to fight in the highest courts in the kingdom, the Court of Session in Edinburgh, and the Houses of Commons and Lords in London.

No sooner had Lord Lovat and Margaret established themselves at Dounie than one summons after another was delivered to Lovat's table, claiming that he (in his role as representative of the Lovat estates) owed monies the previous incumbents had refused to repay. Lovat set to work. He too had allies in the Scottish judiciary. In Duncan Forbes, Deputy of the Court of Session, he found an advocate who, everyone had to admit, acted for him 'with disinterestedness, very rarely to be found in gentlemen of the long robe'.

He had to borrow more. He would take out loans secured on his only asset, his clan lands. When he won, he would get rewards, judgements in his favour, places, gratifications; his financial worries would be over. If he lost, God forbid, his clan would be set on the path to bankruptcy. The words of his old chronicler the Reverend James were wonderful and inspiring; but not in the light of common day, in early 1717, ordinary time, not mythic clan time. If he was to bring his clan out of the penury to which it had been reduced since a Mackenzie woman first married a Fraser chief, he would need to take a more modern approach.

The ordinary men of the clan waited for the change of weather to come in, mixing fine days and foul, to allow them to get back to the land. They waited to know what was going to happen to their cottages and agricultural lands, the farms and hill grazings. At Dounie, land-grabbing lawsuits poured in. The purpose of Lovat's life now was measured in the petty remorselessness of libel actions. How would his chronicler record that and make it a feat of heroism worthy of his ancestors?

At the end of January 1717, Lovat wrote to Duncan about the looming crises. He was driven mad by the thought of how temporary was the King's gift. 'I have several calls from London,' he wrote. Fraser of 'Foyers assures me that the Squade have resolved … to break me as to my commissions, and as to my Gift … I most humbly beg of my dear General to employ Sir Walter Pringle,' an Edinburgh lawyer, 'and whom else you please, and consult together of some legal way of my keeping possession of this estate … which I look upon as the most precarious thing on earth … Either I must keep violent possession, which will return me my old misfortunes,' fighting and outlawry, 'or I must abandon the kingdoms, and a young lady whom my friends … engaged me to marry … if I do not find any legal pretence of possessing the estate but by this gift, which I now reckon as nothing. The thoughts of all this confuse my brain; so excuse my write and style.' Surely, thought Duncan, he was not seriously thinking of returning to France.

Forbes counselled calm. Lovat must fight through the regular channels of the Court and the courts. Duncan would help him to win, he assured him. Lovat told his wife he must pack and leave to fight the legal actions seeking to take their home and country from them.

*   *   *

Were the Mackenzie creditors genuine or fraudulent, that was the question facing Lovat and his legal representatives? Some claims looked very odd indeed when Duncan unrolled them. In far too many, the original debtor was Sir Roderick Mackenzie of Prestonhall, deceased, and the creditor was a cousin. Sir Roderick entered into these debt arrangements when Lovat was in prison in France. The 'express clause' was that Fraserdale and his wife and their baby son Hugh were 'burdened with all the lawful debts' and responsible for any repayments outstanding on Sir Roderick's 'decease'.

Duncan Forbes and Lovat objected that Sir Roderick had died nearly ten years ago, and ever since no creditor had come before the Court of Session and pressed for repayments, or complained about Fraserdale defaulting – until today. Duncan and Lovat were well aware that the scheme in many of these Jacobite prosecutions involved the creditors, who on examination, were all friends and relations of the debtor, but had not pressed their claims for years, suddenly needing all their money back right now. The debtors could not or would not pay and the Lovat estates were signed off to the creditors in lieu of the cash. After a decent length of time, the so-called creditors then reassigned the estates back to their debtor cousin.

Lovat lost. The Court of Session found in favour of the creditors and issued warrants against the Lovats investing the creditors with 'the lands, Lordship' and everything else that they said was legally liable to be seized to pay their debts. This was what Amelia and her backers needed. They appointed a factor, a man called Robertson, to go onto the Lovat estates and lift the rents in cash and kind. They could use violence if the tenantry resisted, and arrest goods to the value of the rent if no rents were forthcoming.

Argyll and the Forbeses told Lovat that since the courts in Edinburgh were so partial and vulnerable to Atholl–Mackenzie influence, he would have to get his case referred to the British Parliament for appeal. Lovat packed his travelling chest. It was ironic. He, who loathed the Union, now sought to use the body at the heart of it, the British Parliament, against the Scottish legal system.

Lovat wrote to Lord Stanhope, who, as Secretary of State, shared almost equal power with Walpole in the leadership of the Commons. He wanted to come to London, he said, 'both to represent the present condition of this country to your Excellency and to endeavour to hinder my enemies from doing anything for the convicted rebel Fraserdale'. Stanhope had to refuse permission. Intelligence about another invasion had been passed to the British and all officers had been ordered to remain at their posts. Lovat had to obey. Meanwhile, 'I hope and beg that your Excellency may protect and support me in my gift, if it comes in dispute before the House of Commons,' he asked the Secretary of State. No one had served them better 'since his Majesty was pleased to give me the bread [gift] that's now taken from me' by the judgement of the Court of Session.

In a postscript, he added some intelligence to keep Stanhope's attention. 'I am certainly informed Seaforth has landed in Lewis, and arms landed … I have been at pains and expense for intelligence this year.' Without salaries they all put in huge expenses claims.

When the threat of invasion calmed down, Lovat was allowed to go to London to listen to the debate about him in the Commons. Afterwards, Culloden wrote of it to his brother Duncan. For over two hours 'Lovat's gift run the gauntlet' of their political enemies 'this day in the House of Commons, by reason of a resuming clause in favour of Fraserdale's lady, presented by Lord James Murray'. The 'Squadrone were pleased to belch out a great many scurrilous reflections against Lovat; but all to no purpose; for the gift subsists as it did, and in a great measure owing to Mr Walpole and honest Mr Smith who … would not desert Lovat.' He had trumped them! He still needed to change the condition of ownership from remaining 'as it did', but it was a start.

Lovat submitted an appeal to the House of Lords to overturn the judgement of the Lords of Session in Edinburgh. He instructed his kinsmen at home to resist the Mackenzie creditors' agents wherever they appeared, whatever justification they offered. But before he could roll up these lawsuits and go to the Lords to rid himself of these phoney creditors, fever struck him down.

TWENTY-ONE

Matters of life and death, 1718–21

'The most sincere sentiments of my heart'
− LOVAT TO THE
GENTLEMEN OF HIS CLAN

Coming back to his lodgings from Parliament, Lovat collapsed in exhaustion. Servants pulled shut the windows of his rented house. The panes kept out the 'gross stinking Foggs, scents and vapours' they believed carried disease in to the patient. Banked up with blankets, temperature rising, he longed to change the foul London air for that of the Highlands. He believed he was going to die. This was the end of his journey, to fall before the finishing post, one foot over the threshold of his home and estates, one foot hanging over the abyss. He worried that he had failed in his responsibilities. After 500 years, the Fraser name would be gone in a generation.

A physician arrived with his bag of 'lancets, boluses, confections, and electuaries'. From the pocket of his frockcoat, he tugged out 'a big sand glass' and counted Lord Lovat's pulse. The first treatment he recommended was a phlebotomising – blood-letting. British people shed more blood in peace than in time of war. The doctor then consulted manuals of the healing arts. For a pestilential fever like this, Lovat could 'have a cataplasm of snails beaten and put to the soles of the feet'. Fevers induced sore eyes. For this he might take 'pigeon's blood hot to the eyes, or a young caller pigeon slit in the back'. Despite trying a selection of remedies, Lovat got weaker. By 4 April 1718, he could barely sit up or hold a pen. It was time to dictate a testament for his people. He must tell them what he died for.

'My Dear Friends,' he said, 'this is the last time of my life I shall have occasion to write to you ... The greatest happiness I proposed to myself under heaven was to make you live happy.' What of lasting value would his words leave? He had produced no son. He enjoyed no permanent and unchallenged possession of his titles and clan territories. 'I designed my poor commons live at their ease and have them always well clothed and well armed, after the Highland manner, and not to suffer them to wear low country clothes,' like trousers, 'but make them live like their forefathers, with the use of their arms, that they might always be in a condition to defend themselves against their enemies, and do service to their friends.' The letter was a manifesto on clanship's values and fears. It was also a detailed picture of Lovat's internal landscape, a vision that combined the imaginary and the historical. To his mind, this way of life was all that preserved them 'from the wicked designs of the family of Tarbat [Mackenzies] and Glengarry, joined to the family of Athol'.

Should the Fraser gentry, 'falsely, for little private interest and views, abandon your duty to your name and suffer a pretended heiress and her Mackenzie children to possess your country ... to chase you by slight and might ... out of your native country ... you will be like the miserable ... Jews, scattered and vagabonds throughout the unhappy kingdom of Scotland.' Their children will curse them in their graves as 'cowardly, knavish men, who sold and abandoned their chief, their name, their birthright, and their country for a false and foolish present gain, even as most of Scots people curse this day those who sold them and their country to the English by the fatal Union which I hope will not last long.' The Scottish nationalist cursed the Union which the British peer served George I to defend. A cash-based economy; private enterprise that favoured the individual over common endeavour – new values were creeping into the homes of the Gaelic-Highland lairds and pushing apart the foundations of their society. Lovat sank back onto his pillows and despatched the letter to the Highlands. He glanced here at the basis of quarrels he had with certain Fraser gentlemen, who had thrown over the bonds of clanship to live and work contentedly under the Mackenzies.

As he lay in what he believed was his deathbed, the Mackenzie creditors contested the authority of the British Parliament to reverse the decision of Scotland's highest judicial body. Under the Articles of Union, the Scottish judiciary was independent and kept jurisdiction in these cases, they said. They asserted they were owed over £6,000 (over £750,000 in today's money). Duncan Forbes responded tartly that the British Parliament was the last resort for all Britons seeking justice, and the Scots were also British. The impasse could not hold. Duncan tried to cheer him up. 'I got your mock letter of my burial,' Lovat thanked Duncan. A month later, Lovat was pleased to report that after taking a vomit he felt better at last. He could not afford to stay away from the Highlands any longer.

Lovat climbed the stone turnpike stair at Castle Dounie, and bent his head to go through a narrow arched door on the first floor, entering the great hall. It gave him the most powerful pleasure to be here. Rooms led off it in the other three corners. One was his. One was his wife's. One was a withdrawing room, the privy. In her room, Lady Lovat sat before a fire. She pushed herself from the chair. Lovat liked the way her swelling belly lifted the belt of her dress. She was delighted to see her Lord back home, but thought he looked careworn, thin and ill.

He greeted Margaret, Castleleathers and Fraser of Phopachy in Gaelic. He had made Phopachy his chamberlain. The clan elite, the *fine*, attended her Ladyship to advise on managing the estates in her Lord's absence. Phopachy and Castleleathers told their chief they were struggling to control the Mackenzies gathered around Amelia. On his own behalf, Phopachy presented his debt for settlement, contracted when Lovat had to flee in 1702. It had fallen due when Lovat was reinstated. Still worn out, Lovat raged that he had nothing to pay with, and it was not matured until he had permanent title to his lands. This he did not have, though Phopachy must agree he was trying as hard as he could to rectify that. Neither of them had foreseen this scenario of temporary restoration when they agreed the terms of the loan. Phopachy must wait. Phopachy demanded something back. The two men rowed bitterly.

Castleleathers's brother-in-law would not climb down. He insisted the two of them, the chief as the debtor and Phopachy the creditor, submit the decision on Phopachy's bond to arbitration. Lovat had to agree. Arbitration had the binding force of Scottish and British law, though it was a native Gaelic regulating structure. Phopachy presented his account. Lovat's defence was quixotic – he said he was mad with fear for his life at the time he entered into the arrangement. He could not be held liable for decisions made during the period of lunacy. The arbitrators heard him out, and declared unanimously for Phopachy. Lovat offered to reissue the bond to Phopachy, with a five-year term. Phopachy accepted it, and even loaned his chief more money.

Typical of a man brought up in proximity to a great house, but not the son of the person responsible for the day-to-day problems of thousands of tenants and their homes and livelihoods, their hundreds of requests and complaints, Lovat lived out an idealised image of his role. The ideal inspired him to achieve the impossible, but made it hard for him to adapt to his role in a changing world. While he had been in exile, Highland society had changed, yet he imagined it was still as he had left it. When the largely self-sufficient members of his clan gentlemen queried his actions, he overreacted to any criticism and dismissed them with impatience. These men should not challenge his authority. Even Castleleathers, who had risked his life to bring Lovat home, now sided with his brother-in-law against his chief.

The following January, 1719, Duncan stepped in to help Lovat win his appeal in the House of Lords. No wonder Lovat had no money. His legal actions passed back and forth between the Court of Session in Edinburgh and the Houses of Parliament. The costs appalled him. Money melted in London. Although finding in favour of Lovat, the Lords issued a proviso. 'Such debts of the creditors … as were real,' were still binding and chargeable against the estates. Always, thought

Lovat, the partial victory, the limited prize to temper his joy. The Mackenzie lawyers fell on the word 'real' debts. It was a terrible tug of war between two evenly matched sides. Both hung on to their claims for dear life. Lovat sent out Phopachy to collect his rents.

Amelia's agent, Robertson, also rode through Lovat's country to collect rents to meet the 'real' debts and the allowance she had to live on. When Phopachy called on the tenantry after Robertson, he was told Amelia's 'receiver' had already taken them, in cash and kind. This could not go on. Robertson's house was within two miles of Dounie. Lovat rode across and ordered him to stay off Fraser lands. Robertson ignored him. Like his mistress, Robertson regarded Lovat with contempt, as an outlaw and a rapist. This *arriviste* chief would be gone the minute his mistress's husband died anyway. Lovat and Robertson quarrelled violently.

In the middle of the night a couple of days later, Robertson woke to the sound of animals in a panic, and the smell of burning timber. Horrified, he roused his household. They rushed outside to see 'corn, barns and other outhouses' collapsing to the ground, 'to the great loss and terror of the owner and his family'. A lot of Amelia's farm rents were in those buildings. The Mackenzies conjectured who was behind the arson. 'Wilful fire-raising is regarded as a crime of a very deep dye, and is punishable as treason,' said a contemporary account. Under feudalism all property was the King's property. To attack his property was to attack his person. Unnerved, Robertson did not stay to press his suit, despite Mackenzie pressure to do so, and left Lovat country.

The previous spring, the death at St Germains of James II's widow, Mary of Modena, exposed how unsettled Britain still was five years into George's reign. Mary's pensions, the subsistence of many leading Jacobites for so many years, died with her. She was the last link with real power for the Jacobites. Her death threw her followers into panic.

Philip V of Spain offered to help. Eager to reassert Spanish authority in Europe, he had diverted a fleet, equipped for him by Pope Clement VI, to be used to defeat the Ottomans. Instead, Philip sent it to seize Sardinia and Sicily. For some time, Spain had also been stopping British shipping on the high seas, demanding to search for contraband. The Spanish suspected the British of trading illegally with Spanish colonies in America. On 17 December 1718, the British declared war on Spain. The Spanish first minister, Cardinal Alberoni, took the war to mainland Britain, and in the spring of 1719 persuaded Philip to fund the Jacobites to invade Britain and return the Roman Catholic 'James III and VIII' to power.

On 7 March 1719, the first wave of the campaign, with the Irish Duke of Ormonde at the head of several thousand men, sailed from Cadiz. When the news reached England, Walpole ordered his intelligence network to find out their destination urgently.

Off Cape Finisterre in Brittany, Ormonde's fleet encountered a severe storm that scattered and damaged it, forcing a return to Spain. The second prong of the attack, a little diversionary fleet to Scotland, knew none of this when the Earl Marischal, the Earl of Seaforth, the Marquis of Tullibardine (eldest son of the Duke of Atholl) and 307 Spaniards reached Stornoway on the Isle of Lewis in late April 1719. They moved to the mainland on the Scottish west coast, landing at Eilean Donan Castle.

Unable to suppress his latent Jacobitism, Lovat wrote in secret to his 'Cousin Seaforth' to 'encourage and desire him to come down with his men; and that he, Lord Lovat, would join with all his'. Lovat hated some of Seaforth's Mackenzie kin as predators to his estates, but he felt affection for their high chief as a devoted supporter of their rightful Stuart King. George I was never more than a usurper; Lovat's support for him was opportunistic. Jacobitism was always with Lovat, though mostly hidden under lock and key.

His next letter was as Governor of the Castle and troops in Inverness. Lovat wrote to Stanhope to ask for arms, men and money to defend the country from the rebel force lying on the west coast. Instead of getting more funds from the Secretary of State, Lovat received a furious reply, reporting some political gossip from their Squadrone opponents: apparently Lovat had offered Inverness to the Earl of Seaforth. The administration ordered General Wightman north at once to take charge of the government resistance to the invasion. Lovat galloped south to defend himself, and deny the allegations. Before leaving he ordered his gentlemen to raise the clan and put themselves under Wightman.

It was not difficult for Lovat to deny the rumour. He had worked with energy and diligence on the government's behalf for nearly five years now, sincere in wanting to serve his political masters well to earn places and positions. His friends and patrons were sure this rumour was a hate campaign by Lovat's political enemies. Among the letters waiting for Lovat in London, however, one made his heart skip a beat. It was from the dowager Countess of Seaforth.

She asked if there was anything the Governor could do to speed her son's pardon with the King? Seaforth had agreed to bring out his clan in rebellion again because he had nothing to lose, she said. A pardon would give him his liberty and property and he would not jeopardise those again. Lovat understood Seaforth's position more perfectly than his mother could imagine. He wrote back. In exchange for pleading Seaforth's pardon, Lovat asked about 'a paper that might be trouble-some to me'. Perhaps 'you would be so kind just as to send it to me?', he asked. She did. When a friend of Lovat's saw it, he said 'there was enough to condemn thirty Lords' in it and threw it into the fire. Lovat knew he must cut out this dangerous spiritual and emotional attach-ment to the Stuarts, or it would destroy him.

By the time Lovat was back on the road towards home, General Wightman had received intelligence about the Jacobites' decision to launch an attack on Inverness, where they counted on raising the supporters who had come out in 1715. Wightman marched south-west, down the Great Glen along the banks of Loch Ness, to meet them on his own terms. He passed through Stratherrick-Fraser coun-try and gathered Lovat's men as he went. Some of Lovat's lairds, such as Castleleathers, himself a committed Hanoverian, noted how his chief went out of his way not to be able to take up arms against the Jacobites, whenever he could.

On 10 June, Wightman appeared at the foot of a hill in Glen Shiel, where the Jacobites and Spanish marines were encamped. They recon-noitred the ground, and Wightman decided to attack a detachment of

Jacobite soldiers placed on the right of the main rebel force, on the other side of the River Shiel.

While battle raged at Glen Shiel, Lovat was at home with his wife who was in labour. Margaret was prescribed 'an hysteric cordial julep which is provoking and whereof she may take a third part when it comes' – labour pains – 'and the other third part (if she is not delivered in the time) two hours thereafter, and what remains two hours after that; in the meantime, let her walk and take snuff or what may provoke sneezing. I wish her a happy hour and safe delivery.' The doctor did not advise lying on her back in a bed. No one would.

Margaret plodded through her labour, sneezing, and drinking vomit-inducing cordials, and eventually gave birth to a healthy daughter. Given Lovat's passion for a male heir, it was disappointing, but this tiny lamb was his first legitimate Lovat child and he loved her for that. Even a wee girl had possibilities. He told his wife they must call her Georgina, and wrote to the King to crave his royal consent to be her godfather. This was no time to be rebelling against a Crown that, however sluggishly, was helping him in his life's ambition after twenty years. King George agreed.

The King's present was a silver christening plate, richly inlaid with gold gilt, twenty inches in diameter, having the Royal Arms of Great Britain and Ireland engraved in the centre, and chased round the circular edge. It weighed a satisfying eight pounds. Lovat sent it to Inverness to be engraved: 'This is the Christening Plate that King George gave as a gift to Simon, Lord Fraser of Lovat when his Majesty was godfather to his daughter Georgina, born at Inverness, the 10th of June, 1719.'

The Mackenzies did not rejoice. In Edinburgh they asked for the entire Lovat estates to be sequestered, and a new factor to be appointed. The Law Lords of the Court of Session, smarting from the overturn of their august opinions by the House of Lords in London, agreed and insulted Lovat further by appointing Fraserdale's old chamberlain, William Fraser, to be the new factor. In Westminster the Lords reacted swiftly, ruling that the Court of Session had contravened the wishes of their King by rendering his gift to Lord Lovat worthless. The Mackenzies were one of the most rebellious Jacobite kindreds, disaffected to his Majesty's rule. Forfeiting the Mackenzie estates (another of the King's wishes) was proving impossible and dangerous. One man was attacked and died in the attempt, and a third was told he also could collect the rent in lead shot. Now members of this tribe were trying to correct the King about forfeits and rents. None of the Mackenzies' actions were acceptable to Lord Lovat or his allies.

It had become obvious over the years that the quickest way for Lovat to get rid of his plague of petitioners was to have the power to act for himself, rather than sue through intermediaries. A general election had been called. If he could become one of the sixteen Scottish peers elected to sit in the House of Lords, or if he could control tame MPs in the Commons, as Argyll and Walpole did, he could speak on his own behalf in the Lords and his loyal MPs would represent his interests in the Commons. That way his business could be done for half the time and half the money.

Yet he continued to play a perilous double game. Lovat could not resist using one of the Jacobite spies, moving between France and Britain, to communicate with James Stuart, who had married a Polish princess (Maria Clementina Sobieska) in May 1719. They resided at Palazzo Muti in Rome under the protection of the Pope. On 31 December the following year, Clementina presented her husband with a son, Charles Edward Louis John Casimir Silvester Severino Maria Stuart, later known as Bonnie Prince Charlie. Now there were two generations of male Stuart claimants to the British thrones to fight for.

In September 1721 Lovat received a pardon from 'James III and VIII' under the Great Seals of England and Scotland 'upon his returning to his duty'. Lovat did not consider he needed a pardon, and he certainly could not return to any duty to James. Jacobitism was a strictly private passion in this climate. The following spring, just weeks before the British general election of 1722, Lovat received from

James a commission as a major-general. Lovat hid away these patents in his charter chest, and locked the lid. They helped cancel out some of the humiliation of those years of imprisonment. In the meantime, Lord Lovat was the loyal servant of King George I and his officers, and they had an election to win.

TWENTY-TWO

Networking from Inverness, 1722–24

'All Inverness is yours'
— LOVAT TO JOHN FORBES OF CULLODEN MP

Comparing himself to Argyll, Lovat felt that a landowner such as the Fraser chief ought to control at least a couple of MPs at Westminster. He could then look after them and someone like Argyll would look after him in return for his votes. When Lovat left Britain in 1702, the new form of government was only fourteen years old. He had not paid attention to it. Twenty years and a handful of general elections later it was assuming the character it would keep for a greater part of the century.

Politics was tied up with the business of patronage: positions, pensions, places, gratifications, commissions, and all the other names for the financial and honorary rewards through which the Crown and government kept their supporters loyal and ensured their policies were carried through. It was how MPs, who received no salary, obtained their incomes. On one side, they promoted the policies of the vested interests that put them in Parliament – usually a landed magnate who sat in the Lords. On the other, they offered to serve the ministers with most patronage to offer, and were rewarded. Out of a total of 12–15,000 government perks, the Treasury (which meant Walpole, the First Lord of the Treasury and Stanhope, the Secretary of State) had seventy-five per cent in its gift – a huge patronage pot with which to buy loyalty. But patronage was not that easy to come

206

by; there were more people after the jobs than even Walpole could satisfy. Petitioners had to come with substantial offers of support.

Lovat's neighbours, the Forbeses – whom he unwisely still considered to be retainers, as they had been a hundred years before – had access to Argyll and Ilay. Ilay grew closer to Walpole every year. Culloden was already MP for Inverness, and voted in favour of every Argyll or Walpolean policy in the Commons. Duncan Forbes, one of the county's leading lawyers, was MP of the Ayr burghs seat – a seat in Argyll's gift, 200 miles away from Culloden. Duncan was looking for a seat nearer to home in the upcoming general election, and Lovat needed an MP who depended on him for his position. Duncan had been very helpful over Lovat's legal actions. Lovat thought about what he had to offer and to whom to offer it. Inverness returned two MPs – one for the shire, the county seat; and one for the burgh. He considered these seats as traditionally in the gift of 'my Lord Lovat'. There were several things not quite accurate about his reading of the situation, but it did not matter just for the moment. He would control the MPs and offer them to Argyll or Walpole in exchange for gratifications.

Lovat knew Culloden received a pension of £500 a year to keep the ministry informed about the state of the Highlands. Culloden did what he could to encourage clan chiefs to remain law-abiding at home. In London he gave his opinion on who should be patronised and who could be overlooked. He did it in concert with Argyll and Ilay, and even Walpole listened to them. No commoner could go higher than Walpole. He was in effect Prime Minister, though the title did not yet exist. At the polls, Duncan fought for himself and his brother. The Forbeses had no sense of Lovat's appraising eye on them. In fact, they assumed he owed them gratitude for their support in 1715, and subsequently in the business of the Lovat estates.

The brothers positioned themselves as intermediaries, brokering information about the Highlands to Westminster, and vice versa. They were trusted. They had the ear of the powerful, and rewards flowed in at a steady pace. Lovat saw how the Forbeses worked the system. In their youth they had been famed as 'the greatest bouzers in the north'. They still networked through conviviality, but were now serious, professional, middle-aged men. They acted with high-mindedness and integrity. This was why Duncan had been prepared to fight in the courts so energetically for Lovat's right to enjoy his gift. He was certain Lovat had justice on his side. Yet in the months coming up to the election, Lovat ran against the sharp edge of Duncan's principles when the Mackenzies came back to court yet again, maintaining Lord Lovat was obliged to maintain Fraserdale's son, Hugh.

As innocent heir to the titles and estates of Lovat upon his father's death, Hugh was legally entitled to a house and land on his inheritance. With these and some supplementary income from the rest of the estates, he could support himself until that day of grief and joy for the Mackenzies, when they lost their kinsman Fraserdale, but regained the Lovat estates for his son. Duncan Forbes supported the young man's claim. He agreed that at present, in law, Hugh Mackenzie was the rightful heir. Lovat could not stomach the hint of it for a second. He was furious with Duncan for such an act of betrayal. Duncan was his ally, and his social inferior. Duncan thinking for himself made Lovat wonder if these Forbeses would be the right men to do his business in Parliament.

As election day, fixed for 13 March, approached, Lovat drew away from Culloden and Duncan. Blood was thicker than lawyer's ink, he decided. He suggested his brother-in-law, Sir James Grant of Grant, contest the Inverness-shire seat with Culloden. As Culloden himself admitted, Lovat's votes had been crucial to his electoral success in 1715. The Forbeses counted on that support; its withdrawal could be crucial. Lovat told the Fraser lairds qualified to vote that John Forbes of Culloden must be ousted to clip the Forbeses' wings. They would support Duncan for the time being. Lovat's brother-in-law, chief of a large and ancient clan, bound to the Frasers by marriage and history, must be voted in. Grant could then offer Argyll and Ilay a very impressive network of Fraser–Grant connections in the north. The gentlemen of both clans would profit by the commissions that came up from London, Lovat promised his lairds, to empower the Frasers and Grants to keep the peace. The Fraser bloc vote moved to the Grants:

Grant was duly returned as MP for the shire seat of Inverness, and Culloden was ousted. Duncan gained the Inverness burghs seat and Lovat congratulated him.

Lovat settled to his desk and reviewed the state of North Britain for his Majesty. As Governor of Inverness, chief of one of the most prominent clans, and pensioner of George I, he felt it his duty to inform the King that things were not all well in his northern British territories. Lovat inferred the King was not kept very well informed by his informants such as Culloden, who were paid handsomely for the job. Lovat complained that the Highlanders were 'very ignorant, illiterate and in constant use of arms', flatly contradicting his letter of wishes from his deathbed in 1718, where he had implored them to stay true to their traditions.

To address these problems, the King must overhaul the system of royal appointments to the positions of Sheriffs, Lord Lieutenants and JPs. As a result of inept distribution of these favours, there was poor local management of the area. 'Robberies go on without restraint', blackmail was a thriving business for some lawless lairds, and undermined the trade in black cattle that gave the weak economy much-needed income, Lovat reported. What regular soldiers there were could not keep order because they were foreigners who spoke no Gaelic and lumbered in the wake of fleet-footed Highland bandits in the hills and moors. Ordinary Highlanders spoke only Gaelic and the English-speaking soldiers could not form any relationship with them except that of occupier and occupied. High county office must be offered to loyal men who were already eminent in their communities, thanks to their birth and upbringing, he said. Centrally, Lovat recommended that the Independent Companies of foot soldiers should be revived. George I had ordered them to be disbanded in 1717, when the threat of an uprising seemed low, many companies were inactive, and many of their captains were using the salaries intended for the soldiers' maintenance to supplement their own private incomes.

Under both systems a group of fighting men were kept in a state of readiness to fight. The failed 1719 invasion reminded the authorities in London that some kind of militia force to guard and police the peripheries of the kingdoms was desirable. Lovat suggested the revived companies be led by loyal Highland magnates of good proven family. All this Lord Lovat humbly submitted to his Majesty for his consideration. The ministers in London thought Lord Lovat's memorial full of stimulating observations, but found themselves tangled up in the many threads of Highland self-interest. They advised George I to send someone north to assess the situation.

In 1724, General George Wade, about the same age as Lord Lovat, arrived in Inverness with a reputation as an internal security expert. His brief was to investigate 'how far the memorial delivered ... by Simon, Lord Lovat, and his remarks thereupon are founded on facts', and how far the 'remedies mentioned' by Lovat were the right ones. This chief was making quite an impression on the King. Lovat's opinions interested George. The noble Lord Lovat's memorial in his pocket, Wade set himself to observe the strengths and resources of the Highlands, and advise on measures necessary to 'civilise' them and cast out 'barbarity' – that is, anything distinctly Highland, Gaelic or clannish.

To Wade's eye, the region existed entirely in 'a state of anarchy and confusion'. He agreed with Lovat that efforts to disarm the Highlanders after the 1715 risings had left the Jacobite clans better armed than before. They had handed in obsolete weapons, which had been bought by the boatload from Holland, and were compensated for their 'losses', while hiding their good guns at home and leaving the law-abiding clans to obey orders properly and disarm themselves. Wade estimated there were about 22,000 fighting men in the Highlands, 10,000 of whom were well affected to King George. Most of the rest stood 'ready, whenever encouraged by their Superiors or Chiefs of Clan, to create new Troubles and rise in arms in favours of the Pretender'.

Wade liked much of what Lovat concluded, and saw several potential security problems in the region. However, the General was extremely puzzled by the Fraser chief. Lord Lovat, MacShimidh, or both, seemed in a way Wade could not quite pinpoint to be as much a part of the problem as the solution.

TWENTY-THREE

Lovat under Wade's eye, 1725–27

'Vain of his clan, the Fraziers,
and ready to sacrifice everything to their interest'
– JOHN CLERK OF PENICUIK ABOUT LOVAT

Wade, the intelligence adviser, had to consider the implications of disclosures from a man who lived at Castle Dounie by standards he claimed to deplore. The two men arranged to meet at Inverness Castle, where Lovat presented himself to the General as Simon Fraser, the 11th Lord Lovat – frockcoat, lace cuffs and legal documents to the fore. Wade was here to advise on the management of what Lovat described as 'that part of Scotland [that] is very barren and unimproven, has little or no trade, and not much intercourse with the Low Country … [where] the people wear their ancient habit, convenient for their wandering up and down and peculiar habit of living, which inures them to all sorts of fatigue. Their language, being a dialect of Irish, is understood by none but themselves.'

The next day, Lovat came as MacShimidh, eighteenth chief of the name Fraser – dressed 'in the ancient habit' and accompanied by a brace of Highland gentlemen. Here was the head and heart of a clanned power that identified itself as Fraser first, Scottish second, and British by shameful derogation of their identity; the head of a kindred who had lived according to the laws of clanship for 500 years, and who dominated his country with the power and mystique of a divinely appointed prince. Wade had to admit that Lovat was uniquely qualified to speak about what motivated the Highlanders.

Feuding and raiding threatened the peace, said Lovat. The clans 'grow averse to all notions of peace and tranquillity – they constantly practise their use of arms – they increase their numbers by drawing into their gang [those] who would otherwise be good subjects – and they remain ready and proper materials for disturbing the government upon the first occasion'. Wade was mindful that a lack of respect for property rights and the rule of law had shown itself in recent troubles involving the Frasers, and the chronic state of imminent feuding with certain of the Mackenzies.

The General dined and was entertained at Castle Dounie frequently. He enjoyed Lovat's company, but it also gave him the chance to compare the laird's recommendations with Wade's own direct experience of a traditional Highland clan in its home environment. Wade's observations would lead him to endorse much of the Fraser chief's analysis, and persuade the government to revive the Independent Companies. One of the first to benefit was Lord Lovat himself, who filled his Independent Company with loyal Frasers. It was a private army at hand when he negotiated with other clans and 'iniquitous' and 'unnatural' Fraser lairds trying to abandon clanship for the modern world.

James Ferguson, the brilliant Scottish astronomer and instrument-maker who was a guest at Castle Dounie, later recalled how much Lord Lovat's life at Dounie differed from an English aristocrat's, to the detriment of the former. 'This powerful Laird' resided 'in a sort of Tower, forming at best such a kind of house as would be esteemed but an indifferent one for a very private plain country gentleman in England. It had in all only four apartments on a floor, and of those, none of them large. Yet he moved like a king.'

Highland chiefs did not need showy palaces, though Lovat liked to collect portraits of his Scottish heroes when he could. Lovat had 'country', 500 square miles of it. The windows of Dounie framed mountains and views extending over many miles. 'He kept a sort of Court,' Ferguson noted, 'and several public tables, and had a very

212

numerous body of retainers always attending.' Lovat led a semi-public life and saw himself as his kindred's servant, in the way a prince served his people. The head of the kin must be available to be seen by his people, to listen to their complaints, and to speak with the most pretentious and the most humble of them. *Dion* – protection – was the abiding virtue of clanship. But Lovat was also princely in the way he brooked no attempt to question or limit his power.

'His own constant residence, and the place where he received company, and even dined constantly with them, was in just one room only, and that the very room wherein he lodged,' the young star-gazer wrote. Lovat slept, worked, received guests and dined in his room, adjoining the great hall. 'His Lady's sole apartment was also her own bedchamber.' The only provision made for 'lodging either of the domestic servants, or of the numerous herd of retainers was a quantity of straw, which was spread every night, on the floors of the four lower rooms in this sort of Tower-like structure – where the whole inferior part of the family, consisting of a very great number of persons, took up their abode. Sometimes, above four hundred persons, attending on this petty court, were kennelled here.' No one was turned away who wanted shelter. It was not too small to accommodate 400, though Ferguson – a self-made man from a very humble background in Banffshire – inferred there was something primitive about 'the family' in the word 'kennelled' and 'herd'.

Outside the castle were 'those wretched dependents' whom Lovat caught breaking the law. Because he had the 'right of regality' – that is, the law in all cases except treason – 'three, four, and sometimes half a dozen, [were] hung up by the heels, for hours, on the few trees round the mansion'. Then they were cut down and taken inside. Ferguson stayed as a guest of the Lovats for several months. Lovat had first met him in Inverness when he had been working as an artist and asked him to come to Dounie to paint him. They discussed the young astronomer's work mapping the heavens, and the motions of the stars using beads and string. Always interested in philosophy, Lovat was intrigued what this new science inferred about the meaning of life; about determinism and divine intervention; about superstition, second sight and omens – such as comets. Ferguson, a future Fellow of the Royal Society, recognised Lovat's power, but the astronomer had left home to become part of the Enlightenment Republic of Letters, where learning and the printed word gave more power and prestige than hundreds of square miles of land and thousands of illiterate, Gaelic-speaking dependants educated through oral culture.

General Wade saw all that Ferguson saw, but did not agree with the young Scot's analysis. Wade found much to enjoy at Dounie. He and his officers wined and dined and celebrated with Lovat when, in October 1726, Lady Lovat was brought to bed and gave birth to a healthy boy, named Simon. Approaching his mid-fifties, his Lordship had a son and heir at last, a direct descendant of the first Fraser chief. He and Margaret had lost their precious Georgina to fever. Lovat confided his pain in a letter to Lord Cowper. Though every parent expected and dreaded the death of children, it did not spare them anguish. And they had two more healthy daughters, Janet (Jenny) and Sibyl, before they got their longed-for son and heir.

Lady Lovat and her son lay in bed, visible to everyone in the hall through the doors of her chamber. Wade loved the Gaelic music and poetry that celebrated the birth and asked for some translations to be made for him. He admired the clan's inclusiveness: the stories of the clan were the stories of them all, not just the nobles at the top of the heap. MacShimidh 'was a man of a bold, nimbling kind of sense', said John Clerk of Penicuik who knew Lovat in Edinburgh; 'very vain of his clan, the Fraziers, and ready to sacrifice everything to their interest'. Wade thought Lovat certainly was pumped with ambition, and understood why he was so motivated. He saw how all this feasting and inter-marrying and shared history in music and song tied these men to each other and their country. He just hoped they would then bond themselves to the fledgling kingdom of Great Britain.

Like Ferguson, some of Wade's men could not see past the lack of sophistication at Dounie. To them it was all on a grand scale, but rather shabby, uncomfortable, and pretentious. All the leading men of the region dined here. One of Wade's officers, Captain Burt, wrote that a 'band of music struck up in a little place out of sight' as they sat to dine. He assumed Lovat 'would have us think they were his constant domestics' but 'I knew they were brought from' Inverness for these occasions. The lower-ranking officers shrank from the noisy gangs of Highlanders who served at table, 'whose feet and foul linen, or woollen, I don't know which, were more than a match for the odour of the dishes'. One remarked that 'many a peruke [wig] had been baked in a better crust'.

At supper, there was rare beef on silver plates and 'a great number of dishes ... almost all cold'. However, Captain Burt could not tell what most of them were as they were 'disguised after the French manner', that is, with sauces. The English officer did not like French food. 'My palate ... is always inclined to plain eating,' he said, pleased with his own humility; but he admitted the wine was 'very good'. Everyone knew that the wine had arrived through illegal channels, what the Highlanders called 'free' or 'fair trade'. A more appreciative guest recorded that MacShimidh gave all his pocket could supply.

Wade's officers admitted that the laird's hunting was good: 'salmon and trout just taken out of the river ... partridge, grouse, hare, duck and mallard, woodcocks, snipes, etc., each in its proper season'. But even this was not quite right: it was all 'to exuberance; rather too much I think, for the sportsman's diversion', while the conversation 'was greatly engrossed by the chief, before, at, and after dinner'. Captain Burt remarked that nothing of note was said. His commander, General Wade, was riveted. Time spent on intelligence was never wasted.

Sitting back, Wade agreed with much of Lovat's analysis of the Highland clans' disrespect for British justice: there were hardly any JPs to keep the peace locally, while three of the Sheriff Deputies had been out for the rebels in the 1715 uprising. Though aspects of clanship offended Wade, his own pleasure in Gaelic culture surprised him. He also recognised that it was Scottish nationalism, not so-called 'Highland barbarism', that rankled with him and London. But how could you make Scottish people not Scottish, or Highland; or make them Scottish or Celtic in a way that blended with being British?

Among the ordinary Highlanders, Wade could not help but notice Lovat's huge popularity. One soldier born on the Isle of Skye, a humble man of the MacLeod clan who knew Lovat's reputation as a *deulnach*, a great Highland chief, had walked from Edinburgh to Castle Dounie just to enlist in Lovat's new Independent Company. Arriving before dawn, he sat on the green in front of Dounie and waited. At daybreak he glimpsed 'a fine-looking tall man' at the window. Lovat moved through the hall in a morning coat. A servant attended, 'throwing open the great folding doors and all the outer doors and windows of the house'. Looking out, Lovat spotted the stranger and came down. He bowed and invited the man in to explain his presence and take breakfast with them. MacLeod followed the chief and saw a huge table extending from one end of the hall to another, covered in various types of meat and drink. The place was soon 'crowded by kindred visitors, neighbours, vassals and tenants of all ranks' and resounded with noise. MacLeod explained he had come to offer himself for Lovat's Independent Company. 'For a thousand men such as you I would give my estate,' Lovat responded and asked him to tell his story. Hearing it, the chief 'clasped him in his arms and kissed him; and holding him by the hand, led him to an adjoining bed-chamber' to introduce him to Lady Lovat.

Since living at Dounie, Lord Lovat had eased into a role described in the chronicles of his people, one he had first heard while sitting by the fireside at Tomich, listening to the Reverend James and his father. He was chief, the heart of the clan. He organised feasts and games and hunting to bring them all together. He kept a bard, a *seanachie* (a tradition-bearer) and a piper. The ordinary clansmen, the backbone of the Frasers, expected this of him. Many Highlanders believed that if the chief lived well, then so did the clan. His capacity to host, to be prodigal, was identified by the clan with its own well-being. Lovat filled the role to bursting point. He was the one around whom it all revolved, and the one who needed to raise funds to keep it all going.

Mediating between his kin and the larger political and social world, Lovat pressed invitations on fellow gentlemen and titled folk to keep abreast of opinions and loyalties. Exiled for so long, he adored the mingling and planning. His ambition was to form an elite group of Highlanders who could act in concert for their mutual security and prosperity. They should negotiate with Westminster as one body – the Gaels, the clans – to create a greater *dìon*: protection of Highland and Scottish interests against Westminster indifference. Even pro-Union Scots like Duncan Forbes did not want to be ruled by London. When George I abolished the position of Scottish Secretary, Duncan celebrated: 'We shall not be troubled with that nuisance, which we so long have complained of, a Scots Secretary, either at full length or in miniature; if any one Scotsman have absolute power, we are in the same slavery as ever.' The 1720s were a good time for the Argyll faction, including Duncan and Lovat. The Earl of Ilay rose to be *de facto* minister for Scotland. Walpole had him made Lord Privy Seal.

Listening to men like Lovat, and his friends and enemies, Wade went further than his initial brief demanded. He addressed the question that was always avoided: What was the longer term policy for accommodating the Gaelic-speaking Highlands into the wider culture of Great Britain? Wade responded by asking for finances to improve the country's infrastructure; to repair and upgrade existing roads and fortresses and build new ones; and to put commercial and Royal Navy vessels on the major lochs. Wade intended to open up the Highlands to immigration and commerce.

Lovat vehemently disagreed with Wade, hating the prospect of his country being overrun by foreigners. They did not need more forts. The chiefs of the significant clans loyal to King George already lived in fortified castles. If funded from central government, these focal points could hold enough men to enable effective local policing. Wade said that was not desirable; for various reasons it would be insulting to Lovat to dilate upon. The forts must be independent of interference by local magnates like Lovat, answerable only to London. Lovat insisted there was plenty of commercial activity in and around Inverness, since the port of Inverness had been a royal burgh for 500 years. It did not need new roads, while the sea lanes were mighty highways, packed with traffic connecting Inverness to the whole world.

* * *

In Inverness, on Church Street, Lovat kept a house. He did business of all sorts here but only kept a small table: the public dining of scores of people at Castle Dounie exhausted his stomach and his purse. He needed to trade with Inverness merchants such as his cousin Bailie John Steuart, who bought the commodities Lovat's estates produced in commercial quantities. The Bailie only wholesaled as a merchant, and had cellars and a warehouse in the town.

The Bailie's ships went all over Europe and brought back everything desired by both the humble and haughty all over the Highlands. Barrel staves, knapwood, timber, iron, window glass, copper, soap, flax and rope came in to Inverness harbour from Danzig, Stockholm, Norway and Frankfurt. Writing paper, flint stones and prunes arrived from the Channel Islands; sago and linen from Hamburg; linseed oil, madder, azure, white lead, verdigris, indigo, linens, muslin, aniseed, cloves, nutmeg, tea, sugar, and cork from Rotterdam; raisins, lemons, oranges, coffee beans, rhubarb, ipecacuanha,* olives, olive oil for burning in lamps, eating oil, and rice from Leghorn (Livorno); and large quantities of brandy, claret, sherry, burgundy, champagne, sack, and other wines from Bordeaux and Guernsey, Rotterdam and Hamburg. Lord Lovat ordered olives, almonds, walnuts, anchovies, coffee beans and 'the best eating oil' and the freshest of fruit. Musty walnuts infuriated him.

For his and his friends' houses and families, the Bailie's captains picked up copper tea kettles, lint hankies, iron pots, metal trenchers, house lanterns, warming pans, pewter dishes, branders, flesh hooks, flamers, leather, dressed calf skins 'soft as cream', silk plaids, clothes for the men and hats for the boys when they were too old for Scotch bonnets. A blue frockcoat the Bailie ordered for himself must have buttons of the latest fashion; and silks and other articles of clothing for all their wives and daughters.

Every time Lovat came to Inverness there seemed to be some change. There were a score of merchants apart from the Bailie. Some

---

* Ipecacuanha is a South American plant that was used as an emetic or to facilitate expectoration in chest infections, very common in the damp Highlands.

were shopkeepers. Lovat's kinsman, Sandy Fraser, sold him necessities for Castle Dounie. Lady Lovat sent a rider to him daily with a list to command tea, coffee, bread, salt, sugar, wheat flour and spices. Lovat added paper, lead shot by the pound, ink, and so on. Broken pots and knives went to the tinkers for repair.

All the latest books could be ordered from men like Allan Ramsay – father of the artist – in Edinburgh. News-sheets like the *Caledonian Mercury* and the *Courant* came regularly when the Bailie's credit was good. To be able to buy in these commodities, the Bailie first had to send out cargos, exporting anything that could be traded and turn a profit. He courted big estate owners like Lord Lovat to sell him whatever the estates produced in excess.

Though Lovat protested against clansmen who abandoned traditional clanship in favour of the modern world, he modernised his estates in order to maximise revenues and preserve the traditional practices such as feasting. He harnessed some of the most up-to-date methods to fish and extract timber on his estates. Timber was taken from Glen Strathfarrar and Strathglass, then rolled into the rivers and floated to Inverness for shipbuilding, processing or export. When he thought his salmon 'was fishing slowly' Lovat invested in improvements. He applied for a £300 loan from the Bank of Scotland to improve his *cruives*, the wicker traps attached to the stone groynes protruding into the river and the firth on the way to Inverness. Wade's soldiers noticed that the rivers were so plentiful in fish on the Lovat estates, they watched 'above a hundred large salmon brought to shore at one haul'. So important was the trade that catching salmon fry was a criminal offence, punished by transportation to the Colonies – except for the little children who caught them for fun on 'a crooked pin'.

The soldiers were puzzled by the seasonal running-in and then disappearance of the salmon. The Fraser Highlanders explained that the fish bred in the Ness and the Beauly went to sea for several years and for some reason returned to the place they were spawned in order to lay their eggs. Analysing their commodity, 'by way of experiment, they clipped their tails into a forked figure like that of a swallow, and found them with that mark when full grown and taken out of the *cruives*'. The Frasers understood the life cycle of this precious asset as well as how to kill it and market it.

Lovat worried that General Wade's plans for improving the infra-structure of the Highlands would undermine the ancient power of the chiefs. Wade sought a scaling back of clan society, much as he enjoyed certain things about it.

Lovat memorialised George I to provoke investment in the Highlands in the form of cash payments direct to local magnates to buy peace, as William III had done in Lovat's youth. Wade reported to King George that investment in improving the infrastructure would improve communications. Improved communications would open the Highlands to penetration by modern British culture. This would increase national security and undermine clanship. Arming clans against one other to preserve the peace through a balance of power was an outmoded policy; it could no longer work. The government agreed with Wade and not Lovat, and gave the General up to £60,000 to start his public works.

Wade's pet project was the construction of a series of metalled roads connecting the Highlands with the Lowlands. Just now, there were none at all. Diggers and engineers, soldiers and officers were sent out on the moors where they stayed for several years. The ordinary soldiers could earn an extra sixpence a day for labouring; the officers as much as two shillings: there were tables to be kept, even in the middle of the wilderness.

The first road to be hacked, thumped, detonated and packed down, cut right through Lovat territory, to the south of Loch Ness and through Stratherrick. Lovat had said he would rather forgo influence in any part of his land than Stratherrick. The Aird of Lovat was better agricultural land and produced good income. Close to Inverness, its people were open to modern ways and values. Stratherrick was his, body and soul; every unyielding, stony inch of it. When Wade completed the road, in 1727, Lovat rode out to look at it. The sight of it made him sick. It connected the government's garrison at Fort

William to Inverness via the newly named settlement of 'Fort Augustus'. Until three years ago, this was *Cill Chuimein*, a village which for hundreds of years had been the meeting point of the drove roads between the east and west coast. Wade renamed it Fort Augustus when he built his huge fort there, recognising the spot as hugely important strategically, being halfway up the Great Glen between Fort William and Inverness. In renaming it Wade claimed it for Great Britain.

It all seemed to be unstoppable, this gradual reeling in of the north closer to the rest of Britain. But Wade's work was paying off. Duncan Forbes wrote to Whitehall: 'I made several small progresses into the Highlands' from Inverness to assess 'the tranquillity of those parts' and 'in the whole of my journey I had not seen one Highlander carry the least bit of arms, neither did I hear of any theft or robbery'. He was determined to maintain his and Culloden's positions as purveyors of intelligence to the government in the face of the competition that was coming from men like Lovat.

Duncan, now Lord Advocate to Scotland, did however agree with Lovat that it was better for the government to feel relaxed about North Britain, and leave local matters to local men. Anxiety would only express itself in an occupying military force. He did not want hundreds of foreign soldiers quartered and garrisoned all over the Highlands for years on end, a focus for resentment, repressing unrest with force, not addressing the causes. Garrisons consumed scarce resources. The quartermasters' list of supplies drove up prices in a semi-subsistence, traditional clan economy. The army created markets but also shortages in the basics of life.

Lovat looked around at what felt like the inevitable melting of the Highlands into Great Britain. He needed to obtain greater leverage in central government if he was going to manage the relationship between the Gaelic-speaking world of the clans and early imperial Britain. On the other hand, Lovat had a wife, daughters, a son and heir, and was chief. In Edinburgh his lawsuits to make his temporary ownership permanent dragged on so slowly and expensively, yet seemed to inch his way. He felt a certain peace and satisfaction.

* * *

On 11 June 1727, George I died at Osnabrück during one of his trips to Hanover. He was sixty-seven, but had felt well before he left. Three days later, Walpole received the news while at dinner and went to salute the Crown Prince as George II. Everyone with a pension, place, salary, gratification, or other financial sign of the old King's favour lost them at a stroke, including Lovat. These were the gift of a Crown that now circled another head. They would have to be reconfirmed, renegotiated, reassigned to another, or simply withdrawn. And there would have to be another general election.

The opposition to the Walpole faction jumped for joy. This was their moment to sweep away the Treasury Lord and his thousands of placemen and pensioners. Lovat got to work, writing to men he knew in the administration, including Duncan Forbes, Argyll and Ilay. He asked them what he could do to ensure his pension was not stopped. He tried to stir up his brother-in-law, Sir James Grant, to political activity. Since his election for the seat of Inverness-shire, Sir James had not been active on his own or anybody else's behalf in Parliament. The only speech he had made was to defend a cousin who was blatantly guilty of fiddling the funds of a charity he was involved in.

Lovat also had his eye on General Wade's position, in charge of defence and development in the Highlands, and the Lord Lieutenancy of the Northern Counties, formerly held by the Earl of Sutherland. Regional power, a budget, salary, control of the armed forces, and the opportunities increased personal prestige and profit offered, came with these posts. Step by step he could acquire land and influence and make himself totally secure. When his lawsuits concluded to his satisfaction, then surely he would become one of the Scottish peers in the House of Lords. He could then represent himself and his clan at the centre of power and interest, the Houses of Parliament at Westminster.

TWENTY-FOUR

Tragedy, 1727–31

'Secure the estate of Lovat to Simon's bairns'
— LOVAT TO DUNCAN FORBES

In the election of 1727, both Sir James Grant and Duncan Forbes held on to their seats. The new Parliament would not sit until November. The following year Lovat wrote to Grant. He had heard the new King might continue the pension he received under his father, George I. It was a great relief. Lovat wrote 'a letter of thanks to my Lord Ilay for obtaining it, being persuaded it was by his means'. He liked to imply that Ilay was his patron.

Lovat needed every penny. The Lovat estates remained heavily burdened with debts and ongoing legal costs meant he could seldom lower the level of debt on his territories. In Edinburgh, Duncan Forbes prosecuted one of Lovat's major cases: his claim that the titles and honours of Lovat reside *in perpetuity* in his own family. He had been fighting in the courts for ten years; it all threatened to grow into one of those interminable actions that drag a family to near penury and distraction over several generations and seems only to satisfy the lawyers.

In Inverness, Lovat called on Bailie Steuart to negotiate the best prices for his salmon, timber and grain. He discussed when his chamberlains would bring in the cattle to be driven to Edinburgh to market. Lovat could hardly hear himself think above the detonations, crashes and bangs of Wade's workmen. They were digging out the gravel at the foot of the hill on which Inverness Castle perched. The path between the hill and the River Ness was very narrow and Wade had ordered his men to widen it to improve access to the river bank. Lovat kept his eyes before him, not wanting to see what was happening. He had lost his governorship of the castle and town with the accession of George II.

Mary Stuart, Queen of Scots, stayed at the castle during her visits to Inverness. Its walls reared high above the town, the tiny eyes of its windows giving a view of all that went on below. Partly ruined, it was in no shape to defend the town. In his day, Lovat had repaired what he could without funds. Three soldiers digging near the main door turned up a long-dead body. One of the soldiers reached down to touch it, and the thing collapsed into dust. The workers dropped everything and ran. As the news of it spread, people came for a look. 'Troth,' an Inverness man decided, 'I dinna doubt but this was ane o' Mary's lovers.'

Day after day, Wade's men dug and carted away the loose gravel at the base of the castle until a road big enough to take a cart opened between Castle Hill and the River Ness.One night, the townsfolk woke to a tremendous cacophony: above a roaring noise came the sounds of shouting and running about, of names being called. People jumped from their beds. Perhaps the town was on fire. Many houses had enclosed wooden staircases running up their fronts, the way up to the private living areas above shops or warehouses. As the shouts and crashes grew louder, men, women and children rushed into their wooden stairwells and looked out through the peepholes, like little birds peeping out of a nest in a wall. There was no sign of fire, thank God. They relaxed and chattered to neighbours.

A boy came running from the direction of the castle; they stopped him to ask what was happening. General Wade's improvements to Castle Hill had given way. The new cart track had fallen into the river. The castle was on the verge of following it. Lovat, always superstitious, called it an omen when the news was brought to him at his town house. Inverness Castle had sat tight above the town for hundreds of years and throughout his time as Governor. In foreign hands it now teetered on the brink of collapse; the land had just slipped away through their greedy grasping fingers.

Certain gentlemen of the clan always bothered Lovat. They turned this way and that, seeking to escape their chief one day, and then serve him the next, looking for a way to make a good living for their families, partly outwith, and in part within the clan. Lovat returned to Castle Dounie one evening to find a letter waiting for him. It was from James Fraser of Castleleathers, informing him that his brother-in-law, Fraser of Phopachy, had prepared a memorial about Lord Lovat's Jacobite sentiments and secret dealings. Phopachy had recently lost his chamberlain's position. Lovat said it was because of sharp practice; Phopachy said it was because he knew too much. Details of Lovat's treason would go to London soon where it would be presented by 'a Lord in the south' to the government. It 'is full of all the crimes that ever was invented, and capable to hang all England if it were proven', Castleleathers explained to his Lordship.

Lovat answered that he feared nothing from this 'wicked calumny', though he would have to go and deny it. He accused Castleleathers and Phopachy of having cooked it up between them, to blackmail him into reinstating Phopachy as chamberlain and into giving Castleleathers a farm. He was outraged that a Fraser should be ready to 'give a scandalous impression of' his chief 'to the world', though he believed he was too secure to be knocked down by anything they could say. This kind of smear could be damaging. Though the accusations of treason were ignored, Lovat found himself out of favour once more. His name was taken off the lists of those recommended for places and pensions from the Crown and government and his pension of £500 a year was not renewed. Such signs of distrust angered him.

In July 1729, Lovat was in Edinburgh on legal business, leaving a heavily pregnant Margaret in charge of the growing family and bustling estates at Dounie.

From his Edinburgh house, Lovat sallied out to the Advocate's library, repository of legal documents. He sat and researched among the records as thoroughly as had Duncan and his other legal retainers, amassing evidence to support his claims to the titles and estates of Lovat in perpetuity. He produced detailed historical examples and precedents in his favour – he would have made a brilliant lawyer. His findings were printed and bound and he gave the book to his lawyers. He paid his respects to friendly Law Lords, especially anyone concerned with the Court of Session. Duncan Forbes received almost daily visits. One judge, James Erskine, Lord Grange – a Lord of Session, and former Justice Clerk – became a close friend.

Grange was one of the judges drawing up the Fraser entail to ensure that, as soon as Lovat regained his estates, they could not be alienated from Lovat's descendants and from male heirs again. Lord Grange 'was understood to be a great plotter ... and supposed to reserve himself for some greater occasions', political and spiritual. As brother of the Earl of Mar, the failed leader of the '15 rebellion, he always carried about the whiff of Jacobitism. His diary teemed with records of his dreams, prognostics and his encounters with persons supernaturally gifted, or possessed by demons. Demonology was a passion. An elder of the Presbyterian Church, it was common knowledge that Grange had a secret life in tandem with his ferocious piety.

In London, where his male friends said he went to indulge Jacobite fantasies and communicate with his exiled brother, he kept a mistress – 'a handsome Scotch woman', named Fanny Lindsay, who ran a coffee house at the bottom end of Haymarket. Grange and Lovat were as complicated and principled, wild and Rabelaisian as each other. It was obvious that their business relationship extended to real friendship. Grange was also fighting for the restoration of a lost inheritance. He wanted the Mar titles and estates, forfeited to the Crown after the collapse of the 1715 rebellion, restored to his nephew. He and Lovat always found much to talk about.

It was with Grange and Duncan Forbes that Lovat shared his joy the day news came from Dounie that Margaret had given birth to another healthy boy. Lovat sent back a command that he was to be baptised Alexander – 'my little Sandy' – after his late brother. It was a good Lovat name. He told Margaret to order the chamberlain to bring champagne and claret from the cellar. They were to drink the boy's health. His sent for his wig and his boy to barberise his head and went out to celebrate.

When Lovat rose the next day, his housekeeper announced the arrival of another messenger. In the parlour stood a clansman. The chief must return immediately to Castle Dounie, he said. Complications had set in after the baby's safe delivery. Margaret was dead. Puerperal fever, plague of the birthing chambers of Europe, had swept her away.

A devastated Lovat poured out his grief in his letter to his brother-in-law, Sir James Grant. 'My loss is inconceivable to any but myself that feels it every hour and every minute,' he wrote. 'If I lost a most affectionate and good wife, I am sure you lost the most affectionate sister that ever was born ... So I hope, my dear brother, that whatever comes of me, you will support my poor infants, your own nephews and nieces, the dear and tender pledges of my lovely soul's affection for me.' He had been married to his 'lovely soul' for thirteen years. So much he had been starved and deprived of in France he had found in Margaret. A clan home without the chief's lady to preside over it and sweeten it with her spirit and style lacked a heart.

Lovat now had total responsibility for four children: two girls under ten, a boy aged three and the newborn Sandy. He packed and made his way home to bury his wife and arrange for a nurse for his 'poor infants'. He found them utterly bewildered, seeking their mother. In exile for so long, he had married late, bred late. His brother-in-law's son, Ludovick Grant, was getting ready to go to university, while Lovat's sons were babies. The funeral cortege stretched for miles from Castle Dounie to the thatched church in Kirkhill.

Margaret had always been there at Castle Dounie, orientating him. Now he was alone and getting old. He found domestic matters did not run as smoothly in his absence as they had under Lady Lovat's control. Servants ran away, and the cellars and grain stores fell into disorder and were continually raided. Using his powers of hereditary jurisdiction, Lovat put out an arrest warrant on one runaway. 'John Fraser, my domestic servant, that plays on the violin and hautbois, a black fellow, about five foot eight inches high, who run away out of my house with his liveries, and with several other things that he stole … both gold and silver and clothes … in order to go and play at the assemblies in Aberdeen', and should be apprehended ''til I send for him, to be tried according to law'. If found guilty, he would be thrust into the pit of Beauly – an underground cell – or strung by the heels for a few hours in front of the castle, as a lesson to the others not to take liberties.

He had no one to listen to his defeats and triumphs in his great odyssey. Margaret was not there to share his joy the following year when Duncan triumphed in the Court of Session in the matter of the Lovat titles. On 2 July 1730, Lovat wrote to John Forbes of Culloden from Edinburgh 'I have this afternoon gained my cause, two to one.' His son, Simon, was the Master of Lovat and heir to the ancient titles after his father. 'I cannot tell you how much I owe to Duncan,' he admitted to Culloden. 'I hope he has established a family that will be forever faithful to the rooftree of Culloden,' he cheered, invoking the alliance of friendly clans that would serve each one by serving them all.

The loss of the titles fatally weakened Fraserdale's chances of keeping the Lovat estates. The Mackenzies were humiliated by losing this case. It signalled that they were judged not to be the heirs. If the courts forced them to hand over the land and houses as well, they would beggar Lovat for them; his family would never recover financially. Though Lovat expected this outcome, it still outraged him. He would have to put the clan in difficult circumstances for decades in order to own what he should have inherited in 1698.

He needed more and more income. Lovat berated his brother-in-law, Sir James Grant, MP for the shire of Inverness, demanding to know why he did not make more capital out of his position. His constituency was vast, and effectively included all Lord Lovat's country, as well as the Grant estates down the north side of Loch Ness, and some MacDonald of Glengarry and Cameron country towards Fort

William. Why was Grant not establishing himself and Lovat with Ilay and Walpole as the key men to patronise in the region? Lovat felt his bargaining position at Westminster would be enhanced by the settlement of the Lovat estates on him and his boys. It would reinforce the impression of an established clanned power. He criticised Duncan Forbes for not getting on with the case, for wasting time on other things.

On Christmas Day, 1730, Lovat was in Edinburgh asking Culloden to find out if 'the infatuate family of Fraserdale are resolved, or not, to agree, really and finally'. Lovat told Culloden '[Duncan] says that they are such mad fools that he can make nothing of them. However he will put the thorn in their side, and make them excuseless before God and man. If you can bring this about … you secure the estate of Lovat to Simon's bairns.'

TWENTY-FIVE

Kidnapping and election-rigging,
1731–34

'Necessity has no law'
– THE CHIEF OF CLAN MACLEOD

In the New Year, Lovat was feeling his age. 'Many marks appear that show the tabernacle is failing,' Lovat wrote to his old friend Culloden. His wrinkled skin did not quite seem to fit him as tightly as it had in his youth. 'The teeth are gone,' he sighed, 'and now the cold has so seized my head, that I am almost deaf with a pain in my ears. Those are so many sounds of the trumpet that call me to another world, for which you and I are hardly well prepared.' They had both led full lives. Stinging ear pain as the sound of the last trumpet sounded horrible.

Complain as he did about his aches and pains, Lovat was fit enough by 1732, after two years of widowhood, to think about finding a mother for his four children, and a helpmeet for himself: someone to keep an old man warm. Going back and forth to his Edinburgh lawyers, Lovat's attention had alighted on pretty young Marion Dalrymple, granddaughter of Lord Stair, Lord President of the Court of Session, where he spent so much time. She was unmarried, though was being courted by an Edinburgh buck. She came with a good dowry and was superbly connected into the upper echelons of the Edinburgh legal establishment. Between the Dalrymples in Edinburgh and Grants in London, Lovat reasoned he ought to be able to get his affairs settled to his satisfaction. If he did not live much longer she might be a wealthy and eligible widow. Lovat hoped she would be kind to his children.

In the spring of 1732, Marion Dalrymple began to receive visits and notes and small gifts from Lord Lovat as he rode between Edinburgh, Dounie and wherever General Wade was currently mustering the Highland Companies. Lovat fell from his horse one day, which should have been a sign he was too old for galloping about playing love and war games. Eventually Marion accepted his proposal. A delighted Lovat announced the banns and rode to Edinburgh to work out the details of their marriage contract with her father, who was younger than his prospective son-in-law. When he arrived in Edinburgh, a letter from North Berwick was waiting for him. Recognising the female hand he tore it open eagerly, only to read that 'after the most serious and deliberate considerations for several months I am fully satisfied that it will not be for the happiness or comfort of either of us to match together'. Marion thanked him 'for the honour your Lordship designed me'. Lovat was stunned. Why had she changed her mind?

Her grandfather told Sir James Grant she had liked his proposal at first. Lovat headed an ancient family, and was a prominent man in Scotland. Yes, he was old, but he was not without glamour. She might even attend Court as my Lady Lovat. Then she went home to 'her other friends'. When Dalrymple saw her next, she had changed her mind, being 'firm and positive in her resolution'. Lovat's lawyer, John MacFarlane, wrote to his Lordship that Marion's 'own natural disposition and the observations she had occasion to make on your Lordship's conduct and behaviour *last winter*' made her change her mind. She was referring to the kidnapping of Lady Grange.

Lord Grange's wife, Rachel Chieseley, kept a cut-throat razor under the pillow, Grange told his friend Lovat when he called on him over a year earlier. Lovat, listening with agitated fascination, could imagine this was not good news. The rumour about a mistress had come to his wife's ears and her mood had darkened. He had tried to placate her, Grange told Lovat. The Grange children noticed that though intimate

231

when seen in public places, in private there were times when for half a year at a time 'there was no intercourse between' their parents at all. The suspicious Lady Grange intercepted her husband's letters, read them and took them to the Justice Clerk Adam Cockburn. Looking for evidence of adultery, she found treason. Lovat winced: Cockburn hated him. Some letters were coded but, the Justice Clerk said, delighted, they burbled Jacobite sentiment. Here was a chance to ruin many of his political enemies. Lovat grew increasingly alarmed as Lord Grange's story developed. Had Lady Grange been listening at doorways as well as reading her husband's post? Getting drawn into a scandal of this nature right now could be disastrous.

Lady Grange's plans to go to London and ruin her husband – and his friends if implicated – were thrown into confusion when Cockburn, her mentor, succumbed to serious illness. Lovat wrote to Sir James Grant. 'I am informed … the Justice Clerk is going very fast and for all his inveterate enmity against me, I am so good a Christian that I wish him very soon in Heaven.' He could not die fast enough – though he lingered on until April 1735. Lovat called in one of his Highland servants and gave him a letter for the chief of the MacLeods on Skye. Lady Grange had become increasingly unstable and embittered. She stood in the streets waving letters and screaming at her husband, and barracked him loudly in church as a hypocrite. The poor woman was terribly unhappy and could be dangerous. Lord Grange decided she must be silenced.

On the night of 22 January 1732, no one noticed a group of men Lady Grange later identified as 'some servants of Lovat's and his cousin Roderick MacLeod', their faces wrapped in plaids, as they pushed open the door of the house where Lady Grange was staying. They grabbed her, gagged her, 'carried me downstairs as a corpse', threw her into a sedan chair, and hauled her out into the night, heading west in the direction of Falkirk. The party disappeared through the gateway of hills into the Highlands, with what someone later called 'the cargo', taking the terrified woman up Loch Ness and then west till they reached the sea. Here they put her on a boat for the Monach Isles, five miles off the west coast of North Uist.

Lord Grange announced that his wife had died of a heart attack and held her funeral. One suspicious soul lifted the coffin lid, and found it empty. Flickering glimpses of the truth emerged. The city of Edinburgh ruminated over the scandal 'for a few weeks only'. It was 'not taken the least notice of by any of her own family or by the King's Advocate', Duncan Forbes. In fact, the gossip was that one of her own sons was part of the kidnapping party. Lady Grange had had an erratic temper. Her father had murdered a judge for making a judgement against him. Grange told anyone who asked that she had been removed for her own safety: 'confining a madwoman ... where she was tenderly cared for'. He professed 'a passionate love' for her always.

People pointed at Lord Lovat and the chief of MacLeod as Grange's accomplices, 'the first as being the most famous plotter in the kingdom, and the second as equally unprincipled, and the proprietor of the island of St Kilda', sixty miles west of the Isle of Lewis, just one of the places she was imprisoned. When Lady Grange's siblings asked the public prosecutors to intervene, they said they could do nothing 'seeing the family were not displeased', although one minister's son noticed that in church on Sundays, Lord Grange would sometimes sit through the entire service in floods of tears. Lady Grange passed the last thirteen years of her life being shifted from one remote island to another, including a spell of six years on St Kilda in a tiny stone hut. She died on Skye aged sixty-six.

There were problems with Lovat's wider reputation too. It was not the first scandal connected to his name. Marion's friends told her that Lovat often accompanied Lord Grange on debauching revels, to drink and carry on freely with 'tapster lasses' in the inns of the town, and talk Jacobite treason. Marion's mind boggled. Enjoying the gossip of the town was one thing; living with one of the most colourful objects of it might be quite another. That, and his age, and the thought of being so far away in the Highlands with servants who spoke only Gaelic (which she did not), woke Marion up from her dream of being my Lady Lovat. 'She believed she could not be happy if she became your wife ... She offered to put in my hands the presents you had given her,' Lovat's lawyer, MacFarlane said, 'but I excused myself from receiving them.'

Lovat threw down the letter. A chit of a girl and her chattering friends had rejected and humiliated him. The marriage banns had been announced. Being Lovat, he had publicised it everywhere. He retired to Castle Dounie and wrote to his nephew, Ludovick Grant. To be refused privately was tolerable, but, 'to have a marriage fully concluded, a contract writ, and every article agreed to, a day appointed for the marriage, to put it back in this manner is an indignity put upon my person and family, that I can hardly bear', he thrashed. He would think of someone else fast, to pour balm on the humiliation. His mind roved over his political allies and came to rest on the biggest, the Argyll Campbells. The Duke's and Earl's first cousin, Sir John Campbell of Mamore, a general in the British Army, Whig, and Presbyterian, had a daughter of marriageable age called Primrose. At the moment, neither Argyll nor Ilay had heirs, and Sir John's family were next in line for the dukedom. She would be perfect. This time nothing stopped Lovat.

The bride had barely left her teens when faced with a sixty-something widower. The marriage went through. Primrose's views on it were expressed by her feet. A few months into married life Lovat looked about and wondered where his wife was. She had not been at home, at Dounie, helping him entertain up to twenty influential Highland men a night in the run-up to the 1734 general election. She had not been mothering and educating his children. She did not run his household and manage servants. She had gone west, visiting family and friends. He wrote to her. She did not respond. He thought her absence a 'shame', and went to fetch her back. She must support him at home while he campaigned.

Lovat sensed things were not quite right in the run-up to this election. For one thing, the Duke of Argyll had added a clause to a forthcoming bill for disarming the Highlands. The clause forbade the wearing of Highland dress. It reflected a belief that after seventeen years of peace there was no need to respect the traditional costume of the Gaels, that marked them as different from the rest of Britons, or respect their need to bear arms to hunt and protect themselves from predation. There was not going to be another uprising. Keeping the Highlanders in arms and in plaids merely reinforced a sense of separateness in them.

Dining at Culloden House, the Highland elite rowed ferociously over their attitudes to this bill, Lovat raging that Argyll, patron of most men in the room, 'will be now the most hated above 60,000 Highlanders, men and women, who will curse him every day of his life, and theirs. And their posterity will curse him and his to all future ages.' The bill showed up fault lines in the Scottish ruling classes, not how much they were assimilated into Britain. They divided over the bill, men like the Forbeses voting for their patron's measure; men like Lovat violently opposed to it.

He was dismayed that his world was being dismantled by its own most ancient and eminent representatives, like Argyll. Lovat remembered Argyll's father fondly, the first duke. He was properly Scottish. This one had been educated at Eton and knew the gentle slopes and ornamental lakes on his English estates in Surrey more intimately than the staggering mountains and lochs of Argyll, and the character and culture of the fiercely independent people that belonged there. One of Lovat's remaining ambitions was to keep the powerful and able men of the Highlands together, fostering a strong feeling for their home and nationality. United, they had some clout with which to negotiate for positions and salaries from Walpole's government and could offer him a bloc vote in exchange.

Ilay understood about tactical voting and grouping, and exploited the Highland lairds' differences to rule them. He did not want a powerfully bonded Highland group that might feel strong enough to turn against him if it suited them. Having two or three factions among his supporters in the north competing for his, and through him Walpole's, favours, balanced power there. No one man could rise too high. Duncan Forbes was Ilay's right-hand man in the north, but from time to time Ilay set out to appoint someone who might 'not be ruled by Duncan', as when Lovat kept asking for the position of Sheriff of Inverness-shire. Against the wishes of Duncan Forbes, Ilay gave it to him. The Sheriff was the leading judge in a shire, civil and criminal. For a nobleman who spent so much time and money in the courts, the post was extremely attractive. Second, the Sheriff was the returning officer on election day. The Sheriff decided who had won the most votes and became elected. This was not a simple matter of counting the thirty to eighty votes cast in the election to Highland seats. Before the election, the Sheriff decided who was eligible to vote, and who could be made eligible with the right paperwork; and who was not eligible, or could be found not to be eligible. The man pushing and pushing for this post was not a man indifferent to politics.

Lovat could see more clearly than any that arguing among themselves played them into Ilay's hands, though he was one of the most belligerent. They were united as Highlanders in defence of their country, and united behind Walpole and Argyll as a group; yet when they entered the arena of their individual needs and desires, the Earl of Ilay divided and ruled them with ease. They should pull together and use their combined power to make the Earl invest more in the area, Lovat said. He worked ceaselessly to unite them, telling his brother-in-law: 'I had four Highland chiefs at dinner with me two days ago. Sir Alexander MacDonald, Mackintosh, McKinnon, and your son, Captain George, Dalrahany, and Grantfield were with us, and we drank heartily to healths of the Duke of Argyle and the Earl of Ilay and to Craigeallachy [a title of Sir James's] root and branch.' The Forbeses also hoped to unite the north, except under their patronage.

Most of Lovat's contemporaries were ageing Highland gentlemen and nobles trying to do their duty by their families, estates, neighbours and country. They wanted a quiet life. Whatever battles life threw them were mostly over, except that of gradually disburdening themselves of responsibilities and passing them on to the next generation. They were living among ambitious young men coming to adulthood with no memory of an independent Scotland and Stuart kings, or of their allies and relations who ruled an independent nation. When Lovat badgered Sir James too strongly, Grant stopped answering his letters, or went on holiday to the South of France.

The rising generation only knew the post-Union Scotland as a peripheral poor cousin to England. They did not fall easily into line behind Lovat's vision of the Highlands as a small state within the former realm. Lovat saw that to attract patronage they must appear to be of importance on the national stage. They must all stand together to make any real impact. They would not be allowed independence, though many in England disliked the Union. Scotland, especially the north, had nothing economically or socially to offer or to threaten to withhold in London's eyes, except good behaviour. The poverty and isolation of their homeland forced most of them into national affairs to make a good living.

At home, even if Duncan Forbes and Lovat had begun to compete over political spoils and the competition was dividing them, Duncan still believed in Lovat's right to his estates and, in two major judgements, helped Lovat, finally, over the winning line. In July 1733, Lord Lovat regained the clan estates.

Duncan and his fellow lawyers settled on £12,000 as fair compensation to Fraserdale and his son for their losses. The financial implications were potentially crippling. Lovat burdened his territories with debts amounting to nearly £2 million in today's terms. It was another reason he could never retire and enjoy his achievements; he needed to compete with all the established and upcoming men in public life. Lovat thought it was a 'terrible' sum, but worth it to secure 'to me, and to my kindred, and to my children, the lands of our forefathers without dispute, and takes us out of the hands of the barbarous Philistines', remarking irritably that most of Fraserdale's advisers were to be found in the Forbes political camp. 'We all met this night for the first time … I never spoke to Fraserdale before.' How odd that this man had affected his life so profoundly – and they had never met.

In the run-up to the 1734 election, Culloden fell extremely ill and it was obvious he could not stand against Grant to try and regain his seat. If Sir James kept his seat in the election, that would at least keep the Grant–Lovat presence at Westminster. But Duncan convinced Sir Norman MacLeod of MacLeod to stand against Sir James and to improve MacLeod's chances, Duncan went to MacLeod's castle on Skye 'to assist him to make twelve or twenty barons, so that he' would definitely win the seat. By the *nominal* transfer of a piece of land to men utterly subordinate to them, who would vote and do exactly what they were told to, big land owners built up a bank of 'parchment barons' or 'faggot votes'.

Lovat watched this development with alarm. 'If your father does not bestir himself and make as many barons as will balance MacLeod,' he will lose, Lovat told Ludovick Grant. Then, Lovat finished, almost shouting with anxiety, 'What will the ministry think of his [Sir James's] interest and mine in this shire?' Their 'interest' was their influence.

Lovat set his lawyers to work to create twenty new voters out of his own obedient kindred. Every one of them cost Lovat money, and every one alienated him further from the Forbeses, as he tried to unite the group around the Grants. At the meeting to validate voters prior to election day, Lovat, as election officer in his position as Sheriff, disallowed several Forbes–MacLeod-made voters (including some who had actually voted in the previous election) and allowed all of Grant's. 'In a straightforward competition in unscrupulousness he had little to fear from any normal man,' concluded one historian of the period. But he was made very anxious by the costs – both the money and the collateral damage to relationships with those he wanted and needed to cultivate. The duty of the successful candidate was to go to Westminster, flatter the ministers who held real power and extract perks for themselves and their followers at home. That was what Lovat was buying here. 'Let us take courage and fight it bravely,' Lovat charged Grant, though the 'fatiguing campaign' left him feeling ill.

As a Forbes supporter, General Wade tried to disrupt the Fraser chief's political activities by repeatedly mustering all his officers and their Highland Companies. A few weeks before election day, Wade ordered the Sheriff of Inverness into camp at Badenoch. Lovat was doubly furious. Interrupted his campaigning, as it was meant to, there was also the larger problem of famine in the Aviemore area in March

1734. John Roy Stuart, a known Jacobite conspirator, came to dine at Dounie and commiserate. When he had gone, Wade appeared 'in a cursed humour; he scolded me horridly ... He swears he will break us all as soon as he comes to London,' Lovat said. Wade believed the Independent Companies were full of Jacobitism and being used for private enterprise.

In England a book appeared called *The Humours of a Country Election*. Hogarth provided the illustrations, satirising all the 'vices attendant on rural election campaigns': feasting, violence, bribery, corruption, menaces, and vote-rigging. The electioneering parties in Inverness encouraged satirical songs to demean their enemies and laud themselves. Lovat was under enormous pressure when he met Duncan in Inverness shortly before election day. Lovat yelled that there were circumstances in which he would not hesitate to cut his throat. It was a little excessive to threaten the life of the principal state prosecutor in Scotland, even for Lovat. Election day dawned with feelings running very high between the influential men of the north.

TWENTY-SIX

A pyrrhic victory, 1734–39

'We are such beggars in this country
that we long after a war'
— LOVAT TO LUDOVICK GRANT

Lovat was uncontainable. Wednesday, 16 May 1734, Lord Lovat's Independent Company of Foot patrolled the streets of Inverness to keep the peace at the polls. Victory today would change the fortunes of the Lovat–Grant axis. Soldiers everywhere attached themselves to voters, and guarded polling stations. Lord Lovat, the Sheriff of Inverness-shire, returning officer for the county and burgh seats of Inverness, presided.

The burghers and magistrates supporting the Forbeses protested that Lovat's men intimidated them. Lovat sent Grant a ballad the Inverness mob was singing about the Fraser versus Forbes contest. Grant quailed before his brother-in-law's vigour.

> The Peer and his clan were there to a man,
> His Lordship looked big, like a Hector;
> No doubt he will vaunt, in the Evening Courant,
> With a hey, Sine Sanguine Victor ...

> Though our story does boast of the Frasers and host
> Before Forbes from Adam came out;
> Yet the fourth of that race, with his impudent face,
> Said, the Grants and the Frasers he'd rout.

240

'The Peer', Lovat, had been a presence since 'before Adam'. The Forbeses only 'came out' as gentlemen of property four generations ago. Before that, as the Fraser chronicles recorded, they were Lord Lovat's 'pastry cooks'. The rest of polling day 'was not then bairns' play', Lovat told Grant. 'I thought to lose my life in the burgh room', where votes were cast. When the booths closed, no voting was private, of course, they all came out of the rooms, and 'I was pelted with showers of stones and clods by the Patriots' mob'. The Patriots were anti-Union nationalists, one of the Whig opposition groups. In another life, they would have been his natural allies.

Parliament was summoned on 13 June 1734. It was made up of 326 ministerial Whigs who unquestioningly supported Walpole's administration. Ilay's Scottish faction was among their number. There were eighty-three opposition Whigs, including the Squadrone men and the new group, the Patriots; and 149 Tories. Walpole's majority had gone down by sixteen MPs. In the north, Sir James Grant kept Inverness-shire, thanks to his more effective vote-rigging, seeing off the challenge from Culloden's replacement, Sir Norman MacLeod. Duncan Forbes kept the Inverness burghs. The gentry had mauled each other verbally. Now, the scrapping for places and pensions began in earnest.

Walpole and Ilay and the other men at the top settled to work out who they wished to patronise, who they had to patronise, and who they could safely ignore. Even the great patronage of the Treasury could not provide enough to satisfy the expectations of more than a third of the old and new faces. 'The people in this country continue in much the same disposition as formerly; their own opinion of their deservings and the liveliness of their expectations gives me some uneasiness', Duncan wrote to Ilay's Scottish campaign manager, Lord Milton.

When it came to the Highlands, Duncan Forbes, the Lord Advocate, never ceased to cultivate Ilay and Walpole, repeating that his family's rise to prominence depended on them. He thwarted Ilay on specific policies or appointments, but consistently supported the ministry by hard, successful work. His reports were to the point, and requests for hand-outs came with offers to do something substantial in return.

Walpole and Ilay wished to patronise Duncan. Sir James Grant toed the Walpole line, but was too patrician and lazy to thrust himself forward and strike deals. Grant did not want to do much work. The ministry could probably afford to ignore him, and his allies. This was a disaster for Grant's brother-in-law. Lovat had thrown himself and his resources into this election in order to come out of it as a beneficiary of patronage. Lovat absolutely believed Ilay and Walpole owed him a seat in the Lords as an elected peer. He badgered Grant to represent him as worthy of any local government post with a salary that came up. As Sheriff of Inverness-shire and captain of an Independent Company he already helped maintain law and order.

By Christmas, Lovat was still looking forward to good news in his letters. He wrote to Sir Robert Walpole to wish him the compliments of the season, and copied the letter to Sir Robert Munro, Ross-shire MP and friend, just in case Lovat's name was mentioned in conversation when Munro saw his political boss. Still nothing came for Lord Lovat.

The election had all but broken Lovat's friendship with Duncan Forbes. Duncan's reports on his activities were losing 'me the favour and countenance of the Duke of Argyll', Lovat admitted to Sir James. The cost of fighting Duncan Forbes, whom Lovat called Ilay's 'sycophant fiscal' in the north, alarmed the Fraser chief. Lovat reckoned he was £3,000 out of pocket (about £500,000 in present-day values). The smaller lairds he had corralled for their votes, now 'dun and importune me' daily for the favours he had promised after the election – cash, appointments, and army commissions. Lovat needed 'support' from the administration to satisfy their expectations, and his creditors, and to build up his 'interest', his group. He would lose face in the Highlands if he did not get something significant out of this election. He had set himself up to be a patron. The great long party of the election campaign ended. Lovat woke up with a sore head and a horribly negative vision of the Highlands and his place in it. Through his sixties, Lovat had laboured with huge vigour to create a united team of influential Highland gentlemen under him, mutually dependent and supportive, the group bigger than the sum of its individual agents. He had the right idea, but it was not the right time or place to do it.

In previous elections, Highland in-fighting died down in the year leading away from the election itself. It did not happen this time. There were just too many dissatisfied men wielding a lot of personal power in the region and no outlet in Edinburgh or London for their energy, ambition and egos. It worried Ilay. Growling discontent in the Highlands had never been something about which a government could be complacent. Ilay considered thinning out the ranks of the combatants, perhaps by bringing some south to Edinburgh or London. Had he made Lovat an elected peer, it would have taken the voracious and capable Fraser chief out of the Highlands more, and exhausted some of his aggression and thrusting in the Houses of Parliament at Westminster, and might have changed Highland history.

But Duncan Forbes and Wade spoke against favouring him to Ilay. The fight for votes had turned too nasty, and they no longer trusted Lovat. In London, they thought Lovat's talk of trouble on the horizon was a bluff to attract inward investment, through him, into the region. In the north, Wade thought investing in the Highlands a sound idea but warned Ilay that local talk increasingly connected Lovat with the Jacobites and he should not be funded. Lovat argued that Wade insulted him to goad him to react with violence and justify stripping him of his Highland Company.

Not promoting him was a mistake. Although well into his sixties, Lovat was capable, powerful and could deploy his talents in one of several directions. All through these years he maintained friendly relations with the Highland chiefs who had rebelled in 1715. Some Jacobites, like Cameron of Lochiel, Lord Grange, Gordon of Glenbuchat, Seaforth and John Roy Stuart were old friends and neighbours. The names that passed through his letters and doors were tinted with Jacobitism.

His failure to find enough favour with the ministry left him struggling to meet his debt repayments. He held back money where he could. He borrowed £4,000 from the Royal Bank of Scotland, thanking his nephew Ludo Grant and Sir Robert Munro for standing guarantors. More bad luck came when Ludovick failed at the third attempt in his hope to get a Lord of Session's robe. 'Bear with patience, temper and a good grace, what you cannot help,' Lovat counselled his nephew. 'Though we are now at a low ebb, I am convinced that in a little time there will be used for chiefs of clans more than people now imagine. You know I have the second sight, and I see a vast rough storm coming on very fast; and it is certain that we are such beggars in this country that we long after a war.' It was as if he had reached a point where, in his heart, he knew the Hanoverian Whig administration could never satisfy him. Perhaps that was what Forbes and Wade picked up on in their friend Lovat. They liked him, and wanted him with them, but they were Unionist Hanoverians by conviction. Lovat had only ever been one of them out of economic and personal necessity.

For the dynamic Lovat, the inert Sir James was a catastrophe. Lovat had thought Grant's passivity would make him malleable, and the two would find good careers on the national stage in Westminster and at home. Now, Lovat considered that he may have backed the wrong horse. He remarked sombrely to Sir James that 'all his life if one interest failed him, he would turn to another'.

Yet about traditional clan and Highland society Lovat's thinking was not at all compromised. As Sheriff and with an Independent Company of soldiers under his command, he still managed and controlled feuds, cattle raids and extortion with natural authority and professionalism, knowing when and who to threaten, and when to cajole and placate. He offered solutions and mediated between warring parties. The peace and well-being of the Highlands mattered to him profoundly. Apart from the election, he was an effective and impartial Sheriff. Traditional structures existed within clanship to deal with law-breaking, such as arbitration panels. Lovat preferred to use those. But he stood ready with soldiers if not. So, it was puzzling that Lovat could not make use of his influence within the Highlands to gain influence in the south. Perhaps the problem was which way he was looking – not his daily activities, but his goal. He did not seek to use his clan status as a springboard to get himself out of the Highlands and into the glamorous maelstrom of British government and society. Rather, he tried to obtain powers and investment from the south in order to strengthen the society and economy of the Gaelic clans in a way that kept them slightly independent of mainstream British society; where they could never be important.

Worse than ignoring him, questions arose about Lovat's loyalty when Wade's troops captured John Roy Stuart. Jacobite spies continually darted through the country, evading Walpole's espionage and intelligence-gathering network. They travelled as cattle dealers and clerics, or disguised themselves as women. Wade committed John Roy Stuart, Jacobite, soldier, spy, poet and song-maker, to Inverness Castle. John Roy broke out within a day and disappeared off the face of the earth. They searched for him but it was useless. Then one day an informant said that John Roy had been taken to Castle Dounie, the Sheriff's own castle, and had stayed there for six weeks.

At Dounie, John Roy and Lovat had feasted, talked and sung. They composed songs telling how 'when young Charlie [son of 'James III'] came over, there would be blood and blows'. They spoke in Gaelic, sang in it, composed verse in it, and plotted in it. Then, smuggled in Lovat's chariot, John Roy was taken back through Inverness, right under the noses of the British authorities, and put on a boat to France. Lovat sent him with a message for the Pretender, it was later alleged. Apparently, Lord Lovat assured 'his King', James, 'of his fidelity'. He 'charged him to expedite his sending his commission of Lieutenant-General of the Highlands, and his patent of a Duke'.

During the days, after recovering from nights such as those with John Roy Stuart, conjuring up intoxicating visions of a remembered fantasy Scotland, Lovat juggled his debts and repayment schedules. He heard at long last from the object of his attentions, the Earl of Ilay. He opened the letter, expecting an appointment. Wade's complaints to George II that the Highland Companies were infiltrated by Jacobitism had led the King to demand action. Wade put Lovat's captaincy forward as the first to go. Ilay hesitated. He did not want to drive Lovat into hostile opposition. Instead, Ilay wrote to Lovat to ask him to send his son, Simon, to him, to be educated in England. Ilay intended to put him where the Master of Lovat would learn sound British values that would help the young man to govern his clan properly, in due course. Lovat controlled his bitter disappointment with difficulty. Lovat thanked Ilay for his concern. At present, the young Master of Lovat, rising ten, was 'so tender and so much threatened with a decay', that he preferred to keep him at home and prepare him and his brother Sandy for school in Edinburgh.

In answer, Lovat heard that Duncan Forbes had been appointed Lord President of the Court of Session, the most senior judge in Scotland. Not even an ordinary Lord of Session's gown for Ludovick Grant, but Forbes had been raised to the Presidency. The Grants were outraged. They retired from public life, went home to Speyside and said they wanted to live privately. To show his disapproval, Sir James Grant moved into opposition to Ilay. This was nothing short of catastrophic for Lovat. He had spent decades working against the political ambitions of Duncan Forbes and his allies, and Duncan was now one of the most powerful men in the country. For the Grants, the game was up. Lovat had encouraged them to carry on for so long, he felt cast down. 'I am but a poor old invalid,' he told his brother-in-law. He recalled his heyday, when 'I was a courtier and I may say a favourite, both of Lewis Quatorze and the late King George's.' These days, he felt old and ill, less able to withstand the wintry gusts of disfavour.

Fraser of Castleleathers continued to bait his Lordship. 'The known notorious common liar and monster of ingratitude, Major Cracks,' came to Inverness, Lovat told Grant in the spring of 1737. Castleleathers boasted that he had informed against Lovat to Ilay. No wonder Lovat made no headway. 'It is the greatest trial that ever my patience met with, that I do not yield to my just passion in allowing his nose and ears to be cut off,' Lovat snapped. Perhaps Grant might plead for his beleaguered brother-in-law. 'Vindicate me against the lies of a rodomontade villain!' with the Earl, he implored. Grant declined, thereby avoiding his terrifyingly energetic Fraser brother-in-law.

Lovat tried to distract Ilay by reporting how well he served as the face of British law and order in his role as Sheriff and commander of an Independent Company. No one disputed that. He avoided mentioning what Wade, Forbes and Ilay thought was his other face – the intriguer with spies from the Stuart Court at Rome. The ghost of old charges of Jacobitism, conspiracy and treason haunted his letters to Ilay.

Grant sensed a change in his brother-in-law's mood. From remorselessly vigorous requests and plots to get places, Lovat seemed more reflective. He thought all his problems flowed from Duncan Forbes who, he maintained, hated him. Grant countered that this was simply not true. Lovat went out of his way to abandon the Forbeses, after they helped him so much when he first returned, and after they had laboured for years over his various lawsuits. Lovat's virulent opposition in the last election upset Duncan profoundly, but the Lord President still admired Lovat's skill and authority in regulating a balance of power among his neighbouring chiefs. As a Highlander, Duncan liked and understood Lovat and his values. As a Briton, he could not.

As 1737 drew to a close, Lovat put a very basic question to Ilay: Would the Earl do anything at all, make any gesture, to stop him doing something irreversible? If Ilay gave him trifles to let him hope, then Lovat would see 'no further difficulty in life' than to 'live frugally in order to pay the great debt I owe for that natural and beloved acquisition of mine, which has cost me above thirty years' purchase … An Arabian would have got it cheaper than I,' he noted. The price of his estates could also be summed up in lost decades of his life, as well as a fortune in legal costs and compensation. When he set out on this path in 1715, he assumed his inheritance would simply be assigned to him after a few years of proving himself in the courts.

Lovat failed to reach Ilay; whether it was Lord President Forbes who blocked him, or Ilay's elected deafness, it was no matter. A year later, Lovat, the British government employee, swore his oaths of allegiance to King George II. Then he travelled to Edinburgh on business, and to arrange his boys' education. While there he put down a marker of his independence and dissatisfaction with his treatment. In an age of clubs, establishment and dissenting, the problem with the one Lovat now joined – as a founder member – was the purpose declared in its name: The Association for the Restoration of the Stuarts. 'I was one of those that entered into a formal association to venture our lives and fortunes to restore the King ['James III and VIII'] and his offspring, and we signed our mutual engagements for this purpose with our hands and seals,' Lovat said later. Lovat was the head of it. With him were Sir James Campbell of Auchinbreck, Cameron of Lochiel the younger, John Roy Stuart, the Earl of Traquair, Lord Perth and his brother, Lord John Drummond. Seven noblemen expressed treason. Soon others joined them.

PART FOUR

Lord Lovat's Lament, 1739–47

Many a blank is found for us
To fill again in Britain,
Which not without unsheathing swords
Can ever be rightly written.
One of them is our fairest gem
The kingdom's foremost hero –
Great Lovat, whom that Parliament
Of ill-will executed ...

We are beneath oppression's heel,
Ashamed are we and weary,
The remnant that survives of us
Is scattered through the mountains
With terror filled before our foes,
Who hunt us midst the islands.
They've made of us but wretched thrall,
'O Charlie come to help us.'

– FROM 'LORD LOVAT'S LAMENT'
BY ALEXANDER MACDONALD, JACOBITE POET

TWENTY-SEVEN

Floating between interests, 1738–43

'I have a clean conscience and an upright heart'
— LOVAT, ABOUT HIMSELF

The members of the Association for the Restoration of the Stuarts met regularly in Edinburgh to air grievances about the government and its policies. Drummond of Balhaldie – an agent running information between France, the Stuart Court in Rome, and Great Britain – was one of their main contacts. He was an active Jacobite and close friend of John Roy Stuart. As Lovat pulled away from his friends in government, Forbes and Wade wondered, and shared their speculation with Ilay, just how many of Lovat's intimates were active Jacobites. Balhaldies, John Roy Stuart, various Erskines of Mar, members of the Perth family, Gordons along the coast east from Inverness towards Aberdeen, Camerons of Lochiel – these rocks formed the foundations of Jacobitism in Scotland.

When Balhaldie's brother died of fever in the West Indies, where he had been a sugar planter, Lovat commiserated but begged Balhaldie not to pursue his plan to go abroad and take up his brother's work. 'Fix your heart upon your home affairs, and wait patiently some happy occasion in which you can show your merit and valour for the honour and glory of your country, and how heroic and glorious it is to venture your person for your dear country, rather than for the sordid dross of the earth, which is as difficult and uncertain to preserve, as it is painful and tormenting to acquire.' Lovat's letters reeked of clannishness, Scottish nationalism, the semi-biblical glamour of fighting for Jacobitism – and treason.

His letters to his friends recounted exhausting socialising at Castle Dounie, trips to Edinburgh, chatter about the boys and whether or not to buy paintings. When a portrait of William Wallace came on the market in Edinburgh, he wanted it but, given his huge debt obligations, his advisers told him he just did not have enough cash. 'Pray tell Evan Baillie,' his business manager, 'that I yielded my resolution of purchasing Sir William Wallace's picture' – Lovat felt a pang – 'for I always loved to preserve the glory and honour of old and ancient families.' It was his life's work. The portrait spoke to him like a picture of any hero. Wallace represented victory, Scottish independence, unflinching resistance to English colonialism, all themes at different times in his life. The painting excited and uplifted him. His ancestor had also died in the Wars of Independence. They were connected in spirit and through history.

Other letters contained messages from his hidden world, where a group of high-born sleeping traitors had banded together, and waited for what might happen. The club was an outlet for their frustrations with the Union and Britishness, and for their personal grievances after they were passed over for jobs and pensions.

As the 1730s drew to a close, a lot went wrong at once for Lovat. After a political campaign that had cost him dear in terms of money and important friends, he had been overlooked by the new administration when it had come to handing out perks after the election. Now, returning home to Dounie he was confronted by Lady Lovat. She demanded a separation.

Primrose had given him another son, Archie, who was now eighteen months old. 'My Lady Lovat, whose head was never right,' in Lovat's view, 'turned entirely wrong.' She looked more like a 'mad woman' than one of 'common sense and religion'. She complained of his frugality and lack of attention. Lovat thought it was 'mad' that she did not want to cut her dress from the mothy shroud of her predecessor's garment. On her side, she had not made this home or this family. It was a borrowed life. Lovat was too set in his ways, and too old, to build an intimate union with a young woman barely into her twenties. She had been dropped into a world of wheeling and dealing, unfinished business at home and abroad, flirting with treason, speaking loyalty and disloyalty. She was supposed to fit in with this man of twists and turns. If Lovat found biddable women in Amelia Murray and Margaret Grant, he could not dominate Primrose – so they had fought.

Lovat's chaplain, his baillie and Mr Donald, the boys' tutor, overheard the rows and tried to persuade Lady Lovat that her place was in the family, as chatelaine of the clan and Fraser country. She cried that she wanted to see her mother. She needed money and asked for £50. Lovat retorted she could have what she wanted from his chamberlain, as long as she made an account of its use 'for the good and service of the family'. She screamed that she had brought a good dowry and wanted an allowance she need not account for – for feminine things – 'clothes, drugs and any other little necessaries that she thought fit'. He scratched his head. 'This is most horrid and puts me to the four corners of my saddle to consider what to do.' He intercepted 'things' that she 'was sending to her mother, with some guineas'. He let the gold guineas go, but kept the Fraser items, including a silk tabard he bought years ago as a christening gown for his daughter Jenny.

The domestic carnage did neither of them any good. You have an 'angel for a wife', Lovat congratulated his nephew Ludovick Grant, Sir James's son and heir, where he had 'a mixture of a devil and a [jack] daw' – a thieving bird. He complained it was hard to have money extorted from him, so she could go 'south ... making a noise and racket among her relations' about his cruelty. Primrose refused to be reconciled to the marriage, and he agreed to give her her independence, though she stayed at Dounie for a while. Lovat asked three household officers to 'cut and carve upon it', ready to 'do anything for peace sake, and to hinder my name and character to be maliciously tossed up and down' and his private life made 'the table-talk of the country'.

Despite the tensions, Lovat was 'almost overwhelmed with company'. Every day, the servants set up 'two tables and above twenty covers ... My whole time is taken up, so that I have not a minute to myself' to think where this was all leading and attend to his clan business, Lovat wrote. He loved the networking and hosting, the feeling his home was the hub of the Highland world of the clans, though. Chiefs and lairds, 'Mackintosh, Drynie, Redcastle and other gentlemen and seven or eight ladies' stayed for weeks, demanding food, entertainment and beds. He knew Wade watched him for a reason to break Lovat's company. This socialising caught his attention.

When his guests left at last, Lovat succumbed to low spirits and 'a very strong roving fever, with a violent cough'. He forced down 'several vomits and doses of rhubarb'. The distemper raged, his body heaving with 'a violent vomiting and purging at the same time'. After such a brutal evacuation, he improved. Lady Lovat heard and her stomach tightened. It was all she could do to hold herself still until she could escape his fortress. Soon enough the day came and she left, leaving her husband a single parent again – in his seventies, organising the clan, his home and raising five children, aged between eighteen months and twelve years.

Being Lovat, he applied his whole attention everywhere, questioning school masters, querying shopkeepers' accounts, ordering supplies daily for the household. 'I have as good Skill myself of Housekeeping as any in the Island,' he boasted. He sent instructions to his Inverness merchant when 'wee Sandy' was ready to be 'breeched' out of nursery pinafores. John Young, 'general of our tailors', will come, he said, 'to take off clothes for my little boy Sandy … I hope his periwig is now ready … and a little hat for him. It must not be very little for he has a good large head of his age.' He was only nine, but already a Highland gentleman, all 'furniture conform', 'periwig' and all.

Then he drove with his beloved Sandy, smart and itchy in his new suit, to put the boy to live with his older cousin Ludo Grant, to see if a break from Dounie might calm the boy's coarse tongue and appetites. The child, unmothered at birth, and then badly mothered, was always a worry to his father. Even now he was very hard to control. On the way, Lovat reflected that if Margaret had been alive, she would have shouldered the burden for loving and teaching their children and tending their illnesses, and controlling the many keys to the stores of a large household, all hanging in a noisy 'chatelaine' from her belt. He felt agitated in his heart. He collected Simon and dropped the boy in Glasgow before going on to Edinburgh, instructing the lad to make sure his handwriting was firm and clear and to keep speaking Gaelic. To placate Ilay, Lovat had agreed to put the Master of Lovat with a Campbell minister in Glasgow instead of in Edinburgh, where he and his Jacobite friends had houses.

From Edinburgh, Lovat wrote to Mr Donald who had temporary management of the household at Dounie, to say he hoped to be home 'in five or six weeks if I am alive and in health'. Until he arrived, 'you will be so good as to keep all the keys of the house, the key of my closet where my strong box is, the key of the press [cupboard] in my room', and so on. 'Little Hughy will have the key of the meat cellar and act as butler till I send home one, and after you take an inventory of what is in the press and little cellar he may get the keys of that too.' When the mutton was eaten up, they should ask for a few hens. 'Hugh Papa will give you [oat]meal and salmon, and John Fraser's wife will send you out grey fish from the town. In short you must have two good substantial dishes when you are alone and three dishes when you have any strangers. Drink as much of the fine ale as you have a mind and when there comes an extraordinary stranger you may give him a bottle of wine. I shall leave instructions with Hugh Papa how to manage the second table.' Tired, he put down his pen and flexed his fingers. If only he had a wife, this would so much less of a burden. But he never stopped, and picked up his pen again as soon as he could.

What concerned Lovat particularly in 1740 were the first reports of the harvest. It was already July. He prayed to God this year would be better than the last. In 1739 the harvest had failed. Some of his 'commons' were in very poor health, and malnourished. From Edinburgh he wrote constantly to his estate factors, asking for updates: 'I am exceeding glad of the account you give me of the corns.' It promised to be an abundant year. 'We should thank God that the poor people will have bread ... As the harvest must be late, the poor people cannot expect a relief from it for three or four weeks, so that now is the time to be charitable towards them ... I find that the spates and the floods in the river this year has wronged my fishing very much, there is no help for it, we should thank God for what we have.

'I am glad you tell me that the hay of Tomich is cared for, but you say nothing of the hay of Lovat, and I am sure it is very good condition before this time …

'I am glad that most of my peats are secured in the peat yard, and I hope no time will be lost to put in what remains when the weather will allow it …

'I will have all the stones that are landed at Dumballach carried near the old castle …' Lovat's chamberlain knew 'better than I do how to manage those rascals the waggoners'. Meantime, he requested them to send south his two cash books 'since I know not what I have paid or what I am owing in this town'.

Back at Dounie he watched for Duncan Forbes's movements, asking one of his Inverness contacts if he knew when the Lord President was coming to his estate of Bunchrew and Achnagairn; whether he would go to dine at Brahan (the Mackenzie stronghold); so 'that my posts may be in good order as he passes'. He needed to keep everything looking as Duncan should see it, without too many Jacobites spotted, coming and going through Fraser country.

When he relaxed back in his carriage and looked about him though, despite some setbacks and failures, Lovat could congratulate himself. He had largely fulfilled the quest given to young Simon Fraser of Beaufort by men like the Reverend James. Taking stock of his achievements old Lovat wrote: 'I have done my part to my family, children and kindred, and I am easy about all the actions of all the great men of Britain. I shall live well with my allies and neighbours, and never desire to have to do with any public people or affairs. I am quite tired of them … but I must have patience till the debt of the estate of Lovat be paid.' His real difficulty meeting everyday expenses was the huge call on his resources caused by having to pay off Fraserdale.

The Master of Lovat's time in Glasgow did not last. Lovat said the Campbell minister charged extortionately for the boy's board and schooling, and so he moved Simon to Edinburgh as soon as he could. Lovat drove himself as hard as ever. The children took up a lot of his time and thoughts. A child of Simon's social standing needed a foot-man. 'I thought William Chisholm was a very fit handsome fellow for him,' Lovat said to Mr Donald, whom he sent to run the boy's house-hold in the city, but 'I know his design is to have little Simon McQuian that used to serve him in this house, and I will humour him in that.' Also, 'I think riding out once a week would be good for his health, but you must make a frugal bargain for horses.'

He told his cousins and kinsmen to take the young Master out into Edinburgh society. 'It is the best piece of education that he can have, for he will learn always something by those that he visits, and it will give him countenance and forwardness in the world, which is very necessary and much more useful to him in his life than all he can learn in schools.' This was the man-of-the-world's philosophy: cultivate charm and interest. Lovat delayed his plan to bring Sandy to Edinburgh for as long as he could. 'The Brig', as he called Sandy, short for Brigadier, Lovat's nickname for his second son, 'is in such a bad situation every way that I cannot send him south till the spring.' Living with the Grant cousins had failed. Simon was 'very ill as to his health, and low in his body; but, which is worse, he is entirely lost and debauched in his education. He hardly speaks a word now without swearing, cursing, blaspheming and lying. So that I am resolved to keep him under my own eye this winter.' The boy worried him terribly, but he could not think what to try now.

The other reason to be in Edinburgh was the Stuart Association. Balhaldies had carried Lovat's requests for commissions, patents and honours to James Stuart. 'His Majesty' was generous enough to give 'a commission to carry to me of General of the Highlanders, which I have; and several letters writ with the King's own hand, that his Majesty would pay all the money I paid Fraserdale, and his creditors, for the estate of Lovat; and, last of all, the King was so good as to give such a singular mark of his favour to me, and to my family, that he created me Duke of Fraser etc.,' Lovat admitted. Until the Stuarts were restored, this was play-acting. Yet if any of his old Whig colleagues got hold of letters calling James 'the King' or 'his Majesty', Lovat could have been executed the next day.

Duncan Forbes's intelligence told him of a dissenting group, and old friends foolish enough to become members. It might be no more than another seditious club: an outlet for like-minded men to air views highly critical of Walpole's administration. There were plenty of those. The Lord President was content to treat it as the fantasy of the dispossessed it was most likely to remain. Meanwhile, he worked to strip its activists of any power that might enable them to endanger the state. This was Walpole's way also: not to challenge enemies openly, just dig out the ground steadily from under their feet.

From the army's point of view, Wade reported to the King that old Lord Lovat embodied the North British problem. At the government's expense, highly politicised, able and powerful chiefs had equipped and trained up their clansmen to create an armed force that combined the discipline of regular British troops with the martial spirit of clanship. Lovat rotated the men of his company so as many as possible capable of bearing arms experienced formal military training. Wade saw potential trouble being trained, at his expense, but there was nothing definite to fix on.

At the beginning of 1740, George II demanded action against the captains of the Independent Companies. Wade stepped in and stripped Lord Lovat of his company of Frasers and put them under command elsewhere. Lovat was mortified. There was worse to come. Wade advised the government to remove Lovat from the office of High Sheriff of Inverness-shire. Lovat complained to Lord Grange's brother. 'I was fitter to be Sheriff of that great and troublesome shire, to keep it in peace and good order, than any one man beyond the Grampians; nay, I may say, than any man in Scotland.' No one disagreed, including Lord President Forbes, but the risks of letting him do the job were too high. The risk in dismissing him was to alienate him further from the establishment. On balance, they could not imagine that would be a problem at his age.

'I have a clean conscience and upright heart,' Lovat comforted himself, and he meant it, this short and infinitely complex statement of his position, adding: 'My Lord Ilay is gone into measures ... to ruin my person and family ... I plainly see the design is to put me in prison upon the first account of an invasion, and then to make a battalion of my name for the good of the government.' Ilay would have been startled to hear him refer so casually to the idea of a foreign invasion. Britain had been safe from that threat for a quarter of a century. That summer the Earl of Ilay and the Duke of Argyll came north and Lovat went again to Edinburgh, to see if there was anything he could do to reverse Ilay's decision. 'If I was such an observer of frights [omens] as I used to be, I would not have taken journey,' Lovat commented afterwards.

Two days before he left, one his coach horses stepped into the paddock and 'dropped down dead as if she had been shot with a cannon ball'. The next day, Lovat was on his way to say goodbye to Fraser of Dumballach and Fraser of Achnagairn and leave them their orders, when 'one of the hind wheels of my chariot broke in pieces'. Then his chamberlain, John Fraser, broke his leg coming back from doing the chief's business in Applecross on the west coast.

The weather was foul the entire journey south. They broke down three times, and Lovat brooded the whole way on the latest political developments. The Whigs under Walpole were in power still, after twenty-five years. In Scotland, Walpole and his managers, including Ilay, Forbes and Wade, aroused hostility and envy of their power and incomes to the extent that other Whigs, not the Tories, were their main opponents. This Whig opposition to the Court Party at present divided into two groups: the Jacobites, and a group called the Patriots. The Patriots wanted independence again. The Duke of Argyll had broken with Walpole and led the Patriots at home and in Westminster. Ilay stayed with the Court Party that served his interests so well, and with Walpole. As he rode south with his daughters, Lovat wondered if he should break with Ilay officially, and side with the Patriot opposition? Or, should he commit himself openly to the Jacobite opposition? He admitted to his cousin, Fraser of Inverallochy, that he was in a quandary.

In Edinburgh, the Duke of Argyll held a levee every morning. Once he had recovered from the journey, Lovat attended. Argyll 'embraced me after his ordinary manner'. The Fraser chief regaled him with his nightmare journey. They both 'laughed heartily'.

Seeing Ilay was a different matter. The Earl shunned Lovat for days, and then summoned him in for a private interview. Face to face, the Earl was cold and unamused by the old chief's news. Ilay and Argyll had saved this man twenty-five years ago. He owed them loyalty, no matter what he thought in his heart. Ilay accused Lovat of Jacobite conspiracies, but denied having a hand in breaking Lovat's company. Besides, the Independent Companies were going to be raised into a British regiment of the line. Lovat waxed on to Ilay that he had been 'as faithful to him as his own heart' over the years. Ilay objected that even if he was, it was also the case that his 'house was a Jacobite house; that the discourse of those in my house was Jacobitism, and that I conversed with nobody but Jacobites'.

'When I came here,' Lovat wrote to Inverallochy after this meeting, 'I was not determined to dispose of myself absolutely for some time.' But then he heard the Duke of Argyll, 'openly proclaiming' that he and the Patriots 'were resolved in any event to … endeavour to recover the liberty of their country, which is enslaved by the tyranny and oppression of a wicked minister [Walpole], I own my heart and inclination warmed very much to that side.' Lovat had come to sound out Ilay, to see if he would offer anything to keep him loyal; but he 'said nothing to me that regarded my person or family'. He just kept repeating that Walpole 'accused me of being a Jacobite … I found that he asked nothing of me.'

This was the point. Asking no favour of Lovat, Ilay did not need to offer favours. He did not even promise Lovat some 'equivalent for my company … I then plainly concluded that he left me to myself to do what I thought fit.'

That was not at all the conclusion Ilay thought he should draw. Lovat should conclude that he was very lucky not to be arrested, but permitted to go home and live out the remainder of his life invisible to the ministry. He had never done that. Certainly, Lovat was now old, and slowing down. Nevertheless, he was still a dangerous man to leave 'floating between interests'. Lovat joined the Patriots.

More than the malice of enemies, Lovat was a victim of the terms of his own success. He had achieved, against all the odds, much of what he set out to achieve in life. But his natural enemy, the Hanoverian regime, had delivered it, not his beloved Stuarts.

To take his mind off his troubles, Lovat asked his son's tutor John Halket to dine, and told him to bring his university friend, a young minister called Alexander Carlyle, with him.

The two young men went to 'Lucky Vint's, a celebrated village tavern in the west end of the town. There 'they found Lord Grange, with three or four gentlemen of the name of Fraser, young Sandy Fraser, and his father, Lovat'. The two old Lords bubbled playfully with Jacobite allusions. Lovat said the grace in French, leaving the clerics distinctly uncomfortable. After supper the claret was put on the table. It 'circulated fast, [and] the two old men grew very merry'. Carlyle noticed that Grange, without appearing to flatter, was very attentive of Lovat, and careful to please him.

Kate Vint, the landlady's daughter, pleased him better. When she brought in more wine, Lovat insisted she stay to dance with him. She was a handsome girl, 'with fine black eyes and an agreeable person'; she 'was very alluring', the young cleric noted, but he could not get near her. 'She was a mistress of Lord Drummuir,' Halket told him, but Drummuir could not set her up in a house, where he could get at her when he wanted, because 'her mother would not part with her, as she drew much company to the' tavern. Lovat and Kate danced until she, observing Lovat's legs as thick as posts, fell 'a-laughing and ran off'. Skipping away from the old man 'she missed her second course of kisses ... though she had endured the first'.

Watching the chief standing in the middle of the room, Carlyle observed that 'Lovat was tall and stately, and might have been handsome in his youth.'

Back home, when campaigning for the 1741 general election got underway, Lovat seemed to hang back. Young Simon was recovering from a serious fever and Lovat could think of nothing but the boy's health. 'I do not think it is proper that he should go to the college this year on account of his health, and the design that my Lord Ilay has to bring him to England – which design however shall never be execute but over my belly. And,' he snapped ominously, 'by all probability things will fall out before that time that will take up the ministry with more essential things than the education of my son.'

When he could not resist the call of electioneering, Lovat finally abandoned Sir James Grant, a Court man, and promoted his cousin Sir Norman MacLeod, a Patriot Party man, for the seat of Inverness-shire. Lovat had given the Grants twenty-five years of support, delivering votes, spending money, dispensing advice, and Grant had done nothing to build a faction to rival the Forbeses for Ilay's favours. On the contrary, Lovat was stripped of his offices. This humiliated and angered the old man.

The whole winter of 1740–41 Lovat was much confined to Dounie and could not canvass much. A 'terrible storm ... which is the greatest that was ever known in this country since the memory of man or by tradition or history', kept him indoors. 'I bless God I stand it out very well. It is true I live in the South of France, for I never go out of my room, and I keep such fires night and day, that my room is a quite different climate from any other room in the house. The question is how to venture out at all.' Lovat formulated a health regime. Stuck inside, hot rooms and cold baths helped keep him vigorous – and dancing. 'Notwithstanding of this extraordinary severe storm ... I take the cold bath every day, and since I cannot go abroad, use the exercise of dancing every day.' He and his teenage daughters, Jenny and Sibyl, jigged and reeled with their servants and friends. 'I can dance as cleverly as I have done these ten years past,' Lovat boasted.

He told Lochiel, the Cameron chief, that if MacLeod got the seat for the Patriots 'my family gets honour and reputation by it'. On the day, MacLeod won, but so did Walpole, fighting off again the challenge to his leadership. The Patriots got no power.

By 1743, Lovat had found contentment in his life. A prominent and successful figure in the Highlands, he seems to have reconciled himself to disappointment in the national arena. He was managing his debts and the estates were in good order for the first time in generations.

Most of his children thrived. Cluny MacPherson, head of a Jacobite clan, married Jenny in 1742. The Mackintosh's son came on a visit 'to see me in this little hut', Castle Dounie. The Mackintosh was an active Jacobite and was out in 1688, and 1715. 'His visit has given me vast pleasure,' Lovat assured the young man's father, adding suggestively, 'I have enjoined my son to live in great friendship with him all his life … I was so lucky as to have here the Earl of Cromartie, and Lord MacLeod, his son, and his Governor, and Dr Fraser' – Jacobites all. 'I never saw more delightful company than they have been and continue so. The Earl and Dr Fraser are enough to make a hundred rejoice if they were in company. There was nothing but mirth and affection among us.'

Lovat said he and the Mackintosh must stay in touch by sending letters via Lovat's Inverness merchant, Duncan Fraser. He ended the letter on a sharp, quiet note, indicating why they might need a quick and reliable method of communicating. 'We expect great news by this post. If I have anything extraordinary, I will acquaint you. I pray God preserve our friends, and restore the liberties of our country.' There was rumour of an invasion.

TWENTY-EIGHT

'A foolish and rash undertaking', 1743–45

'Heroic and glorious it is to venture your
person for your dear country'
– LOVAT TO DRUMMOND OF BALHALDIE

The French had moved to menace the borders of Hanover. Horace
Walpole, Sir Robert Walpole's brother, reported from Florence that
the Jacobites in Italy were telling each other that France would not
pull back from Hanover 'but on conditions very advantageous to the
Pretender's family ... which they interpret to be the dismembering of
Scotland from England and settling themselves there'.

Nearly thirty years earlier, Lockhart of Carnwath, a passionate anti-
Union Scotsman, came up with a scheme whereby the Jacobites and
the French, with help from the Holy Roman Empire, could seize
George I's beloved Hanover and not let it go until he abandoned
Great Britain in favour of James III. Perhaps it was happening now.
The Jacobite interpretation greatly exaggerated the power of the
British King. George II could not, ever, form a policy that hung on
him compromising British security and the very structure of the
nation. The idea was inconceivable to any but desperadoes and revolutionaries. Lovat was neither of these things.

George II looked to his homeland and went to put himself at the
head of his army. At Dettingen, on 27 June, George II led British forces
to victory over the French. It was the last battle in which a British King
commanded his armies in person.

The French reaction was towering anger. They were not at war with England. They menaced Hanover in so far as it was part of the Holy Roman Empire, with whom they *were* in dispute. In retaliation, the French decided against a peaceful withdrawal from the borders of Hanover, and prepared to send a fleet up the Channel to strike back against the British by invading and drawing home their troops. Part of the strategy involved supporting a Jacobite uprising in Scotland.

This then was the 'extraordinary' news Lovat mentioned to Mackintosh. Over the last few years Gordon of Glenbuchat had visited James Stuart several times to urge him to come home to Scotland and forget England. Most Scottish Jacobites were happy to break up the Union. In Edinburgh, the Association for the Restoration of the Stuarts now met with Drummond of Balhaldie and Murray of Broughton, to gather intelligence about the mood and desires of the English and Scottish Jacobites. An English opposition Whig, Philip, Earl Chesterfield, had even visited the Jacobite Duke of Ormonde in Avignon to see if the Jacobites' action might bring down the hated Walpole.

The Edinburgh Association sent a memorial to Fleury and the French Court, exaggerating the level of support in the country. The French answered with a proposal 'to send over 3,000 to be landed in Scotland: 1,500 near Inverness, so as immediately to join with the clan of the Frasers; the other 1,500 to land on the west coast near Lochiel's country'. The Association repeated that French support was a non-negotiable condition of a rising in Britain. They said 10–12,000 troops should be landed as near as possible to London. Drummond of Balhaldie met Lochiel in Edinburgh (where he was renting Lovat's house) and said that if support looked likely from the English Jacobites as well, then 1743 might be a year of great change.

Lovat sounded a warning to his younger conspirators, saying he thought the French, on past form, might drop the Jacobites if they settled their dispute with England. One British diplomat summed up what Lovat already knew about Spain and France's attitude to the Stuarts: 'This family is a tool in the hands of some people and made to believe great things in agitation in their behalf.' Yet no one could afford to trust too much 'to outward appearances ... in a matter of this importance'. That was the problem. The Stuarts were a sideshow that could be moved centre stage. It meant they must all tread with great care in public, said Lovat.

In Lovat's Edinburgh house, Cameron of Lochiel found himself bombarded with post from his friend and landlord, now at home in Dounie. 'You are a very lazy correspondent,' Lovat scolded him. 'You never tell me a word of the Duke of Argyle's death, nor of the Lady Achnabreak's dream, nor of Prince Charles passing the Rhine, nor of King George's beating M. de Noailles, nor of Landes being taken, nor the Germans having their quarters in Alsace Lorraine and Burgundy, nor of the Czarina having sent 40,000 men to assist the Queen of Hungary. You may think little of these events, but I think them very considerable, and would wish to know the sentiments of your great city about them.' He then told Lochiel, all the work of Balhaldie and Murray of Broughton could bring forth was a wash of sympathetic sounds from English friends. They must wait for God to deliver them from 'Slavery', by which he meant the Union, and then they could act. Under all his protestations to Wade or Ilay had lain the old Lovat, instinctively Jacobite and Scottish nationalist.

The Fraser gentry in Edinburgh and London fed the information they gathered into their chief's formidable intelligence network, often via cattle drovers going to and from Edinburgh. Dr Fraser of Achnagairn reported the rumour that John Roy Stuart had turned double agent and gone to Rome to spy for the Hanoverians at the Jacobite Court. Detected, John Roy had to flee to Italy. Lovat was doubtful. Local and European pressures churned together in his head, inseparable. He was not solely a Scot, Gael, Briton, or European, but educated all his life for all these roles. He was the oldest chief around. Few of the younger men had his experience, intelligence, or personal power to draw on.

Sick with the ague, at home Lovat treated himself with Peruvian bark infused in Spanish wine, and got better. The weather, in typical Scottish fashion, compounded the gloom. A severe storm confined him in his room for two months. He thought his constitution must be marvellous to 'have resisted such a close confinement and continual eating and drinking and sitting up without any exercise', since there was no escaping the need to entertain and make plans. Cluny MacPherson came with his wife Jenny and their infant daughter. They brought with them some Camerons, including Lochiel's brother Archibald, MacPherson of Invereshi, and Lachlan MacPherson, Duncan Campbell of Clunes, and the Laird of Foulis and seven of his friends, 'and dined and stayed all night and was very merry, so that my house was very throng', as it was almost every other day this [spring] and summer'.

When his daughter and son-in-law prepared to leave, Lovat begged Cluny to leave the little girl to cheer up her grandfather. Cluny agreed, but then changed his mind. 'He acted the absolute chief,' complained Lovat, 'and carried the poor infant away in a cradle on horseback ... I cannot think that a house ... not finished two months ago can be very wholesome either for the child or the mother. But it seems that Cluny is resolved to wear the britches and the petticoats too.'

Lovat often sat till six in the morning, combining socialising and business. The men who came regularly were the ones excluded by the government. The government favoured the men who dined at Culloden House, where the Lord President entertained and networked as keenly as Lovat did at Dounie. The 3rd Earl of Cromartie, grandson of Lovat's first enemy Tarbat, came to Lovat. He was broke, but ambitious to replace Seaforth as chief of the Mackenzies. Simon called him 'the prettiest Mackenzie alive'. Seaforth was dining at Culloden.

Lovat also kept up a busy correspondence with MacLeod of Macleod, MP for Inverness-shire, whose seat he felt he had bought at great expense. He hoped his cousin (Lovat's mother was a MacLeod) could secure him some advancement, as Sir James Grant had signally failed to do. Lovat wrote to MacLeod in London, saluting him. Lovat had been ill again, but 'it has pleased God to keep me for some more time from the happy society of those brave upright honest persons who were an honour to their king and to their country' – the forebears for whom they were all named, and in whose beds they slept and halls they ate in, and whom he knew he must soon join. 'I pray for my friends as I do for myself, and particularly for the laird of MacLeod ... for I presume to know a little of his private sentiments.' Lovat tickled the Skye chief with MacLeod's emotional Jacobitism and shared feeling for homeland and people. Then he got down to business. MacLeod was his MP, and Lovat addressed him in that capacity. 'I took the liberty to write to you about getting the premium on naval stores.' It was a small customs perk yielding £80 per annum. He also asked MacLeod for newspapers, especially the *London Evening Post* and *Westminster Journal*, and offered to pay him in 'Beauly salmon and good claret' when MacLeod came to stay at Castle Dounie.

By the end of 1743, the crisis between Britain and France was resolving itself without the declaration of outright hostilities. Some malign fate seemed to haunt 'the affairs of poor old Scotland', Lovat observed through the miasma of approaching peace. Yet peace did not come, and in 1744, Britain and France finally declared war on one another. Jacobite hopes revived, yet again. Lovat and his fellow conspirators continually reconnoitred the Highlands to pass on intelligence through their spy network. One thing struck them as being of particular note: their land had been emptied of its effective military presence. The government had undermined most of the work General Wade had devoted his life to since 1724. Wade strove to lay down roads, build up barracks, put galleys and patrol boats on lochs and inlets, and to maintain six well-trained, fully manned Independent Companies. His brief had been to secure the Highlands so they could never again threaten the security of the British state. As Ilay told Lovat, the administration decided to break the six Independent Companies. They were then reformed, expanded from six to ten, and raised into a regular British regiment in 1740. Called the 'Black Watch' to distinguish them from the Redcoats, the Highland Regiment had served to protect the Highlands for three years. Wade was very pleased. The government embodied the regiment specifically for this purpose. At the precise moment when they were needed to discourage the Jacobites and Scottish nationalists alike, to Wade's and Duncan

Forbes's utter dismay, orders came to march the Black Watch south in preparation for embarkation to Flanders, to join the British line in Europe.

From Westminster's point of view, by the end of 1743, the Highlands had been peaceful for nearly thirty years. The region was mostly seen as a source of tax revenue and men to bolster his Majesty's government's policies in Europe. Lovat and his associates alerted the Stuarts that the Highland garrisons had shrunk to skeleton forces, local informers had been paid off, and local soldiers had gone. The situation in Scotland had clearly moved into a much more promising position for potential invaders.

The empty horizon shocked Wade and the Lord President. Resentment that the Highlanders were paying to go to fight a war against the French, during a period of hardship for the country people, began to sour the atmosphere. Lovat ground his teeth as his Company of Frasers were marched from Scotland to Flanders. Lord Perth arrived from France. He asked Lochiel for permission to recruit among the Camerons for the French invasion force. He got away with it for a while and then was politely told to stop by a local government officer. Early in 1744 a French expeditionary force was assembled. Dudley Ryder, the British Attorney-General, noted there was 'certain news that the French intend a descent, and the Brest squadron is reported to be now in the Downs, and they intended to come up the river, had got many pilots … We are very bare of soldiers, cannot collect 7,000 in a fortnight.' You could hear the panic as he scribbled down his intelligence onto paper. Louis XV prepared to send 10,000 troops to land at Malden and, led by Maurice of Saxe, march up the banks of the Thames.

Unbeknown to the French, Charles Edward Stuart, enervated by an existence of nothing more than political gossip, had left Rome at three in the morning of Saturday 9 January. He arrived at Antibes in the South of France on the evening of the 23rd, evaded two British ships seeking to intercept him and reached Paris on 8 February. The Prince's impetuous dash to try and join an expedition made the French very unhappy. They knew his movements would arouse British suspicions about their invasion plans.

The British minister, John, Lord Carteret, asserted that any attempt to 'force a Popish Pretender upon the Protestant nation will produce an universal resentment against the authors and abettors of such a design and at once unite all his Majesty's people in the defence of his person and government'. The ministers knew it was better to rely on soldiers than the people's 'resentment', however, and in England they began arresting Jacobite leaders and suspended habeus corpus.

They need not have worried. Since the French had begun to win battles, and the weather turned against the invading fleet, the French abandoned the invasion, as Lovat said they would.

Lovat dabbled in local political sport. At a meeting in Inverness, Lovat challenged Lord Fortrose, Seaforth's heir, to a duel. The old chief shouted and slapped the young man for spreading treasonous gossip about the Fraser chief, a man twice his age and three times his quality. In the end, Lovat struck him with his cane. Fortrose stormed from the meeting, unwilling to be forced to duel with an old man and the most senior chief in the north. Some of Lovat's Stratherrick lairds followed Fortrose and set upon him in the streets of Inverness. Nothing obviously amiss could be observed among the leaders of the Highlands, but there was terrible tension between them that erupted like this every now and then.

Rain poured down ceaselessly during the summer of 1744. Lovat sat in his room at home while his mind roved abroad. He was semi-invalided and could not walk much unaided, due to arthritis and gout. He heard rumours that General Keith, the best of the Jacobite generals, was going to lead a descent into northern Scotland. Yet he was just as pleased to hear his son-in-law Cluny had a remunerative commission in a new Hanoverian Highland Regiment, which was being raised to defend the Highlands. Wade and Forbes should have asked why no Fraser or Cameron presented themselves as officer material in the Highland Regiment. They thought Lovat was feeling bitter. The dreadful summer weather just went on and on.

In July 1744, Charles Stuart wrote to his cousin Louis XV. He argued that the large-scale despatch of English troops to the Continent had made England vulnerable and asked for support to lead an invasion to Scotland. The following spring, in May 1745, Marshal de Saxe defeated the Duke of Cumberland, Prince William Augustus, George II's youngest son, at the battle of Fontenoy. The British government despatched more troops to the European front line, including Highlanders. British garrisons at home now functioned at dangerously low levels.

In the Highlands, MacLeod of MacLeod kept up a steady correspondence with his cousin and most important constituent. Duncan Forbes also kept in touch, asking Lovat to chase Cluny to make up his company quickly. Lovat did as he was asked. In some ways, even the Jacobite lords hoped this crisis would pass like the others. Lovat was old and settled and ready to hand on his estate to Simon, who was now nineteen. 'Only the arrival of a royal Stuart in their midst was likely to shake' the most important Highland chiefs from their established network of alliances and political alignments, said one historian. Without French support, this divinely appointed apparition was very improbable and totally unwelcome. Therefore, when the Prince's Secretary, Murray of Broughton, in Scotland to stir up the Jacobites, received a letter from Charles saying he 'was fully resolved and determined to come into Scotland ... He was to set out in June; and proposed to come to the west of Scotland; and appointed signals for his landing,' Broughton sent the letter to Lord Perth, one of the Association. It soon found its way into Lovat's hands. He turned the scheme down flat. This was a 'foolish and rash undertaking ... he should not land; and if he did ... none of the men would join him,' Lovat replied. 'He should *not* land, but return,' Lovat repeated, until he brought the French with him. He spoke for all of them. Charles should be aware 'of the bad situation that their country lay under' after too many bad harvests. Lovat was about seventy-three, Charles in his early twenties. At his age, on his mission from St Germains, Lovat would have jumped the gun to shock the Scottish Jacobites into action; but he was older and wiser, and the country had been at peace for thirty years.

Disliking what he heard, Charles ignored them and embarked. He kept his movements a secret from the French and from James, his father. He left Paris and travelled to the French coast near Nantes. There, on 3 July 1745, he embarked on a frigate, the *Doutelle*. Bonnie Prince Charlie's rebellion had begun, and hardly anyone had noticed.

TWENTY-NINE

Rebellion, July–December 1745

'To have bloodshed in our bowels is a horrible thing,
to any man that loves Scotland'
– LOVAT TO DUNCAN FORBES

Imprecise intelligence arrived in London that some Jacobites were embarking from France. General Guest, commanding Edinburgh Castle, wrote to Lord Lovat. Sir Hector MacLean, chief of the MacLean clan, had just passed through his hands, summoned to London for questioning. His two fellow travellers went along with him. 'If they are plotters against his Majesty's government or not I am no judge, but if they are, they are very poor ones, for he had no money to pay for his linen washing the few days that he was here.' MacLean was lame in both feet, and his companion was 'a tall, black man, whose strength does not seem to lie in his head'. Quite likely, thought Lovat, he spoke Gaelic not English, and could not understand what Guest said to him. 'The French King must certainly have a low opinion of us if he thinks *these* are fit to overturn a state,' Guest laughed, 'with Lord John Drummond and his family at their head. If he employs no better, I don't think but the brave Frasers and the best of their friends will be able to give them battle, come when they will!'

Guest called for a postbag, sealed his letter and strolled off to enjoy the sense of superiority he felt from his elevated position on top of the plug of an extinct volcano, one hundred feet above the city. It was impossible to see how a crippled Hebridean bankrupt, his dumb

273

helper, and a motley crew of Jacobite Drummonds in Perth might stage a coup d'état.

No more could he imagine the *Doutelle*, carrying Charles Edward Stuart towards him. On 12 July, the *Doutelle* had rendezvoused with the *Elisabeth*, a 64-gun warship, carrying arms and 700 men of the Irish Brigade. Both ships sailed on towards Scotland. On 20 July, a hundred miles west of the Lizard peninsula they encountered the *Lion*, a British sixty-gunner. The *Lion* and the *Elisabeth* closed on each other for four hours. At the end the *Lion* drifted, a dismasted wreck, 45 dead, 107 wounded out of a complement of 400. The *Elisabeth*, also crippled, could not even heave to against the *Doutelle* to transfer across the 1,500 muskets and 1,800 broadswords she carried, nor, as importantly, the 700 battle-hardened soldiers she had on board.

Charles shrugged this off too. It was just another setback. They were a fact of his life. He sailed on up the coast of Britain, heading for the Hebrides, and the hundred fingered inlets of the coastline of Western Scotland. Not expecting an invasion sailing his way, Sir Norman MacLeod MP sat in Dunvegan Castle on Skye and kept up his gossipy correspondence with his old friend and cousin, Lovat. MacLeod's clan had been out in 1715 for Prince Charles's father, James. Thirty years later, it was not armed rebellion but the usual moans and groans that occupied their chief. It was typical, MacLeod said, a great heap of friends arrived and he, their host, immediately fell ill with a 'feverish disorder'. 'It seems we are to be always out of order in company,' he sighed. I suffered 'a vast feebleness in all my joints and a great disorder in my stomach'. He got better, then relapsed, and now he was better again and thought he must be over it. The friends had gone.

Lovat questioned him sharply about the lack of commissions offered to Frasers in the 4th Earl of Loudon's new regiment, the 64th Regiment of Foot, raised on 28 August 1745. Once accoutred, they would defend the Highlands and also march to support General Cope, commander-in-chief of British forces. The main reason was that Lovat had declined a commission for his son, Sandy, MacLeod explained. 'Want of timeous application' by the rest of Lovat's kin was the other reason. MacLeod promised to try and get an ensign's commission for Fraser of Foyers, but not for 'your Pimp Churgeon', Fraser of Achnagairn, Lovat's bibulous family physician and brother-in-law of Lord President Forbes.

Lovat told Duncan he had wanted an officer's commission for the sixteen-year-old Sandy, to command one of the new companies, but on getting the boy home Lovat was amazed to find the boy was a midget. Forbes dismissed the feeble excuse. He offered not only a commission for Sandy, but was waiting for 'a list from you of the person's names to whom you would have the commissions for Captain, Lieutenant and Ensign given'. Duncan banged the real point home. 'My labour for the best part of thirty years is lost, if I need to employ many words to convince you that I wish your family heartily well.' They were sparring partners, but very old acquaintances. Duncan was desperate for the Frasers to join this Hanoverian regiment. It would send out loyal signals to the disaffected Highland chiefs, many of whom deferred to Lovat, and calm the whole region. Duncan also hoped to protect the old chief.

More important than Sandy Fraser, Forbes wondered what Lovat's intentions were for his son and heir, the Master of Lovat. The Frasers, thanks only to their chief's lifelong effort, now sat firm in the heart of the establishment in the Highlands. The Lord President and many of the Fraser elite wanted the Master to be sent out of harm's way to Leyden, in the Netherlands, fiercely Protestant and a great seat of learning. Fraser of Balnain offered to pay for his first year's expenses if his father did not have the money. After the first year, Lovat could reimburse Balnain, and take over the financing of Simon's Continental education if needs be. Lovat listened, hesitated, and agreed. Next day, he changed his mind. He was in at least two minds and could not act.

The government was confident the French intended this flurry of invasion gossip to divert their attention from Cumberland's campaign in Flanders. As a precaution though, ministers requested Cumberland to send home some troops to discourage the French. No one, including the Association, could see beyond France and did not consider seriously the freelance enterprise darting towards the Western Isles of Scotland.

'That mad and unaccountable gentleman!' Lovat exploded to Lochiel when he was at last informed that Charles had landed, on the tiny island of Eriskay on 25 July, with no evidence he acted in concert with the French. Barely able to stand, Lovat could not contain his excitement and irritation. He hobbled up and down his room at Dounie, letter in his hand, hearing the place and manner of the Prince's arrival from the Jacobite soldier in front of him. No, the Bonnie Prince had no troops: he had had to leave them floating around on the disabled *Elisabeth*. No, he had no strategy or plans to show the arrival and disposition of French support. Most of his weaponry was with the abandoned troops. He had some men, about twenty-five he thought, a very light war chest and a few hundred sword and guns.

MacLeod of MacLeod moved from his fortress on Skye to his house at Glenelg on the mainland, and put his ear to the ground. Completely unknown to his 'dearest friend', Lord Lovat, MacLeod passed his intelligence to Duncan Forbes as well. 'I know from Lovat his forwardness to serve the government,' MacLeod said to Forbes. Yes and no, thought Duncan. Since they all believed this landing was a fiasco, MacLeod was confident he could keep his fellow conspirator at home. Lovat was sure MacLeod would rise if and when French back-up arrived.

'He did not come like a Prince,' Lovat wrote with contempt. The boy should go home. Or, go to France. Go anywhere. He should not come back without serious military support, and until his appearance looked less likely to get them all killed than it did right now. But Charles had no ears for this negative chatter from his family's ancient Jacobite warhorses. He had 'come to make his people happy', he announced in heavily accented English to an assembled group at Glenfinnan, half of whom only spoke Gaelic and did not understand him. He sent out letters ordering all the chiefs to rise and rally to him, to help him bring this happiness to everyone. MacDonald of Boisdale delivered the answer from the Skye chiefs, MacLeod of MacLeod and

MacDonald of Sleat. If the ship was still there, could they 'beg' that he 'go back to France'?

'Return home, sir,' MacDonald of Boisdale advised.

'I am come home, sir,' Charles said, and ordered his ship back to France.

Lovat dismissed the man Charles sent to summon him with the reply that when the French embarked, the Frasers would rise for the Stuarts. Lovat contacted some of the leading clansmen, including his son Simon, the Master of Lovat, and Charles Fraser of Inverallochy, and started to put his clan on a fighting footing. This was exactly the move men like Fraser of Balnain and Duncan Forbes expected and dreaded. If Lovat were unwaveringly loyal, Duncan thought he would have accepted commissions for his sons and gentlemen, ordered the clan to go and muster under Loudon, as repeatedly requested – not have them muster at Dounie under a known Jacobite chieftain, Inverallochy. In the face of great opposing forces, Charles Stuart and his Highland supporters on one side, and government men like Duncan Forbes and the Earl of Loudon on the other, Lovat hung fire.

MacLeod wrote to him. He must have heard 'some of our unlucky neighbours are up in arms in order to support the Pretended Prince of Wales. The consequence as to them must be fatal,' MacLeod said. 'As for you, your loyalty and prudence is so well known that it's easy to guess the part you will act.' MacLeod and Sir Alexander MacDonald resolved, he said, 'as we are armless … to sit quiet at least till we have orders to the contrary, and are enabled to exert our strength if required, in support of the government'. Lovat did not believe this was MacLeod's real sentiment. It was a front. In all their conversations at Dounie and in Edinburgh, the Skye chiefs promised to bring out a couple of thousand men between them, and influence others to bring out more. Yet Lovat did not like this level of explicit rejection of Charles when they could just shuffle about, like him.

They were all 'armless' at present, Lovat agreed, but they waited to rise *for* the Prince, not *against* him when arms came from France. That was what all the hosting and feasting at Dounie over the last six or seven years had been for – preparations for this moment, and agreement on how to act. Lovat wrote a letter roasting his fellow chief. He had put himself in enormous debt to get this man made MP, and keep him loyal to the Highland confederation.

What Lovat could not know was that Duncan Forbes had been blackmailing MacLeod and MacDonald of Sleat. Five years earlier, strapped for cash, the two of them had decided to sell some of their humbler kindred into slavery to American plantation owners. Women and children suddenly disappeared from beaches and hillsides. When the outcry reached the authorities, Duncan Forbes threatened to prosecute and ruin MacLeod and MacDonald. The two chiefs appealed to Duncan, old friend, Lord President of the Court of Session. 'A prosecution would be attended with a multitude of inconveniences,' MacLeod opined. Therefore, it 'ought in my weak judgement to be shunned'. Duncan was 'the only person on earth we would mostly, nay entirely, rely on. Therefore in God's name, do what you think best for us,' he appealed. Duncan thought it best, looking at the wider situation, to stop proceedings, and close the two chiefs in his fist, protected, unable to escape. When Lovat began to question MacLeod and MacDonald now, he could not see that Duncan held these two powerful Highland chiefs in his grip, and was calling in his favour.

Lovat looked out from the battlements of Dounie across the Aird of Lovat. In the closing years of his life, all he had to do was clear the debts from his country and hand everything over to his beloved son. Looking west, where the backs of the hills unfolded like a herd of giant ancient beasts, he knew it was one thing to feel resentment and frustration, and to plot a utopia of restoration to change the balance of things. The reality was terrible to contemplate, win or lose. It would happen here, up against his house sides. Civil war was a monumental clan feud. It would slip all bounds of decency. 'To have bloodshed in our bowels is a horrible thing, to any man that loves Scotland,' he said to Duncan, sombrely. Forbes agreed it was hellish. 'I pray God we may not have civil war in Scotland,' Lovat said, though he prepared for it. Lovat was not a coward. He would face the coming crisis if it did not march around him. This too was his duty.

In England, Flanders and Hanover, news of the landing provoked more irritated anxiety than panic. After thirty years of peace, the news from Scotland was incredible to think of, but the authorities in the Highlands seemed to be handling it efficiently. The arrival of a few mad papists did not threaten a major power. Few could even picture where the menace was. In London there was a run on maps that showed the location, very roughly, of Western Scotland.

As long as the King remained in Hanover, though, his throne stood empty. This made the ministry uncomfortable, but what they took seriously were events across the Channel in Flanders and France. To be safe, the Duke of Newcastle asked Prince William, the Duke of Cumberland, to send home some regiments. Newcastle was worried that 'we have not left enough troops in this country' to fight off 'a smuggling party of one hundred men' let alone an invasion by a foreign power. Cumberland thought there was little danger and the few already at home could deal with a boy and his band of men 600 miles away. Flanders loomed bigger in every way in the Duke's mind.

The government proclaimed a reward for Charles Edward's capture. Not that they really wanted him – what would they do with him? Chop off his head, as they had his great-grandfather? Eventually, the Lord Justices, who ran the country in George II's absence, sent 500 stand-of-arms to Scotland, instructing that the new Duke of Argyll (Ilay) should have as many as he wanted, and ordered General Cope north to attack the Young Pretender. The 2nd Earl of Stair, a Scottish military expert, was sure 'one has little to fear from irregular troops'. Many regarded this landing by Prince Charles as 'romantic and chimerical'. The troops and military investment in the Highlands over the last twenty years should keep the Stuart Prince behind the Highland line. Stair did not realise how much the government had run down the military presence in the Highlands to supply men and arms for the Continental war.

Newcastle asked Cumberland to take the invasion of Charles a little more seriously. Cumberland admitted 'I *am* surprised to see this romantic expedition revived again ... But I don't doubt that Sir John

Cope will be able to put a stop *immediately* to this affair,' and again refused to send any of his troops back to Britain.

On 14 August, a party of Hanoverian soldiers on their way to reinforce Fort William were ambushed. They were roughed up, two were killed and the rest seized by rebel soldiers on their way to join Prince Charles. The first blood of the invasion had been spilled on British soil. At once MacLeod wrote to Lovat to tell him to get the Master of Lovat out of the country before it was too late. Lovat must make a gesture like this to show his commitment to the Hanoverian regime. Or, he must send Sandy to join Loudon's forces, as requested repeatedly. MacLeod said the nonsense about the boy's stature was an insult. 'If his figure is the only objection to his being in the army, if an officer's head and heart be good it avails little what his person be. Marshall Luxembourg was a hump-backed dwarf of a body as ever was seen, but a very great man and officer for all that.' He concluded with his compliments to his cousin Lovat and all with him – 'which I suppose … is not a few, as I hear all the Country is in a moving disposition'. He was aware Castle Dounie thronged with both Jacobite conspirators and government Hanoverians. Lovat disliked the continuing Whiggish tenor of his co-conspirator's letters, and did not reply.

At Glenfinnan, the Prince raised his standard and held a war council. They decided to attack Sir John Cope as soon as possible. A Highland skirmishing type of conflict, continually manoeuvring without engaging face-on, had weakened the Earl of Mar in 1715. It might even have lost him the rebellion, running from here to there, picking up and losing irregular troops. Sieges to take big forts, which Prince Charles was not equipped for, would lose them time and men for no great advantage. The Hanoverians' tactics were based on their hope and expectation that the Jacobites would either skirmish or siege. General Cope left Edinburgh on 19 August and passed Stirling on the 21st, en route for Fort Augustus. He and the Prince were heading for each other.

The Earl of Stair wrote to the Earl of Loudon in Inverness that his course of action would have been, 'preferable to everything, to have disarmed the Frasers, and to have secured my friend Lord Lovat' as soon as news of the Prince's landing reached them. It would have relieved Lovat of difficult decisions. Forbes had secured MacLeod and MacDonald. Securing Lovat as well would have drawn the teeth of Prince Charles's Highland support.

The Lord Advocate, Craigie, added to the pressure on Lovat to use his well-known influence in the Highlands in the government's favour. Craigie knew Lovat had 'ground of complaint … against particular persons'. Surely Lovat could put his complaints aside in a general emergency? Lovat replied: 'I could bring 1,200 good men to the field for the King's service, if I had arms and other accoutrements for them … As you wish I would do good service … order immediately a thousand stand-of-arms to be delivered to me and my clan at Inverness, and then your Lordship shall see that I shall exert myself for the King's service.' They did not trust that the King he had in mind was George II.

Yet, Lovat refused Lochiel's call to arms for the Jacobites as well. 'I pray God we may never see such a scene in our country, as subjects killing and destroying their fellow subjects. For my part, my Lord, I am resolved to live a peaceable subject in my own house and do nothing against the King or government.' He had to mean George II here. 'And if I am attacked by the King's guards and his Captain General at their head, I will defend myself as long as I have breath in me: and if I am killed here it is not far to my burial place; and I will have, after I am dead, what I always wished, the *coronach* of all the women in my country, to convey my body to my grave; and that was my ambition when I was in my happiest situation in the world.' He sensed he would lose all if he got involved again, because the Stuarts could never really come back now. For all Lovat's sedition in Jacobite clubs, this arrival showed him that the recent rebellious talk was only a protest to which this landing was not the answer.

The English commander, General Cope, was struggling. Of an original 4,000 troops he brought to Scotland, the force he marched to the Highlands numbered barely 1,400. He had left garrisons in Edinburgh,

Glasgow and Stirling. Neither the Duke of Atholl nor Lord Glenorchy turned up at Crieff in Perthshire with reinforcements, as arranged. Cope carried a thousand weapons for men that never came. He lost his nerve and retreated to Inverness. He disliked this alien terrain, and lack of reliable information on enemy troop numbers. He believed himself hugely outnumbered. Camped outside Inverness on 29 August to rest 'after so many fatiguing marches', Cope had put himself in a corner.

Prince Charles had observed Cope's movements, and changed his mind about challenging him. Deciding to leave the British Army where it was, he bypassed it, and marched south. By 31 August, Charles was at Blair Castle, the Atholl–Murray stronghold. He was out of the Highlands, and the army sent to crush him was cut off behind him in Inverness. It was a brilliant tactical move. By 4 September, Charles was in Perth, ancient crowning place of the Kings of Scotland. He proclaimed his father, James VIII, King of Scotland. 'The Pretender's son,' Cope told Duncan Forbes, 'is in a fine Highland dress, laced with gold; wears a bonnet laced; wears a broad sword; had a green ribband … a well-made man, taller than any in his company'. Even the British commander sounded overwhelmed by Charles's physical presence. Duncan *had* to prevent his Jacobite neighbours from encountering the Pretender's son.

With Cope on his doorstep, and the Prince 110 miles to the south, Duncan Forbes alerted Westminster to the dangers of shrinking from tackling the rebels. 'As there is no body of forces in their way to oppose them, it is to be feared that their reputation will grow, and with it their numbers.' Recruits flocked to Perth, but not the Frasers. Lovat watched and waited, convinced still of the need for French aid.

In London, at last they reacted with alarm, immediately taking on board the seriousness of allowing Charles to break out of the Highlands. The government demanded troops from Flanders. Cumberland agreed. The first British soldiers reached Gravesend at the end of September. The authorities ordered Catholics to leave London and its environs. Those who would not take the Oaths of Allegiance and Supremacy and the Test Act Declaration had their arms and horses confiscated. Short of interning them, they treated dissenters as hostile aliens. The Lord Lieutenants set about implementing all this across the counties of England.

Intelligence reported tens of ships ready in France and Spain: the British confidently expected a concerted pincer movement now. 'We have hardly any regular force between Berwick and London,' Newcastle revealed. 'There are not in all England of all kinds 6,000 men, guards included … I think people begin now to be alarmed. I heartily wish they had been so a little sooner.' They still did not believe Charles Stuart's mission was personal, not agreed to by his father, let alone the great Bourbon powers of France and Spain. This had coloured their whole reading of it until it was too late to prevent this tiny landing becoming a major rebellion.

In Inverness, Lovat made a great show of his zeal for the government, even as he watched the growth of this enthralling uprising. Duncan requested intelligence from him about the rebels' movements and plans. Lovat said he had made secret enquiries. His information was that all but three clans would rise. He also 'discovered', he said, his own people beginning to stir. 'I have a strong report that mad Foyers is either gone, or preparing to go,' he said, implying he was furious and confiding to Duncan what he knew the Lord President would already know from his own intelligence. Duncan communicated ceaselessly with the chiefs who led out their clans for the Stuarts in previous rebellions. He sent letters every other day to Castle Dounie. A rider delivered them and awaited a reply.

Be sensible and calm, Duncan advised. Lovat should just do what he did in the 1715. Then it was much worse. The Fraser men had already gone out; Lovat's word recalled them. Lovat should prepare his men to march south to join General Cope. It would save the clan. Duncan's heart lurched with dismay when his rider came back without a reply. The Lord President sighed and hoped he could fill Lovat's ears with loyal messages and reminders long enough to prevent him hearing the siren call from the Young Pretender. If the critical moment passed, Lovat would stay true. Nevertheless, the news from Edinburgh was so seductive. Many Highlanders who had gone to see Charles to tell him to go home, had not come back. Something about him, or his cause, or both, put these hardened negotiators under his spell when they came into his presence.

Two days later, Duncan received a letter typical enough to make an old friend, who knew his ancient chiefly neighbour and competitor, smile – but also shudder with apprehension. Lovat informed Duncan: 'My dear cousin Lochiel ... contrary to his promise to me, engaged in this mad enterprise.' On the surface he meant simply that. Beneath the surface, Lovat meant that he and Lochiel had agreed not to engage *until the French landed*. Should Charles defeat Cope, Lovat said prophetically, then he 'will be the occasion of much bloodshed ... I have sent my officers this day with orders to them to be ready. I ordered them to make short coats and hose, and to put aside their long coats, and to get as many swords and dirks as they could find out.' Duncan could not pin him down and make Lovat send them to Loudon, who offered repeatedly to come and secure Dounie and take command of the Fraser fighting men.

Lovat's exchanges with Lochiel told the missing half of the story. 'I fear you have been over rash in going 'ere affairs were ripe. You are in a dangerous state.' Lovat spoke tersely. Cope has 3,000 men 'hanging at your tail ... We have no force to meet him ... If the MacPhersons would take the field I would bring out my lads to help the work and twixt the twa we might cause Cope to keep his Xmas here. But only Cluny' – Cluny MacPherson, Lovat's son-in-law – 'is earnest in the Cause ... Look to yourselves, for you may expect many a sour face and sharp weapon in the south. I'll aid when I can. But my prayers are all I can give at present. My service to the Prince, but I wish he had not come here so empty-handed. Silver would go far in the Highlands. I send this by Ewen Fraser, whom I have charged to give it to yourself; for were Duncan to find it, it would be my head to an onion. Farewell.' Under a certain kind of pressure, Lovat cut to the quick. Had Duncan seen the letters to Lochiel, he would not have been surprised. However, actions were the thing, and Lovat did not act.

Reviewing the progress of the rebellion, the government gave the Lord President power to raise and dispose of new Independent Companies. Did his old friend Lovat want one back, Duncan asked him? Too late, too late, thought Lovat when he read the offer. The right thing came at the wrong moment. He had been increasingly overlooked in the last decade, dealing mortal blows to Lovat's pride and loyalty. The government had left him a laughing stock with his enemies; but they were likely not laughing now.

Duncan pressed on, refusing to lose hope. If Lovat did want a company, he should give the bearer of this letter a list of men the Lord President could commission as captains and subalterns. In the bygoing, Duncan mentioned a rumour. It was bound to be nonsense, but Lovat ought to be fully apprised of events in his own territories. Duncan's sources told him the Stratherrick men were on the point of marching to the rebels. Could Lovat please confirm this was without foundation?

Lovat ignored him and answered that he was retiring from the everyday running of his estates. He, Lord Lovat, was determined to go to 'France for the benefit of my health'. The words rang hollow to the Lord President. 'Sir Robert Walpole and Mr Wade used me so much like a scoundrel or a *banditti*, that I am ever since disgusted at the political world,' Lovat insisted; 'and as I am old and infirm the only desire I have now is to live quietly and peaceably, and to retire to some place where living is cheap and reasonable, where I may spare as much money as will assist to pay my debts, or the portions of my children.' He protested too much, even if there was a corner of him that did feel too old and had had enough of fighting and probably did think like this. Still, his old heart stamped and snorted to charge out, restore the Stuarts and break the Union.

Bonnie Prince Charlie left Perth and headed south. By 16 September he was standing outside the walls of Edinburgh, demanding the city surrender. The Magistrates of Edinburgh rushed round to see Robert Craigie, the Lord Advocate, and pledged to levy enough money to pay for a thousand men for three months to defend them. But the next day, taking advantage of an open gate to walk in to Edinburgh, with 'the Provost secretly helping', Prince Charles's forces took the capital of Scotland. He rode down the High Street and entered Holyrood, the palace of his forebears, the Stuart monarchs who ruled Scotland in an unbroken line for 300 years.

General Guest pulled his regular troops up into the castle at the other end of the Royal Mile from Holyrood. They barricaded themselves in. The Prince proclaimed his father James VIII, and his soldiers pitched camp on the fields surrounding Holyrood. An Edinburgh doctor came to have a look and commented that the ordinary Jacobite soldiers, 'in general ... were of a low stature and dirty, and of a contemptible appearance', though their officers were 'gentleman-like', 'civil,' 'polished and gentle'. The Prince rode among his men, 'a good-looking man of about five feet ten inches; his hair dark red, and his eyes black. His features were regular, his visage long, much sunburnt and freckled,' as you would expect from a Scottish skin nurtured in Continental heat, 'and his countenance thoughtful and melancholy.'

Charles resupplied his army, and a few days later marched it to confront General Cope who was heading his way. Cope had consulted with the Lord President and other Hanoverians in Inverness. They had advised he leave by sea. Cope loaded his troops and left the Highlands, eventually arriving at Dunbar, to the east of Edinburgh, too late to try and prevent the city's surrender. The two sides met at Prestonpans. Cope was decisively beaten within the first fifteen minutes, collapsing before a classic Highland charge. The Jacobites lost about 25 men, Cope around 300. Cope's army, its nerves already shattered by the Highland experience before the battle, was utterly destroyed. The Jacobites took 1,500 prisoners and Cope fled to Berwick. It was to be the last victory gained by swords in Britain.

Loudon had brought his men from Inverness to fight and was fortunate to escape with most of his forces back to Dunbar. A fortnight later, he commandeered a ship and sailed with the rest of his men, arms and money back to Inverness. When Loudon docked at Inverness harbour, Duncan Forbes came out to meet him. They agreed Loudon must greatly strengthen the government's hand in the north.

The Lord Advocate wrote that 'this defeat will make it a dangerous experiment for his Majesty's troops to engage the rebels a second time without a visible superiority'. Cumberland examined every report handed to him, until he grasped what happened and why. He concluded that the superiority they needed was tactical not numerical. British troops must study the Highland charge and develop a tactic to counter it. The shockwaves of the defeat ended meaningful British opposition to the Stuarts in Scotland. Prestonpans brutally dispelled the myth of the inability of irregular troops to meet a regular force in open combat. Some important fortifications held out against Charles at Dumbarton, Edinburgh Castle, Stirling, Fort Augustus and Fort William. The garrisons in these ancient forts were not enough by themselves to support George II's position as King in Scotland. The soldiers needed to come out and engage the enemy in open combat; but after Prestonpans, British troops were understandably reluctant to come out and face the same treatment from Highland broadswords.

The Bailiff of Jedburgh in the Scottish Borders complained after Prestonpans, that 'although our country must now be branded with disaffection, yet I'm sure the government has friends enough amongst us to have prevented things coming this length, if the Disarming Act had not bound up their hands and both deprived them of arms and the warrant to use them'. This was the point that many loyal Scots, including Lovat, made over the last twenty years. Walpole's administration bore some responsibility for Charles's successes.

The battle of Prestonpans shocked and terrified the people of England. Wade was raised to the rank of field marshal, though he feared 'England is for the first comer, and if 6,000 French land before the Dutch *and English* are here, that London is theirs'. Charles raced south.

* * *

MacDonald of Barrisdale and Glengarry galloped north from Edinburgh to Inverness and charged into the hall at Castle Dounie to bring news of the victory from two who had won it. 'A victory obtained, not to be paralleled in history!' Lovat shouted, and raised his glass again and again. Representatives from both sides streamed through his doors. Lord John Drummond came to press Lovat to bring out his clan for the Prince. A group of them talked urgently in Lovat's room. A packet arrived. It contained James Stuart's 'Manifesto and Declaration'. Lovat unfolded it, handed it to his son and 'ordered the Master immediately to read' it. As he listened, Lovat sat in his chair and beat his hand against the arm, repeating, 'his right master' would prevail.

'We see a nation always famous for valour ... reduced to the condition of a province, under the specious pretence of an Union with a more powerful neighbour; in consequence of this pretended union, grievous and unprecedented taxes have been laid on, and levied with severity ... and these have not failed to produce that poverty and decay of trade, which were easily foreseen,' James wrote.

'We will, with all convenient speed, call a free Parliament ... to redress all grievances ... which have been the consequence of the pretended Union ... We will preserve right of worship to Protestants, and schools and colleges ... We are resolved to act always by the advice of our Parliaments, and to value none of our titles so much as that of common father of our people.'

Lovat said that 'whoever looked the Pretender, his lawful King, in the face, he would own he was his only rightful King, as he himself owned him to be'. His loyalty was amazing in some ways, considering the treatment he had received from James in France.

A servant opened the doors to announce supper, and they went through to the great hall to dine. The room teemed with Frasers, Drummonds, MacDonalds, Mackenzies, dogs and servants. Pipers screamed the battle cries of the clans. Gaelic toasts of 'Confusion to the White Horse and all the generation of them' roared round the room. They dipped and soared in and out of English and Gaelic as the subject demanded. Barrisdale and Glengarry kept up the tales of their miraculous triumphs. Young Alexander MacLeod, who had come out in spite of his chief MacLeod's order to stay at home, turned to Lovat. 'All would be well if my Lord Lovat would pull off the mask,' he appealed to him.

Lovat drew himself to his feet. All eyes turned to him. MacShimidh swept off the loose soft cap he wore at home to cover his shaved head, and hurled it to the floor. 'There it is then!' he cried. He was a slightly shocking sight.

Next morning, Lovat entered his room. His secretary, Robert Fraser, looked up from his Lordship's desk. Lovat asked what he was doing. Robert sat back and showed him. Lists of names trailed up and down the page. John Fraser of Byerfield, Lovat's factor, 'ordered me to make a list of the names of all the men capable of bearing arms north of Loch Ness', Robert said. Lovat nodded in satisfaction.

Lovat's lookouts came to say British soldiers were riding towards them. The rebels in the castle quickly withdrew. Duncan and Loudon sent British officers every other day, to make sure the Fraser chief was safe, they said. He expressed his fears due to lack of arms so often, they came to reassure him their eye was always on him and his kindred. Loudon again offered to garrison some men in the Aird, for his better safety. Lovat again declined, but thanked him.

Orders for supplies to be delivered to Dounie arrived daily at the Fraser merchants in Inverness. The town was very unsettled. Hugh Inglis, skipper of the Inverness boat, *Pledger*, was a Jacobite and yet resented the uprising because it ruined his trade. He complained it was absurdly expensive to get insurance for cargos, with the height-ened risk of privateering. Lovat's trading partner, Bailie Steuart, was also Jacobite, but would never rebel. This type of sentiment was what Duncan hoped accounted for Lovat's continued peacefulness; Lovat could indulge his passion for the Stuarts as a comforting pastime. He believed they would hold off civil war. The Reverend MacBean, the Forbeses' favourite preacher and minister in the town, was staunch Hanoverian and Presbyterian, and he was observed chasing his daughter through the streets and physically tearing the white Jacobite cockade off her hat which she had been parading through Inverness.

A blacksmith and a tinker was called out to Castle Dounie and stayed for a fortnight. The clang of arms being repaired and horse-shoes beaten into shape, tolled out across the courtyard. Lovat ordered his agent in the town to send out a man to make bell tents – little 'lodges to keep arms dry from the rain'. Lovat's chamberlain, Fraser of Byerfield, ordered that Lovat's crest be painted on them. The tent maker did not see his chief until the last day of the job. He thought Lovat looked very sick and walked slowly between the tents, taking a colour in his hand and examining it for quality. Lovat was under the most enormous pressure. What should he do?

About 700 men rendezvoused outside Dounie, to see 'who was capable of bearing arms, and who had any'. Women of the clan went about pinning white cockades and yew sprigs on each Fraser bonnet, uniting the Jacobite and Fraser badges – madness if Lovat still intended to signal loyalty to the Crown. The groom from the castle, going out to catch some of Lovat's horses, was amazed to see so many men. The MacDonalds of Barrisdale and of Kinlochmoidart galloped in with their dragoons. Barrisdale's horse's saddlecloth had 'GR' on it. Lovat's groom guessed he had stolen it at Prestonpans. All through the Aird, Jacobite officers lodged in 'farmers' houses, change houses and ale houses', sometimes riding up in the evenings to dine at Dounie.

The Earl of Cromartie and his men arrived to consult him as he lay in his bed. These days Lovat was often bedridden. Fraser of Byerfield never left his chief's side. Lovat asked the MacDonald and Mackenzie chieftains what kind of man was Prince Charles. Barrisdale was tired of anecdotes and pushed impatiently for the old chief to give the order to march, that would finally commit the Frasers. Lovat was waiting for Sir Norman MacLeod from Skye, still unaware he had changed sides. MacLeod had made Lovat promise to wait for the arrival of the MacLeods before he let the Frasers go.

It was now October and the campaigning season was officially over. Impatient, Barrisdale pulled out, and some of Lovat's Frasers followed a couple of days later. Lovat had not given the order, and he brought them all back again. He found these young chieftains hot headed and hard to control. They were fierce and loyal and mad for the excitement of action with no idea of the consequences. From Holyrood, Prince Charles tried to force Lovat's hand, and make it impossible for him not to come out. 'Charles, Prince of Wales, and Regent of Scotland, England, France, and Ireland, and the Dominions thereunto belonging' ordered 'Lord Lovat to apprehend and secure the person of Duncan Forbes of Culloden … We now judge it necessary hereby to empower you to seize upon the person of the above-named Duncan Forbes,' commanded Charles, 'to carry him prisoner to us at Edinburgh.' The order was issued at Holyroodhouse on 23 September 1745. It was addressed to Fraser of Foyers, head of some aggressively Jacobite Stratherrick men. If Charles could force Lord Lovat to come to him with the Lord President in tow, the effect would be explosive.

Lovat wrote to Duncan, fuming about the rumour the Lord President was about to be kidnapped. 'There has been several villainous, malicious and ridiculous reports that vexed me very much.' Lovat truly wanted nothing to do with the kidnapping of his old friend. Duncan answered miserably and angrily. The tales made no more impression on him 'than to induce me to take that sort of care of myself, without which I should have been laughed at', he said. He had fortified and garrisoned Culloden House.

Nevertheless, on the night of 15 October, 200 men descended from Stratherrick, under the leadership of Fraser of Foyers and Lovat's aggressive chamberlain, Fraser of Byerfield. (Foyers's father had gone out with Simon's older brother to fight for James II in 1688.) They crossed behind Inverness, and halted at the bushes by the gates of Culloden House. Some of Loudon's Independent Company were on sentry duty. Out of the scrub charged the caterwauling Frasers. Duncan woke in his bed with a jump to the sound of muskets. The sentries returned fire and turned a cannon on the would-be kidnappers. On both sides, the men dived behind scrub and sniped at each other in the pitch dark. As cannon balls tore into their cover, the kidnappers fled.

Duncan wrote to Lovat a couple of days later. He knew Lovat would have heard all about it. He said he would have written sooner, but for the anguish he knew it would give him to hear of it. It was true. When Lovat heard of the attack 'he was like to go mad; he cursed for a matter of two hours, and we had no peace with him'. Lovat groaned as he read the Lord President's pained and dignified letter. 'No man of common equity,' Duncan said, would think Lovat had anything to do with it. But now Duncan was 'teased every hour' by reports that the failed kidnappers were going to 'pillage, burn and destroy my innocent tenants' to vent their frustration. Duncan said he was only telling him all this so Lovat could do what he needed to 'prevent such hurt to me and my tenants as I undoubtedly should to prevent damage to your Lordship, or to anyone that belongs to you'.

MacLeod wrote to Dounie in appalled amazement. The 'scandalous attempt on the President', Duncan, 'has given me great pain, especially if Stratherrick men were the actors'. Over the years, all his friends had heard Lovat's boasts about the loyalty of his Stratherrick kindred. 'However innocent you are, it has a very ugly aspect,' MacLeod said. 'You owe yourself and the world a more public vindication ... and that is to bring the offenders to public and condign punishment ... So much for a most disagreeable subject!' He added that Lovat was welcome at Dunvegan, were he capable of travel.

MacLeod had discovered that six of his kin had gone to join the Master of Lovat's rendezvous. 'They were entertained in an outhouse of yours, and then sent' on, he said to Lovat. They should have been turned in to the garrison at Inverness. MacLeod's unhappiness was mirrored in the skies. 'The weather is still dismal,' he signed off.

Lovat grew more and more alienated from his old friends. He apologised profusely to Duncan for the 'base, barbarous, inhuman and distracted attempt and behaviour of the Stratherrick men at Culloden'. He then lamented that the Master of Lovat was on the point of leaving to join the rebels, taking hundreds with him, and how the prospect filled Lovat with fear. He was powerless to stop him, he wailed.

Duncan replied instantly. This was the worst news. Duncan agreed a delinquent son was a trial, but insisted it was well within the capabilities of a father of Lovat's quality to stop him. That, Duncan said, was everyone's opinion in Inverness. It mortified Duncan to play these games with a venerable man he had known all his life and worked with for thirty years. He understood the election battles. They had been pushing for the same jobs. However, that this tit-for-tat, skirting the real issues, was what their joint venture to promote the Highlands came down to hurt and angered the Lord President.

Lovat answered it was easy to claim he was a strong father and chief, but the Master 'always flew in my face like a wild cat when I spoke to him against any of his distracted opinions'. Simon entered his father's room in the middle of this exchange of letters, as Robert Fraser was taking down the dictation. He demanded to see the letter. The secretary refused and Simon grabbed it out of his hand. Everyone watched him as he learned of his disobedience, the pain he was giving his father and that his behaviour would be the death of the old man.

When he finished reading, Simon stared at Lovat. 'To call *me* stiff-necked and disobedient! I will set the saddle upon the right horse,' he shouted. Lovat stepped forward to stop him and take the letter. Simon jerked it away and shouted, 'If this letter goes, I will go … and discover all to my Lord President!' A youth of nineteen, he could not understand the underhand dealing. They should just rise and be done with it. Hugh Fraser of Dumballach said, though his opinion had not been asked, he thought 'if the affair could not be entirely dropped', then his preference was, 'that it should be put off for some time'. He did not want to turn traitor. Lovat agreed his opinion had not been asked, adding coldly that 'some people's opinions might be easily read in their countenances'.

Dumballach did not answer. Simon began to cry out in protest, saying 'he had been made a fool of, and a tool from first to last … he had been one day doing and another day undoing; but that now he was determined, that whatsoever resolution Lord Lovat should come to, that he would execute it, let the consequence be what it would'. The young man needed to act, not toss it to and fro, which was in fact the saving of them. But he did not understand an old man's tactics. In frustration, 'the Master rose up, took his bonnet and threw it upon the floor, threw the white cockade in the fire, and damned the cockade'.

Lovat 'rose up in a passion' and asked what could he do? Seeing his son's distress appalled him in some ways. Instead of facing the risk and danger himself, he 'was forcing his son out'. Father and son switched into Gaelic. Mr Fraser the minister stood up to speak on the Master's behalf. Fraser of Byerfield pushed the minister back down. 'What have you to do with it? You have no estate to forfeit,' he said.

In his heart, Lovat believed this rebellion could not succeed, but he also believed 'himself too far engaged to go back'. He told Dumballach in private that 'the conduct of his clan on this occasion would be his ruin, and very probably cost him his life'. At best he might be back where he started, with nothing, isolated, hunted; then all his fighting would have been for nothing, or worse than nothing. Still he would not make a decision.

Into November, Duncan went along with Lovat's prevarications as best he could, warning that if Lovat's 'authority with that kindred for whom you have done so much', retrieving them from the brink of oblivion, 'and who with reason were so passionately fond of you' is not used to pull the clan to safety, it would be a disaster. Make the Master of Lovat desert 'his rash undertaking … to save you and your family from ruin', Duncan appealed, 'as they very remarkably did thirty years ago'. To Thomas Fraser of Gorthleck, Lovat's best-loved Stratherrick laird, Duncan confessed it has 'grieved me cruelly, to see my unhappy and much loved friend on the brink of destruction' over the past three months.

'I am so monstrously tired with writing,' Duncan confided to a friend in London. The weariness of trying to save his neighbours, dealing with restraint with their deceits and struggles, made him feel ill. Yet he did not want his country to suffer for the compromised loyalties of the leaders. He had sympathy with their nationalism, while he loathed their method of expressing it. Forbes wrote to Lovat twice in one day. He would not give up on the old chief. Then, all of a sudden it was too late.

* * *

At Castle Dounie, Lovat stood on the battlements and watched the marrow of his clan, under the Master of Lovat and Charles Fraser of Inverallochy, march away. He then went to his desk in the cold, dark morning of 1 December to tell Duncan what he would know almost the moment it happened. 'My son has left me under silence of last night, contrary to my advice, contrary to my expectations and to my most earnest requests ... The consequences of his doing so are to me terrible beyond expression.' That much was true. Here came the nightmare. Lovat unleashed it and thought he controlled the path of its devastation. He could not. People never ceased to think that once they let slip the dogs of war they could call them off or change their path to suit themselves. Even as the Frasers marched, the Earl of Loudon was still at his desk writing out the terms on which he would leave Lovat in peace.

Duncan told Lovat's Stratherrick kinsman, Gorthleck, that the news sickened him to his stomach. As a way of saving Lovat, Gorthleck asked Duncan to turn a blind eye. 'An expedient which to the end of time would dishonour me,' Duncan answered coldly.

Duncan went to tell Loudon what had happened. Loudon 'stopped short'. Lovat had just put himself beyond negotiation or appeal. Loudon was infuriated that he had swallowed Lovat's blandishments about no one marching.

The Earl angrily accused Lovat with his own words: three months ago Lovat had boasted he 'had the absolute direction of them'. Now Lovat claimed his son 'seemed determined to join the rebels'. The Master apparently had 'twenty times more to say with most of them than your Lordship has'. If so, then none of Lovat's words carried any weight, and he should have been wise enough to say so. Seeing 'with half an eye' what the consequences of rebellion were, 'in place of expostulating with me and using very earnest arguments against' Loudon coming into Fraser country to garrison troops at Dounie when the Earl offered them, Lovat should have been begging him for help. With every word Lovat should have pressed 'me to march immediately to support your authority over your clan, seduced by your son, from the respect due to your Lordship'.

Lovat replied he could not imagine what actions would satisfy Loudon.

'I will tell you in two words,' Loudon snarled. 'Come home.'

Lovat waffled, appealing to Loudon and Duncan to 'be a friend to old, infirm and distressed Lord Lovat ... I resolve to live as peaceable a subject as the King and government has and will do all that's within my power to make my kinsmen that will obey me to do the same.' So many provisos, it made their heads spin.

The day after the Frasers set off to join the rebels, Loudon informed Lovat he was on his way down Loch Ness to Fort Augustus via Stratherrick. If all was quiet and everyone at home, 'I shall not put the least hardship on any man.'

Frost hardened the ground to iron as Loudon led his men down the south side of Loch Ness, through the Fraser country of Stratherrick, towards Fort Augustus. Lovat regarded it as an intolerable abuse of him and his land. The fort was blockaded by the rebels and Loudon intended to break it and resupply the government troops there. Stratherrick men had also blockaded the road between Inverness and Fort Augustus (and the west coast).

The Earl marched through Stratherrick, opening the road again. He stopped and had a proclamation read, to let the people know what was coming if they did not call back their men to turn in their arms, and resume their peacetime way of life. They would be arrested and never come home again. This was not a clan feud, and not 1715.

When he got back to Inverness, the Earl 'gave out a bloody proclamation which was read at the [Market] Cross'. He would go into the lands of those who had risen if they did not stand down at once and surrender. That meant Fraser country. The time for pacification by gentle persuasion was over. The region would be forced to submit. Tell your chief, Duncan told Fraser of Gorthleck, Loudon 'has authority to burn and destroy' their homes to bring them back. 'I shall try and stop him,' Duncan said, and persuade Loudon to finish a letter of terms of surrender for Lovat and his kin, but it 'will be his last'. If that didn't work, it was over. 'From my heart,' he said, 'I wish that repentance may not come too late' to prevent the total destruction of the Frasers.

Exhausted as he was, Duncan wrote to Lovat one final, cool letter, a sort of signing off after all his efforts. 'I can no longer remain a spectator of your Lordship's conduct, and see the double game you have played for some time past, without betraying the trust reposed in me ... Methinks a little more of your Lordship's wonted artifice would not have been amiss,' he said with bitter humour.

'Whatever had been your private sentiments with respect to this unnatural rebellion, you should, my Lord, have duly considered and estimated the advantages that would arise to your Lordship from its success, and balance them with the risks you run if it should happen to miscarry ...

'You sent away your son and the best part of your clan to join the Pretender with as little concern as if no danger had attached to such a step. I say *sent* them away, for we are not to imagine they went of themselves, or would have ventured to take arms without your Lordship's concurrence ... This, however, you are sure can't easily be proved, which indeed, may be true.'

The whole long letter was suffused with passion, anger and terrible sadness, all determinedly controlled. He knew Lovat would have as little incriminating stuff on paper as he could. 'The whole strain of your Lordship's conversation in every company where you have appeared since the Young Pretender's arrival, has tended to pervert the minds of his Majesty's subjects.'

'Those unhappy gentlemen', who came back from exile with the Young Pretender, Duncan found easier to defend than Lovat. Some had been stripped of their titles and honours since 1715. Some, like Lord George Murray, had no expectations, and may have been moved by pity for his brother Tullibardine, who had been in exile most of his life.

'But what shall I say in favour of you, my Lord?' the Lord President cried. 'You, who have flourished under the present happy establishment! You, who in the beginning of your days forfeited both your life and fortune, and yet by the benignity of the government' was not only forgiven but 'even restored to all you could lay claim to.

'But,' Duncan choked with sad foreboding, 'there are some men whom no duty can bind, nor no favour can oblige … If a timely repentance do not prevent it, your Lordship will not unjustly be ranked among that number.' The consequences would be dreadful. There was nothing available to Lovat now than to perform services of such magnitude that would counter the magnitude of the harm he was plotting.

Lovat read it, picked up his pen and dipped it in ink. He thanked Duncan for the letter, musing 'I own I never received one like it.' He paused. What had he done, losing men like this as his companions? He then threw away the chance for reconciliation and truth by insulting Duncan's intelligence. 'I see by it,' he feinted crudely, 'that for my misfortune in having an obstinate son and an ungrateful kindred, my family must go to destruction, and I must lose my life in my old age.' He congratulated himself on having 600 Frasers, who would defend him, and piped up that he was still loyal.

The song was out of tune. When he read this nonsense, Duncan let out a groan and threw it in a drawer, slamming it shut.

Writing to Bonnie Prince Charlie's secretary, Murray of Broughton, Lovat lamented his inability to come out and fight due to his decrepitude. 'I send my eldest son, the hopes of my family and the darling of my life … Instead of sending him abroad to complete his education I have sent him to venture the last drop of his blood in the glorious Prince's service, and as he is extremely beloved, and the darling of his clan, all the gentlemen of my name and clan (which I thank God! are numerous and look well and always believed to be as stout as their neighbours) are gone with him.'

As the old chief sat by his fire, and reviewed his life and achievements, 400 miles to the south, December was setting in hard around the Jacobite army. In the worst piece of timing of his life, Lovat finally sent his men out just four weeks before the Jacobites turned back at Derby. Now they hurried north, pursued by Wade and Cumberland, retreating in the worst of winter weather over terrible terrain and up through the Lake District.

Duncan sent notice to Lovat. The next day, his clerk would begin to note down who was not there, in order to stop every one of the rebels *ever* returning to live at peace in the homes and families they left. It was over, this world Lovat had brought back into being. Let your men know the danger, Duncan pleaded. They had one more day to save themselves – just one. They would never come home once he came into his old friend's country. Did Lovat not feel the reality of that? No reply came from Dounie.

Lovat looked at the list of names. The Master left with the Frasers of 'Struy, Culbokie and Reelig' – heads of the principal families this side of Loch Ness. Also, Foyers, Farraline and Leale-Garth 'as principal heads of the families of Stratherrick and Abertarff ... He has certainly,' Lovat mused wistfully, 'taken with him the flower of my clan.' Loudon ordered a regiment to prepare to go with him to fetch Lord Lovat to Inverness. They should have done it three months ago, and saved him from himself.

THIRTY

A quick victory, and long march to defeat, December 1745–June 1746

'I had rather be hanged than go to Scotland to starve'
— AN ENGLISH JACOBITE
ON TURNING ROUND AT DERBY

Tuesday 10 December: frost and a mist creeping off the River Ness.
Over 800 soldiers mustered on the Green of Muirtown, a field on the
western edge of Inverness, on the road to the Aird of Lovat. Four days
earlier the Jacobites began their retreat from England. In Inverness,
the Earl of Loudon had decided this was the day to bring in Lord
Lovat.

Loudon summoned Lovat's friends and neighbours to fetch him in.
Two companies of Sutherland's men and two companies of Seaforth's
Mackenzies camped near Brahan; two companies of Grants, his
brother-in-law's men, two companies of Munros under the laird of
Culcairn, two of Lord Reay's Mackays, and one company of Loudon's
own Highland soldiers formed up in columns. Nearly 800 men
marched out to Castle Dounie to secure MacShimidh, and disable
him from doing anything else to threaten the regime.

Lovat saw and heard them outside Dounie between three and four
in the afternoon, the light fading fast. The men halted. Loudon sent
in Brodie and Munro of Culcairn to order the Fraser chief to surrender. He was a hostage for the peaceable behaviour of the people of the

Aird of Lovat. Lovat's wild, hunting Highland men from the hills above Loch Ness had gone out, but there was no reason the civilised, low-country farming Frasers should not stay at home. The rumour was that their chief might force them out too. It was not a risk worth taking. Lovat promised to surrender by ten the next morning. He would send out his chamberlain, tacksmen and factor to order the people to come in with their arms and deliver them up. Loudon's men dispersed and billeted themselves among the tenantry around Dounie, asking for hot food and somewhere to sleep.

Next morning Loudon's forces marched back up to the walls of Dounie to collect the chief. Nothing happened. Brodie and Culcairn went back in. After another wait, they came out of the door, and found Loudon. 'Lovat was not that day in good health, and could not march,' they told him. Loudon sent them back in to say he would hear no more excuses. If Lovat did not appear at once, he would use any force to 'oblige him'. He turned to the officer at his side. A shout went out, and the 800 men circled Dounie.

Inside, Lovat raged. He was surrounded. Looking out of the window, he saw a couple of Coehorn mortars levelled at the walls of his beloved home and angrily sent out a servant to beg Loudon for a parlay. Loudon re-entered the castle. Six weeks ago, they had all dined here, listening to the bard and the piper, playing chess and cards, dancing, and laughing at the madness of Prince Charlie's landing to try and take over this land. Lovat 'still insisted to be left, but for one day'.

Loudon refused. 'Pack immediately,' he ordered. Hours later, Lovat was ready. Only then did he call for his carriage to be made ready to go to town. The chief groom, Riddel, and his stable boys dawdled over fetching tack, harness, checking one horse, replacing it with another, playing to the limits of Loudon's tolerance. The Earl had worked hard to avoid this scene, and it was infuriating to have his time wasted by insolent Fraser peasants. Lovat kept looking out across the Aird. No one came.

Loudon barked an order for his sergeants to 'yoke the horses'. They shoved the fiddling Frasers aside. At last they lifted Lord Lovat into the chariot and 'drove him before us' towards the edge of the sea and the road to Inverness. All the way in, the old chief kept asking them to stop. He was in such pain from his joints, he needed to stretch. They let him get out and sit down to rest. Further on, he needed to relieve himself. He asked the coachman to stop for any kinsmen who ran beside the carriage, so he could give them a *bodle* (coin) and ask who and how they were. Sentries kept a peeled eye on the surroundings; his Lordship was obviously waiting to be rescued.

Loudon told Lovat he would remain in their charge to encourage rebels to return. Lovat promised the clansmen around Dounie and Beauly who still had arms would bring them in by the Saturday, 14 December. He could do nothing about the Master and his small band of 'mad young men', riding to their rendezvous with Prince Charles, somewhere between Perth and Stirling. Loudon waited.

'The surrender of the arms was all that could well be expected of him,' Duncan Forbes told Tweeddale, the Scottish Secretary. Duncan told Lovat they had proof of his involvement, while the Lord President admitted in private to his superior that in fact it would be quite difficult to obtain. In which case, 'committing on suspicion a man so aged and seemingly so infirm would have had the appearance of cruelty'. For this reason, and also because he was an old friend, they did not send him up the hill to Inverness Castle. They left him in his town house on Church Street, where it was warm and comfortable, and awaited the delivery of swords and guns.

Nothing came in but excuses. Saturday came and went. By the following Thursday, Loudon had had enough. He could not catch Lovat out, but was certain he had despatched letters to the Master of Lovat and other Jacobites. It was too dangerous to leave him this much space to communicate. Loudon 'clapped sentries on the gate' of Lovat's home and told the Fraser chief he would be confined in Inverness Castle the next morning. Lame as he was, Lovat did not wait. There was a secret passage that led out of his house and down onto the banks of the river. In the middle of the night, loyal clansmen helped Lovat along it. 'An escape in his state of health was what no one dreamed of,' Duncan confessed when he heard of Lovat's flight. They had so often underestimated him. Clansmen rowed their chief upriver to the mouth of Loch Ness, out onto the loch, landing him on the shore and carrying him into the hills. Half a century after his first flight into Stratherrick, he fled again to this wild district, to shield himself from the law.

They carried him to Gorthleck House, sited on top of a small hill, high above the black waters of Loch Ness and about two-thirds of the way towards Fort Augustus. Lovat was in a great deal of pain, and was very angry. His home, possessions, lands, everything, was exposed to the government forces. No one had come to rescue or defend him. Local Jacobites marched to rendezvous with the Prince, who was beating a retreat from England.

An anonymous letter came to Lord Lovat at Gorthleck's house. It appealed for his return to loyalty to King George. He read it. Was it from Duncan? So many anonymous letters circulated from both sides. There were things about it that reminded him of the Lord President, though it could have been one of his own lairds too, like Balnain, who had tried to get him to send the Master to safety. 'I own, my Lord, that if any man living has right to dispose of his estate and clan you have it, as you have recovered the one from almost nothing and the other from bondage and slavery, but will you throw away that estate and clan? ... What will the world say, but that your Lordship is not the man you once were?' All that was very Duncan-like, Lovat smiled. It was true he felt cornered in a way he seldom had in his long life, locked into a crippled body from which he would never escape, while his Jacobitism locked him into this terrible final twist in his life story.

Trapped at Gorthleck's house, he waited to see what would happen. Enclosed too was a letter for his son, also anonymous. Lovat read it. 'For any step you have hitherto taken, you are still safe if you will but hearken to good advice of a parent ... and of friends who have it at heart to do you all the good offices that lies in their power ...

'Break through a rash, ill-digested engagement,' and return. 'My dear Master, be not amused with false reports. The situation of the young Adventurer gives no encouragement to any wise man join him. He is by this time between two fires' – Wade at his rear and Cumberland in front. Lovat worried about where his boy and his men were, and why he had not heard from the Master.

By the time Lovat reached Gorthleck, he knew his son and clan were attempting to join up with a retreating rebel army. Backing away put fear into the Jacobites for the first time since Charles landed. Eventually the Master of Lovat wrote to his father to apologise that he had not sent a body of troops north to keep his father safe, and promote the cause. They could not afford to split up their forces. Simon promised to come when he could, when he had permission from the Prince to do so.

Lovat suggested his son come north to force out the rest of the clan; he was too feeble and they had ignored his call, he said. Young Simon did not believe him. 'I know your Lordship's influence over your clan too well to think that where your orders fail, my presence will have any weight.' Besides, 'that I should, at such a critical time, run home, would look ill; and the pretext (as it would be called) of raising men, would not screen me from an imputation your Lordship would … always wish me to shun.' Cowardice. The father feared for the son though. Lovat had always liked to cover his bases. If he brought Simon home, his letters from the authorities made him confident Duncan and Loudon would pardon the Frasers. The youth refused and Lovat was left holding this heartbreaking and honourable letter, showing him a young man ready to take responsibility for actions he had not sought – a very worthy Master of Lovat.

On the desks of all the important men reports landed every day about the government's strengthening position. The two sides approached the Highlands.

Lovat wrote from Gorthleck's house to tell his son and the Jacobite leadership that he had broken free from Inverness and was on the run from the authorities. There was a search on for him, and he was preparing in case he had to seek shelter 'in hills and woods and inaccessible places'. The next place he would go was to Strathfarrar, the glen that was his channel to the west. He was 'hunted like a fox by Loudon up and down the country', Lovat wrote, 'which, perhaps, would cost him his life by cold and fatigue'. In Strathfarrar a little stone house was being built for him in the middle of Loch Muily. 'That country is the strongest hold in Scotland,' he told his son. He would go there only if all was lost, to make a last stand. 'I will make one hundred good men defend it against all the forces that King George can have in Scotland.'

Then he wrote to Lochiel, who had written to tell Lovat of 'the glorious retreat his Highness made from Derby'. Lovat did not believe a word. The minute he heard the Prince had turned back, he regretted sending out his clan. 'Be so good as to comfort my languishing soul, and drooping spirits,' Lovat begged Lochiel, 'by assuring me that you are the same affectionate Laird of Lochiel to me that ever you was: I truly never had so much need of your comfort and assistance as at this time; for I am in vast distress of body and mind.'

Nearly thirty years after he received his pardon from George I, Lovat was once more an outlaw. He thought he must be dying. His legs had gone. He and Gorthleck could hardly get out of bed unaided, let alone go and lead a revolution. Gorthleck, eighty-seven years old, had kidney disease. 'He lies in the next room to me; we are both much indisposed and invalids,' Lovat told Lochiel. There they lay, the two old men, too ill to participate, too passionate to let it all pass them by.

Lovat sat up in bed, blankets piled high on him. He could not keep warm. On nights of deep frost the moon rose over the loch and a broad highway of light fragments glittered along its length. Sometimes lights flared on the opposite banks as the army searched for him. In Gorthleck's little tower house, he waited. It was as near as he dared be to Inverness and still evade discovery. When his ancestors wanted to come here to visit their Stratherrick kindred, they commanded barges, lit by the torches leaping into the sky. A tail of a hundred men kicked their horses onto the boats, following Lord Lovat, and crossed the loch announced by pipers in the bows. They clattered off the other side and drove their spurs in, to breast the hills above them.

He had come here like a thief in the night, carried in the bottom of a mean little boat, his arms around the shoulders of his faithful kin. This was the man on whom the Prince suddenly reposed his hopes of revival. When Charles was told Lovat was free, he asked him again to come and help lead the rebellion. If Lord Lovat rose in arms, the Jacobite leaders flattered him, 'there is not a man beyond the Forth, however timorous or cautious … but will appear with the greatest alacrity and cheerfulness'. The image of Lovat would give them courage. What the Prince 'above all things wishes and desires is, to have your Lordship with him, to take upon you the command of the army'. How often in the past had he asked to lead the Jacobite forces and been shunned. The Prince 'knows your Lordship's age' made active service as a general an impossibility, 'yet he is sensible that your advice and counsel will be of greater value than the addition of several thousand men'. Charles flattered Lovat with everything he had ever wanted from the Stuarts, and everything he had claimed about his standing in Scotland. It was why Duncan and Loudon had taken such care to try and make him stay at home, to be an equally important example on their behalf. Charles offered him the use of his own coach and horses to ride in. He, Lovat, would sit in the place of the heir to the thrones of Great Britain when he appeared in it.

MacLeod discovered his whereabouts and sent a 'little sneaking gentleman here with his treacherous letters', to ask Lovat to commit himself to King George. Waiting for a reply, Lovat drew himself up. 'I told him to tell his chief that he was a traitor to the King, and a murderer of my son and me, which he might be sure I would resent, if I was able; but that I would never black paper to a man that had so basely betrayed me; that since he went to the devil I would leave him there.' MacLeod's messenger slunk away, Lovat's curses ringing in his ears. He speculated that if MacLeod had kept his oaths and his word, 'I had so managed this part of the north that about 6000 men had marched south to the Prince's service.' If only; they could have drawn out so many lingerers and lookers in the combined wake of Frasers and MacLeods.

Letters kept him connected to the action drawing closer all the time. He wrote to his son daily. 'I have done more against this government than would hang fifty lords, and forfeit fifty estates … Loudon told me the day before I made my escape that he had as much to say against me as would hang all the Frasers of my clan,' he told Simon. 'I shall send you my fine pistols and furniture after I put them … in a new portmanteau; for it would be a pity to spoil them; for there will be few so good in the army' – he still had his gifts from Louis XIV. 'My dear Simon, for Christ's sake, don't be a week without writing to me,' he cried. 'I beg over and over again my dear child to let me hear more often from you.'

By the end of January 1746, the Jacobites were at Bannockburn, between Stirling and Perth. Cumberland was only a few days behind them, and ready to retake Edinburgh. The Jacobite leadership pressed the Prince to retreat further north and not make his stand at Edinburgh. Since they were now heading for the Highlands, the Master of Lovat obtained permission to ride ahead and muster more men from his father's estates. Fraser of Inverallochy took command of all the Frasers, and Simon rode away through the snow.

The Jacobites trudged deeper into a Highland winter. The ladies among them struggled with the conditions. Miss Isabel Stuart, who had come to march with them from her parents' home south of Dunkeld, wanted to go home, as the Jacobites kept their faces heading north into the empty snow-fogged spaces of the Drumochter Pass. Plains of peat bog 1,500 feet above sea level stretched ahead of them, scoured to sour granulated mud and moor grass, ice and water. But 'the storm was too great' for her to go home just yet, Miss Stuart said. She hauled up her skirts and plodded through fourteen miles of frozen mud and the intermittent relief of some time on one of General Wade's roads. Murray of Broughton's wife rode along, but the wind chilled her so badly she had to be taken down off her horse and put in a chaise.

In Inverness, Lord President Forbes and the Earl of Loudon regarded the closeness of the warring sides with trepidation. Inverness lay right in the path of the battle that Charles fled and Cumberland chased. They had been informed that the Prince had reached the Mackintosh house, Moy Hall, just ten miles south of Inverness. Loudon tried a surprise raid on Moy to grab the Prince, but they were ambushed and most of Loudon's troops panicked and fled. With a groan, Loudon collected his remaining men and retreated to Inverness. Casualties of the fighting were tiny. But 200 government soldiers deserted their posts in the hours that followed. The encounter resulted in a loss of confidence in the government officers that they could defend the town. To prevent Inverness being reduced to rubble in a siege and street battle, Duncan Forbes, Loudon, MacLeod of MacLeod and the other officers, decided it was best to make a strategic withdrawal across the Beauly Firth to the Black Isle. Loudon ordered a garrison of 300 up to the castle, marched the rest of his troops to the River Ness, across the bridge and to the harbour area at Kessock.

When the news came to Lovat and Gorthleck in their beds in Stratherrick, they rejoiced. Perhaps all was not lost. The Prince had still never lost an encounter. His Highland army had won several skirmishes and a major battle.

The Prince left Moy and took up a position on the high ground to the south of the town. They could see the government army below them on the flat land by the harbour, and prepared for battle. Miss Isabel Stuart never made it back to Castle Menzies, and her mother and father. Now officers crowded round her and 'gave me some of their watches and purses and other things, their pocket books and anything valuable'. If they fell, she could return the keepsakes to their families. The Highlanders got ready to unleash the juggernaut of their charge down the hill.

Instead of fighting, they watched in amazement as scores of boats came in and ferried the British forces away. The Jacobites streamed down into the town, but the Hanoverian garrison guarded the bridge from the castle, and the tide was too high to ford the River Ness. Loudon and his fellow officers and men kept retreating until Loudon was at Dornoch, 'twenty-eight miles and three' sea crossings from Inverness; and Duncan Forbes and MacLeod were at Dunvegan on the Isle of Skye. Back in Inverness, Major George Grant, a cousin of Sir James Grant, and a cousin by marriage to Lovat, commanded the garrison in charge of the castle. He had a company of Grants and one of Rosses under him, and about eighty regulars from Loudon's men.

The Jacobites reconnoitred the castle; the improvements carried out in the 1720s under Wade had exposed the foundations. Loose rock and sandy ground invited undermining operations. On the morning of 20 February, the Jacobites opened fire and engineers scuttled up under its cover, to mine into the base of the castle walls. The Hanoverians leant out from the battlements to drop hand grenades on them. The grenades fell wide. The Hanoverian soldiers tried without success to retrain their cannon far enough to lower the barrels that they might fire down the walls.

Major Grant could see no option but to surrender or see his ramparts blown up. He did so. Cumberland was furious when he heard. The skirting wall the Jacobites were trying to mine was over five feet thick. Behind it was thirty-five feet of open ground to the wall of the castle itself. Grant could have put up a fight. He might have held the Jacobites down for a few days. Storming the castle, Prince Charles and his men plundered the well-stocked armoury and provisions for much-needed food and ammunition. Then the Prince ordered the flattening of the outer wall and bastions. The mining engineers set to. One charge failed to ignite and set off the gunpowder. A French explosives expert and his dog padded up gingerly to see what was wrong. He fiddled about and found too late there was nothing; the whole thing went sky high, launching the engineer and his dog a huge height. The dog thumped to earth on the river bank, got up and trotted away. The engineer had died.

The rebellion was in Lovat's land, and he had no role. His son was in Inverness with the Prince, but Lovat had not seen him. He knew Simon had been in the Aird trying to make the rest of the clan rise, and threatening to take their plaids and cattle if they would not. The Jacobite leaders argued about whether to pursue Loudon through the north, or go out east to meet Cumberland, now advancing towards them from Aberdeen. The deeper they went into the Highlands, the more the Jacobites suffered desertions as men disappeared home to help their families. Cumberland had issued orders to his officers to 'attack all whom he finds in arms against the government, and to burn the habitations of such who have left them and are with the rebels'. Women and children and the elderly were to be regarded as combatants, and none of the Jacobites were to be respected as soldiers. They were rebels and traitors to their King. He would not give them the rights of captured soldiers to decent treatment under the terms of war. The Duke of Cumberland recorded that this 'has had a very good effect' as the men whose families were made homeless and destitute tended to run off and try to help them. He noticed that harshness sent the rebels home from Inverness, where leniency, as used by the Lord President towards Lovat's clan, was abused.

The Jacobite leaders in Inverness recognised their forces were worryingly thinly spread. Some had stayed around Blair Atholl under Lord George Murray to siege and take it from Murray's brother, the Duke of Atholl. Another force had already gone to chase the Earl of Loudon north of Inverness across the firths and hills of Ross-shire and Sutherland.

When Gorthleck's health improved, Lovat sent him to his son Simon with a letter. Lovat mentioned that Prince Charles was expressing a desire to 'go some of these days, and view my country of the Aird, and fish salmon upon my river of Beauly'. But, 'I do not much covet that great honour at this time,' Lovat continued. 'My house is quite out of order … I am not at home,' he explained, slightly unnecessarily. If the Prince insisted, the Master 'must offer to go along with him and offer him a glass of wine and any cold meat you can get there'. If the Prince went by himself and met with 'no reception, it will be an affront, and a stain upon you and me while we breathe. So, my dearest child, don't neglect this, for it is truly of greater consequence to our honour than you can imagine, though in itself but a maggot. But I fancy, since Cumberland is coming so near, that those fancies will be out of his head.' Even in the shadow of battle, he spoke to his son of the need for hospitality and good manners.

In the hub of the Highlands, in wintry sleet and snow, the two sides ploughed through sodden land for a sovereign cause. No more than

16–17,000 men joined in battle here, small compared with the monumental battles on Continental Europe. But the fight here was bitter, personal and hugely ambitious. Settled in Inverness, the Jacobite forces lost their edge. Eventually the Master of Lovat managed a visit to Gorthleck to see his father, to describe what was happening, and discuss tactics.

It was clear to Lovat that, from being a tightly knit group in Derby, in great spirits and red-hot keen to charge on to London, the Jacobites were now scattered across a huge area of the Highlands, with the Prince at the centre and left trying to pull them all back in for the big confrontation with Cumberland. It had to come soon. Cumberland marched towards them along the coast from Aberdeen. Lovat thought that unless they could gather all the Highlanders back from this dispersed position, they were far too weak to fight a pitched battle and should retreat into the high hills and narrow glens to regroup and recover. The Prince had actually ordered home the men who lived locally. He simply did not have enough supplies to maintain them. There was no money, and soon there would be no oatmeal. Charles could not remain in the town, getting weaker. He decided to send a body of men to Elgin to meet Cumberland thirty miles east of Inverness and hold him up while the Jacobites regrouped. They must all muster at Inverness.

Lovat repeated that they should retire into the hills, but some of Charles's Irish officers thought this was a terrible idea. This was not their country. They had hauled themselves through the sub-arctic desert of those hills in winter. Sparsely populated, ill supplied with meat and meal, how could they keep an army together there? If they broke up into guerrilla groups, how could they communicate and act effectively? That was not the army or the war they wanted.

The Master of Lovat returned to the camp and tried to rally the officers around him. He said to his cousin and fellow officer, Charles Fraser of Inverallochy, that armies often ran short of money. It did not matter they could not pay the men. It was better to pay them in full upon a decisive victory, than drip it out day by day to be spent on drink, food and women in the towns they conquered. Simon then returned home to Castle Dounie, to recruit more fighting Frasers.

By the beginning of April 1746, frost and snow, sharpened by easterly winds, were weakening both sides. When Cumberland's men mustered in the morning, hundreds hunched over with bronchial diseases. They moved painfully, suffering the effects of chilblains on their fingers and toes from being continually icy cold and wet. It was like walking on razor blades. Their split and reddened skin ached and burned. Most of the officers could dry off in warm billets at night, but even some of them succumbed, though mostly to gout. Fevers – flu-like or dysentery – flared up. Disease compounded the struggle to move men, artillery and supplies through the mud. The men were used to being in winter quarters. Cumberland needed to go back to Flanders. He had to bring this to a swift end.

The Duke did not understand the Scots at all. He was here to support the well-affected majority. They did less than support him. Even the many loyal Scots harboured a residual sympathy and respect for the Jacobite elements among them. 'A petty insolent spirit' kept them aloof from admitting defeat, he observed. Cumberland concluded that when he had crushed this rebellion, something, a 'stroke of authority and severity' perhaps, would be unavoidable to subdue this independent-minded part of the Scottish soul for good and all. The Fraser chief, Lord Lovat, whom Cumberland knew from his father's Court, had been loud in his loyal and submissive talk, and also nurtured Jacobites behind his back. Cumberland did not completely trust any of them, including most of those on the Hanoverian side, such as Duncan Forbes.

The part of the Jacobite army that Charles sent out to Elgin was in no way substantial enough to impede the approaching Hanoverians. The Duke of Perth and his brother Lord John Drummond pulled out when Cumberland got near enough to engage and poured back down the road to Inverness. Another Jacobite leader, Colonel O'Sullivan, riding out to meet them, said they retreated too fast. The Prince was not ready. Too many of his officers and their men had not returned from the different parts of the Highlands.

The Prince retired south of the town to Duncan Forbes's home, Culloden House, with his men. Charles lay awake all night and spent the daytime trying to find food and bedding for his men. The Camerons and Lochiel arrived on 14 April, closely followed by the Drummonds and their troops returning from Elgin, forty miles east of Inverness. The Jacobites lined up on the moor outside Culloden House on the morning of 15 April, knowing the Duke was closing on them. Poised to attack, they shouted whenever anyone claimed to have sighted the enemy. Hours passed. Their nerves jangled. Cold and tiredness set in.

All day they waited. He did not come. Cumberland's men were fatigued by their march. He wanted to rest them. This was his twenty-fifth birthday and he ordered them to stay in camp and rest up with a good ration of brandy and rum to celebrate and keep them warm.

As the day ended, the Jacobites stood down. Lord George Murray, in an inspired stroke, proposed a night attack on the enemy camp. They would have the benefit of complete surprise, he argued. Most of Cumberland's army would be in a semi-drunken doze. The cavalry and infantry, camped separately, would not be able to help each other. Throw the enemy into disarray by the maniacal shock of their charge, thousands of them, out of the night, like devils, he said. Then, scythe them down like corn with their broadswords when they panicked. The scheme had all the elements that had helped them to victory in the south.

Though brilliantly inspired, the manoeuvre was a planning disaster. The Jacobite leaders could not work together. The two columns set off as darkness fell, Highlanders at the front, followed by Irish and French. Sleet came down. The north-east wind blew. Halfway to Nairn, the two columns split and lost each other in the black night. Some men went round the woods of Kilravock Castle in circles. The Irish and French lagged behind and lost sight of the leaders.

One column reached within hearing distance of the Hanoverian camp, and waited for the other column, only to be told they were miles back. At 2 a.m., furious, Lord George Murray led them back, utterly exhausted and demoralised, to Culloden.

The men fell to the ground, some never waking till 'they found the enemy cutting their throats'. Others, formed up the next morning, were 'nodding with sleep in their ranks, and at least 1,500 fewer in number than they had been even a few days earlier'. The morning of 16 April, they stood on Drumossie Moor, buffeted by a north-easterly wind and rain, a couple of miles west of Inverness, and waited for the government army to line up opposite them. The walls of Culloden House's enclosures formed part of the defences.

Fraser of Inverallochy, in charge of the Lovat Frasers, was in the front line, between the men of John Roy Stuart and the Appin Stewarts. The Master was still on his way back from the Aird of Lovat with more men.

Battle joined at about 1 p.m. The Highland charge was delayed. The muddle in timing the order to charge exposed the men to a terrible cannonade for a few minutes. Then they were unleashed, and lacked nothing of their habitual ferocity. Cumberland had been training to meet them.

The Duke had noticed that as the Highlanders raised their right arm to strike, the white skin of their chest on that side lay exposed. At least it did if you were standing opposite but slightly to the side of him. If you were directly in front of the lifted broadsword, the enemy's spiked targe protected their bodies, and they merely thrust an extra spear-like point at you at waist height, while their swords descended on your head. 'The instructions given to the soldiers to direct their bayonets, each to his right-hand man of the enemy, will doubtless be entered in the books of discipline as proper against sword and targe. The poor wretches ... never thought of the defensive; they never considered, while they lifted up their broadswords with their right arms, how open they laid their sides to receive their death from the bayonets,' the *Gentleman's Magazine* noted.

In other words, Cumberland had taught his men *not* to attack the man in front of them. Rather, make a slight turn to the right and

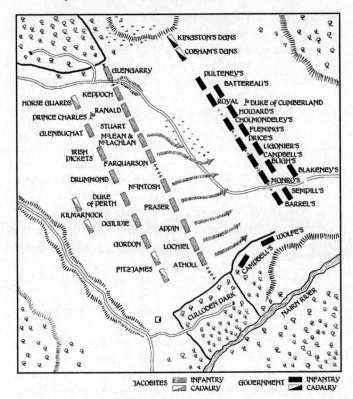

JACOBITES ▨ INFANTRY · ▨ CAVALRY · GOVERNMENT ▰ INFANTRY · ▰ CAVALRY

attack the man who attacked the man to your right, and stick your bayonet under his armpit. It required great trust. You did not defend yourself, but your neighbour, and you in turn were defended by the soldier to your left. It required, in addition, very good training. The Hanoverians had been practising hard. To stiffen their resolve, the second line of Hanoverian soldiers had their bayonets at the backs of their fellow soldier in the front line, to keep him in place in face of the horror of the unhinged Highlander howling semi-naked straight in your face.

'The ranks were packed so tightly that even the men whom the Highlanders had cut to pieces did not fall down, and the living, the wounded, and the dead formed such a solid mass that the Highlanders had to give up any hope of breaking through.' Brutal and obscene, it worked. The artillery and dragoons did the rest.

Lovat's Inverness businessman, Evan Baillie of Abriachan, with William Duff the merchant, Bailie Steuart and other Invernessians, rode out to watch the battle from a small rise near the Prince's command position. On the rise, a handful of schoolboys, the sons of chiefs, lay in the heather next to the Inverness lawyers and merchants. Young Archie Fraser, Lovat's youngest son by Primrose Campbell, was there, aged nine and a half. He searched the sea of men for a sight of his half-brother, Simon, whom he knew should be leading the Frasers below him. The son of Robertson, Laird of Inches, though his big brother was on the government side, stretched out beside Archie. Young Robertson was a cousin of Archie Fraser's. His mother was Lovat's sister. They huddled together with a couple of other friends, discussing the fighting. Archie knew Evan Baillie well. He was often at home with his father.

They saw Inverallochy lead the Frasers bravely into the storm of metal. The men fell as if bewitched. They watched Prince Charles's horse take a musket ball in the shoulder. It bucked and twisted to get its rider off. The Prince's groom rushed up with a fresh mount. Reseated, Charles turned to thank the man, in time to see him beheaded by a cannon ball. Colonel O'Sullivan told Charles to flee. He refused. In the end a cousin of Lochiel's seized his horse's bridle and dragged him from the field of defeat.

The Inverness businessmen 'remained until dislodged by the cannon balls falling about them'. Jacobite soldiers started to break ranks and run for the shelter of farms, hills, the town. The spectators moved. The men told the boys to run back to school as fast as they could. Baillie and the Inverness men dashed back to lock themselves in their houses in case the Hanoverians gave chase. At the bridge over the Ness, Evan Baillie and William Duff met several hundred Frasers crossing the bridge to their side of the town, led by the Master of Lovat. He and his men had missed the battle, but assumed it was still going on and shouted excitedly about going to join their companions and fight up on the moor.

'Fighting, by God, Master!' Evan growled. 'You were not in the way when fighting might have been of service. You had best say nothing about it now.' Baillie's excitement had sickened to fear and anger over the last few hours, watching friends and fellow Highlanders being shot, hacked or blown to death. Duff pulled Baillie away and they went home.

Several chiefs killed, the Prince gone, the Highlanders turned and fled what was coming at them – Hanoverian dragoons, who slashed to left and right and chased them all the way to Inverness. The battle lasted little over an hour. The mopping-up exercise began at once, working their way through the Jacobite wounded lying on the field.

THIRTY-ONE

The beginning of the end, 1746–47

'There fell the fine Stars'
— JOHN ROY STUART

At first, they knew nothing at Gorthleck House. For days, Lovat watched the women of Stratherrick cook and brew for their victorious Jacobite men. On the day of Culloden, they could not bear to wait at home. White cloths, newly washed, bleached by frost and sun, had been strewn across the hedges for days. The women carried them in, full of the coconut scent of gorse, and laid them on trestles. Salted meat, a little fresh mutton, but not good, it being too early for spring animals to have fattened, lay on trenchers. Plenty of barley bannocks, oatcakes, ale and wine covered the cloths by late morning of 16 April. Beakers and plates and knives, a few glasses for the nobles, all waited. All ready to celebrate the victories from last July to now. Unable to wait, gaggles of chattering people set off up the road to Inverness. It was a horrible, wet day, but in their excitement they did not feel it. Gorthleck House settled into deep silence.

Approaching footsteps broke it. A runner brought a rumour that things were going well for the Jacobites. Others arrived and the news changed. The house began to fill with people anxious to hear about their husbands, sons, brothers, fathers. More people left to go back up the road to Inverness to hear something from those who had been watching the battle. Soon only Lovat sat there, alone, staring into the fire, waiting. A door clicked and he looked round. A small girl stepped out of a cupboard, put there, she said, to stop her getting under everybody's feet. The quiet frightened her. She thought she had been forgotten, and came out to see. She went over to the window. Below, she began to make out shapes. She caught her breath. 'The fairies,' she said to Lovat. The plain below the house was a famous rendez-vous for the spirits and sprites. Neither the old man nor the child moved. People believed that the sight of fairies disappeared when you blinked. The old chief shook his head – men. The girl shut her eyes quick and then flicked them open. He was right. Not supernatu-ral beings, just women tearing their head scarves off, and men lying about.

A door crashed and women ran into the house. They grabbed the cloths smoothed with pride on the tables, and ran out with them flap-ping behind, as if they were being chased by ghosts. They tore them up and bound wounds, invoking God's peace on the suffering men, questioning. 'The intended feast was distributed in morsels among the fugitives, who were instantly forced to disperse for safety to the caves and mountains of Stratherrick.'

Back on the battlefield at Culloden, when a kind of peace fell at last, the Redcoats stopped for lunch, sitting down among the dead, wounded and dying. Local people feared to touch the bodies of their dead men till the soldiers had moved to the town.

Cumberland separated the Highland soldiers from the foreign ones. Charles Fraser of Inverallochy, leading the Frasers on the field of battle, had fallen, but with a wound that was not going to be fatal. He hitched himself up on his elbow, looked about and waited to be picked up and given quarter. Someone like him could be ransomed with his kin. He watched General Henry Hawley as he rode through the field with his junior officers. Surrounded by soldiers, Hawley ordered them to pistol or bayonet anyone they thought might still live. The finishing blow delivered to so many wounded revolted Inverallochy. The Jacobites had been careful to be merciful during their whole campaign. These were fellow Scots and Britons. Inverallochy prepared his sword to give up in surrender.

Hawley spotted the young gentleman, a month from his twenty-first birthday, his cocky head propped up, staring at their work. He turned and rode across, halting above him. His horse's breath was warm and intimate on Fraser of Inverallochy's face. What party did he belong to, Hawley asked. 'To the Prince,' Inverallochy replied.

General Hawley turned to Major Wolfe,* the officer at his side. 'Shoot me the Highland scoundrel who thus dares to look on us with such an insolent stare.' Major Wolfe refused. He would fight as a soldier, not an executioner, he said, and offered Hawley his commission.

The General barked down at a foot soldier to empty the contents of his musket into the dog. Without hesitation, the man approached to point-blank range and fired. The leader of the Frasers fell to the ground to join the corpses of his men. Near him, a Stratherrick man, Alexander Mackintosh, lay with twenty wounds, waiting to be rescued, and taken prisoner. His head 'which is almost all over in one wound', swam in a pool of blood. His elbow stuck out at the wrong angle, wounded as it protected his head. His broadsword had snapped in two and he had raised his arm as a sabre came down on him. Redcoats moved through the wounded, killing and stripping them all nearly naked. Mackintosh was 'reckoned amongst the dead'. He woke 'out of his swoon' later to the sound of a party of dragoons with fixed bayonets, looking for wounded and discussing him.

'Let us try if this dog be quite dead,' one said. The dragoon bent and thrust his bayonet deep into Mackintosh's buttock. 'I happily received [it] without any shrinking or emotion,' he said afterwards. 'I had resolved beforehand, under God, upon hearing their language, to endure, if possible, any shock they might put upon me, without showing any signs of life. So they rode off, declaring me dead enough.' He

---

* Major Wolfe, a general ten years later, was despatched to Canada and died on the Heights of Quebec. Simon, the Master of Lovat, en route to Culloden, would be one of his senior officers; the Frasers accompanying him would serve Wolfe and King George II with courage and loyalty. Serving also would be Inverallochy's younger cousin, Simon, and the Fraser lairds of Culduthel, Balnain, Belladrum, Errogie, and hundreds of Lord Lovat's ordinary kinsmen now fleeing into the hills.

fainted again, 'came to himself' several hours later – and 'got off the field in dead of night', dragging himself towards Inverness on his hands and knees. Two sentries stepped into his path. To either side of them bodies waited to be cleared. Mackintosh reached into his sporran and brought out two shillings sterling. He held them up, one for each, in exchange for his life. The soldiers took them and told him to move on. They called after him they could easily have taken the money and his life. He did not risk another encounter, and began the twenty-mile crawl back to Stratherrick.

As the battle ended, the dragoons galloped down the road to the town to hunt fleeing survivors. The road to the town was strewn with bodies. Unlike Bailie Steuart, some who came to watch their men did not leave in time. Women and children heaped up like a pile of laundry, all mixed together, mangled among their dead soldiers. Bailie Steuart and his friends, especially the Jacobites, sat silent in their houses and prayed and prayed for this fury to be taken away from them. The bells of the town began to ring out unsteadily to let Cumberland know they thought this was a victory.

Cumberland ordered the town secured, Redcoat prisoners released and 'the cavalry to pursue the enemy as fast as they can', to be sure few escaped. The town braced itself. A servant girl, Margaret Grant, did not get off the street quickly enough. Two unarmed men ran into a cottage as she passed it. A dragoon following them shouted at her to halt. At first, she could not properly understand him. He spoke in English, and in her fright she could not tune her ear to his language. When he merely tossed her the reins of his horse, she almost wept. The town bells grew louder. The cavalryman went in. Miss Grant clung to the horse for dear life, restraining the urge to bolt with it. She knew the moment the dragoon found the hiding men: voices rose as he 'hash'd them with his broadsword to death'. The cavalryman emerged 'all blood', grabbed the reins, mounted and left.

Parallel with the aftermath, some life went on as usual. Robertson of Inches died of natural causes in the week before the battle of Culloden. The family home at Lees lay between the battlefield and the town. Robertson's relatives listened to his funeral service start up 'as the cannonading began on Drumossie Moor'. The youngest son was lying next to his cousin, Archie Fraser of Lovat, watching the battle begin from under a plaid. The clergyman had no choice but to press ahead. Mrs Robertson buried her man and two days later the widow went home to a scene of unimaginable horror.

Prince Charles had led his party away from the battlefield and the immediate consequences of defeat. They rode westward, going south around Inverness and entering Strathnairn. The straths and glens lay in rows running east–west. Strathnairn began south of Inverness and at the western end it emerged at a slight angle into Stratherrick, Lovat's place of safety. They galloped up into Stratherrick, seeking Lord Lovat at Gorthleck House.

Meeting his Stuart Prince at last, the Fraser chief rose and bowed as deep as he could, and repeated his vows to the Scottish royal line. Lovat took Charles's hand and drank in the features. He knew his father; the colouring was the same, and the height, and certain aspects of his face. The Prince thanked him, and said they must all take to the hills and hide as best they could. Drawing back, Lovat held the young man in his gaze. 'Remember,' he said, 'your great ancestor, Robert Bruce, who lost eleven battles and won Scotland by the twelfth.' This was no time to run. His Highness must think of his cause and of the people committed to death for him, who had nowhere to run, and needed to be led and defended. Charles must calculate and scheme without emotion. They must regroup in the hills, beyond the reach of the Redcoat army. He and Charles dictated a letter to be sent to Cluny MacPherson, telling him to muster at Fort Augustus by Friday at the latest, where the Prince would review his troops and speak of 'something in view, which will make ample amends for this day's ruffle'.

The Prince could not imagine guerrilla warfare among the heather and stones. He had come 2,000 miles from Rome, led an army south into battles, and reached within eighty miles of his thrones. Lovat feared for the innocent in their homes around Dounie, waiting for their men to return. If they did nothing to draw off Cumberland, these people were lost. The Duke had been told 'the Pretender's son ... lay at Lord Lovat's house at Aird, the night after the action'. Brigadier Mordaunt was marching with 900 volunteers to go into Fraser country, to destroy all the rebels he found there and investigate the rumour that the Old Fox, Lovat, and the Young Pretender were holed up there. Despite the killing on Drumossie Moor, nearly a thousand were keen to volunteer to go and see if they could trap the fox in his lair. Cumberland said he wanted to meet this old Highlander, 'the Oracle of his country'. His men strained at the leash to hunt him down for the prize.

Up to now, Fraser lands had been protected by Loudon and Duncan Forbes, hoping Lovat might help them now as he had thirty years ago. The impatient Redcoats knew Lovat's estate was wealthy and offered rich pickings. It was in their interest to gather as much plunder as they could. Cumberland released his troops and they discussed the day ahead. Some wanted to hide little souvenirs; they would be flogged in front of the whole camp if caught. Petty pilfering ruined the esprit de corps and honour of an army. Public flogging reinforced it.

Brigadier Mordaunt's orders were to burn everything that could not be carried away. What would not burn, must be pulled down and scattered. The glen, from the River Beauly to the hills above, must be laid waste to teach these villains the only lesson that counted – never again. 'I find them a more stubborn and villainous set of wretches than I imagined would exist,' Cumberland remarked. He was astonished. His friend, the Duke of Richmond, egged him on. 'Nothing but force will ever keep that stinking corner of the kingdom quiet ... Most joyful it is to think that so many of those villains are destroyed, and indeed the rope must finish those that are escaped with their lives and are fallen.'

The sight of Castle Dounie and its outbuildings provoked whoops of joy from Mordaunt's soldiers. He smiled indulgently at their boyish high spirits. 'One thousand bottles of wine, three hundred bolls of oatmeal, with a large quantity of malt, and a library of books to the value of £400, was all brought to Inverness. His [Lovat's] fine salmon weirs were destroyed.' The troops waded into the Beauly and hauled apart the cruives. As they did so the river gushed in, nearly knocking them off their feet. 'Salmon in abundance' lay in them and they were 'brought into the camp and divided among the soldiers'. All this destruction, one volunteer said, 'was very cheerfully undertaken and performed', as if they were being asked to help a neighbouring squire clear some waste land for cultivation.

The Frasers' peat stacks smoked, the fuel for heat and cooking for a year gone up in a day. Once emptied, they set fire to Castle Dounie. Over the next few days, it hollowed out into a blackened crown. Any man who had returned from Culloden fled west until Mordaunt was satisfied and gone. Ploughshares, harrows and other farm equipment too big to move went on the bonfires, as did people's tables and chairs. Their little querns, small millstones for grinding corn to make bread and porridge, were thrown into the river, hammered in half, or rolled down rocky slopes to split them.

Nor did the women and girls escape the soldiers' attentions. After a couple of days the troops marched back to town tired and happy, followed by horses and wagons laden with Lovat's possessions and stores. Officers, who lifted a bottle or two from the carts and examined them as they passed, praised the Old Fox's cellar. When Lovat's possessions reached the quartermaster, they bought Lovat's Madeira at two shillings a bottle, and claret for one shilling and eightpence a bottle. Some of it they consumed. Some they sent south, to inspire the anecdotes of this extraordinary time and out-of-the way country, that they could share with friends when the job was done. Good stories attached to Lovat's things; of this horrendous place and its brutal overlords, and Lord Lovat, tyrant chief and the wickedest of them all.

At the Market Cross, soldiers turned salesmen offered 'all manner of plaids, broadswords, dirks and pistols, plaid waistcoats, officers' laced waistcoats, hats, bonnet blankets and oatmeal bags'. Women badgered soldiers in the streets wanting the plaids on the soldiers' arms. Some of them simply asked to buy back what had been taken from them.

Once they had gone into the Aird, Gorthleck and the other lairds forced their chief to move. It was too dangerous for him to lie in a house on the road to Fort Augustus, in the middle of rebel country. If they did not find MacShimidh in the Aird, the next place they would look was here in Stratherrick. He must go to the glens. The Stratherrick lairds constructed a litter for their chief. When it was ready they gently put him into it and ferried him across Loch Ness, and up into the hills, passing near the Aird of Lovat in darkness. Lovat called for them to stop to watch the glow like a sunset over the Aird. Flames spewed up out of the towers of Castle Dounie into the night sky.

When Dounie did not yield Lord Lovat, Cumberland made plans to launch boats onto Loch Ness with men and supplies, and to march with fifteen battalions and some dragoons through Stratherrick to Fort Augustus. He would penetrate the Highland heart along Fraser veins, Mordaunt through the Aird of Lovat and up the rivers into Fraser country; Cumberland down Loch Ness.

The Argyll Militia and the Independent Companies were to shadow Cumberland's flotilla on the loch. They had to thread through the hills on both sides of the Great Glen, in pursuit of rebel Frasers, Grants and MacDonalds, expanding a cordon sanitaire, clean of rebel Highland filth, around the Highland capital. Another piece of intelligence said that Lovat had fled across the loch and into the Grant country around Glenmoriston, leading away from the north side of Loch Ness. Thorough and severe search parties were ordered up into their country. Pain would make the Highlanders vomit up the Fraser chief. It was full springtime now, the loveliest time of the year in the Highlands. By the middle of May the sun did not set until ten in the evening.

Behind the reek of burning and unseen rotting things, wild bluebells shimmered in the breeze, ready to open and carpet the floor with vibrant blue in the cool of the woods. Deep yellow flag irises shook their pennants along the banks of burns and ditches. Any other year, the young women of the clans would be preparing to take their sheep and cows up to the shielings, the summer grazings, to fatten their beasts and make butter and cheeses to last the next winter. The young men used to come and find them there, and sit beside them in the evenings and court them. For now, the shieling might provide the young men with temporary safety from the hunters.

At Dunvegan Castle on the Isle of Skye, two days after the battle of Culloden, Duncan Forbes handed two shillings to 'Lord Seaforth's servant that brought a letter', with news of the great victory that let Duncan come back to the home that had hosted the battle. On 23 April, the Lord President set off from the Western Highlands, and by the 26th he stood on the Black Isle looking across the Firth to Inverness. He took the ferry and crossed to the town, full of apprehension.

Ten days after the battle, the business of the town still revolved around the buying and selling of the spoils of war. The bridge over the Ness seethed with traffic carrying goods plundered from forfeited estates. Duncan heard the soldiers had gone into the Lovat estates the previous week. The news about the condition in which they left them made him feel ill. He rode up to Culloden with increasing misery. His home, where the Prince lodged in the days leading up to Culloden, was a scene of chaos, but had not been plundered – though his unexpected royal guest and his officers had emptied the cellar of sixty hogsheads of claret. Many of the Highlanders would know well where to find it. They had dined here with Duncan and Culloden scores of times over the years.

The borders of his estates were something else. Blood, weapons, bodies, clothes, dead animals, and the pervasive, nauseating reek of rotting flesh soaked into his land and home. Duncan rode back into the town. The main army camp spread over the part of the town called the Crown, a flat-topped piece of ground overlooking the town below. The castle stood on the hill between the Crown and the River Ness. All Duncan's work was mocked by the carnage on his own doorstep. Between Culloden House and Inverness, the land was speckled with corpses. He would see them again whenever his eye strayed that way in springtime. He had to go and congratulate the Duke of Cumberland on his decisive victory. Looking and listening, he intended to press him to temper justice and authority with mercy for the losers.

'As yet we are vastly fond of one another,' Cumberland wrote to Newcastle, 'but I fear it won't last.' Duncan 'is as arrant Highland mad as Lord Stair or Crawford'. They were all foreigners in their way. They were compromised by their loyalty to their homelands and way of life. Britain had been brought to the brink of civil war. They were traitors and deserved no mercy. 'He wishes for lenity, if it can be done with safety, which he thinks probable(?), but I don't.' Cumberland trusted his instincts. Duncan might be the Lord President, the senior state prosecutor in Scotland, but martial law marched over his arguments for the time being.

The civilians had not prevented this. Lord President Forbes had tried every kind of diplomacy. Cumberland was trying everything he knew for a while. Utterly exhausted, Duncan forced his sore head and body on to beg for justice with mercy. Cumberland took no risks. Even loyal Invernessians found their accent inclined to condemn them. John Hossack, Duncan's friend on Inverness Council, told the Lord President the problem of achieving anything that would restore order was that 'we are all accounted rebels ... We have no persons to complain to, nor do we expect redress.' None were to be trusted. Most were to be crushed.

Hossack and the town's Provost, a Fraser, also went to pay their respects to Cumberland and repeat Duncan Forbes's request. The Town House and Tolbooth were operational headquarters for the occupying force. The two Highlanders moved among the staff officers, trying to speak to them so they could talk of their fellow Highlanders in other ways than as actual or potential prisoners and corpses. They overheard an officer give out an order to kill all the wounded prisoners wherever they were found. Hossack stepped up to the man. He 'could not witness such a prodigy of intended wickedness without saying something'. Hossack asked the officer to mingle 'mercy with judgement'.

Old General Hawley boggled and shouted, 'Damn the rebel dog!' at him. Hossack harboured no rebellious thoughts, and opened his mouth to speak again. Hawley silenced him with an order to 'Kick him downstairs and throw him in prison directly.' The junior officers pushed him towards the top of the stairwell. The last one 'gave him [such] a toss that he never touched the stair until he was at the foot of the first slate of it'. His friend, Provost Fraser, ran to his aid. Soldiers grabbed both of them and threw them into the Gaelic church, commandeered for a gaol.

They had pushed hundreds of men into the church and locked the door, taking the instrument bag from a Jacobite surgeon, forbidding him on pain of death to treat any of the stripped and wounded men. The prisoners consoled themselves that at least they were not in the prison ship with the pretty name, *Jean*, that lay at anchor in the harbour. The Hanoverians had had to tow it far enough out into the firth for the town not to be troubled by the growing smell from it. It grew more rank by the day, despite the salt sea air blowing through.

Eventually, Lovat arrived at the little stone house on the island in the middle of Loch Muily in Strathfarrar. Mountains rose over 3,000 feet on either side of the glen. The wide valley was good land for cattle and some corn, with the line of the River Farrar drawn in a squiggle down out of the hills, and along the valley bottom, falling towards the east coast, the Aird of Lovat and Beauly. It was fertile enough to sustain several hundred people on small farms and clustered in tiny townships. Lovat's kinsmen pulled out into the loch and rowed him across to the island. There was no sound but the splash of oars and the breeze. The silence was enormous. By his passion for the Stuarts, he had contributed to the making of this story, in its entirety, including the final act. Many Highlanders simply did not want to be ruled by Germans in London. His anger grew. They could not give up without a fight. Perhaps this was a setback, not the last act of the drama.

Murray of Broughton and Lochiel came to meet him in Strathfarrar. They stood on the shore watching Lovat being rowed to them. From the top of Sgurr na Lapaich, at over 3,500 feet the highest mountain in the glen, you could see the smoking ruins of the Aird thirty miles away. Standing at the foot of the mountain, the chief and his fellow Jacobites were dots in the middle of a vast flat plain in the centre of the Highlands.

Lochiel did not expect Lovat still to be there. He came for the Fraser chief's 'advice and assistance'. Lochiel had sent a couple of men to Dounie for any wine or food that might be left. The men returned with news that the Redcoats were coming into the glen to look for Lovat. The two clan leaders sat to decide what to do. Lovat could not stay. He had to move on, and it had to be soon. They decided to meet at Lochiel's house, forty miles to the west.

Fraser clansmen carried Lovat further and further from home. He did not know where his boys were. Simon, the Master, was on the run; so too was Sandy. Jenny was at her husband's home, trying to keep out the military raiding parties, while Cluny hid in the wilds of Badenoch. Sibyl, his youngest daughter, stayed in Inverness with friends. Lovat heard her half-brother, young Archie, was with her. He hoped so. Their home was gone and all their things, while men hunted their father. It was not safe to be anywhere near to the heart of Fraser country.

They met at Loch Arkaig – Lord Lovat, the MacDonalds of Barrisdale and Clanranald, Murray of Broughton, old Gordon of Glenbuchat, John Roy Stuart, Cameron of Lochiel, and his brother Dr Archibald, with whom Lovat had been lodging en route to the west coast. Lovat said he might escape to France, as he had nearly fifty years ago. Everything was coming full circle, like a noose. Some of the most wanted men in the land were here, with high prices on their heads. Most of them had had brushes with search parties. Providence and their kin concealed them. Lovat had a plan. He always had a plan. The country would protect them. They must gather a tight cadre of 3,000 men. These must be brought into the mountains. Forget the House of Stuart. If the Prince was still running to the islands, then all he had left for them was death and devastated homes. Their royal master was abandoning them without a backward glance.

Our duty is 'dying sword in hand', Lovat argued. They would play cat and mouse with Cumberland. His troops performed poorly in this terrain. Cumberland had said he wanted the job complete within six weeks so he could go back to Flanders. Making him stay longer might bring him to the negotiating table.

Nothing like the number they hoped for appeared when they met again at Achnacarry, home of the Cameron chief, Lochiel, two days later. There were only 4–500 in total. They had no choice now but to split up and save themselves. At his age Lovat saw no place to rest. He worried all the time about his kindred and family. The only thing to do was try to make for France from his estates on the west coast. He must go there and hope a boat might pick him up. From France he could help them. He climbed back on his litter. His men carried him towards Morar.

The Atlantic bounded Fraser country. The short neck of the River Morar, only a mile long, separated Loch Morar from the sea. The people were Roman Catholic, loyal to Lovat, and lived out of the way of rebellions and battles. Small islands studded Loch Morar. The deepest loch in Britain, it plunged in the centre into a hole 1,700 feet deep, much deeper than the Atlantic seabed at its western end. Tales abounded of monsters nurtured in its dark womb. At the eastern end of the loch, the mountains shot down precipitously to the black water. Waterfalls and small Highland rivers gouged out cracks in the hillsides as they threw themselves downhill. Winds created treacherous conditions for fishing boats along its eleven and a half miles, but particularly at the eastern end among the bowl of hills. At the western end, little green islands lay quiet near where the loch ended in a sandy bay on the coastal side. They descended to Morar at the end of May. Lovat was rowed to one of these islands. It would have been safer had he been nearer to the churning and forbidding eastern end.

Lovat lay by Loch Morar, half asleep, half dreaming. Since 1688, when a teenage Simon Fraser of Beaufort heard in his chief's hall that God's anointed King, James II, had been chased away and was not invited back, and that Mackenzies and Murrays had dismissed his father and kindred, the stories of clans and nations had inspired him.

Everything lately had unravelled so fast. A year ago, he was at home, anticipating handing over to Simon a clan and estate unencumbered by debt, free of intruders for the first time in generations. Now he was told the news that the Master of Lovat had surrendered and been committed to Edinburgh Castle.

Castle Dounie had gone, dissolved in the air; gone too were so many of the things he had loved and lived among, touched and admired and used every day. Some of his friends had sent their chamberlains to Inverness to buy items taken from their friend Lovat's home, lying in the mud by a soldier's boot. The Baillies of Dochfour had (and still have) his casement clock. The Earls of Cromartie bought one of his bedposts (now a standard lamp). By these things he could be recalled home.

Cumberland was determined to break the Highlanders' loyalty to their homes, rather than the Duke's father, the King. That link had to be smashed so they could bend at the knee to gods other than chief, clan, country. The Highlanders must look to their conquerors for life, not each other. Camped at Fort Augustus, Cumberland gazed about and reviled the wilderness. He had planned to be out of here in a few weeks following his victory at Culloden. The verminous clansmen scurried into so many cracks in the land, flushing them out took longer than he anticipated. Some of them were even breeding there. His men found women and children, waiting for their men, making a home of a cave, dropping babies onto the floor. Cumberland thought the prettiest things about his surroundings were the British forts. They were ornaments, pearls in the Highland muck.

The people stampeded through the hills, brought down by musket shot, or brought in. This formerly useless landscape would soon be exploited properly, as a nursery for the armed forces. What Sir Norman MacLeod began as a cottage industry when he sold his people to the plantations, would now go ahead on a proper commercial footing. Chiefs could farm kindred, once the land had been cleansed of its vicious streak, its troublesome elements culled. Regular warfare would breed out any insurrectionary instincts, and turn them into a desire to obey. He and that old woman Duncan Forbes at least agreed that the Highlanders would make very good soldiers in the end.

In June, two government sloops, *Terror* and *Furnace*, spent several weeks nosing in and out of the inlets and bays along the west coast of Scotland. They poked their prows among the Western Isles, seeking the Young Pretender and his senior command, coming eventually to Loch Morar. Captain Fergusson of the *Furnace* had intelligence that the loch was worth probing more deeply. Fergusson ordered his men to tow a boat up the mouth of the River Morar. Then they set about their search. One island beckoned more than the others. Small boats creaked on their moorings on the edge of it. Yet there was no sight or sound of human life. The sailors trod soft through the undergrowth. Suddenly it opened out and they caught their breath – a little house and a popish chapel.

A commotion of breaking branches made them turn. A group of men leaped into their boats, loosed them and were pulling as hard as they could away from the island and up the loch. Some of the Redcoats on the banks ran up each side to catch them where they landed, but the boats were too fast. All but one man escaped. The soldiers brought down a brother of MacDonald of Morar and marched him back to the coast.

The troops on the island 'quickly gutted and demolished' the 'popish bishop's house and chapel'. It was a seminary, withdrawn from the world; a MacDonald Catholic bishop had worshipped God here, said Mass, and trained up any young man who came thinking they had a vocation for the life of a hermit living close to nature. The soldiers got busy, 'merrily adorning themselves with the spoils of the chapel'. They took back church relics, vestments, chalices and plates, sacred vessels, but no rebels of note, to their captain, waiting on the bridge of the *Furnace*.

The men on the banks of the loch, hearing that there were no rebels to be taken off the island, pressed forward away from the coast and in towards the steep hills that rose higher as they got nearer the eastern end. If Lovat had been helped this way he was not going far. No lame old man could attempt those hills.

In the end, they nearly walked onto him. He was lying on 'two feather beds not far from the side of the lake'. Captain Campbell, the officer in charge, stepped forward and seized hold of an old man reclining in the heather. 'I surrendered my sword in the Desert of Morar,' Lovat said. 'Desert' was his own English translation for *fasach*, the Gaelic word for the Highland wilderness. He gave up his other weapons and his strong box, full of his precious papers.

The captain who received them was serving under John Campbell of Mamore, a decent man, government officer and Highlander – and Lord Lovat's father-in-law. They put Lovat into one of their boats and rowed him down the loch, then carried him down the short stretch of the river to the sea. Local Frasers gathered. Some wept as he was put in the boat. Pipers came, and as he was rowed away, the pipers 'all the while playing the tune called "Lord Lovat's March", with which his Lordship pretended to be pleased'. He smiled and his hand beat time, too much a chief to sink into despond in public. Lovat watched the pipers as the boat rose and dipped, till the music faded and silence fell.

Men hung over the edge of the man o'war to see the prize. Unable to climb the rope ladder, they lowered a sling for him. Two men hauled him up in jerks, swung him over the bows, and lowered him onto the deck. He was taken below, while they kept up the hunt for others who might be close by. One young officer guarded Lovat. He sat and talked with him to pass the time. After a while, he plucked up the courage to ask him why he engaged with the Prince after 'having received so many favours from the government?' He replied that 'he did it more in revenge to the ministry for having taken away his Independent Company, than anything else'.

On the deck of the *Furnace*, the captains of the two British ships, Fergusson and Duff, discussed what to do. They decided they should open Lovat's strong box. It might give hints as to what the rebel leaders planned to do next, and where they might find others. The captains instructed another officer, David Campbell, to take an inventory of everything in the chest. A thick pile of letters covered the bottom.

Campbell reached in and took them out. The captain told him to read them all. Campbell sighed. Lovat assured him he would find nothing in the box that had to do with the rebels. Nearly all of them concerned the ownership and management of the Lovat estates. It was dreary stuff. At its base, under the procedural papers of a chief's domestic life, was a letter written to his son, Simon. Campbell picked it up with a bit more enthusiasm, and scanned its contents.

He caught his breath. In Campbell's hands was Lovat's attempt to explain to his son what he had done and why. It told so much about how he joined the Jacobites years earlier, and what they should do to overturn the government and change the regime. A masterwork in treason going back over decades, it declared ancient and undimmed love and allegiance to the House of Stuart. Campbell looked up at the old chief. 'I think your Lordship had better not have had this letter here,' he murmured. Lovat said Campbell was right.

Orders arrived to take Lovat to Fort William to see if he might be persuaded to reveal the whereabouts of other rebel leaders. The authorities needed someone close to the top to turn King's evidence and bring down the rest.

The Duke of Cumberland sent his Private Secretary, Sir Everard Fawkener, a man well into middle age, a big London silk merchant in peacetime. Sir Everard came to talk with him, but Lovat was disappointed to find he had no hope of mercy to hold out in exchange, just a clean conscience, as the government saw such things. Lovat refused to deal. He merely boasted of his influence in the Highlands. He complained of the humiliation of being deprived of his public offices and, worst of all, losing his Independent Company of Highland soldiers. He could still render service to the government, Lovat insisted. Fawkener agreed he could – by giving evidence to use against the rebels.

Lovat meant 'no more than to bring his clan for the future into the service of the government, instead of employing them against it'. The government had tried that course of action for thirty years.

One thing struck Sir Everard in particular. Lovat spent a long time trying to make him understand that it was possible to reconcile 'his principle of loyalty to the family of Stuarts, and the services done for the late King [George] and royal family'. In Lovat's head he negotiated a way of living with these contrary pulls on his loyalty, while keeping his good name and honour.

If only he could get back to the clan, he might protect his people and begin to rebuild his estates. He could help re-establish the peace, and civil society again. Lovat asked for pen and paper, and wrote to the Duke of Cumberland pleading for his life. What would it add to the government's honour to execute a crippled old man?

He recalled Cumberland to when Lovat was in high favour at Court. 'I carried your royal highness in my arms in the parks at Kensington and Hampton Court,' Lovat reminded the young prince. Cumberland ignored him, and sent Lovat's letter to London. It was published to universal mockery, provoking ballad versions from the presses that ridiculed Lovat with his own words:

> When first the proud Scotchman rebelled,
> In your great, good old grandfather's days,
> He loved me and did all he could
> Both my fame and my fortune to raise ...

It harked back to the 1715 uprising and Lovat's pardon from Cumberland's grandfather, George I:

> 'Twas then, I remember it well,
> Your Highness was wondrous pretty,
> And what is more wonderful still,
> Though a child, most exceedingly witty.
>
> Who then in more favour than I?
> Who hugged you and kissed you like me?
> And can you behold your old nurse,
> Who thus fondled you, swing on a tree?

The Duke's answer to the last was in the emphatic affirmative. Cumberland gave orders to move Lovat south, writing to Secretary of State Newcastle with relish. 'I imagine that the taking of Lord Lovat is a greater humiliation and vexation to the Highlanders than anything that could have happened.' They had not got the Bonnie Prince yet, of course, but Lovat was a very big fish. The Prince was a fleeting and remote image of an ideal Scotland and Gaelic nation. MacShimidh Mor, the 11th Lord Lovat, was a man many had known of by experience or repute in Scotland all their lives. 'He is dignified with great titles, and ranks high in command,' Cumberland went on as if writing Lovat's obituary. 'They had such confidence in his cunning, and the strength of the country, that they thought it impossible for anyone to be taken who had these recesses open, well known to him to retire into, especially as they had a high opinion of his skill to make the best use of these advantages.'

The Duke had been determined to prove that the hills and glens would be no barrier to British law, and Lovat's capture confirmed it. He gave orders to take all the prisoners at Fort William to Inverness for imprisonment, trial and sentence, transportation to the Colonies or execution. They made up a cradle, strapped it between two horses and put Lovat in it. The party of guards and prisoners made their way north-west, up Loch Lochy and along the road by the River Oich to where it flowed into Loch Ness at Fort Augustus. Lovat was back in his country.

The government garrison came to look at the prodigy of evil. 'Yesterday I had the pleasure of seeing that old rebel, Lord Lovat, with his two aide de camps, and about sixty of his clan, brought in here prisoners,' one wrote. 'He is seventy-eight years of age and has a fine comely head to grace Temple Bar, and his body is so large that I imagine the doors of the Tower must be altered to get him in. He can neither walk nor ride and was brought in here in a horse litter, or rather a cage.' Looking into his face the man thought he looked 'as hardened as ever'. The hardness was on both sides. Lovat showed no fear or pain. They would show no mercy.

*　*　*

The 20th Regiment of Foot, under their colonel, Thomas Bligh, clattered into Fort Augustus after several weeks pacifying the surrounding area, 'burning houses, driving away cattle and shooting those vagrants who were to be found in the Mountains'. The term 'vagrants' covered any non-combatant who looked suspicious. The 20th Foot brought in hundreds of cattle and cartloads of meal and property. One of Bligh's men watched Lovat in the few days he was there. 'He had been a great courtier and a great knave,' he said, 'but how[ever] abominable for ever his character is represented in England, 'tis not half so bad as his North British countrymen make it,' he concluded. The English press made a monster of him for the British people. His Highlanders portrayed him as an unconquerable terror to the government. Here he was, suffering quietly and with dignity.

The procession restarted and they trudged up Wade's road on the south side of Loch Ness, onto the high ground through the Glen of the Birds, and into Stratherrick. There, the Frasers who were left after the incursions by the government army, slowly gathered and joined in procession behind him. They began to sing and lament as if it was his coffin passing them, not a cage for a living man. The women began to keen the clan lamentations, elegies to mark the rite of mourning. One man swore he would not shave again in memory of his attachment to MacShimidh. Lovat's *seanachie*, his family chronicler, chanted aloud the heroism of the Frasers for hundreds of years, embodied in the person of the chief. He was them; they were him. The family mausoleum at Wardlaw kept a place for him. It was an odd feeling for Lovat. He was a pre-emptive spectre at his own funeral.

They would not kill him here, their priceless piece of plunder. They carried him south. His litter rocked between the horses. People came out to stare at the mythical beast, half-fox, half-lion, in his wickerwork cage. They walked south out of the Highlands to Stirling and then across to Edinburgh.

At Edinburgh Castle they dared not leave him alone in case Jacobites or clansmen moving anonymously in the capital tried to release him. Somewhere imprisoned in the castle was his son, but he was not allowed to see him. Lovat's heart ached horribly. Two

Highland women slept at the head of his bed, to attend to his needs, and two Highland men at the foot. The old chief lay 'in a hundred flannel waistcoats and a furred nightgown'. The officer in charge of the castle assigned an officer, Captain Maggett, to his Lordship, and ordered him sleep at the foot of his bed every night.

Soon the journey resumed, through Berwick-upon-Tweed, across the border and into Northumberland. There were hostile demonstrations near Newcastle, followed by a peaceful journey south. They had to pause often to let the old man rest. No one wanted him dead on arrival. They had to get him to the altar of state power, to Westminster. One young Redcoat officer wanted to see the 'great Leviathan', terror of the Highlands, but Lovat kept his cradle's curtains drawn. He was not to be gawped at by the onion-crunching crowd. He heard the officer approach, knowing what he wanted, lay back and shut his eyes. The young man crept up and pulled back the veil, and gazed on the architecture of that huge body. Lovat's arm shot up, he grabbed the youth's nose and tweaked it till his eyes watered, then slumped back laughing.

When they could, they stopped at taverns and hotels. At St Albans, a day's journey north of London, Lovat sat having his head and chin shaved in a room at the White Hart Inn. The door opened and Hogarth came in. Lovat turned and when he saw who it was, he erupted from the chair, and came to embrace the artist. They had met before in London, in better days. When he drew back, both men looked at each other, the two of them lathered in Lovat's shaving cream. Hogarth asked for Lovat's permission to make a portrait. All London was agog to know what he actually looked like. Lovat graciously agreed. He cleaned his face, pulled on his wig, well down on his forehead, and leaned forward. Hogarth moved him about a bit and began.

Lovat's left index finger tapped the thumb of his right hand, as if he enumerated some point. It might have been the number of clans who would rise and rebel. It might have been the men he could count on subverting. It was any old argument from a man who had spent his life in debate. Big, beautiful hands stuck out from the gathered wrists of his linen shirt. His legs were lumpy from gout and the amount of flannel wrapping them up. His feet squeezed into buckled shoes. Above his necktie, his face thrust short-sightedly forward at Hogarth, to see better what was coming. He might have been short-sighted for decades, but he appeared to stare, his eyes hooded, watching, penetrating. Hogarth told a friend 'that the muscles of Lovat's neck appeared of unusual strength – more so than he had ever seen'. It lent to the sense of leonine force that emanated from the man.

Hogarth returned to London, reproduced his oil painting as an engraving, and offered it for sale. The impressions could not roll off fast enough, the printers worked all through the night to keep up with demand. It earned Hogarth £12 a day for many weeks, and became one of his most popular prints. English news-sheets crowed about the 'monstrous papist' of the north, now coming to the capital. The composer Handel was commissioned by his patron, George II, to celebrate Great Britain's 'release from danger' and wrote an oratorio, 'Judas Maccabaeus', to toast Cumberland's victory. It included the triumphant song 'See, the Conquering Hero Comes!' Elsewhere a verse was added to 'God Save the King' in honour of General Wade. It was sung in the inns and on the streets, though the old soldier Wade had been superseded as supreme commander of British forces by the King's son.

> God grant that General Wade
> May by Thy Mighty aid
> Rebellious Scots to crush
> And like a torrent rush
> Seditious plots to crush
> God Save the King!

At last, Lovat's prison convoy reached the City of London, and went straight to the Tower. In the courtyard before the building were the bumpy planks of an old scaffold. The Earls of Kilmarnock and Balmerino, Jacobite peers captured at Culloden, were to be beheaded for their roles in the uprising. Having attended his own funeral procession as he left Stratherrick, now Lovat was given a vision of how he would die.

He turned to his attendants: his approaching end brought back his life. He spoke to them of its ups and downs – his youth spent dodging the Murrays around the mountains; his life at St Germains and Versailles and the dreary French prison houses; his return and restoration and final grasp on his inheritance after fifty years of trying. It had all come to this.

In the Tower he wrote to his solicitor William Fraser, in Inverness. Lovat prepared for his trial. 'I am sorry that you are not with me,' he said. 'Your presence here is necessary, and your presence there is necessary, but I am so unlucky that I cannot have you in two places at the same time.' He asked that 'Thomas Mor G_____', probably Gorthleck, who knew too much, be kept out of the witness box.

'According to the laws of England … women are sufficient and credible witnesses,' he told William Fraser, odd as it seemed to both of them to ask irrational creatures to follow a line of reasoned argument. He asked his solicitor to find witnesses in Scotland who will 'be very proper to give evidence in my defence'. He could do so little from the Tower. 'I hope God will reward you … for I cannot.' Lovat thought there might be a case for moving the trial to Edinburgh. The crimes of which he was accused had been committed in Scotland and the Scottish judiciary was independent of English law. But Parliament passed a law that they could try traitors to the British Crown in other countries than those in which the treason was committed. This special Act only affected those who had taken up arms and fought to bring down the Crown. He had not taken up arms, he said.

On 11 December, almost a year to the day after the Earl of Loudon escorted Lovat from his room at Castle Dounie, Articles of Impeachment were moved and carried in the House of Commons. Along the Thames, in the Tower, Lovat received the news.

On 13 January 1747, the Governor of the Tower accompanied his Lordship to the House of Lords to answer the Articles of Impeachment. Lovat stood and lodged a petition. He denied the charges, and complained that 'the factor appointed on his estate had not complied with the orders of the House' to let him have income for his expenses here. Moreover, his strong box had not been returned since it was taken at Morar. These two problems meant he had none of his papers, and was without money to buy things to be sent to his room in the Tower and make life tolerable. How could he pay his barber? His wig dresser? How to get decent food and drink? He requested that he be allowed to see certain friends.

His old patron Ilay, now Duke of Argyll, rose and looked at him. 'Something more was couched in this petition than appeared openly,' Argyll said to his fellow peers. 'It was meant to throw dust in their eyes.' As far as the factor of the Lovat estates not paying him an allowance was concerned, he could give Lovat nothing because there was nothing to give, due to the rebellion and its aftermath. This was something for which the defendant was in part responsible.

Lovat 'seemed to be very much moved on the order for his withdrawing. There was a very full House of Commons, and his Royal Highness the Duke attended, as did almost all the members of our House in Town,' reported MacLeod of MacLeod. Lovat had hoped to be one of the elected members of this House. He came among them now as a fugitive. So many old friends and sparring partners were here – Wade, Cumberland, Ilay/Argyll, MacLeod, Grant. The Commoners stood in the gallery. The Lords sat on their benches. It was very odd, to be sitting there awaiting the trial for his life before them. His old friends were miserable, but resigned.

The Duke of Argyll proposed that Lovat's solicitor have access to his chief. The Lords granted the request, and rose. Lovat was to be impeached for high treason. MacLeod told Duncan Forbes, who was very ill at home, that everything happened rightly: that is, according to 'the laws of England … of nations … and of common sense'. The elision of ideas rolled forward, crushing the Gaelic nation beneath it.

Impeachment was a mongrel legal weapon, a mixture of 'popular proscription' and 'judicial trial'. It was a way for the state to deal with enemies who might not be contained by the regular legal tribunals. Something of it was close to *salus populi suprema lex* – the will of the people is the supreme law. Mob rule was its less illustrious expression. In special cases, it took precedence over the strict rules of courts. Impeachment by your peers allowed for the thrilled recounting of rumours, and the excitable speculations of all sorts of individuals, and conjectures that would have been disallowed in a regular law court.

In the Highlands, as soon as a date for impeachment was set, the Earl of Loudon set himself to find evidence against Lovat. He had a court erected at Inverness 'for taking evidence and proof against the Lord Lovat'. The Master of Lovat's old tutor, Mr Donald, was summoned from his manse at Kiltearn on the Black Isle. There was a lot of fear and fury, doubt and anger. It was very difficult to get anyone to speak in a clear and convincing way.

People confined in the gaol in the Gaelic church in Inverness, on the prison ships and in the Tolbooth; many who might be used to condemn Lovat, had died in the last six months. The prison ship *Liberty and Property* had received 157 prisoners since Culloden. Only forty-nine came back ashore alive. When the officer opened the hold to haul out a few witnesses for Loudon, 'what a scene open to my eyes and nose all at once; the wounded festering in their gore and blood; some dead bodies quite covered over with piss and dirt, the living standing to the middle in it'. Up to their waists in excrement, urine and decomposing bodies, the men stared ahead, like men being sucked alive into the grave. The officer regretted approving the use of these ships for this purpose.

The men proving too wretched to be witnesses to anything except the horror of their experience, on 14 January another court set up in a separate place in the 'suburb of the Green of Muirtown'. Hugh Rose of Kilravock was judge. Eventually, they interrogated Mr Donald again about Lord Lovat. He signed what 'they thought proper to insert of what he said', not all he actually said. When he was finished, Mr Donald protested that the enquiry was not asking all the questions. If they did, he could, 'from proper knowledge, say many strong things in his exculpation and favourable' to Lord Lovat. The court dismissed him. Mr Donald hung around all day. The next day he went with the court when it moved back into the town of Inverness. Those coming out spoke to the spectators thronging around the courthouse. 'Lord Lovat was undone by the scrutiny,' they said. Soon enough the day appointed for the trial, Monday 9 March, arrived.

THIRTY-TWO

Dying like a lion

'Justice is an excellent virtue'
— OPENING REMARK IN
THE TRIAL OF LORD LOVAT

Invitations went on sale; the tickets sold like hot cakes. Westminster Hall's hammer-beam roof formed an arch over the crowds coming in for Lord Lovat's trial. There was beauty to this rite, the cool process of law taking the sting out of killing a traitor.

The public assembled in the upper galleries, and stared down on the scene. Below, Hogarth waited with paper and ink to make sketches. He greeted journalists and hacks, the men who bought up trial reports to turn them into publishing gold. They jostled with members of the smart set – the aristocrats, wits, rich merchants; all classes greeting each other and gossiping. It was very English, one of the democratic hot spots, like St James's Park, where you even saw 'the first ladies of the Court mingling in confusion with the vilest of the populace'. Parliament brought Lovat to trial to fight to the death to defend this wonderful semi-democratic 'confusion'. It was a pearl without price.

First entering the floor of the hall were the most humble players. 'The Lord High Steward's gentlemen attendants, two and two.' Then followed 'the clerk's assistant to the House of Lords; and the Clerk of the Parliament, with the Clerk of the Crown in the Court of Chancery'. Then, the Masters in Chancery, two and two. The judges, two and two. The peers' eldest sons, two and two, Then the peers themselves. And so on. Last to come was Philip, Lord Hardwicke, the Lord High Steward, representing the Crown. When all were assembled, two places stood empty – the dock and the throne. Hardwicke read. The King, 'considering that justice is an excellent virtue', has appointed Hardwicke to impeach Simon, Lord Lovat, for high treason.

Then the Garter, and the Gentleman Usher of the Black Rod 'jointly presented the white staff to his grace the Lord High Steward'. Hardwicke sat and gave the White Rod to the gentleman usher of the Black Rod on his right hand. He would not need the White Rod again until the end. It was the ritual by which the state would visit a horrible death on the prisoner. Lovat waited in a small antechamber to emerge before his fellows. They were ready, and summoned him to the bar. Then the old man entered, lame, escorted by the Deputy Governor of the Tower of London. In front of him the Gentleman Gaoler carried the axe. He stood on the prisoner's left with the axe's cutting edge symbolically 'turned from him'.

Lovat approached the bar, bowed three times, and got down to his knees. Hardwicke told him to sit. He unrolled the Articles of Impeachment and handed them to the prosecutor to read aloud the account of Lovat's actions over the last few years. Throughout Lovat shook his head and denied the articles jointly and severally.

The Commons were present also and upheld the Lords' charges. Lovat squinted at them, slowly recognising the scores of familiar faces. They were all here. He turned back to hear the continuing accusations: Cope's defeat at Prestonpans and the march south into England. At the moment of penetration of Britannia by a hostile force, 'a noble spirit immediately arose throughout the nation', the prosecutor said. 'Not an artificial false clamour for liberty, but the true old British spirit of liberty, the true Revolution spirit, that exerted and signalised itself, out of hatred to Popery and arbitrary power.' And, 'thanks be to God, it still remains in its full vigour amongst us: it cries aloud in our streets for justice against those that would have made them slaves and papists; it cries aloud for justice against the prisoner at the bar'.

An emotional crackle of approval went up from the audience. Lovat needed big shoulders to carry all their fury.

One MP, Sir William Young, accused Lovat of helping to bring 'civil wars: a calamity of all others the most to be dreaded'. Voices muttered agreement. Tying Lovat and civil war together damned him. In addition, Young asked them to 'remember the distress of public credit, the stagnation of trade, the loss of our manufacturers, the reasonable, yet dangerous apprehensions, which seized on the minds of all the loyal inhabitants of these great and opulent cities of London and Westminster'. The City certainly had imploded with panic.

What will be the standing of Britain in Europe if the armies 'employed abroad to humble the pride of an assuming nation, her fleets to protect our trade, or to annoy our enemies', are liable to be called home to deal with domestic upheavals, the Commons representative wanted to know? Civil strife meant no forces available to protect 'our trade' and 'annoy our enemies. What pretence can we have to be umpires in the common cause of Europe?' he asked. Britain could 'justly claim that title' when at peace with itself. Even now, the British wanted to be thought of as this – not one of the hotheads, but the cool-headed umpire, holding the casting vote on the world stage.

After the scene-setting – half-reason, half-melodrama – Sir Dudley Ryder, the Attorney-General, rose to begin prosecution proper. He went back to Drummond of Balhaldie being sent to Rome and then to France by seven chiefs who had banded into the 'Association for the Restoration of the Stuarts' in 1738. They had planted treason a decade ago.

And so the trial began, and went on, from 'Monday the 9th Day of March, and continued on Tuesday the 10th, Wednesday the 11th'. On the Thursday, Lovat begged a day's respite, given his age and infirmities. Granted. Proceedings would resume on 'Friday the 13th, 20 George II. AD', the twentieth year of the reign of King George II. That day, the case for the prosecution would begin.

Horace Walpole went home and wrote with a sigh that 'it hurt everybody at old Lovat's trial, all guilty as he was, to see an old wretch worried by the first lawyers in England, without any assistance but his own unpractised defence'. On the morning the trial was meant to resume, Lovat again asked for a break in the proceedings: 'I fainted away thrice this morning before I came up to your Lordships' bar; but yet was determined to show my respect ... or die on the spot.' The last thing they wanted was to deny the hungry axe its moment to swing its averted head in towards Lovat. They gave the old man another rest.

Then the Attorney-General produced his witnesses, starting with the defendant's kinsmen, including Robert Fraser, Lovat's secretary for the last two years of his freedom. Their evidence described life at Dounie over the last few years, including during the period leading up to the rebellion. They recorded Lovat's discontent, but they had no hard evidence of treason.

Then their star witness was led in: John Murray of Broughton, Private Secretary to Prince Charles Edward Stuart. Lovat had egged on the Prince to invade, busied himself as an important agent of the rebellion, stirring up people at home and abroad, for he, Murray, shared every secret of his Prince. He was in the position of most intimate trust. Once caught, Murray of Broughton ratted to save his own life. One of the ladies who came to watch the trial each day remarked that Murray of Broughton and Robert Fraser made very good evidences (witnesses) but very bad secretaries. A private secretary knew all his master or mistress's business, and practised complete discretion.

When Lovat saw Murray he knew he was done for. This man had written evidence enough to kill him. Lovat knew what was coming if Broughton had handed over his letters. He had. An unpleasant atmosphere hung about the man. Lovat had dignity in his decrepitude. Murray shifted about and laid blame as hard as he could, reeling off lists of names. In Murray's shadow Lovat did not dye blacker. He had not tried to buy his life with that of his friends and Jacobite comrades. Sir Everard Fawkener had tried to get him to turn coat. Lovat refused. But Murray of Broughton accepted. He became the high-profile witness the Crown had sought. The loathing in the hall for Murray of Broughton was palpable.

After five days of the case for the prosecution, the sixth day, Wednesday 18 March 1747, Lovat was called to defend himself against the charges. 'The most abandoned of mankind,' Lovat began, Murray was there 'to patch up a broken fortune upon the ruin and distress of his native country ... Today stealing into France to enter into engagements upon ... the most sacred oaths of fidelity ... Soon after ... he appears ... to betray those very secrets, which he confessed he had drawn from the person he called his Lord, his Prince and master.'

Yet Lovat too had taken and broken oaths to George II. Lovat separated oaths sworn from the heart from oaths sworn to get a job – a company of Highlanders, the Governorship of Inverness, the Sheriff's job. You could not hold positions in government unless you swore. He had often said a man must be practical and not 'over fine' in his moralising. He told Ilay's man in the north, Lord Milton, success in the world came to men of action not 'fine words'.

'I am now fourscore years of age,' Lovat complained. 'I hope in your Lordships' hands my old life is safe; and that your Lordships ... cannot find me guilty upon the evidence of such witnesses as have defiled your bar.' He added that bringing forward witnesses for the prosecution who were themselves due to be tried, 'to me, who am no lawyer ... appears extremely strange'. He knew that deals had been cut.

The Solicitor General, William Murray, a relative of Lovat's old enemy Atholl, countered that Lord Lovat 'perseveres in denying the charge', but 'has called no witnesses, but rests his defence altogether upon complaints, observations and objections to the force and credibility of the evidence against him'. William Murray thought there could be little left to say. Lord Hardwicke intervened to point out to Lovat that he must call witnesses in his defence, not just object to the prosecution's. Lovat retorted he wanted to call witnesses to testify that they had been intimidated not to appear. Hardwicke had had enough. He called a halt. He asked each of the Lords present to pronounce their verdict in the case. Each one found him 'Guilty, upon my honour'.

*   *   *

Next day, Lovat was brought back from the Tower by coach. Hardwicke told him to stand. He had previously addressed him with the presumption of innocence, but 'now must address you as a guilty person', he said. What gave bulk to the dreams of 'abandoned traitors' like Lovat, he said, was the nature of society in North Britain. The security of the nation called aloud for clanship to be crushed. Cumberland was already getting on with the job.

Finally he pronounced 'that you, Simon, Lord Lovat, return to the prison of the Tower; from thence you must be drawn to the place of execution; when you come there, you must be hanged by the neck, but not till you be dead, for you must be cut down alive; then your bowels must be taken out and burnt before your face, then your head must be severed from your body, and your body divided into four quarters, and these must be at the King's disposal'.

'Would you offer anything further?' Hardwicke asked. It would have been crueller to let him live and see everything he lived for taken from him – his position in society stripped from him, his titles, honours, lands, people, home, all gone and Lovat left to wither to death in impoverished solitude.

The sentence left Lovat unmoved, relieved as he was of the burden of having to fight any more. He made a short speech asking for clemency but seemed far from desperate. Beyond this, there was 'nothing', he said, 'but to thank your Lordships for your goodness to me. God bless you all, and I bid you an everlasting farewell: we shall not meet all in the same place again.' He believed he was heading straight to heaven and his forebears – 'I am sure of that.' He bowed, and nodded. He was ready to go.

Lovat was taken from the bar and silence called for. Then the White Rod, 'being delivered to the Lord High Steward by the gentleman usher of the Black Rod upon his knee, his grace stood up uncovered; and holding the staff in both his hands, broke it in two, and declared that there was nothing further to be done'. The hall emptied, two by two as it had filled.

* * *

Back in his room, the Major of the Tower came in to see how he was doing. 'Why – I am about doing pretty well, for I am preparing myself, sir, for a place where hardly any majors and very few lieutenant-generals go.' His wide mouth and still well-cut, curved lips, moved between humour and seriousness. The Major nodded. The old man seemed prepared in himself.

A few days later, the Major had some news. His Majesty had commuted the sentence to a beheading, thank God.

The trial fascinated Londoners. For the previous ten months, his presence in the Tower, unseen but present in rumours and the stories of the leading rebels, had brought Lovat to the public eye. The Lords Kilmarnock and Balmerino were dead, but they still had Lovat. Any scrap of gossip, any anecdote, was on everyone's lips as they waited for the final execution. Lovat's rumoured Roman Catholicism bloomed into stories that he had been a Jesuit or a monk, and that debauched young women came to him to confess while he lived in France. One story had him seduce a maid, then use the maid to seduce the young mistress while the maid looked on. No story was too salacious. It built up a great enthusiasm for the day when their man would appear on the scaffold. They would all get a piece of him to look at and talk about and judge.

In the days before his death, Lovat travelled in his mind to the Highlands. He could hear the sound of the pipes playing the chief's *pibroch*, Lord Lovat's Lament, as they drew his coffin to the family chapel at Wardlaw, with thousands in attendance. All the pipers from John o'Groats to Edinburgh were to be paid to pipe his body north. Should the government forbid it (they hated the pipes, symbol of the clans, and the effect they had on Highlanders) then the women of his clan would extemporise keenings for the chief. 'And then,' he said, 'there will be old crying and clapping of hands, for I am one of the greatest chiefs in the Highlands.'

The warrant came to the Tower to execute him the following Thursday, 9 April, almost a week's time. The Governor apologised for bringing the news. He was obliged by law to announce it to him formally. Lovat stood and squeezed his arm: 'God's will be done.' He took the man's hand and drank his health. He was 'so well satisfied with his doom', he said, 'he would not change stations with any Prince in Europe'. They shared part of a bottle of wine, let down with a little water.

At ten at night it was the warders' habit to come and undress him. One crouched to unbuckle his shoes. 'Not long now, my boys,' he said. He would be leaving this world next Thursday.

Lovat slept well and was awake before 7 a.m., to say his prayers, as was his habit. He lay in bed, glass on a table by his side, eyes closed in prayer, memory, contemplation. Talking about his life, he said he had been involved in every scheme to restore the Stuarts since 1688. He wrote to the Master of Lovat, still in prison in Edinburgh Castle. 'You are always present with me, my dear Simon,' he told him. 'It is the blessed Trinity, Father, Son and Holy Spirit, that can deliver you and me from our present melancholy situation. We have provoked God by our sins, which most certainly have brought those troubles upon us.'

God acted in the world to balance the books. A belief in submission to the will of God sustained him. He had sought to be 'the greatest Lord Lovat' that ever was. If young Simon went on to live a good life, Christ 'will certainly bring you out of all your troubles and make you the happiest Lord Lovat that ever was', and you will 'bring God's blessing upon yourself, your family, and your kindred', the trinity of blessings a chief wished for.

For himself, Lovat was confident he was destined for heaven, and had very little time to wait. He decided he should rehearse his execution, as his neck was so broad and thick. He puffed up a pillow into a block shape and leaned forward to see what it felt like. He shuffled backwards and forwards, kneeled up and told his warders 'he believed by this short practice he should be able to act his part in the tragedy very well'. He asked the warder whether he thought the executioner would be reliable about taking his head off with a single blow? He'd heard that Lord Kilmarnock suffered some awful hacking about before they got it off. 'I have reserved ten guineas in a purse,' Lovat told a gentleman who was visiting and watching the little rehearsal. 'He shall have [it] if he does his business well.'

'I'm sorry you should have occasion for him at all,' the man muttered. Lovat nodded. He showed him the letter he had written to young Simon, wanting to know what he thought of it. 'I like it very well. 'Tis a very good letter,' he told him.

"Tis a Christian letter,' Lovat said. There were other letters to write, but it was too late, and they might not be delivered further than the government censor.

On his penultimate night on earth, Lovat was restless. By two in the morning he was awake and praying, calling on the Lord for mercy. Eventually, he slept until about six then woke to his ordinary routine. Dressed, breakfasted, he seemed happy. He sang part of a Gaelic song and declared himself 'as fit for an entertainment as ever he was in his life' – he had enjoyed some wild entertainments in his days.

More friends visited to say goodbye. They smoked a pipe and took some wine, and discussed business. There was a bill going through Parliament to break the power of the clans. Lovat disliked it and wished a bad dose of dysentery on those who wanted to vote it in. Then they might be in the privy when the vote was called. Sir Hector Munro and Lovat's nephew, Ludo Grant, both MPs, appeared in the door to take their leave of him. Lovat kissed their cheeks and welcomed them in. They had come from the House of Commons where the anti-clan, anti-Gaelic legislation was being debated, and would be passed. Lovat said 'if he had his broadsword by him, he should not scruple to chop off their heads' if he thought they had gone along with the bill 'for destroying the ancient jurisdiction and privileges of the Highland Chiefs'. He looked hard at them. They would not fight with the old Lord now. 'For my part,' Lovat told them, 'I die a martyr for my country.'

That night he ate very well and then called for his pipe. 'Now Willy,' he said to his lawyer and friend William Fraser, 'give me a pipe of tobacco, and that will be the last I shall ever smoke.' The Governor came in again to check on his important prisoner's spirits. Lovat got up and offered him his chair by the fireside. The Governor refused, apologising that he had disturbed the old man from his seat. It was clearly a terrible struggle to rise. Lovat laughed, 'I hope you would not have me unmannerly on the last day of my life.'

He talked 'a good while' with Willie Fraser and James Fraser, one of Phopachy's sons, now an apothecary in Chelsea, about family affairs and the management of his funeral. They discussed his conversion to Roman Catholicism. 'This is my faith,' he shrugged, 'but I have charity for all mankind, and I believe every sincere honest man bids fair for heaven, let his persuasion be what it will, for the mercies of the Almighty are great, and his Ways past finding out.'

He reached into his coat and pulled out a silver crucifix and kissed it. The men looked on in Protestant disgust. 'Here's a crucifix.' He handed it about. 'Observe how strong the expression is, and how finely the passions are delineated.' He noticed their discomfort. 'We keep pictures of our best friends, of our fathers, mothers, etc. Why should we not keep a picture of Him who has done more than all the world for us?'

In the end they each stood and shook Lovat's hand and embraced him and wished him a good journey. He ordered a piece of veal minced for his breakfast and asked them one last favour. Would they 'go upon the scaffold with me'? They had been with him all week. He could not be without them now, 'and not leave me till you see this head', he pointed, 'cut off this body'. They promised to be back early.

Those among his friends who defended his actions accounted his deeds as 'the Machiavellianism of a Prince, not simple transactions between man and man. He was endowed with the privileges of a monarch, who is not to be tried by the ordinary rules applicable to a subject; and with whom deeds that amongst mankind at large are called treachery and falsehood, take rank as kingcraft and state policy.'

Very tired, Lord Lovat retired about 9 p.m. The warders undressed him. His breeches, stockings and shoes off, he liked to stand before the fire and warm his rump and feet. After a while they asked, was he ready for bed?

He looked round and raised a hand. 'I will warm my feet a little more first.'

The man bent down to blow up some heat into the dying embers. Looking up, he said he was sorry tomorrow would be such a bad day for his Lordship. Lovat brushed away the man's fears from in front of his face. 'Bad! ... Do you think I am afraid of an axe? 'Tis a debt we all owe, and what we must all pay ... Don't you think it better to go off in this manner than to linger with consumption, gout, dropsy, fever, and so on? Though,' he said, slapping his sides, 'I must needs own my constitution is so good that I could have lived twenty years longer, I believe, if I had not been called hither.'

Some time later, the warder reminded him he was still out by the fire. 'I had forgot that I was so far from the bed,' Lovat said. 'You might have forgot it too, had your head been to be cut off tomorrow.'

The day of his death dawned dreary. He woke at three and saw it in with prayers and a glass of wine and water, lying up in bed. His helpers thought he 'seemed still as cheerful as ever'.

At 7 a.m. they helped him to his chair by the fire. He examined his wig, and sent it back with the barber that he might 'have time to comb it out in a genteel manner'. Then he counted his money and called for a purse for the executioner. The warder brought two – a green knitted silk one, and a yellow canvas one. Lovat said either would do, no man could dislike any purse with ten guineas in it.

The warder observed him closely to try and gauge his mood. 'He had a great share of memory and understanding,' the warder thought, 'and an awful idea of religion and an afterlife', but he saw not a shadow of 'fear or ... any symptoms of unease'. This was in the Tower. It would all change when they went out into the cart and faced the thousands of people scrapping now to get a good place.

The Sheriffs of London called for his body at 11 a.m. They helped Lovat into the Governor's carriage and it moved slowly to the great entrance gates. There he was extracted from the coach with great difficulty, crippled with the pain in his joints. The Tower guards handed him over to the Sheriffs of the City of London and the County of

Middlesex. Lovat had been Sheriff of Inverness-shire, he said, and greeted his fellow officer bearers. They put him in another coach and took him through the roaring crowd to a little house near the scaffold.

Its inside was lined with black linen and the walls lit by sconces. He shuddered. It was like a sepulchre. His friends and kindred were denied entry. Lovat immediately turned to call to the Sheriffs to allow him his relations and friends at this extreme moment of his life. One Sheriff, Mr Alsop, went and called them back. He did not mean to torment the old man as well as kill him. Lovat thanked him and said, 'it is a considerable consolation to me that my body falls into the hands of gentlemen of such honour'. Give the command, he said, and he would obey. He had been an officer in the army many years, he said, and was good at obeying orders. Lovat asked someone to help him kneel so he could pray. He bowed his head and asked one of the Frasers to read a prayer. He then murmured a private prayer, inaudible to anyone, and looked up and asked to be seated. Then, 'I am ready,' he said, affirming the Clan Fraser motto, *Je suis prest*.

'I would not hurry your Lordship,' said the Sheriff, 'there is a half hour good – if your Lordship don't tarry too long upon the scaffold.'

'I hope my blood will be the last spilt on this occasion,' Lovat prayed.

They opened the exit, letting in a wall of light and sound as he came to the doorway, leaning on the men on either side of him, looking up a narrow passage between thousands of yelling heads, and gripping the arms he leaned on. The scaffold rose up huge behind the yelling heads. Lord Lovat stepped across the threshold. The door shut behind him.

NOTES

Abbreviations used in the Notes

BL – British Library, Collection of Lovat papers

CALENDAR – HMC Calendar of Stuart Papers belonging to His Majesty the King ..., Vols 1 & 2 (London, 1902–20)

HLA SCOTS PLOT – 'The House of Lords Enquiry into the Scots Plot of 1704', House of Lords Archives

NA – The National Archives, Kew, London

NAS – The National Archives, Scotland

NLS – National Library of Scotland, Lovat papers

STATE TRIALS – *Cobbett's Complete Collection of State Trials ...*, comp. by T. B. Howell Esq., Vol. 18

TGSI – *Transactions of the Gaelic Society of Inverness*

MAJOR MS – James Fraser, *Major Fraser's Manuscript*, Fergusson (ed.), 2 Vols

MEMOIRS – *Memoirs of the Life of Simon Lord Lovat; written by himself in the French language ...*

WARDLAW MS – Master James Fraser, *Chronicles of the Frasers, the Wardlaw Manuscript ...*

xxiii   *Lord Lovat is to lose ... a serpent may bite them.* See Appendix to Major MS.

  7   *from his numerous family ... wealthy circumstances.* BL Add MSS 31249, f1.

 10   *Grizzled Duncan's organ ... knob-kerry.* See William Gillies, 'The Gaelic poems of Sir Duncan Campbell of Glenorchy (I)', *Scottish Gaelic Studies*, 13/1 (Aberdeen, 1978), pp. 18–45.

 11   *Sir Simon 'the Patriot' Fraser.* Wardlaw MS, p. 13.

13 *I passed to English ground … such another.* Graham, *Social Life of Scotland in the Eighteenth Century*, Vol. 1, (1899), p. 2.

13 *Like Cromwell … extra men.* Paul Hopkins, *Glencoe and the End of the Highland War* (Edinburgh: John Donald, 1998), p. 438 – a wonderful book on this period of Scottish history, and the brutal manoeuvrings of magnates and lairds to get favour and positions from the King.

15 *discourse in arguing … Colleges now.* Most of these quotations are from letters written when Lovat was thinking about his own children's education and comparing it to his own. They are in various manuscript sources, the most accessible transcriptions are in volumes of the *TGSI*.

19 *of extreme ruthlessness … bigots and embezzlers who.* Hopkins, *Glencoe*, pp. 3, 7. For the Revd James's commentary on this period see his *Chronicles of the Frasers* (Wardlaw MS). The modern historical commentary owes a particular debt to Hopkins's *Glencoe*, and Bruce Lenman's *The Jacobite Risings in Britain, 1689–1746* (Eyre Methuen, 1980).

22 *All through the winter … a free parliament.* See Hopkins, *Glencoe*, pp. 120–21 for the politics of this period in Scotland; James Miller, *Inverness* (Edinburgh: Birlinn, 2004); and *Inverness Burgh Records* for the reaction in the Inverness area.

24 *Amongst … died of his wounds.* There was a colourful rumour that Alexander survived and shortly after stabbed a piper at a ceilidh near Beauly for playing the tune *Tha Biodaig aig MacThomais* ('Thomas's son has a tiny blade'), in his presence. He was said to have stabbed the man's pipe bag but reached too far, penetrating his chest and killing him. As a result, Alexander fled to Wales and raised a family. In the early nineteenth century, a man came forward claiming to be Alexander's heir and claimed all the titles and estates of Lovat. Case dismissed.

25 *prove but spies … no good of it.* Wardlaw MS, p. 512.

25 *In January 1692 … blighted King William's rule.* This whole ghastly episode is dealt with quite brilliantly in Hopkins's *Glencoe*, see especially p. 328ff.

30 *Simon approached the Scottish capital.* Among the accounts of life in late-seventeenth- and early-eighteenth-century Edinburgh, Graham's *Journey through the North* still ranks among the most lively and informative, especially when filled out by the poems, songs,

engravings and diaries of some of the inhabitants. Lockhart of
Carnwath (*The Lockhart Papers*) is good on the political scene, and
the Presbyterian kirk session is a fund of comment on the moral
conduct of the people.

32 *In public ... a Jacobite clan.* The feelings of the Murrays are expressed
in letters kept at Blair Castle. A good selection of them is published in
John, 7th Duke of Atholl's *Chronicles of the Atholl and Tullibardine
Families*, 5 Vols (Edinburgh: Ballantyne, 1908). In addition, there are
Lovat's own recollections of the time, his *Memoirs* (1746) for the
period to 1714. These are less reliable, being retrospective, nuanced
by his desire to blacken the Murrays and Mackenzies, ingratiate
himself with the Stuarts up to 1714, and to excuse his misdeeds.
Nevertheless, there is plenty of accurate material in them. Lovat and
his correspondents' letters at times verify and at other times
contradict the narrative in his *Memoirs*.

32 *if one were ever needed.* Hopkins, *Glencoe*, p. 446.

35 *The living wearied of burying the dead.* See D. N. Mackay (ed.), *Trial of
Simon, Lord Lovat of the '45*, in *Notable English Trials* (Edinburgh and
Glasgow: William Hodge & Co., 1911); Hopkins, *Glencoe*, and Alan I.
MacInnes, *Clanship, Commerce and the House of Stuart* (Tuckwell,
1996). Up to 15 per cent of the Scottish population died in the last
five years of the seventeenth century, the result of a combination of
the factors outlined – economic and political collapse, harvest failure
and famine.

35 *I hear the angel ... life of the child.* See Martin Haile, *Queen Mary of
Modena, Her Life and Letters* (London, 1905), p. 320. The emerging
narrative at this time, of the Jacobites as the rightful monarchs,
ruling by right of intimate bond with the land, touches on the issue
of absolutism and the divine right of kings, for which James II's
father was executed. It soon evolved into a discourse of a Messiah
and a Second Coming, to be centred in 1745 on Bonnie Prince
Charlie. This symbolism draws on Gaelic mythology in which the
chief lives in a sacred union with his land. In some songs he is
married to it.

35 *in an assassination.* See Lovat's *Memoirs*, and John Macky, *A
Journey through Scotland* (London, 1732, 2nd edn), p. vi. Macky
the spy travelled through the country recording impressions of
any public figure the government suspected of Jacobite
intriguing.

37 *Come at a crown ... home in the dark.* In *Jacobitism and the English People, 1688–1788* (Cambridge: CUP, 1989), Paul Kleber Monod writes at length of the extent of Jacobite sympathy throughout England.

39 *Lord Lovat obliged ... the heirs male.* See *Lovat Peerage Casebook* (Edinburgh, 1729).

42 *My father ... the estates.* Lovat in a letter to William III, making the case for the Beauforts' inheritance of the titles and estates of Lovat, in BL Add MSS 31251.

42 *in a trustee's name ... legal guardian.* William Carstares, William III's chaplain, writing to the King with his opinion of the Lovat inheritance mess, in Joseph McCormick (ed.), *State-Papers and Letters addressed to William Carstares* (Edinburgh, 1774), pp. 432–50. He was a friend of the Earl of Argyll and enemy of Tullibardine and the Atholls.

43 *Having drunk to a good pitch ... shaking with emotion.* The account of this meeting is recorded by Lovat in his *Memoirs*. It is likely it is simplified and overlaid with wish-fulfilment. I suspect he tried to strike a bargain and compromise, but given what follows, his attempts to prevent the Lovat estates falling under Atholl–Murray control clearly maddened Tullibardine.

44 *if the Secretary of State ... his commission.* Lovat fed Livingstone's suspicion that Tullibardine aimed at control of Scotland through an oligarchy under an Atholl–Hamilton leadership.

44 *By favouring him so completely ...* After the Restoration of Charles II, an Atholl-backed prosecution led to the beheading of Argyll's father, so there was no love lost between the two magnate families.

44 *If Tullibardine ... Highland affairs.* Argyll to Carstares in McCormick, *State-Papers*, pp. 432–50. These two staunch Presbyterians were political and religious allies and used this incident to force a wedge between William and Tullibardine, and undermine the latter's influence with the King.

45 *Tullibardine did not meet ... hot and headstrong.* See George Lockhart Esq. of Carnwath, *The Lockhart Papers*, ed. Anthony Aufrere (London, 1817). A politically active Jacobite in the last years of Scottish independence, Lockhart loathed Tullibardine, and his records on the proceedings of the Scottish Parliament in this era, and on the denizens within it, are very entertaining.

45 *Highland feuds never die.* Wardlaw MS, p. 513, and it was too true. One feud involving the MacDonalds persisted through several

hundred years, and ended up with the feuding parties wasting each other's lands to the point where they had to eat their horses, and then their cats and dogs.

45 *the Highland clans … he read his daughter's letters.* Lovat's assertions about his Highland lairds' loyalty in his *Memoirs* (p. 50) is borne out, angrily, in the letters between the Atholl Murrays and from their officers quoted throughout this chapter.

47 *Simon and his lairds … swore the oath and fled.* This account is put together from Lovat's *Memoirs*, the account by Major James Fraser of Castleleathers (Major MS), who witnessed Saltoun's fit, and the subsequent trial of Thomas, Lord Lovat and Captain Simon Fraser of Beaufort, as they were cited to appear in the case brought against them by the Murrays.

49 *However, the Murrays … hesitated.* Robert A. Dodgshon (*From Chiefs to Landlords: Social and Economic Change in the Western Highlands and Islands, c.1493–1820*; Edinburgh University Press, 1998); Paul Hopkins (*Glencoe*); and Alan I. MacInnes (*Clanship*), first-class historians of the Highlands in the seventeenth and eighteenth centuries, outline the dynamic of struggle for power at work here.

51 *Simon did not stop to think … towards Inverness.* This whole episode produced a flurry of letters, a trial, witness statements and memoirs. In the scene that follows I make extensive use of Sir William Fraser of Ledeclune and Morar's *Trials of Simon, afterwards Lord Fraser of Lovat, 1698, 1701* (London: Chiswick Press, 1880); Major MS; NLS 3161; Lovat's *Memoirs*; Atholl's *Chronicles*; and McCormick, *State-Papers.*

56 *Her refusal to come to court …* Or might there have been another reason for her reluctance? In a letter dated 9 December, the Marquis of Atholl told Tullibardine that Tullibardine and Amelia's mother was given such a terrible shock 'upon a discovery concerning your sister' when the two met that it made her sick with worry for days (*Atholl Chronicles*, Vol. I, p. 421). Atholl said no more, and it is no more than speculation, but perhaps Amelia was pregnant. She had already had eight children, and was only just into her thirties, still young enough to bear more. If she was pregnant, she miscarried.

57 *the most tempestuous weather … in their goods.* Quoted in Alexander Mackenzie, *History of the Frasers of Lovat* (Inverness: A. & W. MacKenzie, 1896). British Army officers tried to resist the injunctions of the Marquis of Atholl that they stop at nothing to torment the

Frasers into giving up Simon. The clan would not yield. As far as Lovat's actions go, he knew what his goal was, but not how to achieve it. He had to think on his feet and could not make considered decisions, which must make him less coolly calculating at this time than Hopkins (*Glencoe ...*) concludes.

64 *William listened ... humiliated fury.* Tullibardine's political enemies worked hard to thwart his ambitions. His high-handedness invited opposition from too many men. See *The Lockhart Papers*.

67 *Sir James Stewart ... profitable trade.* William's ministers too often told him what he wanted to hear, not what was actually the case. William's poor management of Scotland led to a deepening and broadening of Jacobite sentiment.

76 *Lovat's first contact ... Amen.* Multilingual, multi-denominational, multi-cultural, these men played with words, allusions, images and other references freely in their letters. See BL Add MSS 31251.

76 *Before Louis XIV ... each façade.* A major exhibition on the Stuart Court in exile resulted in much graphic and written detail of the period, especially the observations of members of the French Court on their neighbours. A good starting point is the catalogue, *La Cour des Stuarts à Saint-Germain-en-Laye au Temps de Louis XIV* (Paris, 1992).

77 *tells a story ... while he professed it.* There was a vast network of spies and informers, the main source of inside information to intelligence ministers, before the days of hacking and tapping.

78 *Middleton's secretary ... so fatal to him.* The tragedy of the 'James II and III', was the lack of guile. Sincere and passionate Roman Catholics, they simply could not politic their way back onto the thrones, keeping private belief and public policy well apart; though hundreds of thousands wanted them back. Even Samuel Johnson, as late as the 1760s, would write that, if polled, the majority of Britons would recall the Stuarts, though they would not give a penny to bring it about. This comment is from HLA Scots Plot.

79 *He bemoaned ... a miracle.* See *La Cour des Stuarts*, p. 165.

79 *There is a party ... would be restored.* See James Macpherson, *Original Papers, containing the Secret History of Great Britain, from the Restoration, to the accession of the House of Hanover* (London, 1775); Lovat's *Memoirs*; and Macky, *Journey through Scotland* for the arguments about strategy in the next few pages. The fascinating vacillations of the Jacobites in France, and of Queen Anne's most

important ministers, illustrates how fundamental to British politics were the internal and external debates men conducted about who should rule, and how and why. It engaged them at the deepest levels of their hearts, heads and souls.

81 *Brother McLoghlan ... the Highland clans.* BL Add MSS 31250–53 has much of Lovat's correspondence at this time, showing him petitioning and working feverishly for the restoration of the Stuarts, via an independent Scottish monarch, in part as an image of his own restoration to the Lovat estates and titles.

83 *Addressing the King ...* In BL Add MSS 31250–52; and Lovat's *Memoirs*, Lovat flatters and cajoles Louis XIV to mount an invasion of Scotland.

87 *the most effectual ... Crown of Scotland.* See Macpherson, *Original Papers*, but this was the rock on which Jacobite factions split: English Jacobites could never consent to the implied dissolution of the Union of Crowns.

88 *doggerel.* BL Add MSS 31251 ff214 has several examples of these *jeux d'esprits*.

88 *In Scotland ... daughter-in-law and grandsons.* This was an old-fashioned piece of chicanery for obtaining control of property – buy up the debts and foreclose, knowing the person could not, or in this case was told not to pay, and assign them to your representative. The handiwork is traced in NLS Dep 327: 182 – Roderick Mackenzie, Lord Prestonhall; fB17.23; fB17.4; fB17.7; f no number, and so on.

89 *By the spring of 1793 ... Their decision.* This doomed fantasy showed how out of touch Middleton was – the most influential minister at St Germains.

91 *under sentence ... would converse.* See *The Lockhart Papers*, p. 81. This was Lovat's problem. The writer was a Scottish Jacobite and natural ally, but many people distrusted Lovat, even on his own side, since his actions made him an outlaw in Scotland.

91 *Eventually they sneaked away ...* The months covered by the beginning of this chapter, including the Northallerton escapade, is recorded in Add MSS 31252 especially ff88–93, and Lovat's *Memoirs*.

95 *At Northumberland ...* Lovat reported back to Mary of Modena and Middleton on the lack of solid commitment, in Macpherson, *Original Papers*, p. 641ff.

96 *Mary of Modena ... averse to it.* See HLA Scots Plot, which is full of witness statements about the Scots, or Queensberry Plot, with Lovat

at the heart of it. Queensberry comes out of it as a devil or a decent man depending on your politics. *The Lockhart Papers* take the devil/ Jacobite line, and Clerk of Penicuik (in *Memoirs of the Life of Sir John Clerk of Penicuik, Baronet, baron of the Exchequer, extracted by himself from his own journals, 1676–1755*: Scottish Historical Society, 1892) takes the government line – that Queensberry did a decent job in a thankless situation. Thereby Lovat is a litmus test for political allegiances in Britain in 1704. Renaudot's views, essentially Louis XIV's, are expressed in Haile, *Queen Mary of Modena*, p. 386ff.

97 *It was apparent … Hanover and Union.* For one record of the debates see *The Lockhart Papers*, p. 64ff.

100 *On 11 August … the Parliament again.* This was the first outward sign of Lovat's change of heart, see Macpherson, *Original Papers*, Vol. 2, pp. 4–5.

101 *They were perfectly ravished … lives in the cause.* Lovat's *Memoirs* emphasise their enthusiasm but the dangers that would arise if they moved from passive support to active participation were decisive. They had too much to lose. Hate William as most of them did, he had pensioned many into peaceableness.

102 *Under cover of darkness … incriminating material.* There is a wealth of primary and secondary textual commentary on these events. Lovat features, sometimes prominently, especially in HLA Scots Plot; Macpherson, *Original Papers*; W. C. Mackenzie, *Simon Fraser, Lord Lovat, His Life and Times* (London: Chapman & Hall, 1908), and BL Add MSS 15398 ff229–33.

104 *Summoning the leading … control of the game.* See Macpherson, *Original Papers*, Vol. 1, p. 643ff, in which Lovat's memorial to Mary of Modena is printed. The original is BL Add MSS 31252 ff101–04. The memorial aims at a more definite commitment to act from the Stuarts, to provoke the British Jacobites to respond in kind. The witnesses appearing in the HLA Scots Plot record – who, by the next spring needed to persuade the government they never intended treason – of course said the opposite. See also Macky, *Journey through Scotland*, and *The Lockhart Papers* for more contemporary reactions.

111 *We are come safe here … victory at Speirs.* Macpherson, *Original Papers* gives the reaction he wanted the British to hear, in the person of Queensberry. Add MSS 51252 f98 is for his French masters. These contradictions make sense in the light of his one unifying desire – to get home and take possession of his titles and clan and estates.

113 *The Fraser party ... rumours from England.* Comments in Major MS, Vol. 1, p. 138ff; Lovat's *Memoirs*; Macpherson, *Original Papers*, p. 643ff; Haile, *Queen Mary of Modena*, p. 378ff; and Colonel Nathanial Hooke, *Correspondence of Colonel Hooke in 1703–1707* (London: Roxburghe Club, 1870), p. 113ff.

114 *Despite all this ... Court of St Germains.* This was the feeling of Bishop Burnet, a politically alert cleric observing his fellows in the House of Lords.

117 *Lovat was as aghast ... stay put.* See Lovat's *Memoirs*; BL Add MSS 31252 ff163–65.

119 *the following morning to the hospital.* Lovat's letters about the event are in BL Add MSS 31252, ff172–84, 187–88; also Lovat's *Memoirs*, p. 293.

120 *on néglige le reste.* See Hooke, *Correspondence*, Vol. 1, p. 155.

120 *At Angoulême ... No one came.* Lovat correspondence in BL Add MSS 31252 f198ff.

121 *By 1706 ... final elimination.* Letter reproduced in Mackenzie, *History of the Frasers*, pp. 292–93.

121 *Frantic to go home ... responded wearily.* Correspondence between Lovat and French ministers in BL Add MSS 31252 ff203–06, ff218–19, f 245.

122 *cette Union infernelle* in BL Add MSS 31252 f281.

123 *The years at Angouleme ... to Saumur.* See Lovat's *Memoirs*, p. 326.

123 *At Versailles ... unfortunate enterprise.* Jeremy Black, *Culloden and the '45* (Stroud: Sutton, 1993), p. 16, Macpherson, *Original Papers*; Lovat's *Memoirs*; and BL Add MSS 31252.

125 *It seemed ... unfortunate star.* Lovat's *Memoirs*, p. 381.

126 *Leven had turned ... executed.* See Macpherson, *Original Papers*; W. C. Mackenzie, *Simon Fraser*.

127 *Major James Fraser ... decisions ahead.* As well as Lovat's *Memoirs*, and BL Add MSS 31252, much of the story of Lovat leaving France is drawn from Major MS, a highly entertaining account of Major James Fraser of Castleleathers's journey to retrieve his chief. The Major was the son-in-law of Lovat's old chaplain and clan tradition-bearer, the Revd James Fraser of Wardlaw.

129 *No Hanover! No cuckold!* See Paul Monod's fascinating study of how widespread was Jacobitism throughout England, *Jacobitism and the English People, 1688–1788*.

129 *James III and VIII ... the trust was gone.* See Duncan Warrand (ed.), *Culloden Papers* (London: Cadell & Davies, 1815), p. 30, and the

volumes of *More Culloden Papers* (also edited by Duncan Warrand) for the correspondence of the Forbeses, Lovat's neighbours in Inverness and a family that rose to prominence in the first half of the eighteenth century. John Forbes of Culloden was a British MP. His brother Duncan became both a British MP and the Lord President of the Court of Session, the highest civil court in Scotland, a vital contact for anyone involved in disputes over property rights.

131 *Now a British MP … full remission.* See Sir William Fraser, *The Chiefs of Grant* (Edinburgh, 1883),Vol. 2, pp. 282–83.

133 *On 19 November … before me.* Ibid., Vol. 2, pp. 283–84.

134 *a knife being plunged into his neck.* Ibid., Vol. 2, p. 286.

134 *When Mackenzie of Fraserdale … further trouble this way.* See Warrand (ed.), *More Culloden Papers* (Inverness: Robert Carruthers, 1923–30), Vol. 3, p. 4; Atholl, *Chronicles*, Vol. 2, p. 179; Lovat's *Memoirs*, p. 463.

135 *The King's ministers … remission with King George.* Major MS, Vol. 2, p. 12, Lovat's *Memoirs*, p. 465.

136 *The Forbes brothers … cannot so easily lay.* See Fraser, *Chiefs of Grant*, Vol. 2, pp. 289–90; Warrand (ed.), *More Culloden Papers*, Vol. 2, pp. 57, 60, 65.

137 *The money was at last … nothing would come of it.* Warrand (ed.), *Culloden Papers*, pp. 338–39.

137 *Spring drifted … on the run from the law.* Major MS, Vol. 2, p. 14ff.

139 *They looked on it … lead a rebellion.* See John Master of Sinclair, *Memoirs of the Insurrection in Scotland in 1715* (Edinburgh: Abbotsford Society, 1858), p. 36, and Field Marshal James Keith, *A Fragment of a Memoir …, 1714–1734* (Edinburgh: Spalding Club, 1843), p. 393ff.

139 *Go with what you can get … come to his aid.* Calendar, Vol. 1, p. 377.

140 *Just 'make the best … the Fraser chief.* See Sir William Fraser, *The Sutherland Book* (Edinburgh, 1892), Vol. 2, p. 205ff.

142 *In Inverness … her fields and granaries.* See Miller, *Inverness*, p. 118, and Major MS, Vol. 2, p. 25.

143 *the gateway to the north.* See Daniel Szechi, *1715: The Great Jacobite Rebellion* (Yale University Press, 2006), p. 184.

144 *had no idea what to do after they failed to take Newcastle.* Ibid., p. 171.

145 *in his late thirties and still in his prime.* See Michael Fry, *Wild Scots, Four Hundred Years of Highland History* (John Murray, 2005), p. 48.

145 *On his way home ... clan's survival.* Major MS, Vol. 2, p. 42.

146 *Also in Stirling ... entire rebellion.* Szechi, *1715*, p. 185; RH 2/4/305/27 and 46, State Papers Scotland, NAS; Fraser, *Chiefs of Grant*, Vol. 2, pp. 357–58ff.

147 *My Lord Lovat is now gone ... determined on that.* Fraser, *Chiefs of Grant*, Vol. 2, pp. 357–58ff, and Major MS, Vol. 2, p. 46ff.

147 *Edinburgh now ... it bore.* Szechi, *1715*, p. 14, and Ramsay, *Scotland and Scotsmen* (Edinburgh, 1877), Vol. 1, p. 169.

149 *The night gave them some cover ...* Much of this journey north is covered in Major MS, Vol. 2, p. 46ff.

152 *He sent a message ... theatre of the rebellion.* RH 2/4/307/83b, State Papers Scotland, NAS; Szechi, *1715*, p. 185.

153 *hardly any men to command.* RH 2/4/307/83b; Miller, *Inverness*, p. 119; and Major MS, Vol. 2, p. 73ff.

153 *Lovat then met in council ... occupied Inverness on 12 November.* Major MS, Vol. 2, p. 73ff.

155 *The next day, Sunday 13th ...* The best account of Sheriffmuir is in Szechi, *1715*.

156 *Neither side gained much ... the Jacobite campaign.* Keith, *A Fragment ...*, p. 394.

156 *I find Lord Lovat's ... to make a diversion.* Argyll to Townshend, SP 54, State Papers Domestic, NA.

162 *Lovat stressed to Townshend ... to British justice.* Lovat to Townshend, ibid.

163 *The Earl of Sutherland ... joined me.* Sutherland to George I, in Fraser, *Sutherland Book*, Vol. 1, pp. 335–38.

164 *From the government camp ... fifty miles of the town.* Calendar, Vol. 1, p. 482; Fraser, *Chiefs of Grant*, Vol. 1, pp. 363–64 and Vol. 2, p. 189.

165 *we are resolved ... the key of the north.* SP 54, State Papers Domestic, NA.

165 *My presence will inspire ... slow-moving, considered.* Calendar, Vol. 1, p. 484; Mar State Papers, p. 488.

166 *Lovat has it now ... to make the work easy.* Calendar, Vol. 1, p. 490ff.

166 *Now he held the key to the north.* See Hooke, *Correspondence*, Vol. 1, p. 91 fn, and Calendar, Vol. 1, pp. 500–01.

167 *He offered Lovat a dukedom.* Hooke, *Correspondence*, Vol. 1, p. 91 fn.

168 *From London, King George I ... steadily Lovat's way.* Fraser, *Sutherland Book*, Vol. 2, pp. 27ff, 52–53; BL Add MSS 14854 f71.

171 *The Reverend James ... their surviving stem.* Wardlaw MS, pp. 24–27.

171 *Lovat's allies urged Westminster … his pardon.* SRO/GD 220/5/630/1, NAS.

172 *The Flying Post.* BL Burney collection, 175b, Box 2.

173 *He would not usually … Fraserdale's camp.* Fraser, *Sutherland Book*, Vol. 2, pp. 53–61.

174 *guarantee the peaceable behaviour of their people.* Lovat to Cadogan, SP 54, State Papers Domestic, NA, March 1716.

176 *Lovat's heart surged with joy.* Warrand (ed.), *Culloden Papers*, p. 44.

176 *Lovat set off … Argyll was their patron.* Warrand (ed.), *More Culloden Papers*, Vol. 2, p. 102.

176 *Sutherland was as good … Independent Company of Foot.* Calendar, Vol. 2, p. 225.

177 *I can hardly believe … which I hope is not true.* Atholl, *Chronicles*, Vol. 2, p. 250.

177 *Lovat took it from him.* Warrand (ed.), *More Culloden Papers*, Vol. 2, p. 81.

177 *The coffee houses and the other public places are the seats of English liberty.* Anthony Lejeune, *White's: The First Three Hundred Years* (London: A. & C. Black, 1993), p. 34.

178 *expenses he claimed he incurred defending King George.* Lenman, *Jacobite Clans*, pp. 77–78. £14,000 is about £1,250,000 in today's money.

178 *adjust matters betwixt them.* Fraser, *Sutherland Book*, Vol. 2, p. 217.

180 *Whilst in London, Lovat had received news of the death of his brother.* Warrand (ed.), *More Culloden Papers*, Vol. 2, p. 119, and Calendar, Vol. 2, p. 87.

182 *On Saturday 23 June … he meant the Squadrone.* Warrand (ed.), *Culloden Papers*, p. 55.

183 *women are children of a larger growth.* See Roy Porter, *English Society in the Eighteenth Century* (London: Penguin, 1991), p. 24.

183 *secure them the joint interest of the north.* Warrand (ed.), *Culloden Papers*, p. 75.

183 *confident they would not be 'out' for long.* Warrand (ed.), *More Culloden Papers*, Vol. 2, p. 124.

183 *I don't know what will become of me.* Ibid., Vol. 2, p. 125.

184 *The news of the dismissal … reached Inverness.* Ibid., Vol. 2, p. 128.

184 *He was merely to be impoverished.* Warrand (ed.), *Culloden Papers*, p. 57; Calendar Treasury Papers, 1714–19, pp. 222–23.

185 *do what you can to have it stopped.* Atholl, *Chronicles*, Vol. 2, p. 254.

185 *My dear General you must be active in it.* Warrand (ed.), *More Culloden Papers*, Vol. 2, p. 126.

187 *it must be a curse rather than a blessing.* Fraser, *Chiefs of Grant*, Vol. 2, p. 291.

187 *to put her in the handsomest manner of my hand.* Ibid., Vol. 2, p. 354.

187 *for quantities of provisions.* Ibid., Vol. 1, p. 351.

189 *to anyone who would listen.* BL Add MSS 6116 ff87–93.

191 *in this he failed.* NLS, Dep 327.

192 *gentlemen of the long robe.* 1746, *Lives of Lord Lovat*, Vol. 2, p. 65.

193 *Lovat wrote to Duncan about the looming crisis.* Warrand (ed.), *Culloden Papers*, p. 70.

193 *this gift, which I now reckon as nothing* ... For Lovat's escheat from the King see Mackenzie, *History of the Frasers*, pp. 349–50.

194 *that was the question facing Lovat and his legal representatives.* NLS 327 fB23(5).

195 *the bread that's now taken from me.* SP 54 f134.

196 *shed more blood in peace than in time of war.* Graham, *Journey through the North*, Vol. 1, p. 49.

197 *the fatal Union which I hope will not last long.* Mackenzie, *History of the Frasers*, pp. 352–53.

198 *after taking a vomit he felt better at last.* Warrand (ed.), *More Culloden Papers*, Vol. 2, p. 188.

200 *Robertson's house was within two miles of Dounie.* *Lives of Lord Lovat*, p. 60.

201 *he, Lord Lovat, would join with all his.* See *State Trials*, Vol. 18, p. 586.

202 *Perhaps you would be so kind just as to send it to me?* BL Add MSS 28239 f63.

202 *threw it into the fire.* See *State Trials*, Vol. 18, p. 588.

203 *I wish her an happy hour and a safe delivery.* Edward Dunbar, *Social Life in Former Days, chiefly in the Province of Moray* (Edinburgh: Edmonston & Douglas, 1865)

203 *It weighed a satisfying eight pounds.* Catalogue for Lovat Sale, Lot 571.

207 *the greatest bouzers in the north.* In *Memoirs of Duncan Forbes* (London, 1748), p. 11.

208 *contest the Inverness-shire seat with Culloden.* Grant was sitting MP for Elginshire but the Inverness-shire seat, the hub of the Highlands, was more prestigious and in the right hands should command more patronage.

211 *by standards he himself deplored.* Lovat's memorial to George I and Wade's response are reprinted in Edmund Burt, *Letters from the North of Scotland, 1754*, Vol. 2 (London: William Paterson, 1876), p. 258ff.

212 *This powerful laird …* Ferguson, quoted in Edward King, *Munimenta Antiqua; Or, Observations on ancient Castles, including Remarks on … the Progress in Great Britain and on … the Changes in Laws and Customs* (London: G. Nicol, 1799–1805) p. 63.

214 *a man of a bold, nimbling kind of sense … sacrifice everything to their interest.* See Clerk of Penicuik, *Memoirs*, pp. 208–09, one of the commissioners who brought in the Act of Union.

215 *many a peruke had been baked in a better crust.* See Burt, *Letters from the North*, Vol. 1, p. 85.

215 *rather too much, I think, for the sportsman's diversion.* Ibid., pp. 64–6.

215 *rankled with him and London.* In *Jacobite Clans*, Lenman uses Lovat as his paradigmatic example of how the great Highland chiefs tried to negotiate the transition from clannishness to capitalism and the modern age.

216 *the clan with its well-being.* Dodgshon, *Chiefs to Landlords*, p. 85.

217 *we are in the same slavery as ever.* Warrand (ed.), *More Culloden Papers*, Vol. 2, p. 322.

218 *Bailie John Steuart.* See Bailie John Steuart, *Letter-Book of Bailie John Steuart of Inverness* (Edinburgh: Scottish History Society, 1915), pp. xxii–xxiii.

219 *cruives.* See Burt, *Letters from the North*, Vol. 1, p. 67.

221 *neither did I hear of any theft or robbery.* Warrand (ed.), *Culloden Papers*, p. 97.

223 *in perpetuity in his own family.* Fraser, *Chiefs of Grant*, Vol. 2, p. 296.

224 *ane o' Mary's lovers … the castle was on the verge of following it.* Burt, *Letters from the North*, Vol. 1, pp. 20, 22, 35.

226 *the whiff of Jacobitism.* 'Bobbing John' Mar was the hopelessly indecisive leader of the 1715 uprising.

226 *Demonology was a passion.* Dr Alexander Carlyle of Inveresk, *Autobiography of Dr Alexander Carlyle …*, ed. Hill Burton (Edinburgh: Blackwood, 1860), p. 8ff.

227 *my lovely soul's affection for me.* Fraser, *Chiefs of Grant*, Vol. 2, p. 298.

228 *serve each one by serving them all.* Warrand (ed.), *Culloden Papers*, p. 113.

229 *you secure the estate of Lovat to Simon's bairns.* Ibid., p. 117.

231 *Why had she changed her mind?* Fraser, *Chiefs of Grant*, Vol. 2, p. 300.

234 *an indignity put upon my person and family, that I can hardly bear.* Ibid., p. 304.

234 *Lovat sensed things were not quite right* … The significance of this election, and Lovat's part in it, is well explored in Lenman, *Jacobite Clans* and Grant papers, SRO, NAS.

237 *to be found in the Forbes's political camp.* Grant papers, SRO, NAS; and Fraser, *Chiefs of Grant*, Vol. 1, pp. 315, 325.

238 *he had little to fear from any normal man.* Lenman, *Jacobite Clans*, pp. 106–07, and Grant papers, SRO, NAS.

238 *famine in the Aviemore area in March 1734.* Grant papers, SRO, NAS.

240 *the Grants and the Frasers he'd rout.* See Fraser, *Chiefs of Grant*, Vol. 2, p. 380.

241 *they would have been his natural allies.* Ibid., p. 358.

241 *their expectations gives me some uneasiness.* Warrand (ed.), *More Culloden Papers*, Vol. 3, p. 10.

244 *if one interest failed him, he would turn to another.* Quoted in Lenman, *Jacobite Clans*, p. 118.

245 *or disguised themselves as women.* See *State Trials*, Vol. 18, p. 558.

246 *for school in Edinburgh.* Fraser, *Chiefs of Grant*, Vol. 2, pp. 345–46.

246 *the wintry gusts of disfavour.* Ibid., p. 348.

248 *Lord Perth and his brother, Lord John Drummond.* See *State Trials*, Vol. 18, p. 759.

253 *fit in with this man of twists and turns.* Fraser, *Chiefs of Grant*, Vol. 2, p. 366ff.

254 *until she could escape his fortress.* Ibid., pp. 363–64.

254 *ordering supplies daily for the household.* *TGSI*, Vol. 11, p. 341. The accounts of daily life are in the Grant books; in the Lovat correspondence reproduced in *TGSI*; originals in NA and Laing MSS, Highland Archives, Inverness.

259 *for the good of the government.* For letters to Inverallochy see *Miscellany of the Spalding Club*, ed. John Stuart (Aberdeen, 1842), Vol. 2, p. 4.

260 *Lovat joined the Patriots.* Hill Burton, *Lives of Simon* …, p. 217.

261 *Alexander Carlyle with him … might have been handsome in his youth.* See Carlyle, *Autobiography*, p. 57ff, for 'Jupiter' Carlyle, the famous Scottish church minister's memoirs of his youthful encounters with this behemoth from another age.

262 *The Patriots got no power.* *TGSI*, Vol. 12, p. 373.

264 *and settling themselves there.* SP 78/44/526, State Papers Foreign, NA.

265 *1743 might be a year of great change.* See *State Trials*, Vol. 18, p. 653.

266 *You may think little of these events. TGSI*, Vol. 12, p. 367ff, Oct 1743.

268 *shared feeling for homeland and people. TGSI*, Vol. 11, p. 379.

268 *the miasma of approaching peace.* Lenman, *Jacobite Clans*, p. 145.

269 *a French expeditionary force was assembled.* Black, *Culloden and the '45*, pp. 56–58.

270 *The dreadful summer weather just went on and on.* Lenman, *Jacobite Clans*, p. 143.

271 *to lead an invasion to Scotland.* Black, *Culloden and the '45*, pp. 63–64.

271 *after too many bad harvests.* See *State Trials*, Vol. 18, p. 662.

273 *summoned to London for questioning. TGSI*, Vol. 14, p. 2ff.

274 *a feverish disorder. TGSI*, Vol. 14, pp. 3–4ff. The most recent, and outstandingly good, scholarly account of the '45, is Christopher Duffy's *The '45* (London: Cassell, 2003). I acknowledge my debt to this book as the background to Lovat's correspondence and experience during this period. It is printed in letters to and from his fellow Highlanders in *TGSI*, Fraser, *Chiefs of Grant*, Vols 1–3, and Warrand (ed.), *Culloden Papers*, etc.

275 *Captain, Lieutenant and Ensign given.* Warrand (ed.), *Culloden Papers*, p. 221.

275 *he could not act.* See *State Trials*, Vol. 18, p. 697ff.

276 *if and when French back-up arrived.* Warrand (ed.), *Culloden Papers*, p. 208.

277 *ordered his ship back to France. Scottish Diaries*, Vol. 2, p. 421.

281 *put his complaints aside in a general emergency?* Hill Burton, *Lives of Simon …*, p. 223.

281 *the King he had in mind was King George.* Warrand (ed.), *Culloden Papers*, p. 210.

281 *when I was in my happiest situation in the world.* See *State Trials*, Vol. 18.

282 *taller than any in his company.* Warrand (ed.), *Culloden Papers*, p. 220.

282 *shrinking from tackling the rebels.* Black, *Culloden and the '45*, p. 78.

283 *the growth of this enthralling uprising.* Warrand (ed.), *Culloden Papers*, p. 211.

284 *take command of the Fraser fighting men.* Ibid., pp. 214–15.

285 *please confirm this was without foundation?* Ibid., p. 222.

285 *The words rang hollow to the Lord President.* Ibid., pp. 409–10.

285 *a thousand men for three months to defend them.* Black, *Culloden and the '45*, p. 80.

286 *his countenance thoughtful and melancholy.* Carlyle, *Autobiography*, pp. 153–54.

288 *streamed through his doors.* See *State Trials*, Vol. 18, p. 591.

288 *that of common father of our people.* Ibid., p. 780.

288 *he had received from James in France.* Ibid., p. 592. Accounts of life at Castle Dounie in this year are from the witness statements recorded in *State Trials*, Vol. 18.

290 *consult him as he lay in his bed.* Ibid., p. 685.

291 *wanted nothing to do with the kidnapping of his old friend.* Warrand (ed.), *Culloden Papers*, p.228.

292 *we had no peace with him.* See *State Trials*, Vol. 18, p. 691.

292 *or to anyone that belongs to you.* Warrand (ed.), *Culloden Papers*, p. 230.

292 *So much for a most disagreeable subject!* TGSI, Vol. 14, p. 9.

292 *the Stratherrick men at Culloden.* Warrand (ed.), *Culloden Papers*, p. 232.

293 *everyone's opinion in Inverness.* Ibid., p. 231.

293 *against any of his distracted opinions.* Ibid., pp. 234–35.

293 *When he finished reading ... still he would not make a decision.* See *State Trials*, Vol. 18, pp. 599ff, 718.

294 *as they very remarkably did thirty years ago.* Warrand (ed.), *Culloden Papers*, p. 237.

294 *my unhappy and much loved friend.* Ibid., p. 451.

295 *Charles Fraser of Inverallochy, march away.* Ibid., p. 436ff.

295 *he would leave Lovat in peace.* TGSI, Vol. 14, pp. 17–19ff, 22.

296 *I shall not put the least hardship on any man.* Ibid., p. 23.

296 *and never come home again.* See *Scots Magazine, 1745*, p. 589.

298 *The song was out of tune.* Warrand (ed.), *Culloden Papers*, p. 238.

298 *are gone with him.* See *State Trials*, Vol. 18, p. 749.

299 *No reply came from Dounie.* Warrand (ed.), *Culloden Papers*, p. 257.

300 *to the Aird of Lovat.* Fraser, *Sutherland Book*, Vol. 2, p. 93ff.

303 *to send the Master to safety.* TGSI, Vol. 14, p. 31.

304 *They could not afford to split up their forces.* See *State Trials*, Vol. 18, p. 763ff.

305 *the glorious retreat his Highness made from Derby.* Ibid., p. 754.

309 *launching the engineer ...* Christopher Duffy, *The '45*, p. 448.

310 *the terms of war. The Gentleman's Magazine*, Vol. 16 (March 1746), p. 205.

310 *the hills of Ross-shire and Sutherland.* Ibid., p. 204.

312 *to recruit more fighting Frasers.* Cumberland Papers, 13/327, NA.

312 *succumbed, though mostly to gout.* Walter Pringle, *Memoirs of Walter Pringle of Greenknow, written by himself* (Edinburgh: W. Hamilton, 1751), p. 44.

314 *to receive their death from the bayonets.* The Gentleman's Magazine, Vol. 16, p. 244.

316 *to give up any hope of breaking through.* See *SHAT* (*Service Historique de l'Armée de Terre*), Paris, A1/3154.

316 *He was often at home with his father.* John Prebble, *Culloden* (London: Penguin, 1967), p. 62.

318 *things were going well for the Jacobites.* Anne Grant of Laggan, *Letters from the Mountains*, (London: 1806).

320 *declaring me dead enough. Scottish Diaries*, Vol. 2, pp. 28–29.

322 *scheme without emotion.* See *Scottish History Society*, Vol. 26, p. 265.

322 *make ample amends for this day's ruffle.* MacLaren, Moray, *Lord Lovat of the '45, The End of an Old Song* (London: Jarrolds, 1957), p. 198.

323 *the night after the action. The Gentleman's Magazine*, Vol. 16, p. 210.

323 *Young Pretender were holed up there.* 'Historical Manuscripts Commission Report', Vol. 10, pts 1–2.

323 *escaped with their lives and are fallen.* BL Add MSS 32707 ff128–29ff; 281; 381ff.

325 *buy back what had been taken from them.* Prebble, *Culloden*, pp. 166–67.

326 *soaked into his land and home.* Ibid., p. 61.

327 *Cumberland trusted his instincts.* BL Add MSS 32707 ff128–29.

327 *nor do we expect redress.* Miller, *Inverness*, p. 147.

328 *at the foot of the first slate of it.* Ibid., p. 145.

328 *Lochiel came to meet him in Strathfarrar.* See *State Trials*, Vol. 18, pp. 664–65.

333 *In the end, they nearly walked onto him.* The other story of his capture said he was taken on the island. A sailor spotted two feet. They appeared to fall out of the bottom of a hollow tree trunk. He came closer. Two gouty legs, wrapped in masses of flannel, were stuffed into the shoes. He peered inside and looked up the body into Lord Lovat's face. With great difficulty, some men had manoeuvred him inside the hollow tree. He stood there, concealed in wooden armour and imprisoned by it. They had him. The man let out a holler of triumph. His fellow soldiers rushed over, and they dragged the old man out onto the ground. See *State Trials*, Vol. 18, pp. 739–40.

333 *with which his Lordship pretended to be pleased.* See *Scots Magazine,*
1747.

333 *for having taken away his Independent Company, than anything else.*
See *State Trials,* Vol. 18, p. 740.

335 *to execute a crippled old man?* See *State Trials,* Vol. 18, p. 715.

336 *to make the best use of these advantages.* SP 54; *Gentleman's Magazine*
16: 381.

336 *They would show no mercy. Gentleman's Magazine* 16: 325.

337 *He was them; they were him.* Anne Grant of Laggan, *Letters from the
Mountains.*

337 *spectre at his own funeral.* Warrand (ed.), *Culloden Papers,* 30 Oct
1746.

339 *one of his most popular prints.* John Nichols, *Anecdotes of Mr Hogarth*
(Leipzig, 1783), p. 282.

341 *the defendant was in part responsible.* Warrand (ed.), *Culloden Papers,*
pp. 301–02.

342 *to find evidence against Lovat. TGSI,* Vol. 14, pp. 33–36.

344 The trial and execution of Lord Lovat are covered in many of the
news-sheets for March and April 1747, in the contemporary 'Lives of
Lord Lovat' in the *Gentleman's Magazine,* and in the official record,
State Trials, Vol. 18. I have recreated this last act of Lovat's dramatic
life from these, respecting the bias of the writer while trying to see
Lovat at the centre of the often conflicting versions of events.

SELECT BIBLIOGRAPHY

Unpublished Sources

ARCHIVES

British Library, London: Collection of Lovat papers covering period in France up to the early years of his incarceration, BL Add MSS 31249–53; BL Add MSS 6116: Letters and reports of trials after the 1715 rebellion; BL Add MSS 23289; Lovat memorial to William III: BL 20310; Burney collection of early British newspapers on microfiche

Highland Archives, Inverness: Burgh Council Minutes; 'Historical Account of the Family of Fraser' manuscript; 'Laing manuscript'

House of Lords Archive, London: papers relating to the Lovat inheritance case up to 1730

Lochaber Archive Centre, Fort William: Lovat Papers, CL/6/–

National Archives, Kew, London: State Papers Domestic and Foreign, SP 54; SP 78

National Archives of Scotland, Edinburgh: State Papers Scotland, Volumes RH 2/4–

National Library of Scotland, Edinburgh: NLS Dep 327: Fraser family papers, Lovat and Strichen; NLS 987: Lovat's time in France, 1702–25; NLS 2963–69: Forbes family correspondence; NLS 3161: Letter Countess of Findlater to David Crawford describing marriage of Simon and Dowager Lady Lovat; 'Remarks for Simon Fraser Lord Lovat on the Information for Hugh Mackenzie ...', 1730

Published Sources

NEWSPAPERS

The Courant
The Gentleman's Magazine
The Scots Magazine

BOOKS AND PERIODICALS

Anderson, John, *Historical Account of the Family of Frisel or Fraser, particularly of Fraser of Lovat* (Edinburgh: Blackwood, 1825)

Arnot, Hugo, *A Collection and Abridgement of Celebrated Criminal Trials in Scotland, from AD 1536, to 1784. With historical and critical remarks* (Edinburgh: 'The Author', 1785)

Atholl, John, 7th Duke of, *Chronicles of the Atholl and Tullibardine Families*, 5 Vols (Edinburgh: Ballantyne, 1908)

Bevan, Bryan, *King James the Third of England* (London: Robert Hale, 1967)

Black, Jeremy, *Culloden and the '45* (Stroud: Sutton, 1993)

Book of the Lamentations of Simon, Prince of the Tribe of Lovat (London: M. Cooper in Paternoster Row, 1746)

Buchan, John, *A Lost Lady of Old Years* (London: Thomas Nelson & Sons, 1950)

Burns, William, *Simon, Lord Lovat of the 45: Has he been defamed by history?* (Inverness, 1908)

Burt, Edmund, *Letters from the North of Scotland, 1754*, 2 Vols (William Paterson, 1876)

Caesar, Julius, *De bello gallico*, trans. by S. A. Handford (Penguin, 1951)

Carlyle, Dr Alexander of Inveresk, *Autobiography of Dr Alexander Carlyle, containing a Memoir of the Men and Events of his Time*, edited by Hill Burton (Edinburgh: Blackwood, 1860)

Catalogue of Antiques, Curios etc, which belonged to the late A. T. F. Fraser, Last male Descendent of Simon. Lord Lovat of the '45' (Inverness: J. T. Paxton Auctioneer, 1884), Part 1

Catalogue of Books, Charters, Letters and other family Papers, Mineralogical Cabinet, Philosophical Instruments, Arms, China, and Pictures, which belonged to the late A. T. F. Fraser Esq of Abertarff (Inverness: J. T. Paxton Auctioneer, 1884), Part 2

Clerk, Sir John, of Penicuik, *Memoirs of the Life of Sir John Clerk of Penicuik, Baronet, baron of the Exchequer, extracted by himself from his own journals, 1676–1755* (Edinburgh: Scottish Historical Society, 1892)

Cobbett's Complete Collection of State Trials and Proceedings for High Treason and other Crimes and Misdemeanors, from the Earliest Times to the Present Times, compiled by T. B. Howell Esq. (London: T. C. Hansard, 1813), Vol. 18

Cockayne, Emily, *Hubbub: Filth, Noise and Stench in England* (Yale, 2007)

Collection of Original Papers about the Scots Plot (London, 1704)

Collection of Papers in Lovat Cases (Edinburgh, 1729)

Corp, Edward, and Cruickshanks, Eveline (eds), *The Stuart Court in Exile and the Jacobites* (London & Rio Grande: The Hambledon Press, 1995)

La Cour des Stuarts à Saint-Germain-en-Laye au temps de Louis XIV, various (Paris: Editions de la Réunion des Musées Nationaux, 1992)

Devine, Tom, *The Scottish Nation, 1700–2000* (London: Penguin, 2000)

Dictionary of National Biography: From the Earliest Times to 1900, edited by Sir Leslie Stephen and Sir Sydney Lees (Oxford: OUP, 1917 onwards)

Dodgshon, Robert A., *From Chiefs to Landlords: Social and Economic Change in the Western Highlands and Islands, c.1493–1820* (Edinburgh: Edinburgh University Press, 1998)

Duffy, Christopher, *The '45* (London: Cassell, 2003)

Dunbar, Edward, *Social Life in Former Days, Chiefly in the Province of Moray* (Edinburgh: Edmonston & Douglas, 1865)

Field, Ophelia, *The Kit-Cat Club* (London: Harper Perennial, 2009)

Forbes, Duncan, Lord President of the Court of Session, *Memoirs of the Life of the late Right Honourable Duncan Forbes of Culloden, etc.* (London, 1748)

Fraser, Charles Ian, *Clan Fraser of Lovat, A Highland Response to a Lowland Stimulus* (Edinburgh and London, 1952)

Fraser, James, late of Inverness, *A Genuine Narrative of the Life, Behaviour, and Conduct, of Simon, Lord Fraser of Lovat* ('printed for B. Cole in King's-Head-Court, Holbourn, 1747')

Fraser, James, *Major Fraser's Manuscript*, Fergusson (ed.), 2 Vols (Edinburgh, 1899)

Fraser, Master James, *Chronicles of the Frasers, the Wardlaw Manuscript, entitled 'Polichronicon seu Policratia Temporum', or the True Genealogy of the Frasers, 916–1674*, edited by William Mackay (Edinburgh: Scottish History Society, 1905)

Fraser, Sir William, *The Chiefs of Grant*, 3 Vols (Edinburgh, 1883)

—— *The Sutherland Book*, 3 Vols (Edinburgh, 1892)

Fraser, Sir William of Ledeclune and Morar, *Trials of Simon, afterwards Lord Fraser of Lovat, 1698, 1701* (London: Chiswick Press, 1880)

Fry, Michael, *Wild Scots, Four Hundred Years of Highland History* (London: John Murray, 2005)

Gatrell, Vic, *City of Laughter: Sex and Satire in Eighteenth Century London* (New York: Walker & Co., 2006)

Genuine Memoirs of the Life of Simon Lord Fraser of Lovat (London: printed for M. Cooper, 1746)

Gillies, William, 'The Gaelic poems of Sir Duncan Campbell of Glenorchy (I)', *Scottish Gaelic Studies*, 13/1 (Aberdeen, 1978)

Graham, Henry Grey, *The Social Life of Scotland in the Eighteenth-Century*, Vols 1–2 (London: A. & C. Black, 1899)

Grant. I. F., *Highland Folk Ways* (Edinburgh: Birlinn, 1997, rpt. 1st pub. 1961)

—— *Every-Day Life on an Old Highland Farm, 1769–1782* (London: Shepheard-Walwyn, 1981 rpt. 1st pub 1924)

Grant of Laggan, Anne, *Letters from the Mountains; being the real Correspondence of a Lady [i.e. Mrs Grant of Laggan], between the Years 1773 and 1803* (London, 1806)

Haile, Martin, *Queen Mary of Modena, Her Life and Letters* (London, 1905)

Hill Burton, John, *Lives of Simon Lord Lovat and Duncan Forbes of Culloden* (London: Chapman & Hall, 1847)

Historical Papers relating to the Jacobite Period (1699–1750), edited by Col. James Allardyce (Aberdeen: New Spalding Club, 1895)

HMC Calendar of Stuart Papers belonging to His Majesty the King …, 8 Vols (London, 1902–20)

Hooke, Colonel Nathanial, *Correspondence of Colonel Hooke in 1703–1707* (London: Roxburghe Club, 1870)

Hopkins, Paul, *Glencoe and the End of the Highland War* (Edinburgh: John Donald, 1998)

Hume, David, and Smollett, Tobias, *The History of England*, 3 Vols (London: James S. Virtue, 1860)

Jacobite Correspondence of the Atholl Family (Edinburgh: Abbotsford Club, 1840)

Jacobite Peerage, Baronetage, Knightage and Grants of Honour (London: Charles Skilton Ltd, 1974), a facsimile of the original edition of 1904 with an added introduction by Roger Ararat

Keith, Field Marshal James, *A Fragment of a Memoir of Field-Marshal James Keith, written by himself, 1714–1734* (Edinburgh: The Spalding Club, 1843)

Lejeure, Anthony, *White's: The First Three Hundred Years* (London: A. & C. Black, 1993)

Lenman, Bruce, *The Jacobite Risings in Britain, 1689–1746* (London: Eyre Methuen, 1980)

—— *The Jacobite Clans of the Great Glen, 1650–1784* (Aberdeen: Scottish Cultural Press, 1995)

Lockhart, George Esq., of Carnwath, *The Lockhart Papers*, edited by Anthony Aufrere (London, 1817)

Lovat, Lord, *A Free Examination of a Modern Romance, entitled, Memoirs of the Life of Lord Lovat* (printed for W. Webb, near St Paul's, 1746)

MacInnes, Alan I., *Clanship, Commerce and the House of Stuart* (Tuckwell, 1996)

Mackay, D. N. (ed.), *Trial of Simon, Lord Lovat of the '45*, in *Notable English Trials* (Edinburgh & Glasgow: William Hodge & Company, 1911)

Mackenzie, Alexander, *History of the Frasers of Lovat* (Inverness: A. & W. MacKenzie, 1896)

Mackenzie, W. C., *Simon Fraser, Lord Lovat, His Life and Times* (London: Chapman & Hall, 1908)

—— *Lovat of the Forty-Five* (Edinburgh & London: The Moray Press, 1934)

Macky, John, *Memoirs of the Secret Services of John Macky Esq., during the reigns of King William, Queen Anne, and King George I* (London, 1733)

—— *A Journey through Scotland* (London, 1732, 2nd edn)

MacLaren, Moray, *Lord Lovat of the '45, The End of an Old Song* (London: Jarrolds, 1957)

MacLeod, Donald, *Memoirs of the Life and gallant Exploits of the Old Highlander, Serjeant Donald Macleod (1688–1791)*, Reprinted from the original edition of 1791, with an Introduction and Notes by J. G. Fyfe (London & Glasgow: Blackie & Son, 1933)

Macpherson, James, *Original Papers, containing the Secret History of Great Britain, from the Restoration, to the accession of the House of Hanover* (London, 1775)

McCormick, Joseph (ed.), *State-Papers and Letters addressed to William Carstares* (Edinburgh, 1774), especially Martin Martin, *A Description of the Western Isles of Scotland, 1716*, pp. 432–50

McLynn, Frank, *France and the Jacobite Rising of 1745* (Edinburgh: Edinburgh University Press, 1981)

Memoirs of the Life of Simon Lord Lovat; written by himself in the French language; and now first translated from the original Manuscript (London: printed for George Nicol, Bookseller to his Majesty, Pall-Mall, 1797)

Memoirs of the Life of Lord Lovat ('printed for M. Cooper at the Globe in Paternoster Row, 1746, anon. attrib. to Duncan Forbes, Lord President of the Court of Session')

Michael, Wolfgang, *England Under George I: The Quadruple Alliance*, Studies in Modern History series, edited by L. B. Namier (London: MacMillan & Co., 1939)

Miller, James, *Inverness* (Edinburgh: Birlinn, 2004)

Miscellany of the Spalding Club, Vol. 2, edited by John Stuart (Aberdeen, 1842)

Mitchison, Rosamund, and Leneman, Leah, *Girls in Trouble: Sexuality and Social Control in Rural Scotland, 1660–1780* (Edinburgh: Scottish Cultural Press, 1998)

Monod, Paul Kleber, *Jacobitism and the English People, 1688–1788* (Cambridge: CUP, 1989)

Newton, Michael, *Handbook of the Scottish Gaelic World* (Dublin: Four Courts Press, 2000)

Newton, Norman, *Life and Times of Inverness* (Inverness, 1996)

Oxford Dictionary of National Biography: from the earliest times to the year 2000, edited by H. C. G. Matthew and Brian Harrison (Oxford: OUP, 2004)

Petrie, Sir Charles, Bt, *The Jacobite Movement* (London: Eyre & Spottiswoode, 1959)

Pittock, Murray, *The Myth of the Jacobite Clans* (Edinburgh: Edinburgh University Press, 1995)

Porter, Roy, *English Society in the Eighteenth Century* (London: Penguin, 1991)

Prebble, John, *Culloden* (London: Penguin, 1967)

Pringle, Walter, *Memoirs of Walter Pringle of Greenknow, written by himself* (Edinburgh: W. Hamilton, 1751)

Ramsay, John of Ochtertyre, *Scotland and Scotsmen in the Eighteenth-Century, from the Manuscript of John Ramsay of Ochtertyre*, 2 Vols (Edinburgh Blackwood, 1888)

Riddell, John, *Inquiry into the law and practise in Scottish Peerages, before and after the Union; involving the questions of jurisdiction and forfeiture; together with an exposition of our genuine, original Consistorial law* (Edinburgh, 1842)

Robertson, Honorable Alexander of Strowan, *Poems on various Subjects and Occasions* (Edinburgh, 1752)

Saint-Simon, de Rouvroy, duc de, *Duc de Saint-Simon, Memoirs: A Shortened Version*, Vol. I, *1691–1709*, edited and translated by Lucy Norton (London: Prion, 1999)

Sankey, Margaret, *Jacobite Prisoners of the 1715 Rebellion: Preventing and Punishing Insurrection in Early Hanoverian Britain* (Ashgate Publishing, 2005)

Scottish Diaries and Memoirs, Vol. 1, *1550–1746*; Vol. 2, *1746–1843*, arranged and edited by J. G. Fyfe (Stirling: Eneas Mackay, 1942)

Seccombe, Thomas (ed.), *Lives of Twelve Bad Men: Original Studies of Eminent Scoundrels by Various Hands* (London: T. Fisher Unwin, 1894)

Sedgwick, Romney (ed.), *History of Parliament, The House of Commons, 1715–1754*, 2 Vols (London: History of Parliament Trust, 1970)

Selection from the Papers of the Earls of Marchmont, Illustrative of Events from 1685 to 1750, edited by Sir G. H. Rose (London: J. Murray, 1831)

Sinnott, Patrick, J., *Simon the Fox: Being an Account of the Activities of Simon Fraser … in his Early Twenties* (London, 1956)

Somers, John, Baron, *A Collection of scarce and valuable Tracts. Selected from an infinite number in print and manuscript, in the Royal, Cotton, Sion, and other Public, as well as private libraries; particularly that of the late Lord Sommers. Revised by eminent hands, especially* 'The Visions and Prophecies of the Right Honourable Simon Lord Lovat, which were revealed to his lordship when he was skulking in the Island of Morar, by the late Lord Strathallan, 13 May 1746' (London: F. Cogan, 1748)

Steuart, Bailie John, *The Letter-Book of Bailie John Steuart of Inverness, 1715–1752* (Edinburgh: Scottish History Society, 1915)

Steven, Maisie, *Parish Life in Eighteenth Century Scotland: A Review of the Old Statistical Account* (Edinburgh: Scottish Cultural Press, 2002 rpt. 1st pub, 1995)

Szechi, Daniel, *1715: The Great Jacobite Rebellion* (New Haven: Yale University Press, 2006)

Thomson, Katherine, *Memoirs of the Jacobites of 1715 and 1745*, 3 Vols (London: Richard Bentley, 1845)

Tracts on English History, 'The Proceedings of the House of Lords, concerning the Scottish Conspiracy, and the Papers Laid before that House, by Her Majesties Command, Relating thereunto' (London, 1704)

Transactions of the Gaelic Society of Inverness (Inverness, 1871–2004), Vols 1–63 ('Unpublished Letters of Lord Lovat, 1739–43'; C.

Fraser-Mackintosh, *TGSI*, Vol. 11; 'Some Unpublished Letters of Simon Lord Lovat of the '45 to Cameron of Lochiel', Mr Cameron of Lochiel, *TGSI*, Vol. 12; 'Two Letters by Simon Lord Lovat', William Mackay, Vol. 14; 'Minor Highland Families, No. 5 – The Frasers of Foyers', Charles Fraser-Mackintosh, Vol. 18)

Trials of Simon, afterwards Lord Fraser of Lovat, 1698 and 1701, edited by Sir William Augustus Fraser (London: Whittingham & Co., 1880)

Warrand, Duncan (ed.), *Culloden Papers* (London: Cadell & Davies, 1815)
——— (ed.), *More Culloden Papers*, 5 Vols (Inverness: Robert Carruthers, 1923–30)

News Letters of 1715–16, edited by A. Francis Steuart (London & Edinburgh: W. & R. Chambers, 1910)

INTERNET

www.arts.st-andrews.ac.uk/beauly/pdfs/SURVY1.pdf ('Placename survey of the Parishes of Kilmorack, Kiltarlity and Convinth, and Kirkhill, Inverness-shire' by Simon Taylor, Department of Medieval History, University of St Andrews, 2002)

ACKNOWLEDGEMENTS

I am greatly in debt to my predecessors. Lovat provoked wildly contradictory responses. One writer saluted him as the 'last of the great Scoto-Celtic chiefs', while another recorded with ill-concealed satisfaction that 'seldom has a more horrible old man met a more deserved end'. In addition, I could never have approached his life without consulting the works of scholars of late-seventeenth- and eighteenth-century Scottish and British history. Their labours mine gem after gem from archives all over Europe, and their great intelligence cuts and polishes them. Any biographer owes them huge gratitude. I should also like to acknowledge the influence of Ronald Black, Professor Donald Meek, Professor Robert Mullally and Dr Wilson MacLeod, who trained a full-time mother to produce intellectually rigorous work at the University of Edinburgh Celtic Department. My gratitude goes also to Professor William Gillies for permission to quote from his translation from *The Book of the Dean of Lismore*. The staffs of the British Library, of the National Library of Scotland, and of the Reference Room at Inverness Library; of the National Archives at Kew, and the Scottish Record Office are always helpful and generous, providing books, manuscripts and guidance on locating obscure items with incomplete and outdated citations and references. In the Highlands of Scotland, Alastair MacLeod, Chief Archivist at the Highland Archives, is a mine of information on the region's history. Even closer to home, Sue Thompson's work on the history of the Aird of Lovat has produced masses of information about Fraser country.

At HarperCollins, the commentary of my excellent editor Arabella Pike made me produce a sharper perspective and refine a baggy early draft into a coherent narrative. I thank Kerry Enzor for ensuring the manuscript reached the printer complete and Lucy Howkins for marketing advice. Kate Johnson not only contributed some fine editorial suggestions, but, while she empathised, kept recalling my mind to work during a very black period in mine and my husband's lives. On that note, I want to thank the medical and therapeutic teams under Professor Anthony Rudd at St Thomas's Stroke Unit. I want to congratulate Dr Matthew Wright of the Cardiac Unit at St Thomas's: 1.9 seconds is fantastic. Ongoing, Jackie Albert, Jamie Clark, Liz Edwards, Sally de la Fontaine, Sally Ghibaldon, Richard Jefferson, Maia Parker and Laura Slader have been towers of strength to Kim and me.

I am blessed to have the tremendous David Godwin for an agent. I want also to thank William Dalrymple for his great generosity and encouragement when I first ran the idea past him. Closer to home, for too long Angie, Sandy, Vita and Calum had to tolerate a mother who appeared to be concentrating on their conversation while actually thinking of other things. Thank you. The biggest thanks go to my husband Kim. He has lived with this book with me, and his support and encouragement never fail. He was always ready to discuss it, read large parts, and unfailingly his comments cut straight to the point.

With regard to textual housekeeping, orthography has been modernised in the interests of narrative pace. The spelling of certain names, such as Argyle/Argyll, Athol/Atholl has been standardised. Letters in French have been silently translated.

INDEX

387